THE DUBLIN AND MONAGHAN BOMBINGS

DON MULLAN is the author of the acclaimed bestseller *Eyewitness Bloody Sunday* (Wolfhound Press, 1997), which played a crucial role in British Prime Minister Tony Blair's decision to establish a new Bloody Sunday Inquiry in 1998. Don Mullan is a native of Derry and was educated at St Joseph's Secondary School, Creggan; the Development Studies Department, Holy Ghost College, Kimmage, Dublin; and Iona College, New York. Aged fifteen, he witnessed the Bloody Sunday massacre while attending his first Northern Ireland Civil Rights march. His involvement with the Northern Ireland Civil Rights movement led him to work on civil and human rights issues around the world. In 1980, aged 24, he became Director of AFrI (Action From Ireland), a Dublin-based justice, peace and human rights organisation. In 1983–4 he worked as a volunteer in Recife, Brazil. In 1994, he attended the inauguration of President Nelson Mandela, as the guest of Archbishop Tutu. He worked with Concern Worldwide for almost two years, beginning in July 1994, during which time he visited Rwanda and Zaire. He now works as a freelance journalist/writer/broadcaster.

The Dublin and Monaghan Bombings

Don Mullan

John Scally
Interview Assistant

Margaret Urwin
Research Assistant

WOLFHOUND PRESS

First published in 2000 by
Wolfhound Press Ltd
68 Mountjoy Square
Dublin 1, Ireland
Tel: (353-1) 874 0354
Fax: (353-1) 872 0207

© 2000 Don Mullan

British Library Cataloguing in Publication Data
A catalogue record for this book is available from the British Library.

ISBN 0-86327-719-5

10 9 8 7 6 5 4 3 2

Front Cover Photo: Courtesy Tom Lawlor (*The Irish Times*)
Back Cover Photo: Courtesy D.J. McEnroe
Cover Design: Wolfhound Press
Typeset in Century Schoolbook by Wolfhound Press
Printed in the Republic of Ireland by Betaprint, Dublin

Contents

Acknowledgements   11

Prologue   15

Introduction   19

Chapter One: From Troubles to Tranquillity   25

Chapter Two: The Day of the Bombings
    Eyewitness and Survivor Accounts   37

Chapter Three: The Dead:
    Personal Stories of the Bereaved   84

Chapter Four: Government and Police Reaction   132

Chapter Five: *Hidden Hand: The Forgotten Massacre*   146

Chapter Six: The Media Response to
    Hidden Hand: The Forgotten Massacre   172

Chapter Seven: The Political Response to
    Hidden Hand: The Forgotten Massacre   179

Chapter Eight: UVF — Ourselves Alone   202

Chapter Nine: RTÉ *Prime Time*   219

Chapter Ten: Forensics   229

Chapter Eleven: The Garda Síochána
    and British Intelligence   248

Chapter Twelve: The Holroyd Notebooks   271

Chapter Thirteen: The Victims' Commission Report   285

Conclusion   293

Afterword: History of the Campaign   303

Appendix I: Extracts from Interview with
    Dr James Donovan, Director of the
    Forensic Science Laboratory, Dublin, 24 March 1999   311

Appendix II: Extracts from Interview with John McCoy,
    27 April 1999   317

Appendix III: Telephone Conversations, 2 July 2000,
    with Suspected Parnell Street Bomber, and Owner of
    Farm Suspected of being Launch Base for the Dublin
    Bombings   328

Appendix IV: Statement of Dublin/Monaghan Bombing
    Families and Wounded   330

Bibliography   331

Index of Statements   333

Picture and Text Acknowledgements   336

Abbreviations used in the Text

CID	Criminal Investigation Department (central police detective department)
CIÉ	Córas Iompar Éireann (Irish Transport Authority)
DPP	Director of Public Prosecutions (chief state prosecutor)
DUP	Democratic Unionist Party
FCA	Fórsa Cosanta Áitúil (local defence force in Republic)
INLA	Irish National Liberation Army (republican paramilitary group)
IRA	Irish Republican Army (biggest republican paramilitary group)
LVF	Loyalist Volunteer Force (loyalist paramilitary group)
MBE	Medal of the British Empire
MI5, MI6	British Secret Service organisations
NYPD	New York Police Department
OBE	Order of the British Empire
RTÉ	Radio Telefís Éireann (Irish national television)
RUC	Royal Ulster Constabulary
SAS	Special Air Services (British undercover commando organisation)
SC	Senior Counsel (member of Irish inner Bar)
TD	Teachta Dáil (member of An Dáil — the Irish Parliament)
TUC	Trades Union Council
TV3	Irish commercial TV station
UDA	Ulster Defence Association (loyalist paramilitary group)
UDR	Ulster Defence Regiment (British Army regiment, Northern Ireland)
UFF	Ulster Freedom Fighters (loyalist paramilitary group)
UUUC	United Ulster Unionist Council
UUP	Ulster Unionist Party
UVF	Ulster Volunteer Force (loyalist paramilitary group)
UWC	Ulster Workers' Council (loyalist-controlled group)
VUPP	Vanguard Unionist Progressive Party
YTV	Yorkshire Television

Stay Strong

Friday the 17th May,
Began like any other day,
We ate the cereal and the toast,
Ran to the door and checked the post,
Who could have said who could have foretold,
The terrible tragedy that was about to unfold.
I remember that morning,
Mammy brushed my hair,
Planted a kiss on my cheek
And said 'don't forget your prayer'
I chased out the door as happy as a bee
Not a thing in my secure world troubling me.
Around 5.30 that evening we heard the blast
Not knowing my secure world was a thing of the past
Daddy rang to say 'Tell Mammy I'm fine
I'm going to be late, I'll be home before nine'
The traffic was crazy, the place in a state,
That's why we all thought Mammy's so late.
By some strange twist of fate, Mammy decided that day,
To go into town to collect Daddy on her way,
But her good deed was costly,
Her timing all wrong,
Her life was taken,
God it's hard to stay strong.

Fiona Ryan
(Daughter of Maureen Shields,
killed in Talbot Street bomb, 17 May 1974)

'... sing out a chorus, give voice to the silence,
That shames our fair city as never before.'
From 'A May Day in Dublin' by Pete St John

Acknowledgements

I am deeply grateful to a great many people who contributed to the creation of this book. Primarily, I must thank all of the families who lost loved ones in the Dublin and Monaghan bombings. Their courage, dignity and determination were a privilege to encounter. Their co-operation with this volume was often painful and a clear sign that despite the passage of time, their loss is still acutely felt. My gratitude to the families of the following people who died in the bombings is profound: Marie Butler, Patrick Fay, Antonio Magliocco, John, Anna, Jacqueline and Anne Marie O'Brien, Edward O'Neill, Breda Turner, Josie Bradley, Anne Byrne, Simone Chetrit (including Helena and Eamonn Gunn, her host family in Ireland, and Betty and Tony Shortall), Concepta Dempsey, Collette Doherty, Breda Grace, May McKenna, Anne Marren, Dorothy Morris (including, Sr Ellen and her neighbour, Carmel Hayden), Marie Phelan, Siobhan Roice, Maureen Shields, John Walshe, Anna Massey, Christine O'Loughlin, Patrick Askin, Thomas Campbell, Thomas Croarkin, Archie Harper, Peggy White, Jack Travers and George Williamson. It was with profound regret that I failed to locate the families of John Dargle and Elizabeth Fitzgerald.

I must also thank the survivors of that day who have contributed their eyewitness testimonies: Derek Byrne, Liam Sullivan, John Molloy, John Byrne, Bridget Fitzpatrick, Una Candon, Mr F, Christopher Keane, Frank Goss, Kevin Roe, Marian Keenan, Rosaleen Mussen, Joe O'Neill, Noel Hegarty, Bernie McNally, the late Martessa Ní Cearnaigh, Marie Sherry, Denis Barror, Phil Lawlor Watson, Nora Fitzsimmons, Catherine McLaughlin, Bernadette Bergin, Josie McCormack and Joan Ann T. Hourigan.

A profound debt of gratitude is owed to Margaret Urwin who acted as a research assistant throughout. Her knowledge and extraordinary eye for detail, her unbounded generosity of spirit and, above all, her compassion and commitment to the families of the deceased and the wounded, have contributed greatly to the birth of this book.

I am deeply grateful to John Scally who travelled across Dublin and throughout Ireland to meet and interview many of the bereaved. John's gentle nature and empathy contributed enormously to the goodwill which we received from the families of the dead.

Thanks are also due to the legal team who act on behalf of the families and wounded and whose advice, insight and support is greatly appreciated: solicitor Greg O'Neill, barrister Cormac Ó Dulacháin, Gerard Hogan, SC, Kevin Brophy and legal secretary Ger Bell.

I am grateful to artist Robert Ballagh who was responsible for sowing the seed of this book.

To the Lough Swilly bus driver; to Tom Lawlor, John Burke, and Mr Kevin Walshe, an old Dubliner who refused to forget.

Thanks are also offered to the staff of the National Library, Dublin; Linen Hall Library, Belfast; and the Central Library, Derry. Also Fr Raymond Murray, the Pat Finucane Centre and Paul McGuill whose MA Thesis 'Political Violence in the Republic of Ireland 1969–1997' (UCD 1998) should be published.

The search to find the family of Simone Chetrit in Paris owes much to the support of two French friends, Laurence van der Haegan and lawyer Aude Catala. I am especially grateful to Aude Catala who now acts as legal liaison between the

Chetrit family and Ireland. I am also indebted to M. Raphael Siev of the Irish/Jewish Museum, Madame Laurence Segal, the French Embassy, Mesdames Boury, Magyar, Klein Lieber and Meir Waintrater, editor of *l'Arche* magazine and his colleague, Myriam Ruszniewski.

I am deeply grateful to Italian journalist Silvia Calamati who accompanied me to meet the family of Antonio Magliocco at Atina, Italy.

The following families who are also struggling for justice and truth offered important encouragement and support to the Justice for the Forgotten Campaign: The Bloody Sunday families, in particular, John Kelly, Micky McKinney, Gerry Duddy and the Bloody Sunday Trust; Geraldine Finucane and her brother-in-law Martin Finucane; the Bradshaw, Duffy and Douglas families who are entitled to the truth about the 1972 and 1973 Dublin bombings; the family of Seamus Ludlow; and all victims of unsolved political murders in the Republic of Ireland.

The following journalists and publications are acknowledged for support and encouragement: Glyn Middleton of Yorkshire Television whose time in answering my many questions was always given generously, with courtesy and a genuine desire to help the families of the bereaved and the wounded to achieve truth and justice. I am also indebted to Ian McBride of Granada Television, and my colleagues, Mark Redhead and Paul Greengrass. Brendan O'Brien, RTÉ *Prime Time*, who, despite a very heavy schedule, was also generous with his time and support. Anne Cadwallader and Ken Whelan of *Ireland on Sunday*; TV3 and in particular, 20/20 Producer, Garrett Harte and his colleagues Bernice Burnside and journalist Catherine Hogan; Frank Doherty and Frank Connolly of the *Sunday Business Post*; author and journalist Sean McPhilemy, Katie Hannon of *The Irish Examiner*; *The Irish Times*, the *Irish Independent*, the *Irish Press* and in particular, Dr de Valera, *The Derry Journal*, *Magill* magazine; Pat Kenny and Catherine Cahill of *Kenny Live*; Gerry O'Callaghan, Philip Bouchier Hayes, Róisín Boyd, Paul Larkin, Seamus McKinney of *The Irish News*, Pat Coyle and Liz Curtis.

I am grateful to the following politicians and civil servants: An Taoiseach, Bertie Ahern; Wally Kirwan and Paul McGarry of the Taoiseach's Department. Ruairí Quinn, TD, Patricia McKenna, MEP, and her Press Secretary, Sophie Rieu, Trevor Sargent, TD, Tony Gregory, TD, Austin Currie, TD, and Caoimhghín Ó Caoláin, TD. Kevin McNamara, MP and Martin Collins, Dr Norman Godman, MP and Lord Merlyn Rees. Thanks are also expressed to the Republic's Victims Commissioner, John Wilson and his assistant, Eamonn Mulligan.

I am also grateful to lawyers Peter Madden, Desmond Doherty, Paddy McDermott, Michael Mansfield, QC and Professor Sam Dash, Georgetown University Law Department, for advice and support. Jane Winter of British Irish Rights Watch is acknowledged for her advice and support to the Justice for the Forgotten Campaign.

Indebtedness is also expressed to Congressmen Christopher Smith, Joseph Crowley, Peter King, Donald Payne, Ben Gilman and Richard Neale. I am especially grateful to Mary McDermott Noonan. I am grateful to the NYPD's Bomb Squad, in particular, Officer Denis Mulcahy. Special thanks are extended to former NYPD Officer, Ken Dudonis and US Military bomb expert, Ed Komac.

I am indebted to so many generous friends and supporters in the United States. These include: Amelia Penny, the backbone of Aer Lingus in the US, and her colleague, Clare Barry. Very special thanks are expressed to the following, whose friendship, hospitality and generosity over several years is greatly appreciated: Brian C. Meagher; Todd, Helen and Missy Allen; Ron and Linda Stout; Rita Mullan; Owen Rodgers and Nora Wertz; Pete, Mary and Coleen Quinn; Matt and Maire Reilly; Jim Gallagher; Dave Burke; Arthur and Ali McCabe; Eva S. Sevian;

Robert K. O'Neill, Burns Librarian, Boston College; Michael J. Cummings; Thomas J. Fox; Kevin John Meara; John Kissane; Frank Durkan; Jim Cullen; Annie Deignan; Pat Donaghy; Bob Mulrooney; Fionnuala Flanagan and Dr Jack Worrell — all genuine and deeply caring friends of Ireland. Br Jack Driscoll (President Emeritus, Iona College), Br Harry Dunkak and Sr Kathleen Deignan, CND, who, in over a century of combined service to education, dedicated themselves to investing in the goodness of people and not the grandeur of monumental building projects. Last but not least, Kit DeFever, whose support, encouragement and generosity over the past five years have made an important contribution to the success of my work.

I am especially grateful to the following people whom I either met or corresponded with in the course of this project: Lt. Col. John Morgan, Retired; Commandant Patrick Trears, Retired; former Captain Fred Holroyd, Colin Wallace, John Weir, John McCoy, the Garda Press Office, Garda Officer-in-Charge, Commandant Eoghan Ó Neachtain, Defence Forces Press Officer, the RUC Press Office, in particular RUC Press Officer Tim Hedgley and Tanya Berry, RUC Security Statistics.

The following people made contributions of varying degrees, all of which are greatly appreciated: John Wallace, Annegret Kopp, Kim Phuc, Sr Helen Prejean, Nora Comiskey, Cormac Breatnach, Osgur Breatnach, Bill Rolston, Mairead Gilmartin, Dublin Fire Officers Richard Delaney and John Daly, the priests of Sean McDermott Street and the Pro-Cathedral, Dublin, Paddy Behan, Dermot Beatty, Jim O'Halloran, SDB, Richard Moore, Angela Feeney, Pete St John, Conal McFeeley and Anne Molloy, Barry Pimlott and Ernie Pimlott, Tony O'Byrne, Linda Roddy, June Nash, Emma McAteer, Therese Mullan, Seán Ó Murchadha, Betty Walker, Michael Grennan, Fr Spellman, St Peter's Church, Phibsboro, Brendan O'Malley, Smithfield Corporation Fruit Market, Tommy McCarthy, Fr Desmond McCaffrey, ODC, St Joseph's Parish, Berkeley Road, Vivian Cavanagh, Fr Seamus Reihill, St Patrick's College, Buchlyvie, Stirlingshire, Scotland; Bernard Feeney, Joe Murray, Lorcan McGeough, Breandán MacCionnaith, Jennie Lawlor, Gracie Neary, Anne Shanahan, Stewart Reddin, Kevin and Audrey Curtis, Willie Ryan, Darach MacMathúna, Caitriona Ruane, Susan McHugh, Brendan Malone and Jack Hynes.

A very special word of thanks to Brian O'Brien, Tracy Quinn and Susan Murtagh of Prontaprint, Greenhills Road, Dublin 12, whose generosity and support have been invaluable to the Justice for the Forgotten Campaign.

I wish to thank the staff of my publisher, Wolfhound Press, especially Seamus Cashman for his valued support and encouragement over the past four years, Shay O'Reilly, Sales and Marketing Manager, and Wolfhound's Managing Editor, Emer Ryan, who invested enormous energy, commitment and personal care in crafting the book for publication.

Finally, I wish to thank my family who have sacrificed much in the course of my research and the writing of this book. My wife Margaret spent hundreds of hours transcribing recorded interviews and testimonies, while our children, Therese, Carl and Emma, were immensely patient, understanding and tolerant of my many absences and intensity in the course of its preparation.

Prologue

The blurring of brutality is too easy. We remember snippets of a news story, perhaps a searing image, but the details are like clouds — always changing, always receding.

Only those who have been intimately touched by brutality remember — often traumatically — the consequences of an uninvited, unimagined and unexpected violent intrusion into their lives. Unlike a snapshot, which captures a moment in time, the maimed, the bereaved and those left to cope often face a never-ending nightmare of torment and deepening sadness.

There are images from the past thirty years of civil unrest and repression in Northern Ireland which have remained etched in my own memory. I remember the brutality of the RUC in the early days of the Civil Rights Movement in my home town of Derry, especially 5 October 1968. As I saw pictures of baton-wielding police officers cracking open heads and emptying lungs of air, I asked 'Why?' I was twelve, and it was the first political question I ever asked.

I remember Bloody Sunday and the chilling and murderous barbarity of members of the 1st Battalion, the Parachute Regiment, that afternoon, 30 January 1972. I shall never forget finding, the following day, our blue and white civil rights banner, heavily stained by the blood of an unarmed and innocent man.

I remember finding off-duty RUC Reserve Constable Stanley Wray (50) on the morning of 20 May 1979, moments after his execution by a young Provo gunman, as he walked home from Sunday worship. I shall never forget the sight of his teenage son and daughter, clasping one another in shocked horror, as they looked down upon the still-warm body of their slain father.

I remember my near and dear neighbour, Maureen Doherty, sealed for seventeen years in a black hole of unimaginable pain, after a stray bullet, fired by a young Official IRA sniper, missed its intended target — a British soldier — and almost completely severed her spine. I can still see her sickly ashen face when I called to see her on a visit home from college — her perspiring brow contorted with pain and despair. I still feel her fingers digging into my wrist as they tightened in unison with the sound of her sucking air in a desperate effort to ease yet another wave of throbbing agony. I remember her tortured eyes, glazed with a look of virtual insanity, penetrating my soul as she confessed her deepest desire for relief. 'Don,' she divulged, 'I wish I was dead!' And who would dare condemn her for such thoughts? When death eventually enveloped her, it was almost too late.

Another image I have never forgotten is from the IRA's bombing of the La Mon House Restaurant, near Belfast, on Friday, 17 February 1978. It is of the charred and mangled remains of what was once a human being, garnishing a police poster, like an old piece of bog oak.

Scenes from other IRA and dissident-IRA outrages are played over and over again on our televisions — Enniskillen, Warrington and Omagh; the carnage of Remembrance Day, 8 November 1987, followed by interviews showing the extraordinary compassion and forgiveness of the late Gordon Wilson who lost his 20-year-old daughter, Marie; the devastation of Warrington in March 1993, followed by interviews with the father of 12-year-old Timothy Parry, courageously working to ensure that the legacy of his son might be a new-found friendship between British and Irish people. One eyewitness testimony from Omagh haunts me to this day. It appeared in an *Irish News* report on 17 August 1998, two days after the bomb:

> I saw one little girl who had lost her hand. She was maybe about 11 or 12. She was in a bad state, panicking. She was by herself, walking along the road. No one helped her. I think everyone was scared of her.

As the father of a little girl of the same age, imagining her in the shoes of this child made me sick to the core.

But what of the greatest single loss of life in any one day of the so-called 'Troubles'? Why have the victims of the 1974 Dublin and Monaghan bombings been so abandoned, so rejected and so abused? Why have they been officially banished to virtual oblivion? The scenes of carnage were no less horrific than those outlined above. The dead included two infants and one, possibly two, pregnant mothers. The bomb killed young and old, and mostly women. Words of courage, forgiveness and compassion were to be found similar to those uttered by Gordon Wilson and Colin Parry. Yet neither the media nor the Irish establishment conferred celebrity status on those who spoke them.

The Omagh massacre brought it all back in a stark and sickening way. All of those interviewed for this book talked about the pain and suffering of Omagh penetrating the rawness of their own open wounds. They felt for the people of Omagh. They prayed for the people of Omagh. Some of them developed friendships with the people of Omagh. They supported the resounding clamour nationally and internationally to assist the victims of the Omagh bombing in coping with the enormity of their sorrow and loss. But there was, and remains, one question that haunts many of the victims of the 1974 Dublin and Monaghan bombings: 'Why were we abandoned?'

It is a question asked not out of bitterness or resentment, but out of confusion. The injured and bereaved were left with a sense that somehow they were to blame for the sorrow and suffering that had so mercilessly engulfed them. Was it, perhaps, because the Dublin and Monaghan bombings didn't fit the stereotype? Was it the fact that republicans were not responsible?

Time will tell what only truth can heal.

Introduction

I was a 15-year-old witness to the Bloody Sunday massacre.

It was carried out in broad daylight in full view of hundreds of eyewitnesses, including independent media witnesses. Irish people, north and south, knew that Paratroopers had murdered unarmed civil rights demonstrators in cold blood. Yet, at the highest level of the British political and judicial establishments, a cover-up was concocted, resulting in the report of Lord Chief Justice Widgery. On the twenty-fifth anniversary of the massacre, Catholic Bishop of Derry, Dr Edward Daly, succinctly spoke of the Widgery Report as having 'found the innocent guilty and the guilty innocent'.

My book, *Eyewitness Bloody Sunday*, published in January 1997, has been credited by the Bloody Sunday families and their legal representatives as a catalyst which helped lead to the establishment of a new Bloody Sunday Tribunal of Inquiry. The impact of the publication of the book was enhanced by powerful investigative work by journalists from Channel Four News and the *Sunday Business Post*. The new Tribunal of Inquiry was announced by Prime Minister Tony Blair on 29 January 1998.

The Irish Government, under the auspices of then Taoiseach, John Bruton, TD, subjected all of our research to an evaluation. That assessment was careful in its appraisal of so-called 'new' evidence — none of it new to the British authorities, since almost all of it resided in British files, carefully concealed from the families and their legal representatives for over twenty-five years.

In recent years, as the campaign for the Dublin and Monaghan bombing victims has gathered momentum and become a formidable voice of conscience in this jurisdiction, much emphasis has been placed on 'new' evidence as the key to the establishment of a tribunal of inquiry, or the successful conclusion of the Garda investigation which, we are repeatedly reassured, is 'ongoing'.

This approach reached ludicrous proportions when the families of the deceased met with a former Minister for Justice who suggested that if they (the families) could come up with any 'new' evidence, it would be investigated.

The truth is that just as all the evidence that could have eased the suffering and anguish of the fourteen bereaved Derry families was in official British files for twenty-five years, so too, much of the evidence which would allow closure to the families bereaved by the Dublin and Monaghan bombings has been in the files of An Garda Síochána, the RUC and British Military archives for over twenty-five years. The suffering of the bereaved has been particularly compounded by official silence and resistance in this jurisdiction.

The Search for Truth and Justice

Because of my work with the families of Bloody Sunday, artist Robert Ballagh asked me to assist the families of Dublin and Monaghan in their search for truth and justice. I came to the issue somewhat reluctantly, knowing that I already had a heavy workload with the new Bloody Sunday Inquiry. Furthermore, as with Bloody Sunday, I sensed that the 1974 Dublin and Monaghan bombings would have an underbelly that would not be easy to expose to the full light of day. In many respects, attempting to understand the truth about what happened is similar to being given a six-thousand-piece jigsaw to solve, only to discover, once started, that only a thousand pieces are available. In the circumstances, a book such as this can only attempt to find a few connecting pieces to contribute to our understanding of an emerging pattern. It is hoped, however, that, in consort with the work of other journalists and legal advisers, it will act as a catalyst, leading to the full public cross-jurisdictional tribunal of inquiry, which the bereaved and wounded now demand.

This book is not conclusive nor is it definitive. Just as with Bloody Sunday, it will be several years before a definitive work on the Dublin and Monaghan bombings can be produced. I have merely pierced the surface of a very disturbing event. We should be very clear that, if true, the suspected involvement of British

Military Intelligence in assisting loyalist paramilitaries to place no-warning bombs in the Republic of Ireland dwarfs Bloody Sunday in its implications.

The Victims

As I began to meet the wounded and the families who lost their loved ones on 17 May 1974, I very quickly realised that all of them, without exception, were ordinary, decent citizens — citizens who considered themselves doubly wounded by their prolonged abandonment by those whom they expected to be compassionate guardians of their inalienable rights, namely, the politicians and police force of the Republic of Ireland. I determined to help them in their search for peace of mind, founded on truth.

I also realised that, in addition to thirty-one Irish citizens losing their lives in the bombings, so too did a French citizen and an Italian citizen.

In March 1999 I travelled to the village of Casalattico, in the south-central Italian Appennine mountains. According to the widow and children of Antonio Magliocco, who died in the Parnell Street explosion, I was the first Irish person to visit them and Antonio's grave in almost twenty-five years.

I found a genuine love for Ireland amongst the community of Casalattico and was surprised to discover that St Patrick's Day is celebrated every year because sons and daughters from here have emigrated to Ireland over several generations to open traditional fish and chip shops and cafés. But I also found a deep hurt amongst the community, and in the Magliocco family in particular. Antonio's sister, Savina Borza, summed up their experience following his murder when she said, 'We feel very abandoned.' Her comment was phrased in the present tense.

For over eight months I tried to find the family of Simone Chetrit, a young French woman killed in Talbot Street. On 2 October 1999, I travelled to Paris to meet her brother, Elie.

Simone was born into a Jewish family in occupied France at the height of the Holocaust. When Stephen Spielberg had finished making *Schindler's List*, he established 'Survivors of the Shoah Visual History Foundation' to chronicle the firsthand accounts of survivors, liberators, rescuers and other eyewitnesses of the Holocaust. Elie Chetrit, Simone's brother, was one of 50,000

Jewish people worldwide who testified to the Shoah project about his family's experience during the Holocaust. Elie's grandmother, died in the concentration camps, along with other family members.

The idea of a Jewish mother giving birth to a baby in the midst of the Holocaust seemed to me at once a supreme act of faith in the survival of the Jewish people, and a consummate act of defiance against Hitler's 'final solution'. What an irony that Simone Chetrit should lose her bright, young life on the penultimate day of a very happy month spent in Ireland.

In describing the feelings of the family following the murder of Simone, Elie repeated the sentiment of all the bereaved I have met: 'We were abandoned.' As was the experience of the Maglioccos, I was the first Irish person in twenty-five years to come to speak and sympathise with the Chetrit family.

Lack of Official Accountability

During my investigations into the circumstances surrounding the deaths of Simone, Antonio and the thirty-one men, women and children of my own nation, I became increasingly appalled and deeply disturbed. For me, the crux of the matter is the lack of accountability on the part of the Garda authorities, the Royal Ulster Constabulary, and both the Irish and British governments.

Over the past two years I have spent considerable time working with the Justice for the Forgotten Campaign[1] and its secretary, Margaret Urwin. Throughout that period, the most remarkable transformation I have witnessed has been a growing confidence and determination among the bereaved and wounded to achieve the establishment of a process of public accountability. Whereas previously they were focused solely on discovering the *who* and *why* of the atrocity, they are more concerned now with calling to accountability those agents of the State who bore the grave responsibility of protecting its citizens

---

1   Justice for the Forgotten was founded by the bereaved and the wounded of the Dublin and Monaghan bombings, to 'appeal for — and demand — our right to know the truth as to how and why our loved ones (including French and Italian citizens) lost their lives and so many of our fellow citizens were maimed.'

and subsequently of bringing to justice those responsible for their murder and mutilation.

How and why those agents failed in their responsibility is a matter of urgent public concern and warrants a transparent process of accountability similar to that demanded by the Irish Government in the case of Bloody Sunday and, more recently, in the cases of murdered solicitors, Pat Finucane and Rosemary Nelson, and Portadown man, Robert Hamill. Indeed, the fact that the Government was contemplating a 'private' inquiry into the Dublin and Monaghan bombings caused deep disquiet and unease amongst the Derry families and the Finucane family.

Conclusion

In his foreword to *Eyewitness Bloody Sunday*, the Rev. Terence McCaughey quotes from an El Salvadorean commentator. His words are very appropriate to the historical settlement which we all hope and pray will be copperfastened throughout Ireland in the months and years ahead:

> Unless a society exposes itself to the truth, it can harbour no possibility of reconciliation, reunification and trust. For a peace settlement to be solid and durable it must be based on truth.

In my conclusion to the second edition of the book, I quote from Dr Martin Luther King, Jr., whose words have a deep resonance with the plight of the Dublin and Monaghan families:

> We merely bring to the surface the hidden tension that is already alive. We bring it out in the open, where it can be seen and dealt with. Like a boil that can never be cured so long as it is covered up but must be opened with all its ugliness to the natural medicines of air and light, injustice must be exposed, with all the tension its exposure creates, to the light of human conscience and the air of national opinion, before it can be cured....

I can think of no better way to conclude this introduction and set the tone for the rest of the book. As equal and law-abiding citizens of Ireland and two other EU states, the victims of the Dublin and Monaghan bombings deserve to have the double injustice done to them exposed, with those responsible called to account for their actions and omissions.

Don Mullan
Dublin, 1 September 2000

Chapter One:
From Troubles to Tranquillity

Bernard Feeney was one of the unsung heroes of Bloody Sunday. Several photographs of the day capture him darting back and forth in his Knights of Malta uniform, in a desperate effort to help the wounded and dying. He was sixteen. On 11 September 1973, Bernard Feeney and I left our native Derry, along with another young man, Pat Meenan, to begin studying for the priesthood. We travelled to Buchlyvie, Stirlingshire, Scotland, where we joined eighteen other men from Ireland, Scotland, England and Africa.

We left behind a city and province in deep political turmoil, and entered the tranquillity of a rural environment where silence was broken only by the sounds of nature. The peace of Buchlyvie could not, however, shut out the political battlefields of Belfast and Derry, which Bernard, Pat and I had left behind. In the months leading to our departure, the seeds of the Sunningdale Agreement were being sown. A quarter of a century later, Séamus Mallon, deputy leader of the SDLP was to describe the 1998 Good Friday Agreement as 'Sunningdale for slow learners' and, indeed, the similarities are there, both in terms of content and resistance to its implementation. One wonders how many thousands of lives and limbs could have been spared had the initial experiment been given the opportunity to find its feet.

On 20 March 1973 a Government White Paper, entitled *Northern Ireland Constitutional Proposals*, was published. It had several contentious aspects. For example, because of the ongoing IRA campaign, security arrangements would remain unchanged and anti-terrorist legislation, such as internment without trial and special courts, would continue. An attempt to soften these hard-line measures was made through the announcement of a Charter on Human Rights and proposals to outlaw discrimination.

The paper announced the establishment of a Northern Ireland Government under the Secretary of State. It was to have a single-chamber 78-seat Assembly, elected by Proportional Representation, from which a power-sharing Executive would be chosen.

For unionists, the most contentious aspect of the White Paper was the matter of a Council of Ireland, in exchange for official recognition and acceptance by the Republic of Ireland of the status of Northern Ireland within the United Kingdom. The paper did not elaborate on the nature and extent of the Council but stated that details were to be agreed at a conference involving not only the British Government and Northern Ireland parties, but also, crucially, the Irish Government.

Support for the paper's proposals was predictable. The SDLP and the Alliance Party welcomed it, while the leader of the Ulster Unionist Party, Brian Faulkner, hedged the bets of his party with the announcement that they 'neither reject it totally nor do we accept it totally'.

Opposition to various unpalatable proposals contained in the paper was voiced by loyalist paramilitaries, the Orange Order and Republicans. William Craig, the former Minister for Home Affairs, announced the setting up of the Vanguard Unionist Progressive Party, supported by the Ulster Defence Association. At a 60,000-strong rally in Belfast, he openly talked of liquidating 'the enemy' should politicians fail the Protestant community of Ulster.

Elections to the new Assembly were held on 28 June 1973. The results revealed a chasm within unionism, with anti-Agreement unionists taking 26 seats and pro-Agreement unionists, led by Brian Faulkner, winning only 24. The SDLP took 19 seats, the Alliance Party won 8, and the Northern Ireland Labour Party just one. Spurred by pressure from London, Faulkner agreed to the formation, along with the SDLP and Alliance, of an Assembly Executive. His decision was helped by the SDLP's declaration that there could be no change in the status of Northern Ireland until another poll was held some ten years later. The Assembly Executive was to be formed by 5 October.

On 24 September 1973, the Irish Minister for Foreign Affairs, Garret FitzGerald, informed the UN General Assembly that the Irish and British Governments had agreed, amongst other matters, the reform of the RUC, the formation of a power-sharing executive and the establishment of a Council of Ireland.

For most unionists, after half a century of absolute control, the prospect of power-sharing was unpalatable enough, but the idea of a Council of Ireland, giving the Government of the Republic of Ireland a role in the internal affairs of Northern Ireland, was tantamount to betrayal and the first step on the road to a United Ireland. Attitudes were hardening and the position of moderate unionists who supported a power-sharing executive was eroding.

In nationalist areas such as the Creggan, Bogside and Brandywell from which I and my seminarian friends came, the war had intensified dramatically since Bloody Sunday. Internment was still in place, and hundreds of Irish nationalists and republicans continued to be held in prisons throughout Northern Ireland. The presence of British soldiers on the streets was resented and opposed at every opportunity. News from home inevitably informed us of riots, bombings, shootings and house raids.

On 14 November 1973, the 'Troubles' caught up with us in Stirlingshire. Bernard's 14-year-old cousin, Kathleen Feeney, was shot dead by an IRA sniper who had opened fire on an army patrol. Bloody Sunday and other tragedies had bonded us with an understanding of the trauma of sudden death by violence. In a sense, we were a world apart from the rest of our small community.

As November progressed, political developments at home continued to unsettle both communities. The formation of the new Northern Ireland Executive was announced. The Rev. Ian Paisley, leader of the Democratic Unionist Party (DUP), and William Craig were gathering steam in their campaign of opposition to any agreement which included an Irish dimension.

On 22 November, the Secretary of State, William Whitelaw, announced that a power-sharing executive was to be formed with Brian Faulkner as leader and Gerry Fitt as deputy leader. The executive would consist of eleven members: six unionists, four SDLP and one Alliance. A cross-jurisdictional conference, involving London, Belfast and Dublin, would be held in England on 6 December 1973, to develop, amongst other matters, the Council of Ireland dimension to the Agreement. The conference was to be held at Sunningdale in Berkshire.

From its inception the Assembly was beset by conflicts within unionism, and between nationalists and republicans over the continuation of internment without trial and the exclusion of republicans from the forthcoming Sunningdale conference.

On the same day that the Secretary of State announced to the House of Commons the establishment of the Northern Ireland power-sharing executive, he also warned:

> There are those in this House and outside who are ... determined that we should fail. They are, clearly, entitled to pursue their aims by constitutional means. But ... they are not entitled to blur that line between constitutional action and force.

It was a remark directed not only at republicans who claimed the right to wage war against the British presence in Ireland, but also at 'constitutional' politicians like Paisley and Craig, who were fomenting loyalist anger and appearing in public with masked men dressed in combat fatigues.

Francis Pym replaced William Whitelaw as Secretary of State for Northern Ireland on 3 December. The new Secretary of State found himself responsible for the highly sensitive negotiations of the Sunningdale Agreement, which required, amongst other skills, an intimate knowledge of Irish politics and its key players, and an ability to read the shifting sands of the local landscape. Pym lacked the knowledge and insight required. The removal of Whitelaw was seen by many as yet another example of Irish interests being on the periphery of British concerns.

The Sunningdale Agreement

The Sunningdale Conference opened on 6 December 1973. Participants included the political leaders of the Republic of Ireland (led by the Taoiseach, Liam Cosgrave), of Britain (led by Prime Minister Edward Heath) and of Northern Ireland (led by Brian Faulkner, Ulster Unionists; Gerry Fitt, SDLP; and Oliver Napier, Alliance). Anti-Agreement leaders, including Ian Paisley and William Craig, were, at the insistence of the participants, locked outside the Sunningdale negotiations.

As the Sunningdale Conference began, the four most powerful opponents within unionism vowed to destroy the Agreement. Ian Paisley, William Craig, Harry West and John Taylor announced the establishment of an umbrella organisation, the United Ulster Unionist Council. Their determination hardened on 9 December as details of the Agreement were publicised. These included:

- *A two-tier Council of Ireland* to include a Council of Ministers (seven from each side) and a Consultative Assembly with sixty members (thirty from Dáil Éireann and thirty from the Northern Ireland Assembly). All decisions would have to be unanimous and the Consultative Assembly would be primarily concerned with economic and social co-operation.

- *The consideration of nationalist demands for major RUC reforms.* These would be considered by the 14-member Council of Ministers who would also be consulted on appointments to both the RUC and An Garda Síochána.

- *A review by the British of the policy of internment without trial.* Releases were to begin by Christmas.

In a move aimed at securing Brian Faulkner's political future, Conference delegates from the Republic of Ireland announced that:

> The Irish Government fully accepted and solemnly declared that there could be no change in the status of Northern Ireland until a majority of the people of Northern Ireland decided to change that status.

An Anglo–Irish Commission was also promised, to examine the contentious issue of extradition from the Republic to the UK.

With almost immediate effect, the new power-sharing Northern Ireland Executive was to be formed, taking office on the first day of 1974. It consisted of eleven members:

- Brian Faulkner (Unionist), Chief Executive
- Gerry Fitt (SDLP), Deputy Chief Executive
- Herbert Kirk (Unionist), Minister of Finance
- John Hume (SDLP), Minister for Commerce
- Basil McIvor (Unionist), Minister for Education
- Austin Currie (SDLP), Minister for Housing
- Leslie Morrell (Unionist), Minister for Agriculture
- Paddy Devlin (SDLP), Minister for Health and Social Services
- Roy Bradford (Unionist), Minister for the Environment
- Oliver Napier (Alliance), Minister for Law Reform
- John Baxter (Unionist), Minister for Information.

Just four days after the Executive took office, the Ulster Unionist Council voted to reject the Sunningdale Agreement. The First Minister's position within the Ulster Unionist Party was now untenable. Brian Faulkner resigned from the Party on 7 January and immediately formed the Unionist Party of Northern Ireland. Harry West succeeded him as Leader of the UUP.

Faulkner's position was weakening by the hour. The SDLP had 19 seats in the Assembly while Faulkner managed to bring only 17 of his pro-Agreement supporters to his new party.

On 1 February, the new Northern Ireland Executive and the Irish Government met at Hillsborough Castle to set up the Anglo–Irish Legal Commission to study the extradition issue.

Storm clouds mounted on the horizon with the announcement, on 7 February, of a British General Election three weeks later.

The timing was a disaster for Faulkner, coming as it did so close to his departure from the Ulster Unionist Party. His new party was ill-prepared to fight an election. The Unionist Party of Northern Ireland, in its political infancy, could field only seven candidates.

The parties in the United Ulster Unionist Council (UUUC) agreed a pact and nominated only one candidate in each of Northern Ireland's Westminster constituencies. Their campaign slogan was clever and precise: 'Dublin is just a Sunningdale away.' The only pro-Agreement candidate to win a seat was the Deputy Chief Executive of the new Northern Ireland Assembly, SDLP Leader Gerry Fitt (West Belfast). The UUUC won all eleven remaining Westminster seats. Those elected were:

- William Craig (VUPP-UUUC)   East Belfast
- John Carson (UUP-UUUC)   North Belfast
- Rev. R.J. Bradford (VUPP-UUUC) South Belfast
- Rev. Ian Paisley (DUP-UUUC)   North Antrim
- James Molyneaux (UUP-UUUC)   South Antrim
- Harold McCusker (UUP-UUUC)   Armagh
- James Kilfedder (UUP-UUUC)   North Down
- Willie Orr (UUP-UUUC)   South Down
- Harry West (UUP-UUUC)   Fermanagh–South Tyrone
- William Ross (UUP-UUUC)   Derry
- John Dunlop (VUPP-UUUC)   Mid-Ulster

The overall election was won by the British Labour Party. Historian and political commentator Tim Pat Coogan, in his book *The Troubles*, contends that this was 'a factor which was to prove the ultimate downfall of the Sunningdale experiment'. On

5 March 1974, Merlyn Rees was appointed Secretary of State for Northern Ireland.

Faulkner struggled on with weakening resolve. He hoped to win favour within the wider unionist family with his campaign to have the Irish Government repeal Articles 2 and 3 of the Irish Constitution which claimed jurisdiction over the territory of Northern Ireland. In an effort to save Faulkner's political neck and copperfasten the Agreement, the Taoiseach, Liam Cosgrave, said in the Dáil on 13 March 1974:

> Northern Ireland ... is within the United Kingdom and my Government accepts this as a fact.

On 19 April, Prime Minister Harold Wilson made his first visit to Northern Ireland and stated that there was no alternative to the Sunningdale Agreement.

United Ulster Unionist Council (UUUC) Conference

Encouraged by their electoral success and a decisive swing of unionist support in their favour, the UUUC held a three-day conference at Portrush, County Antrim. Loyalist paramilitary organisations attended, including leaders from the Ulster Defence Association. Also in attendance was former British Conservative MP, Enoch Powell, who was beginning to eye Ulster as a potential sundown for his idiosyncratic racist politics.

The UUUC Conference was very clear about its immediate political aims. It wished to see the establishment of a Northern Ireland regional parliament within a federal United Kingdom. At the end of the conference, on 26 April 1974, it declared its immediate political objectives. They included:

- the scrapping of the Northern Ireland power-sharing Executive,
- immediate new local elections,
- the return of security to a new Northern Ireland parliament, following the elections,
- more spending on security.

The conference threatened widespread industrial disruption of Northern Ireland if Westminster failed to agree.

To achieve this, the Ulster Workers Council (UWC), which was founded in 1973, began to take centre stage. As the political crisis deepened, the UWC leadership engaged in the quiet recruitment of workers in key industries and services.

On Tuesday, 14 May 1974, the UWC called a strike in support of mainstream unionist politicians working to destroy Sunningdale. From the outset, intimidation of workers who did not support the strike was widespread. Crucially, the organisers moved to prevent the delivery of fuel to all but 'essential users'. The decision as to who constituted essential users rested solely in the hands of masked men who openly flaunted the law.

Merlyn Rees, the new Secretary of State for Northern Ireland, seemed struck by paralysis. Masked men in camouflage jackets were given virtual freedom to do as they wished while the British Army stood and watched. There were widespread suspicions that MI5 was supporting the anti-Agreement camp.

The UWC strike began on 15 May. A pan-unionist front was established to manage the strike, with a co-ordinating committee which included Ian Paisley, Harry West, William Craig and representatives of seven loyalist paramilitary groups, including the UVF and the UDA. Ulster Vanguard Assembly member Glenn Barr headed the committee.

The following day at Westminster, Merlyn Rees warned unionist MPs that their loyalism would lead them to come up against British troops.

17 May 1974

In Buchlyvie, May was a particularly busy month with exam pressures, but on the evening of the bombings, many of the students, including myself, gathered as usual to watch the 5.45 BBC News. The main stories included the UWC strike, the French Presidential elections, the Middle East conflict, and the deportation of the Great Train Robber, Ronald Biggs. At some point during the programme, newsreader Richard Baker announced that reports were coming in of bombs exploding in Dublin city centre. Several fatalities and injuries were suspected but no further details were available.

In spite of initial panic among students from the Republic, none of their relatives were affected and life continued as usual for them. Sadly, however, a hundred miles away the news was very different for student nurse Margaret Marren, who was studying midwifery at Cresswell Maternity Hospital in Dumfries. Her sister Anne, an employee at the Department of Posts and Telegraphs, had been mortally wounded in one of the bombs. The following morning as we arose to a new day in Scotland, Margaret was en route to Glasgow Airport and the sad journey home to her sister Anne's funeral.

I was sickened to the core when I read in one of the newspapers a quote from the UWC press officer, Sammy Smith (UDA):

> I am very happy about the bombings in Dublin. There is a war with the Free State and now we are laughing at them.

I could find nowhere a rebuke or a condemnation from his committee colleague, the Christian minister, Ian Paisley. Amongst the dead and injured were a young mother who was nine months pregnant and a young family, enjoying a walk in the sunshine. The idea of anyone laughing at the unfathomable suffering inflicted by such carnage is beyond comprehension.

The effectiveness of the UWC strike was being felt across Northern Ireland. Gas and electricity supplies were greatly reduced. On 19 May, Merlyn Rees declared a State of Emergency. I recall a letter I received from my mother at the time, in which she informed me that my father had built a small campfire in the back garden of our Creggan home, for the purpose of cooking.

The first sign of a crack in the dam came when the Minister for the Environment, Roy Bradford, called on the Secretary of State to open talks with the Ulster Workers Council. His call was sharply criticised and resisted by the SDLP. Merlyn Rees, with the backing of Harold Wilson, refused to negotiate.

As bodies were being buried throughout the Republic and as the families of Simone Chetrit and Antonio Magliocco arranged the return of their remains to France and Italy, anti-Agreement politicians called for an intensification of the strike with a half-page ad in the *Belfast Newsletter* on Monday, 20 May 1974.

The following day, the TUC General Secretary, Len Murray, arrived in Belfast to lead a 'Back to Work' march. In a climate of open and hostile intimidation only 200 workers lined up alongside Murray. The march was described as a 'flop'. However, the courage of the small contingent of anti-sectarian trade unionists, who, literally, risked life and limb, should not be forgotten.

On 23 May, the Secretary of State confronted anti-Agreement unionist MPs at Westminster, accusing them of setting up 'a provisional government in Northern Ireland'. He accused Ian Paisley of being 'a democrat here and a demagogue in Northern Ireland' (Hansard. Vol: 874 c. 616–618).

The following day, one week after the bombing of Dublin and Monaghan, a crisis meeting was held at Chequers, involving Prime Minister Wilson, the Northern Secretary, British Defence Secretary Roy Mason, British Attorney-General Sam Silkin, and the leaders of the three pro-Agreement parties in Northern Ireland — Brian Faulkner, Gerry Fitt and Oliver Napier. While acknowledging that the UWC was effectively in control of Northern Ireland at that moment, Faulkner expressed the belief that the situation could be rescued by a determined government response. In their book, *Northern Ireland — A Chronology of the Troubles 1968–1993*, Paul Bew and Gordon Gillespie state:

> Later the British cabinet holds a special meeting at which it is apparently agreed that troops can go into the power stations if Rees so decides. It is also suggested that the army might attempt to run petrol stations and oil supplies. The army leadership in NI, however, is reluctant to use troops to confront the strikers. With the senior ranks of the NIO holding a similar opinion it seems unlikely that Wilson will risk confrontation with the Protestants to defend the executive.

Quite apart from the suspicions that elements of the British security forces and intelligence services were involved in the bombing of Dublin and Monaghan, the role of the British military throughout this period deserves special attention by British parliamentarians today. When I interviewed the then Secretary of State for Northern Ireland, now Lord Merlyn Rees, on 18 January 2000, I left the Palace of Westminster with the abiding impression that he had, effectively, been reduced to observer status and that decisions had been made by the military and intelligence services without his consultation or knowledge. This may or may not be an accurate impression. However, in any democracy, where the decisions and intentions of an elected government are suspected of having been subverted by army generals, a dangerous precedent has been set. Such suspicions should, at least, be tested and if they are found to have substance, appropriate safeguards should be installed to prevent any repetition. These same issues also pertain to elements within the Garda Síochána, as discussed in Chapter 11 of this book.

Irrespective of any hidden agendas, the reality is that the British Army stood aside while democracy and the rule of law were being sabotaged in a sector of the United Kingdom which they where charged with defending. It was only in their language that the Prime Minister and the Secretary of State managed to get tough with the anti-Agreement factions of Ulster unionism.

I recall sitting in the television room at Buchlyvie on the evening of 25 May to listen to Harold Wilson's well-publicised speech. The Prime Minister called the strike organisers (elected Westminster MPs and loyalist paramilitaries) thugs and bullies. He accused them of 'using undemocratic and unparliamentary means for the purpose of bringing down the whole constitution of Northern Ireland so as to set up a sectarian and undemocratic state, from which one-third of the people would be excluded'. He continued:

> The people on this side of the water, British parents, British taxpayers, have seen their sons vilified and spat upon and murdered. They have seen the taxes they have poured out almost without regard to cost — over £300 million a year this year with the cost of the army operations on top of that — going into Northern Ireland. They see property destroyed by evil violence and are asked to pick up the bill for rebuilding it. Yet people who benefit from this now viciously defy Westminster, purporting to act as though they were an elected government. [People who] spend their lives sponging on Westminster and British democracy and then systematically assault democratic methods. Who do these people think they are?

In considering the tone employed by the Prime Minister and the implications of what he was stating, one can only wonder why the Army was not ordered to move against the strike organisers as it had moved against nationalists in the no-go areas of Derry and West Belfast in 1972. It is, to say the least, confounding.

According to Bew and Gillespie:

> One of the loyalist politicians on the strike co-ordinating committee had been warned by contacts at Westminster that strike leaders were to be arrested immediately after Wilson's speech and as a result the strike co-ordinating committee had gone to ground in east Belfast. In the event no attempt was

made to arrest them and they returned to their headquarters at Hawthornden Road, Belfast, the following day. (*Northern Ireland: A Chronology of the Troubles 1968–1993*, p. 86)

Wilson's address to the nation had echoes of the address made by William Whitelaw, on Sunday, 30 July 1972, the eve of 'Operation Motorman', when 12,000 troops with centurion tanks, armoured vehicles and bulldozers had dismantled the barricades of the republican and nationalist 'no-go' areas of Derry and Belfast.

Loyalists were apparently expecting a similar move to break the strike. Given that strike co-ordinators went into hiding, the warning must have come from a reliable and sympathetic Westminster source. In the absence of a parliamentary investigation, historians of the future will be anxious to study political and classified military files from the period to learn what happened in the wake of Wilson's speech. Did the British military mutiny against their government's intentions on the night of 25 May 1974? The only British Army move was to take control of twenty-one petrol stations across Northern Ireland. The UWC defiantly responded by threatening to choke already depleted electricity supplies further, and the strike leaders re-emerged from hiding unperturbed.

The death of Sunningdale occurred on 28 May 1974. Anti-Agreement unionists celebrated with dancing and bonfires.

Faulkner had resigned as Chief Executive of the Northern Ireland Assembly, along with all other pro-Agreement unionist members, on the basis that the Secretary of State had refused to negotiate with the UWC strike leaders. Plans were put in place to prorogue the Northern Assembly and end the Council of Ireland.

The following day, 29 May 1974, the UWC strike ended.

Reflecting on the collapse of Sunningdale in 1996, SDLP leader John Hume, Minister for Commerce in the 1974 Assembly, said:

> The establishment of power-sharing was a tribute to the political courage and imagination of the then Conservative government in Britain. Unfortunately, the Labour administration which succeeded it early in 1974 showed no similar courage, and in May of that year, in what was one of the most squalid examples of government irresponsibility, it surrendered its policy in the face of a political strike organised by a paramilitary minority on the Unionist side (*John Hume: Personal Views — Politics, Peace and Reconciliation in Ireland*, Town House, 1996).

Chapter Two: The Day of the Bombings

On both sides of the Irish border, people rose to a beautiful sunny morning on 17 May 1974. In Dublin and Monaghan, on the southern side, thirty-three men, women and children who awoke would not live to see the sun set. In Antrim, Armagh and perhaps Derry, on the northern side, twenty or so people rose to execute a bombing mission, which would end in the biggest mass murder in the history of the Republic of Ireland.

For many citizens living beyond the border regions of the Republic, the northern 'Troubles' might have been a million miles away. There had been a number of unexplained happenings south of the border. Since the 'Troubles' had begun, bombs had exploded in Dublin and in border towns, killing twelve, but people preferred not to dwell too deeply on the subject. They left these issues to the politicians, and went about their daily lives as normal.

Parnell Street, Dublin

As usual, Eddie O'Neill arose at 7 o'clock at his north inner city home in Dominick Street, Dublin. His wife, Martha, was six months pregnant with their sixth child. There was great excitement around the house: it was the ninth birthday of their eldest child, Denise, while seven-year-old Billy and six-year-old Angela were due to make their First Holy Communion the following day.

Eddie brought breakfast up to Martha in bed. He was doing some roof-contracting work with her cousin that day, but planned to take the afternoon off to bring Billy for a haircut. Martha had paid a deposit on a new pair of shoes in Henry

Street and he promised to buy them after he had collected his wages at lunchtime.

Before he left for work, Eddie watched Denise open her birthday card and present. She still treasures the gold charm bracelet she received for her ninth birthday. At 8 o'clock, Eddie O'Neill kissed Martha and their five children goodbye and left.

As Eddie O'Neill left his home in Dublin, 62-year-old William Scott was finishing work in Belfast where he was employed by Securicor as a night watchman at the Public Records Office on Balmoral Avenue. He lived alone and arrived home at around 8.30. At approximately 10 o'clock, when Eddie O'Neill was on the roof of the Dublin pharmaceutical factory, William Scott was in his upstairs bedroom at 27 Torrens Road, when he heard feet on the stairway. In a statement made to the RUC later that day, he said that he had left his front door open and, a few seconds later, two men, wearing 'some sort of mask', confronted him. One of the men was 'a big fella' who brandished a pistol in his right hand. He described him as thin, about 5 feet 10 or 11 inches, in his twenties, with, he thought, a sallow complexion. He also thought that he wore a grey coat and a green jersey.

According to Scott's statement, the tall man pushed him onto his bed and told him that they wanted no trouble, just his car. His companion, Scott says, was also in his twenties, about 5 feet 7 inches and stoutish. He was wearing a dark suit jacket, shirt and black gloves. He too had a pistol. A third man, also about 5 feet 7 inches joined them. Scott was unable to describe how this man was dressed and makes no mention of a mask. He said he did not have a gun, but also wore black gloves.

The 'big fella' took the keys of William Scott's car, saying it would be returned in two hours. He then left. After that, Scott was ordered by the other two men to stay upstairs while they went downstairs to play cards. He said that both men took off their gloves while playing cards.

The 'big fella' and the other car thieves would have had no trouble driving the car through Belfast that morning and down to South Armagh. According to authors Richard Deutsch and Vivien Magowan, there were no paramilitary roadblocks on 17 May 1974.

'At 4 o'clock,' Scott continued, his captors 'said they were going and told me not to come out for half an hour or I'd be shot.

I came out at 4.20 and informed the police. They said I'd get my car back either in Buller Street or Bootle Street....'

By 4.20 p.m., Scott's metallic-green 1970 Hillman Avenger, registration number DOI 4063, had been prepared for its deadly mission in an Armagh farmyard and was on the outskirts of Dublin. Eddie O'Neill, meanwhile, had returned home to collect his son, Billy, and, unknown to his wife, Martha, their four-year-old son Edward, to bring them to the barber's. They left in Eddie's work van, calling first at a butcher's shop where he bought a large joint of meat, and then going on to Henry Street to pick up Martha's shoes. He parked the van between Brendan Doyle's hardware shop and the Venezian Café on Parnell Street at around 4.30 p.m., and brought the boys into a busy barber's shop next door to Doyle's.

Out on Parnell Street, a woman sat in a car outside the Welcome Inn. At approximately 5.10 p.m. her husband returned and sat into the driver's seat and turned the key. There was space behind, she recalled, so they found it somewhat strange when a green car with a northern registration pulled up alongside them. Its driver seemed arrogant and impatient and was clearly anxious for them to drive off so he could park his car. As they pulled away, the driver of the green car reversed into the space they had left. According to the woman, who had been irked by the driver's arrogance, he was aged between 45 and 50. It was 5.12 p.m.

Talbot Street, Dublin

Friday, 17 May 1974, was the last full day of Simone Chetrit's month in Ireland. It was also to be the last day of her life. Simone was 30. Four weeks previously she and twenty other students had arrived in Dublin to learn English. It was a two-week course but Simone and another student, Dominique d'Amiens, had decided to stay an extra two weeks to improve their English.

Simone stayed with a young Irish couple, Eamonn and Helena Gunn, in Raheny on the northside of Dublin. Eamonn had already left for work when Simone surfaced at 8 o'clock. She joined Helena and 18-month-old toddler, Sheena, in the kitchen, for breakfast.

In Belfast, at around 7.30 a.m., according to an RUC/CID memo dated 18 May 1974, a 46-year-old motor mechanic left for work at Wordie Cowan Ltd. His route to work always brought him to the traffic lights at the junction of Duncrue Street and the M2 motorway. If the lights were red, as they were that morning, his normal practice was to drive along the M2 to Fort William and then enter Duncrue Street from that end.

The mechanic routinely parked his car, a metallic blue Ford Escort, registration number 1385 WZ, on Duncrue Road shortly before 8 o'clock. On this occasion, he noticed another car in the vicinity — a yellow Ford Capri with a black roof. Its occupants, he recalled, were two men aged about 60. He did not think they were acting suspiciously.

At 9 o'clock, a workmate commented that his car wasn't outside, but the mechanic thought he was joking. However, at 10.30 a.m., having agreed to lend his car to a fellow employee, he discovered that it was missing and reported it to the police.

By midday, when Simone Chetrit and Helena Gunn were sitting down to lunch, the mechanic's car was being checked over in the Armagh farmyard.

Because of a bus strike in Dublin, Simone and Helena had agreed to meet Dominique d'Amiens at Kilbarrack train station at 1.30 p.m. The three women, together with baby Sheena, took the local train to Amiens Street (Connolly) Station. They parted company at the junction of Talbot Street and Gardiner Street, close to Guiney's store, where Simone would be killed a few hours later.

There are no eyewitnesses to the Belfast mechanic's metallic blue Ford Escort being parked outside O'Neill's Shoe Shop on Talbot Street. However, according to documents received from Yorkshire Television, there is firm evidence available from people interviewed that the vehicle was there by 5.15 p.m. It is probable that it was parked at approximately the same time as the Parnell Street and South Leinster Street bomb cars.

Dominique d'Amiens and Simone Chetrit had bought flowers and chocolates for a farewell party to be held at the Gunns' house that evening. Close to 5.30 p.m., their shopping done, they started walking down a busy Talbot Street towards Amiens Street to catch the train back to Kilbarrack.

South Leinster Street, Dublin

Anna Massey and her twin sister, Muriel, had celebrated their twenty-first birthday on 12 May 1974. On Thursday evening,

16 May, Anna and her fiancé, Tommy Geoff, sat with her parents, Annie and Frank, and sister, Catherine, writing wedding invitations. Anna and Tommy were to be married on 26 July. Anna was to be the first of the Masseys' seven daughters to get married.

Because of the bus strike, the Massey household rose half an hour earlier than usual on 17 May. Frank and three of his daughters had a mile or so to walk from their home in Sallynoggin on the southside of Dublin to Sandycove train station. Frank had already left for work when Anna, Terry (19) and Catherine (17) rose at around 7 o'clock.

After a quick breakfast, the three young women left the house. Annie Massey remembers watching her three daughters walk down the path. Annie called to Anna to pull her coat up around her since there was a damp haze in the air coming off the bay. 'I'll see you later, Mam', she shouted back. 'I'll be home with Tommy.' Tommy was getting a new car and was to meet her at the station.

Anna Massey worked as a personal secretary to the manager of Lisney and Sons, Auctioneers, on Stephen's Green. The train brought her to Westland Row (Pearse) Station, from where she walked along Westland Row, Lincoln Place and on to South Leinster Street. She continued along the side of Trinity College to the junction of Nassau Street and Kildare Street, where she crossed the road and walked to Stephen's Green and her place of work. She was sitting at her desk by 9 o'clock.

Meanwhile, William Henry was sitting in the offices of Ariel Taxis in the Shankill district of Belfast, where he worked as a taxi driver. He told the RUC that at 9 a.m. a man aged about 30, around 5 feet 4 inches in height, and wearing a black jacket, came in and asked to be taken to Sandy Row. When Henry and his fare went outside to the taxi, another man joined them. He gives no description of this man who, it appears, remained silent throughout the unfolding drama.

According to Henry, the man who ordered the taxi sat in the front passenger seat while the other man sat in the back. As he started the car, he asked the man beside him if he wanted to go via Northumberland Street but he was told to go by the city centre. As he proceeded down Agnes Street, the man beside him asked that he pull into Woburn Street, as there were others to be picked up. As soon as William Henry stopped his taxi, two men came around to his door and pulled him out, forcing him into the back of his cab and onto the floor. The two men then climbed into the back along with the silent passenger and all three sat with their feet on Henry's body. His statement is not clear as to whether the front-seat passenger sat into the driver's seat or a fifth man took over. However, the car took off and was driven for three or four minutes before it stopped.

A hood was put over Henry's head and he was taken into a building that seemed to be through a gateway. He was put into a room, his hands were tied behind his back, and he was made sit on a chair. He later told the police that he became hysterical but was told not to worry. His captors reassured him that they only needed a car. Henry was forced to remain in this place until nearly 2 o'clock when he was driven to Boyd Street by two men. He gives no description of these men but says that one drove the car away while the other followed him up Shankill Road to ensure that he followed their instructions. He had been told to go straight home and remain there until 3 p.m., at which point he was free to go to the RUC and report his ordeal.

By 3.20 p.m. when William Henry sat opposite Detective Constable Kennedy at Tennent Street RUC station, Belfast, his taxi, a lagoon-blue Austin Maxi 1800, registration number HOI 2487, was on its way to Dublin.

Monaghan Town

While William Henry was making his statement at Tennent Street RUC station in Belfast, a young couple parked their green 1966 Hillman Minx, registration number 6583 OZ, in West Street car park, near Woodhouse Street, Portadown. They returned, an hour later, at 4.25 p.m., to discover their car missing. They reported the theft of the car to the local RUC at 4.30 p.m. Curiously, in addition to the details of the couple's car, the RUC statement also gives personal details about the owner of the car, namely, the owner's family background, his employment and a brief account of his life over the previous four years. It also notes that he was a member of People's Democracy and was involved in the Northern Ireland Civil Rights Movement.

An hour before the theft of the green Hillman Minx, a church minister had spotted three men attempting to steal a car from

West Street car park. He later picked them out from police mug shots. All three were prominent loyalist paramilitaries from Portadown.

Paddy Askin worked as a sawyer at Patton Saw Mills in Monaghan Town. His wife, Patricia, recalls him kissing their four sleeping children goodbye before leaving for work at 7.30 that morning. Friday afternoon was typical for Paddy Askin as he worked to the sound of rotating blades slicing through wood. Having finished work at 5.30 p.m., he walked with some workmates to the town centre, where he entered Greacen's Pub to have an end-of-week pint and catch the evening news. Silence descended upon the staff and customers of the busy pub as news came through of the bombings in Dublin. By then, the Dublin bombers and their accomplices were making their escape.

According to a former RUC officer, John Weir, the green Hillman Minx containing the bomb was driven to Monaghan by a man who later told him he intended to park the car outside a certain pub. However, a Garda officer on the beat, unaware of what the driver and his gang were intending to do, moved them on. They left the car outside the most convenient public house, which happened to be Greacen's, a Protestant-owned establishment. Two of those killed by the bomb were Protestant.

The Bombs Explode

As shops and offices began to empty, close to 5.30 p.m, the first bomb exploded in Parnell Street, just around the corner from the Department of Posts and Telegraphs. Less than a minute later, the second exploded in Talbot Street, outside O'Neill's Shoe Shop. The third detonated in South Leinster Street, close to Dáil Éireann. According to Yorkshire Television, all three bombs exploded within 90 seconds.

Survivors of all three explosions recall a blinding flash, followed by a deafening roar and a shockwave which hit them like a ferocious hurricane. Then, for what seemed like an eternity, all was dark and silent, before the first sounds and movements began.

Rescuers ran to the scene and began to search through rubble and wreckage in a desperate attempt to find people with varying degrees of injuries. Many had limbs blown off. Scores were bleeding profusely, their bodies having been punctured and lacerated by flying glass and debris. Others were suffering from blast burns and concussion. Some were dead, others dying. The nightmarish sounds of screams of terror and despair haunt many of the survivors to this day.

Even those who were not physically injured were shocked and traumatised by the scenes of carnage they witnessed. Speaking to an *Irish Times* reporter at Parnell Street, Fr John Killen, chaplain at Berkeley Road, said, 'I rushed here immediately. I anointed about five people, including a child. It was diabolical.' The first member of the Garda Síochána on the scene had been directing traffic at the junction of Parnell Square and Upper O'Connell Street. 'There was a blast,' Garda McKenny said. 'I knew it was a bomb. I rushed down and saw a man lying beside a car. I don't know if he was dead.' The reporter described seeing shops and houses, on both sides of the street, with windows blasted. Staff, some crying, others visibly shaken, were being comforted. Gardaí, firemen and doctors called into every premises on the street, searching for injured.

The *Evening Press* reported the following day that in Parnell Street five people had been killed outright; others died later in hospital:

> The body of a man lay on the street beside the wheels of a car; at least two more mangled and torn lay half buried in rubble in a garage and a baby was blasted into the cellar of a public house. A young woman had her toes blown off.

Fifteen-year-old Esme Crabbe came with an ambulance from Leeson Street. She took the pulse of the man lying beside the car, but 'he was dead'. Leo Kennedy, on his way to work at the Welcome Inn, helped firemen to take a child from the basement.

Fears that a whole Dublin family might have been wiped out in the blast grew as there had been no enquiries about two young children killed in the Parnell Street explosion. Tragically, both parents were already at the city morgue, awaiting identification.

So ferocious was the blast caused by the 150lb bomb in Talbot Street, that a Morris Minor car had been hurled through the plate-glass window of Guiney's. From under its wheels, lying on the rubble of a shop floor, protruded the legs of a man.

Geraldine Kennedy and Nigel Brown, writing in *The Irish Times*, reported that cars within 50 yards of the blast were wrecked, and windows shattered along Talbot Street and Lower Gardiner Street. They describe the dead and injured lying on the pavement, in the roadway and inside shop windows. A fleet of ambulances, private cars and a single-decker bus took the dead and injured to city hospitals. Several bodies, they wrote, were covered by newspapers from a nearby newsboy's stand. A girl was decapitated and another had a leg blown off. Two bodies had been so badly mutilated that they were fused together when blown off the pavement, through a door and into a basement. Several pedestrians were 'thrown through shop windows by the force of the blast.' The air smelt heavily of burning and fumes.

Dr John Cooper, an anaesthetist at Belfast's Mater Hospital, had come to Dublin to attend a conference at the Royal College of Surgeons. He was just 30 yards away when the car exploded in Talbot Street. He told the *Irish Independent* that the scene was 'horrifying'. He had seen a woman decapitated and another with a piece of car engine 'embedded in her back'. He also saw a man 'dying with an iron bar through his abdomen'. Together with another unknown doctor who was passing the scene, Dr Cooper attended the injured, some of whom had lost limbs, while others had broken limbs. He said, 'All we could do was patch them up with rough splints from broken timbers picked up from the street. We tied the splints with pieces of torn clothing.'

Irish Independent reporters described the scene as 'daylight hell' A young priest, Fr Pearse Duggan of Donnycarney told them: 'Inside the past 30 minutes, I have anointed 22 people, as far as I can remember.'

RTÉ's Maurice Cowan was on the scene in South Leinster Street within minutes of the explosion. He told the *Evening Press* (18 May 1974) of seeing a girl who had been burnt to death and another killed instantly by the blast. The paper also reported that one of the critically injured was an elderly man who had both legs blown off. He was found lying in a mass of blood in Leinster Lane. 'A young man is thought to have lost a leg and a young girl had serious leg injuries,' the paper reported.

Dublin Fire Brigade alerted hospitals that the Emergency Disaster Plan was to be immediately put into operation. The Mater and Jervis Street Hospitals on the northside of the city, and

St James's and Sir Patrick Dun's Hospitals on the southside, had responsibility for dealing with most of the victims. Several nurses and doctors from the Rotunda Maternity Hospital were immediately released to go to the scene at Parnell Street to render assistance. Dublin Fire Brigade also alerted the Red Cross, St John's Ambulance Brigade, the Knights of Malta and the Civil Defence whose personnel rushed to the various bomb-sites. All hospital ambulance services were placed under the control of Dublin Fire Brigade.

Despite the Disaster plan, medical facilities were overwhelmed. It was not simply a case of treating the horrific injuries sustained from the explosions, but also of dealing with distraught relatives and friends. As soon as news spread of the bombings, off-duty staff from all hospitals involved in the emergency plan turned up to help colleagues cope with the avalanche of dead and injured.

An immediate appeal was issued for blood donors. Hundreds of citizens responded. So great was the response, that at 9 p.m. Pelican House, headquarters of the Blood Transfusion Service, turned several hundred people away. They were asked, however, to listen to the radio for further appeals over the weekend.

The Irish Times reported that from the time the first casualties were being treated in the hospitals, Garda cars, taxis, private cars escorted by gardaí on motorcycles, and the Service's own vehicles, were kept at full stretch, delivering the blood and plasma to the various hospitals.

In Jervis Street Hospital, which was trying to cope with victims of both the Parnell Street and Talbot Street explosions, Dr Anthony Walsh, a resident surgeon, came to the waiting room of the casualty department on several occasions. He called out names of people admitted to the hospital, identified through either verbal confirmation or documentation found in their possession. He did not indicate whether they were dead or injured. Occasionally small family groups, having recognised a name on the list, would be led quietly away to be informed of the death or horrific maiming of a loved one.

Victims of the South Leinster Street and Talbot Street bombings were brought to Sir Patrick Dun's Hospital. Initial reports stated that the hospital had admitted two dead and was trying to deal with several severely injured people. Relatives and friends of suspected victims openly wept as they awaited news. For many families, it was the beginning of a long and lonely vigil.

Unlike in Dublin, where the dead and wounded had to be identified later, in Monaghan some victims were immediately recognised. According to the *Northern Standard* of 24 May 1974, one of the first on the scene was Fr Maurice Holland, a curate from Ballybay. He rendered assistance and spiritual aid to the dying. In addition to the devastation caused to Greacen's pub, McGlone's café was on fire. Brian Swift went into the café and helped out a woman and her child, probably Nora Fitzsimmons and her son, Jerome. Mr McGlone was also helped out of the café. Paddy Askin was pulled out of Greacen's and appeared to be very badly injured. Another man was lying underneath rubble at the foot of the bar, and two bodies were lying on the footpath outside. A man in a car nearby was severely injured.

The dead and injured were rushed to Monaghan General Hospital. As in Dublin, off-duty staff returned to their posts to provide support for overwhelmed colleagues. Some of the more seriously injured were sent on to Dublin hospitals for treatment.

Denials

Before the day ended, both the UDA and the UVF had denied responsibility for the carnage. The UVF statement read:

> We want to make it quite clear that we are appalled by these explosions. It is indiscriminate and definitely against our policy. At the present time the UVF have made a firm declaration that we will not engage in any physical activities including bombings and shootings. We, at the moment, are engaged in the political field of Northern Ireland and we believe that the political solution to NI can only be found democratically by the people of NI within NI. Therefore, we are not concerned with the policy of Eire or, indeed, the dictates of Westminster politicians.

The Saturday edition of *The Irish Times* reported a UDA spokesman as saying that the organisation 'completely deny any connection with this'. He suggested that the Republic should look 'a bit closer to home' for the culprits.

The Irish Times also reported a warning received by their Northern office from a man claiming to speak on behalf of the Red Hand Brigade. The man warned that the bombings would be intensified throughout the night and would go on 'until something was done about Sunningdale'.

In his book, *The Point of No Return*, journalist Robert Fisk reports the words of a certain loyalist politician, who he describes as 'a well-known, generally respected figure ... who played an important part in the UWC strike'. When asked about his reaction to bombings, this man said that while he could not condone such things, his reaction to the Dublin bombings had been: 'Slap it into you fellas — you've deserved every bit of it'.

Eyewitness and Survivor Accounts

Parnell Street

DEREK BYRNE

Derek Byrne was 14 and working as a petrol attendant when he was badly injured in the Parnell Street bombing. So bad were his injuries that he was pronounced dead. He woke up in the morgue.

It started when I left the house at 8 o'clock to go to work that morning and I got to the job around ten past eight. I was working away until the time of the bombing in Parnell Street. That was about half five when the bombings happened. I was serving a customer with petrol outside. There was a big explosion.

I remember waking up about three weeks after in James's Street Hospital. Actually, when I was brought out of the rubble I was rushed to Jervis Street Hospital and pronounced dead on arrival. I was sent into the Dublin City Morgue. It was an awful experience to go through but it was the after-effects after it, the nightmares, the whole lot.

I couldn't describe them, they were so bad. Not alone that, as I was growing up — I'd be going to discotheques and I wouldn't be allowed in because of the scars on my face and that. I got the ear sewn back on and then there were facial scars and the scars are mainly all on the left-hand side of my body.

It was a very scary thing to wake up in the morgue. I was just lying on the table. It was full of bodies. I just let a scream. The mortuary attendant then let a scream. She went and got doctors and nurses and I was brought up to the theatre....

When I woke up I was unable to stand up. I couldn't move. I was covered in blood. I hadn't got a clue what happened. I was told after that I was nineteen hours in theatre and I got 28 pints of blood because as soon as they were giving me the blood, it was just flowing out. Too many lacerations. But the surgeons said I was very lucky to be alive. It was touch-and-go at one stage.

I was in Jervis Street for three months and then I was transferred to Our Lady's in Dún Laoghaire for six months and then I was let out and was back and forwards as an outpatient for so many years. I am still waiting to go back in to have the knee done again.

When they took the stitches out of my face I got an awful shock because of the scars.

It was a bad experience for my family. They couldn't find me. It was a local priest, Paul Lavelle, he found me after searching the hospitals. And the *Irish Press* had it in the next morning, 18 May 1974, that I was dead. They then went up to my parent's house to tell them I was alive. My father was in bad health and, in fact, had to retire from work. It was an awful shock on the whole family. But my father only lasted a year after. He died in 1975.

I was very keen on soccer, and I had to give up ... after that.... My mother took it very badly. She wasn't in the best of health after the bombing herself. It was only when I came out of hospital that I was told what had happened. I had to go and see psychiatrists and they told me. But you never get over a thing like that. I could just picture the thing going off ... and you see bodies, the blood. I live in the area where there are two monuments dedicated to the victims that died, and when you're passing by you just can't help thinking about it.

The Irish Government has an awful lot to answer for regarding not pressurising the English Government for the evidence. Where did the crime originate? Who was involved and who was behind it?

I would like to see whoever planted these bombs, and whoever is still alive, brought to justice. I would like to see them get whatever justice is coming to them. And I'd like to see also the victims being properly recognised — proper compensation for them for a start and a letter of apology from the British Government and the Irish one. The families want justice — they want to know who killed their loved ones.

JOHN BYRNE

On 17 May 1974 I went into Parnell Street to buy an evening paper because it was my father-in-law's death anniversary on 17 May. I then went into the Metro pub in Parnell Street to have a pint and to read the paper. I was sitting at the counter near the front of the pub and within a few minutes there was a dreadful explosion. The front of the pub came crashing in. I was blasted off the seat, hurting my back. I was so shocked and frightened. I then crawled to the back of the shop, to the toilets and told some people to do the same. When I came out of the shop, minutes after, it was complete carnage. I was so shocked. I did not stay at the scene because I just wanted to go home to my wife and son where we lived in Gardiner Street, just around the corner from where the other bomb exploded in Talbot Street. It is a day I will never forget. For the people who died and was injured. My injuries — I am suffering since the bombing: shock flashbacks and trauma. My thoughts and feelings — I don't think the politicians give a damn after all these years. I hope the people who planted the bombs that day, person or persons, are brought to justice.

UNA CANDON

On 2 July 1954 I started a hairdressing business at 91 Parnell Street, Dublin. The rented premises consisted of four large rooms on the first and second floors, which included a hairdressing salon and also my

home. On that morning I invited Fr Kelly, SJ, from Gardiner Street
to come and consecrate the premises to the Sacred Heart. This he did
and from that day forward I kept a light in front of the Sacred Heart
picture in the hairdressing salon. I built up a successful business and
enjoyed many happy years there with a very loyal clientele and
numerous friends calling to see me as it was so central, until 17 May
1974 when three of us had a miraculous escape with our lives.

In May 1974 there was a bus strike in Dublin. During this
period business was slow. Time just dragged along, very boring. I
remember that fateful day ... very well. I had two clients in the
afternoon and my sister Maureen was with me most of that day. I
felt tired and bored and at 4.45 approx. I decided I would go
upstairs and lie on the bed. Luckily Sr Rosaleen, a friend of mine, a
Little Sister of the Assumption, came in and asked me if I would
shampoo her hair as she was going to Roscommon for the weekend
and was running in a new car which was given to her by a cancer
patient whom she had nursed. She later asked Maureen if she would
put a coin in the meter. This Maureen did, not realising there was a
car in front of Sr Rosaleen's car which contained a 100lb bomb. It
was directly outside my premises. This was approx. 5.10 p.m. I
proceeded to wash Sr Rosaleen's hair and while she was under the
dryer I noticed she was saying the rosary. During this time Maureen
and I stood, one at each window, admiring Sister's new car and
discussing how wise and thoughtful her patient [was] to give this
dedicated nursing sister a new car to help her in her nursing career.

At approx. 5.25 p.m. I took Sr Rosaleen from under the dryer
and was combing her hair when I suddenly got a wallop on my
forehead which almost stunned me. I got no warning. Next I heard
the crashing of glass and screams of the people. Apparently I was hit
by the wood of a window frame. The place went black and we
couldn't see one another. None of us spoke, too stunned. I couldn't
stop shaking. Everything was smashed, partitions dividing rooms
were moved out of position. Ceilings collapsed upstairs. I later
realised how lucky I was that I hadn't gone to bed at 4.45 p.m. We
managed to crawl out and down the stairs. There seemed to be
beams of wood all over the place. I remember stepping across the
hall door which had been blown in to the bottom of the stairs. We
eventually got on to the street which was a frightening sight,
injured people all over the place screaming. We got separated from
one another. I ran into a friend's house opposite, grabbed a towel,
wrapped it around my head. I also had facial injuries and bled a
good deal. Maureen was seriously injured, her jugular vein was
scratched. Her pullover was saturated in blood. She also got severe
stomach and wrist injuries and had to have a lot of surgery.
Sr Rosaleen got a little bit of glass in her little finger, that's all. All
three of us were taken to hospital. Sr Rosaleen to the Mater, Maureen
and I to Jervis Street Hospital. I was later transferred to the Eye and
Ear Hospital where I first met Bernadette McNally who was injured

in the Talbot Street bomb blast and who was in the bed beside mine.

When the initial shock passed somewhat, realisation dawned on me that in seconds I found myself both homeless and helpless. This caused me greater suffering and anxiety than my physical injuries.... Were it not for my kind friends and neighbours who quickly became aware of my plight and acted immediately, rescuing all of my personal belongings, etc., from the premises, I wouldn't have recovered so quickly.

Offers of help came from all sides. Everything necessary was done for me. A solicitor was sent to see me at the hospital. A builder friend (now deceased) Jim McCullagh from Draperstown, Co. Derry came and told me he would put my premises back together again, irrespective of whether I had the money to pay him or not. There were two phones going and I was from one to the other with offers of help especially offers of accommodation in their homes. Next comes Sr Frances, sister in charge of the Little Sisters of the Assumption. At that time their convent was in Camden Street, now at Mount Argus. She was like Santa Claus, she brought me everything I needed, slippers, underwear, dressing gown, radio, toiletries, etc., plus an invitation to their convent for as long as I needed accommodation. I gladly accepted her offer and she came and collected me by car. When we arrived, there were twelve nuns waiting on the steps to welcome me. When I went to my bedroom, there was one beautiful red rose in a vase plus a card signed — WELCOME Una.... My stay at the convent was the happiest few months of my life, since I left my home in Co. Sligo at 20 years of age. I would like to say these nuns refused to take any reward for their help. I returned to my home which had been restored to its original by Jim McCullagh but, alas, things were never the same. A lot of my clients had gone elsewhere and some thought we were killed, others thought we would never come back after our terrible ordeal.

BRIDGET FITZPATRICK

I was after collecting my children from school, gave them their dinner, cleaned up and took two of my sons, Derek and Tommy, along with my sister Kathleen to Hamill's clothes shop in Parnell Street to collect Derek's Holy Communion clothes. It was a happy day for my boys. They knew I would buy them a treat and we were excited. We got the Communion clothes and walked back up Parnell Street, making our way home. I started to cross from one side of Parnell Street to make my way down Marlborough Street. I was in the middle of the road facing Westbrook Garage, holding my sons by each hand, and Derek's clothes under my arm, when this horrible bang went off in my head. At that very same moment I could see the front walls of the garage coming out and what I can only describe as some kind of a baby's pram lifting into the air. Then, in panic, there was nothing to do even though I knew I was badly hurt, with every thought I had to run as I realised it was a bomb. I grabbed my sons' hands as hard as I could and ran through thick blinding smoke and glass, cutting my legs, straight for the Rotunda Hospital. My poor son Tommy was shouting 'Ma, Ma, stop. The bomb got me in the leg.' He was only 5 years old. He used to watch the news. I could not believe he knew it was a bomb. I recall people screaming, 'Stop that woman!' I did not know it was myself they were screaming about. When I got inside the door of the Rotunda Hospital I was taken into a room and put on a bed. My boys were being looked after by nurses. I saw a young man on the floor. The top of his head seemed to be gone. An elderly woman sitting on a chair with a pair of glasses but the glass was sticking in her eyes which were bleeding, and a nurse washing a young boy's arms covered in blood.

My thoughts about my two sons. My other five children at home — was I going to die as I was losing a lot of blood from my ear? I got a punctured lung. As I walked into the hospital I felt a raw pain in my back and put my hand around and pulled a piece of metal from my back. It was about 8 when my family found out. The staff at the Rotunda did everything they could for me and my boys. Tommy had to have stitches in two parts of his leg. Derek had cuts. They were crying. I could not see them. They were not allowed see me. A doctor was sent for me from the Richmond Hospital to look at where the blood was coming from out of my ear. He explained I had a perforated ear drum and I also had a punctured lung and two deep cuts on the back of my right knee. I was anointed by a priest from the Pro-Cathedral. A bandage was put on my leg and I was told to go to the Mater Hospital next day and bring my boys to Temple Street Hospital. I went to the Mater Hospital the next day and was examined by an ear specialist and told I would more than likely be deaf by 40. I am now. I brought Derek and Tommy to Temple Street Hospital. They were given a tetanus injection. That was it.

Do I feel traumatised? That's a joke. I lost my lovely son Tommy and I hibernated from every one and had a broken marriage.... I am one of the forgotten victims. It's fifteen years ... since I was last in town.

MR F

On Friday, 17 May 1974, I travelled with my wife from our then home ... into Dublin City. I parked my car adjacent to Westbrook Motors in Parnell Street at 3.30 p.m.

My wife was pregnant and complained of tiredness. I put five pence in the parking meter and went to purchase vegetables in Moore Street. It was our intention to stay for one hour in the area. We walked back towards my car at 4.32 p.m. I noted the time, as I feared I might obtain a parking ticket. Walking ahead of my wife with the parcels, I noticed a green car, obviously seeking a car space. I indicated to the driver I was moving out. As I was placing my parcels in the car boot, I noticed the driver of the green car becoming agitated. By this time my wife had reached my car and I held the door open for her. The driver of the car became even more agitated. I went to his driver's side and remonstrated with him.

Strangely for a warm early summer's day, he kept the windows closed. I remember this incident very clearly.

We drove away, dropping off a Nilfisk cleaner into the service department at Wicklow Street. This cleaner belonged to my mother, now deceased. As we were approaching home I had the radio tuned into RTÉ. We listened to *Cinnlínte na Nuachta* read by Maurice O'Doherty. He told the listeners there had been a series of explosions in Dublin city centre.... He repeated the news in English immediately afterwards.

Towards 6.30 p.m. on that same evening, 17 May, RTÉ Television showed pictures of the scenes of carnage. To my shock I noticed one of the scenes of the incidents was in fact Parnell Street where I had vacated my car space for the man in the green car. In response to the requests from the gardaí, I immediately drove back to Parnell Street which had been cordoned off. I spoke with the inspector-in-charge who asked me to go to Store Street Garda Station and make a statement to a plain-clothes officer. I did not hear from the gardaí until August 1974 when two detectives arrived at my home and asked me to identify one of three pieces of car metal, all coloured green. Later, in October 1974, two more detectives called to my house with a mock-up of Parnell Street and asked me to place a Dinky toy car in the spot where I parked my car at 3.30 p.m. on 17 May 1974.

I remember clearly the gardaí saying 'That's first class' and then they left. I was never questioned by gardaí again since that date. Also, I was never asked to co-operate with a photo-fit of the suspect.

I believe I am probably the only person to see the bomber and more particularly speak with him, albeit he did not reply to me audibly.

Mr F first spoke to me at an ecumenical service, commemorating the twenty-fifth anniversary of the bombings on 17 May 1999. The above statement was made, at my suggestion, on 18 May 1999. It was forwarded to Mr Justice Hamilton's 'Independent Commission of Inquiry' in July 2000 by solicitor Greg O'Neill, with a request that the author would be furnished with the original statement he made to An Garda Síochána on the evening of 17 May 1974. To his surprise, Justice Hamilton returned two statements allegedly made by Mr F. One was dated 18 May 1974, and the second dated 27 May 1974. The author of the account published above says that he made a detailed statement to the Garda on the evening of 17 May 1974, not 18 May. He further asserts that he did not make a second statement. He insists that his first statement was much more detailed than the one retrieved by Judge Hamilton from the Garda files. He disputes key elements of both statements — in particular, a short sentence in the alleged testimony dated 27 May 1974, which states, 'I would not know this man [the Parnell Street bomber] again'. In a letter to Judge Hamilton dated 25 July 2000, solicitor Greg O'Neill wrote:

> [Mr F] has informed us that he would have been in a position to pick the man out from an identity parade and to assist in a substantial way with the construction of an identikit picture. [Mr F] was never invited by the Gardaí to assist in either way.

In September 2000, Glyn Middleton of Yorkshire Television told me that, when he was interviewing the gardaí, he asked whether they had a statement from Mr F. The gardaí said that Mr F's name was not on the file.

JOHN MOLLOY

How jubilant I was on that day, 10 May 1974. I had just turned 19, a pre-leaving certificate student with future promise, excellent health, caring family and loving girlfriend. Having taken leave for study before exams in June, I sought a peaceful place in the public library in Capel Street....

4 p.m. I left the library and walked the short distance into the city centre (O'Connell Street)....

5 p.m. ... I made a right turn from O'Connell Street into Parnell Street, purchased an evening newspaper and entered Lowe's Bar on the corner of North Great George's Street.... Indulged myself in a half pint of ale shandy and lost myself completely in the newspaper readings. Minute by minute clocked by until criminal psychopaths of an evil force were to shatter the course of my life for ever....

All hell broke loose when a massive high explosion was heard all over followed immediately by a strong gravity-of-earth movement under my feet. Windows, walls, doors and ceiling came flying in all directions at high velocity never experienced. Oh Jesus — it was hell in the making.

I lay unconscious for a short time among the debris until I was helped to my feet in a daze by some fellow customers. We were all in a trance and covered in dust and appeared like human figures of a living dead. Slowly I made my own way out of the premises and before my eyes was ... a half-axle with wheel tyre on fire from a vehicle; across the street ... was the dreadful scene of the no-warning car bomb explosion. I could only stand there helpless in severe traumatic shock....

People lay on the ground moaning. Some [were] severely injured with no limbs, others were dead, with local priests by their side administering the last rites and blessings. Soon ambulances, fire brigade and Garda arrived and took full control with the utmost of speed in their respective fields....

I was taken by the St John's Ambulance to Jervis Street Hospital, a short drive away, and the carnage there in the O.P.D. section was a surgical battlefield of torn-up bodies, blood, screams of the innocent and an opened room mortuary close by for the innocent dead (RIP). This room was guarded by one single garda.... I had one deep laceration to one of my legs that required stitches and other minor lacerations to legs that received surgical dressings followed on by anti-tetanus injection. (Jervis Street Hospital staff on that dreadful day, eternal praise).

At 9 p.m. approximately, I got my discharge from the hospital and was sent home in a taxi. Our apartment, the house and the whole area had their windows all smashed in. A complete air of silence was felt over the place. I met with my mother who broke down and cried with her two arms around me saying, 'Thank the good Lord, you're safe'.

12 midnight, I visited the scene.... The Garda had the area sealed off and one could see them on [the] ground and rooftops with plastic bags either picking up part remains of human bodies or car-bomb debris. I stood there in silence and in prayer. Next morning close neighbours and friends called to our home, some half-shocked to see me and others shocked with delight.... 'God bless our innocent dead'.

The last days of May, I had stitches removed and other wounds healed all within three to four weeks going to and from hospital and then my final discharge. June came and I went into exams at College of Commerce, Rathmines. During same all I could do [was] sit there and silently cry with most papers only half written up. Results [were] inevitable: 'failed'.

A total withdrawal from the human race followed on for the next three years of my life. I became a housebound recluse with friends gradually falling away and most sadly even my girlfriend (... someday, we planned matrimony). Yes, my whole character began changing from the aftermath of the Parnell Street bombing. (Symptoms were severe post-traumatic shock).

My mother (God bless her) cared for me in those three years of agonising hell. Here I done my purgatory on earth, by her religious ways. I discovered a channel of some help to escape through with the helping hand of the Divine Master God, scripture reading and prayer and with the odd visit from the local clergy too.

Through a contact with medical profession I gained a porter job in a hospital in March 1977. Ironically I found that working with the sick helped me overcome my mental state of disorder and gradually restored confidence. August 1990 I took a position in Ambulance personnel and that too was a mighty step to further self-recovery and ironically I see myself reversing trends.

The year 2000 is now here and I do find life remaining shattered because I do still have intervals of nightmares, depressions, memory lapses and post-traumatic shock. Disappointments, yes. In government failure to recognise the needs and wants of the victims and families of the dead in the 1974 bombings. Their failure to find closure to that very serious bombing open case....

EDWARD O'NEILL

I ... remember the day of the bombings very well as it was a bright sunny day. The family was very excited as my brother Billy and sister were both due to make their communion the next day and the flat had a great buzz of excitement about it. That particular day at about 3 p.m. my dad said that he was bringing Billy out to get his hair cut.... I got somewhat upset and started to cry and pleaded with him to let me go as I always loved going out with him in the van he had. I remember him smiling and laughing with me and telling me that he would be back later and he would bring me back some sweets. I still wanted to go and cried some more. My mother's cousin was there with my dad. We all called him Uncle Brian..... They asked our next-door neighbour to look after me while they went. I ran down the stairs after my dad and stood in front of his van crying and asking him to take me with him. He eventually said okay, and much to my delight I got in the van with my brother and dad and Uncle Brian.

We went into the barber's shop on Parnell Street and my father went to talk with the barber. His name was Liam Sullivan and he was in the same karate club as my dad....

Myself and my brother sat on the bench just beyond the door ... and my dad said that him and Brian were going into the pub to have a 'lemonade' and that they would check on us every few minutes. Before they went into the pub my dad brought us back some crisps with explicit instructions to behave for Liam. We both thought that this was great — being left on our own, that is — and we made the most of the opportunity. As good as his word, it seemed like every ten minutes either my dad or Brian would come into the shop and see if we were ready.... He paid Liam and they stopped to talk for a few moments to discuss a Bruce Lee poster which he had got from a guy. It was apparently the only one of its kind in Dublin, and as my father was a martial arts fan they talked for a while. When we went outside my brother was getting swung by my dad and I held his other arm....

Billy grabbed a hold of a button which was attached to the lapel of my dad's jacket and it fell off and rolled along the pavement and into the gutter. Billy went running after it and bent down to get the button back. At that second it appeared, the bomb exploded. I remember clearly the flames rolling towards us. My dad looked panicked and seemed to freeze for a moment. Billy was bending down but my dad gave me a look which haunted me for many years. He tried to push me behind him, to shield me from what was coming toward us. I think the only way to describe it is that it was the last thing he could do for me, his look was desperate.....

I do not remember anything else for a while but the next thing I do remember is being held in someone's arms. I remember looking down and seeing that one of my legs was a very odd shape. Years later I was told that when I was brought into the hospital my left leg from the knee down was hanging only by skin and a little bit of bone. I was put into something (a car, which I also found out some years later) with my legs placed upwards because they were bleeding very badly. It was, I think, at that time that I got a very bad smell which made me feel very sick. Years later I got to smell cordite and it was the same type of smell ... only worse. I do not remember any pain, just a feeling of calm. There was I remember another person with me in the seat and I heard that person crying. I remember being bumped around in the vehicle which I was in....

Myself and my brother Billy were in a small ward off the main corridor and one day when the nurses came to take out some stitches from my legs I got very upset.

Billy was sitting in a wheelchair and came over to my bed and started to sing our dad's favourite song to me. It was written by Rolf Harris I think but it goes something like this: 'Two little boys had two little toys, each had a wooden horse, daily they played each summer's day, warriors' bows and toys'.... We also used to race our wheelchairs down the corridors of the hospital....

I also remember another day when my mother was with us when the doctor came and told her that Billy could go home ... I got hysterical in the bed because I thought Billy was going to leave me all alone. It was eventually decided that Billy was to stay with me to keep me calm and he ended up staying in the hospital far longer than was actually necessary.

Some years later I developed the most curious complaint. I could not look at any bright light at all because I had the sensation that my eyes were burning. My mother took me to see many doctors, but one in particular ... said that it was all in my head. Every time I seen a bright light I seen the flames of the explosion.

At that time I was also going back to the hospital regularly to see the plastic surgeon....

When I was entering my early teenage years I began to get very depressed. I would never go out at all.... I used to wake up on a regular basis screaming that I was on fire.... More times than not it was Billy who stayed with me until I went back to sleep. We used to talk amongst ourselves about that day but never to anyone else.

A good friend of mine once asked me why I never joined the IRA to get revenge for what the loyalists and the British done to me and my family.... but the memory and good name of our father means more to me to dishonour it in such a way....

I know who killed my father and my sister (my sister was born stillborn at six months) and that ... at the end of the day everyone of us will have to meet our maker.

I have a son now who is nearly two years old. I am going to tell him the entire circumstances of how his grandfather was murdered on the streets of the city that he loved.... I am hoping that I will be as good a father to my son as my father was to me, but most of all I am going to instil in him that to tell the truth is better and that all liars have to in the end have a good memory.

LIAM SULLIVAN

As far as I can remember on 17 May 1974 we were kept busy in the hairdressing salon all day. As it approached the evening a good friend of mine, Eddie O'Neill, who I had trained with for a couple of years at the martial arts, came into my barber's with his two children to have their hair cut. One of the boys was making his Holy Communion the following day. While Eddie was waiting for the boys to be finished he was in great form as we were having great crack about the previous week's training, free style and sparring with one another.

As Eddie O'Neill and his two sons were leaving my shop I gave the two boys a few bob between them. As they were about to go out the door Eddie stopped and gave me a tip and shook my hand and thanked me. Within seconds after the door was closed I heard the explosion. At that moment I realised I had been injured as I could feel blood coming down the side of my face. I knew then something terrible had happened.

All the customers were injured. The whole shop was completely destroyed. But for the fact that there was a form of perspex instead of glass in the window, there would have been more lives lost; the fact that it came in but did not shatter — it saved lives.

Just after the terrible bang as I was leaving the shop with my father, a friend of Eddie's, Brian [Caffrey] came in and asked me was Eddie and the kids all right and I said I didn't know. The shock and horror I felt as I made my way onto the street, when I saw bodies and blood everywhere and buildings destroyed, has never left me. It was later on that evening I heard about Eddie's death and also the children's injuries. While I was in hospital at that time I felt very distressed over Eddie and the kids.

I have to say up to this day, but for the fact that Eddie was a friend of mine he may not have been in my shop that day. He would have been alive today, and the thought often crosses my mind.

Talbot Street

DENIS BARROR

On 17 May 1974 I was working in Clare Street, which is a continuation of South Leinster Street. Under normal circumstances I would have been walking down past Trinity College on South Leinster Street on my way home at the time the bomb exploded there. However, on that particular day I had an appointment with a solicitor in Marlborough Street. That solicitor was late for the appointment by about twenty minutes. Having concluded my business ... I was walking home to Glasnevin, towards Parnell Street, when I heard a loud bang. Because of the glass that I saw falling from the old Post and Telegraphs building at the top of Marlborough Street, I thought it might well have been a gas explosion. However, I then noticed the smoke rising above the buildings on Parnell Street and I thought to myself it might well be a bomb. I was walking home at the time because there were no buses.

I decided then to avoid (as I thought) any possible trouble by turning down Talbot Street with the intention of walking up Gardiner Street.... As I walked down Talbot Street, on the left-hand side in the direction of Gardiner Street, I became more nervous, and distinctly remember looking in a shop window to see if I looked as pale as I felt. I became so nervous that there might well be a bomb parked in one of the cars in Talbot Street, that I said a 'Hail Mary'. I had just finished the prayer when all hell broke loose.

I discovered afterwards that I was standing right beside the car on the same side of the street, within, I would say, approximately 18 inches to 2 feet of it, when it exploded. It was for all the world like somebody opening the door of a furnace and I can well remember the unmistakable booming sound and the tiny particles of debris flying past my face. I distinctly remember being spun to my left and being thrown to the ground by the force of the blast. I do not actually remember hitting the ground. I do remember waking up and the street was for all the world like a still out of a movie. Suddenly everything seemed to come to life after that split second of stillness and I found myself roaring at the top of my voice. I then gathered my senses to an extent and realised that I at least was still alive, and that roaring at the top of my voice like a bull would not help anybody else in distress, so I decided to say a prayer aloud for the benefit of those around me, who ... were badly injured.

I was lying face down, facing back towards the direction of Henry Street, and I was afraid to look at my legs, as I was afraid that they might not actually be there. With a great deal of effort I forced myself to look at my legs and fortunately they were still attached and did not appear to be badly injured. I did notice one lady whose leg was completely severed from the shin down, lying face down near me. At that stage, a young man came rushing into the street with a motorcycle helmet on, asking me was I all right. I suggested to him that he might cover up the leg of the lady that was lying on the ground beside me, so that anybody else coming in would not be too shocked. I distinctly remember him walking through a shop window and pulling a piece of net curtain from it and putting it over the lady's leg. I saw one other lady motionless pinned under the canvas awning of a shop nearby.

A Garda van then came around telling people to clear the area as there had been warning of another bomb. The motorcyclist who came in to help me suggested that I get out quickly. I wanted to collect my briefcase which was lying on the footpath. In somewhat unparliamentary language he told me not to mind my briefcase and just to get out of the place. I felt myself that the safest place to be would be a garda station, so I made my way down to Store Street Garda Station on foot. I did not realise it at this stage but the coat that I had been wearing was in complete and utter flitters, as if somebody had got a scissors and cut it into thin strips from the collar down....

I was brought by ambulance from Store Street to the Mater Hospital. The trip in the ambulance was frightening enough because of the speed at which it was travelling. Each time it took a corner every pill and loose contraption in the ambulance was scattered.

When I arrived at the Mater Hospital I was one of the walking-wounded, so I walked in, only to meet my best friend who was a medical student at the time. He was too busy to say anything other than, 'Jesus, Barror.' My head was stitched and a wound to my leg was passed as being not too bad to let me go home. It transpired three days later that there was a piece of metal in my leg and I had to have that operated on. I was within twenty-four hours of developing gangrene at the time, as this metal had lodged extremely near the bone in my leg, and had not been detected....

I do not feel traumatised at all by the events. I consider myself to be the luckiest person alive. I did feel slightly nervous for a month or two after the bomb, walking down a street with cars parked, but I never did have any bad dreams or nightmares or experiences subsequently....

I believe it is essential that the truth about the bombing in Dublin should be made public. It is a dreadful injustice to those that were traumatised by the bombings that they have not been told the truth, however difficult or shocking it might be. At least then they would be dealing with a certainty rather than an uncertainty. To me it must be like not being able to locate the body of a victim of a crime or a drowning....

I have great admiration for the police who at the time visited me the day after the bomb in order to question me.... I cannot blame the politicians in the Republic for their lack of interest. I do believe there was almost a feeling that the Republic had paid its due for the havoc released by the IRA in the North of Ireland, and that the politicians, in common with an awful lot of people in this country, almost felt personally responsible for the depredations of the organisation that carried out bombings in the North in the name of the Irish Republican Army.

The whole Justice for the Forgotten movement in relation to this bombing and in relation to the demand for the truth merely confirms the resilience of the human being, and the tenacity of those who seek the truth.

I have no anger or bitterness towards those who planted the bomb even if it transpires that they have not been brought to justice because of collusion (thought to be expedient at the time), between those security forces North and South. It was a difficult time for everybody.

There are however no excuses now for hiding the truth.

FRANK GOSS
On 17 May 1974 I was coming home from work at 5 o'clock. I was standing outside O'Neill's shoe shop in Talbot Street when I heard a

loud bang and the car I was standing beside exploded in front of me. There were people running everywhere. My clothes were in tatters. I kept asking someone to help me. I met a friend who brought me to hospital by car. I had leg injuries and lost the hearing in my left ear.

NOEL HEGARTY

I was working as an apprentice tailor in Liffey Street. I got off work early that day to meet my sister in Parnell Street. Lucky enough she didn't turn up and the bomb just went off. I ran from there down into Talbot Street and ran straight into the other one as it went off. There are bits and pieces and I suppose one image which remains in my mind and always will was of a man just lying in front of me and I take it he was dead. That memory always comes back to me. He was badly. He was well dressed. He had a suit on him and he had a briefcase still in his hand.

I was unconscious for I think five days. It was two days before they located me in the hospital, my parents that was.... I just kept taking blackouts for years and years.

The Omagh bombing brought it all back. That triggered it off. I mean after the Dublin bombings, it took me a couple of years before I went back into town. I was so distressed that on a couple of occasions I tried to end the torment of it....

I never received counselling. None whatsoever. I could understand to a certain extent what was happening and over the years I suppose I developed a shield. You withdraw into yourself. I think that it was when the Omagh bombings happened it was the first time in a long time that everything came crashing back in one go. I ended up going on the drink for two months because of it. I don't know whether it was fear or post-traumatic stress.

I was attending a counsellor ... after the Omagh bombings and she more or less said it was. I just stopped going after a while ... it done a certain amount of good but it wasn't really the answer....

You always seem to be searching. I know when I was interviewed after the Dublin/Monaghan bombings the guards came to the house and when they went I felt as though I had done something wrong. I was interrogated and I was only a child. I was fourteen at the time. Just going on fourteen. That was it, there was no such thing as 'I'm sorry for your troubles' or 'Hope you get well', it was 'What were you doing there, why were you there and who were you with?' I mean, that stays in my mind as well.

I was on my own. They brought me into the sitting-room on my own. There were two of them. They were fairly middle-aged. They interviewed me I suppose for about 20 minutes or so and that was it, they just left then. You were left to pick up the pieces then yourself....

I was in hospital for about a month and a half or two months. The Richmond Hospital. I was transferred from Jervis Street to the Richmond. I was anointed, I think, three or four times....

I'd say for [my family] it was traumatic as well.

It was two years before I even went back into town. That was it. That was that career out the door. I never went back to it again. I was doing the group cert at the time of the bombings but that went out the door as well.

I would like to see the truth coming out.... I asked for help then and I suppose at the time I ended up in Portrane and the help that they gave us was electric shock treatment — to a fourteen-year-old. That in itself is another episode of my life. Six times I got electric-shock treatment. I can remember every one of them. As plain as day. A horrible sensation. You're asleep but you're not asleep. As soon as it hits your temples, you're awake. A terrible pain in your head.... It should have never been allowed. It's their way of saying 'Forget about us.'

I'm angry at the government here for treating people the way they have treated us. I'm angry at those responsible because I know in my heart and soul that it was the English government who were responsible for it and I mean so does so many other people yet they don't want to do anything about it. I mean, like, it was a crime against humanity and the crime against humanity still went on and has been going on for the last twenty-five years. Hopefully some day it will come to light and justice will prevail....

I suppose you just want to forget about things and you just want to get on with life. I'm lucky in respect that I have a good wife and three children and a nice home. They are something that I achieved for myself without anybody else's help. I suppose that's about it really.

Christopher Keane (New Zealand)

I remember how busy the city was on that day, due to the bus strike, I suppose. I finished work a little late that day and ran hard to get to Talbot Street to meet my friends who were to give me a lift. We had arranged to meet at 5.20 p.m. but unknown to me they had tried in vain to find parking in the Talbot Street area and as it was so congested they had to move on.

I waited outside Guiney's store, leaning against the window, speaking to an acquaintance.... I asked him the time — [he] replied that it was 5.30 by his watch. I can remember thinking that I'd have to walk home, feeling annoyed that I'd missed my lift. It was so far to walk all the way to Finglas from the city. I turned to walk away from Guiney's store window when the bomb went off. I was lifted off my feet and blown sideways. I felt a force push me from behind and debris hitting me from all sides. Bodies being flung on top of me, all around me. There were a couple of bodies — dead, what was left of them. I blacked out and when I woke up I felt pain, searing pain in my face, like my skin was on fire. I heard voices screaming in agony, children crying. Smoke — smoke so thick I couldn't see through it. Eerie screaming voices. I heard people shouting and I got to my feet and I heard voices screaming, 'Another bomb! Another bomb!' There were panicked voices all around me. This woman panicked, screaming, screaming she was. I managed to get her to the ground thinking another bomb was going off. Such carnage, such devastation. I managed to get to my feet again and as I walked forward some people had come to my aid and took me to some buildings in a side street. They carried me. It was then I was unconscious again. I woke up in the shop on the corner of Talbot and Gardiner Street — a photography shop I think it was; here other injured people also lay. Again I went unconscious. I awoke to people slapping me in the face to awaken me. Buses arrived and people were transported to hospital by bus. There were so many injured the ambulances couldn't cope. I remember holding my head like it was going to explode. The pain in my head. I could feel my face swelling up. Once on the bus I remember holding an old lady — they had put her into my arms. Her legs were blown off and she looked close to death. She looked in my face and murmured, 'I have a son your age', and then she slumped sideways and closed her eyes; she never said another word to me. As we travelled to the Sir Patrick Dun's Hospital — the look on people's faces.... How it must have looked to them. A bus full of maimed and injured people — like something out of a war movie.

The whole hospital experience is a blur. I do remember lots of people, people crying, people running around. I was obviously in shock. I don't know if I was checked for head or internal injuries. I was in shock. I was kept in overnight but I wanted to get out of there as soon as I could. There was human misery all around me.

After arriving home it was from then on that the nightmares began. My body would shake with nervousness. I couldn't even hold a cup. I was too afraid to venture outside. It got so bad that for weeks I couldn't go to work. My employer was very understanding. He even tried to pick me up to take me to work but it was no good. I couldn't do it. Sometime later I had to resign from my job, my career. The nightmares were so intense that I would wake up to my family holding me down for my own protection. Years later my neighbours were to tell me that they could often hear my screaming from the nightmares through the walls. These went on for years.

The doctors put me on medication for my nerves and so began years of medication and drugs to help me forget, to stop my body from shaking, to block out the bad memories. I just wanted to escape. This led to stronger drugs until drugs became my life.... I needed the pills when I woke up and when I went to sleep....

[At 21] I had a complete nervous breakdown. For several weeks I was in the Mater Hospital. When I came out my life was still upside down. Sometime later I was back in the Mater again because I made an attempt on my life. I was there for several more weeks, this time receiving psychiatric care. This was the lowest point....

I was unemployed for a year and that's when I decided to go ... to London [for a second time since the bombings]. My life just spiralled down again and I got more into drugs to dull my senses. This went on for years. During the late '70s and early '80s there were a lot of bombings in London which made me very nervous. At times I would not even leave my flat.

Then somehow I started to confront my problems. I started to see some good in life. During this time I met my wife Maree — a positive spark in my negative world. From then on through sheer determination I started to get my life back on track. The nightmares started to ease slightly, my body started to feel better. I eventually stopped taking dependency drugs in 1981, just before I got married.

When I married my wife Maree I decided that I would live in New Zealand — her home country. This was a turning point for me. I have made a good life for myself. In the nineteen years I've been living in New Zealand I've been back to Ireland three times to visit my family and each time I went back ... the fear resurfaced and it wasn't easy for me to go into the city. The last time I went was for the Christmas/New Year of 1999/2000. It was then that I felt it most. The fear, the anguish, now that I had my children with me each time I entered the city.

I don't think I could live peacefully in Ireland in my heart. Maybe because every time I go back to Ireland the memories come back again. But I know now I have come full circle since that horrible day in 1974 which ripped apart my life. It stripped me of a good ten years of my life that I will never be able to have again. But I want to say after all of this, thinking back and going through all of that, how important it was for me to have the love of my family and the love of my friends, especially the love and support of my mother who went through this nightmare with me. I say to the people responsible — you took all those years away from me but not the strength and love of my family and it is that you will never take away from me. I have asked myself many times why, why would anyone want to kill and maim innocent people? Why those innocent children? I can still hear their crying screaming in my head when I think about it. That torment will never go away. What will heal my torment would be to see those people responsible being brought to justice and to be put away where they belong. I find it gut-wrenching as to why those people we call our politicians with the Irish Government in 1974 did not bring those people responsible to trial.... I hope some day I will find out, not only for myself but for those who were killed and for those like myself who survived. God willing, I do know one thing — those people who are responsible — they have no God. The only God they have is violence which in the end will give them no peace, even until the day they die. And that's not the God I believe in.

MARIAN KEENAN

17 May 1974 was the last day of the second year BA term in Maynooth. I left home early in the morning to go with a friend to a hotel in Dublin for an interview for summer work. I clearly remember one of my house-mates waving goodbye from the top bedroom window as I walked into Maynooth to catch the bus. I cannot remember the interview at all. My friend and I had coffee and a bun in a café after it and then said goodbye.

My friend went down the Quays and I turned left down North Earl Street. I met Anne Marren just at the corner. She asked me to wait for her while she bought tights in Dunnes Stores. I waited outside.

We walked down the street happily chatting. We met Josephine Bradley. Anne introduced us: 'a friend from school and a friend from work,' she laughed. Then we heard a loud bang. It was the Parnell Street bomb. I remember a van racing by and a man with long hair holding on to it. Then the bomb in Talbot Street exploded. There was total silence around me. I couldn't get up. My right arm was numb. I felt dusty. I didn't see anyone around me. I only remember the people who approached me, the old Dublin lady who wrote down the number of my local shop to let my mother know; the young boy from Guiney's who helped me onto the bus and laid my legs carefully on one seat and the rest of my body on the other. I remember the weakness of my body which came from the blood loss.

In Sir Patrick Dun's Hospital I lay in a corridor while they took off my clothes. I remember them talking about the dead people. I knew Anne was dead. It was the silence. I didn't get to theatre until 10.30 and was four hours in theatre. I spent six weeks in hospital. I was showered with love and attention and this helped me to make a remarkable recovery. I am scarred all over. I have shrapnel in my head and legs. I feel, however, that I am lucky, I have been so lucky. I feel guilty about the girls — guilty that they died and I lived. I write about my experience only to document the last moments of Anne and Josephine. They should not be forgotten.

TOM LAWLOR

In 1974, photographer Tom Lawlor worked for The Irish Times. *He was the first photojournalist to arrive in Talbot Street, coming on the scene within thirty seconds of the explosion. In this reflection he records the horror of his experience as he attempted to do the work of his profession.*

I lift my camera to my eye and shoot. The moment captures the crowd in the street turning in panic. A young man struggles with his scooter. Couples hold each other as they rush past me. In a moment I'm standing alone. Behind me the shouts and screams of the crowd, before me a landscape of horror. The air is filled with tumbling litter and smoke ropes lifting from a vortex of hell. My feet crunch on the mayhem carpet as I move forward. My fear holds me back, my job pushes me on. In a shattered shop window I see three women lie together. The explosion has stripped their clothes away. I see the labels of their underwear still white against their blackened skin. I lift my camera to my eye and shoot.

A figure is lying against a silver power-box at the edge of the footpath. The blast has destroyed their identity. Neither male nor female can be identified from the ribboned rags that hang about the upper body. The end of the leg is a bloodied stump. A fireman comes to rescue the figure. I lift my camera to my eye and shoot.

My eye sweeps the street. The smoking metal flesh of the cars drifts upwards. In the silence a voice speaks from the radio of a Garda motorcycle. Rescue is arriving. Blue lights pulsing from the rescue crews. White coats contrast against the blackened scene. I lift my camera to my eye and shoot.

Two men support an elderly lady between them. Her walking stick swinging loosely from her bloodied hands. They move in silence, not a word is exchanged between them. They pass behind a truck. It has the word 'Sláinte' painted on the bodywork.

To my left I see a movement. A young woman lies on the pavement. Her position suggests sleep. Her hair is moving dark and long about her shoulders. Her coat is fitted at the waist and flares below her hips. There is no panic in her posture. She seems to be resting. Her blood fills the seams of the paving slabs that frame her shape. She could be my sister. She could be my mother. There is a home somewhere that expects her. Someone is waiting for her. I lift my camera to my eye and shoot.

MAYDAY MAYDAY MAYDAY.

ROSALEEN MUSSEN
I was in Boylan's opticians in Talbot Street being fitted for contact lenses. My husband, Ciaran, was with me. He was in reception, sitting with his back to the window. He was holding our eight-month-old son, Garrett....

Mr Flanagan [the optician] was examining my eyes when I heard the Parnell Street bomb. I jumped and said 'Christ, there's a bomb!' He said, 'Not at all, you're not in the North now, you know.' A few seconds later there was an unmerciful bang and the place came in around us. I remember looking at Mr Flanagan while the plasterboard, light fittings, etc., fell around him. I remember thinking that I was going to die. I thought this is how it is in Belfast and I pictured people digging through the rubble looking for our bodies.

When the plaster and timber, etc., stopped falling I went into reception. There was an unearthly silence. I saw a person coming from the front door. It was my husband. His first reaction was to get out but when he had reached the door he remembered the baby. We found our son underneath a desk. Ciaran lifted him and he began to cry.

The optician suggested that we should go to the basement in case there might be another bomb but when we got to the second or third step we saw that it had caved in. Ciaran then said that it was unlikely that there would be another bomb and so we all went outside.

When we went outside the silence had been replaced by people screaming and the scene was that of devastation. People were lying injured and dying, cars and buildings were wrecked and people who were not so physically injured were screaming and shouting and waving their hands. I remember thinking that they were having epileptic fits.

I remember seeing a woman lying face down just outside the optician's shop. My first reaction was to go towards her. I heard her groan but then I remembered my baby and knew that both he and my husband had to get to hospital. Mr Flanagan later told me that the woman died.

Ciaran had been cut on the left side of his head and there was a lot of blood. A man approached us and identified himself as a doctor (from Belfast). He examined the baby and assured us that he would be okay and said that most of the blood covering the baby had come from the gash in Ciaran's head.

A little further up Talbot Street (we were walking in the direction of Connolly Station) a young man, probably in his twenties, approached us and told us to get into his car and he would take us to hospital. He took us to Temple Street Hospital. Ciaran was taken away to be stitched and I stayed with Garrett while the doctors examined him. Garrett was kept overnight in Temple Street Hospital.

Garrett was allowed home the next day (Saturday) and seemed to be none the worse. Ciaran's sister and her husband came down to visit us on that evening. They drove from Downpatrick to Dublin and were totally amazed that they had not encountered a single roadblock.

The following day Garrett was back in hospital. He was moved to St Ultan's hospital and spent about two weeks there suffering from spinal injuries. He was very sick and very listless. He lost all his weight and at one stage we were very worried but then one day he rallied and within about four days was allowed home.

We left Dublin a few weeks later and went to live in New York.

In recent times we have spoken to many of the relatives of the victims of the Dublin bombs and we realise how lucky we were.

MARTESSA NÍ CEARNAIGH
Martessa Ní Cearnaigh (Tess Kearney) was a stalwart in the Justice for the Forgotten Campaign. John Scally interviewed her in June 1999. Sadly, Martessa passed away in early February 2000.
I was just preparing to leave the office when I heard an explosion. I'd said to my workmates that that sounded like a car bomb. It was actually the bomb going off in Parnell Street. I was the only one that left the office. I ran down the stairs and just opened the hall door when the bomb opposite went off. I immediately threw myself on the ground, as I had known that this was the usual thing to do, coming from my home town of Derry.

I lay on the ground for a few minutes and then went to get up and found that I wasn't able to see. This gave me a terrible fright but in a few minutes I got the sight back again and I had just got as far as Lenehan's window when there was a second explosion much smaller than the first but it completely blew out the large plate-glass window of Lenehan's with the glass showering all over me. I had many small cuts on my head, neck and damage to both of my legs. The one thing that I really remember in Talbot Street, the one thing that sticks out more than the other horrific scenes around me was a man holding up an infant. That was something I will never forget.

I made my way home as quickly as I could because we had just suffered bereavement ten days earlier. The effect that the bomb had on me I didn't discover for some time later. I had been in and out of different hospitals and eventually went over to a hospital in London where I was transferred to the neurological hospital where they told me I had actually got epilepsy from my injuries. This has changed my life and changed it forever. It even meant me having to give up my job, as I could no longer drive a car.

Up to this very day I am still receiving treatment. A doctor calls to my home every second week to treat me for post-traumatic stress. I hope that some day the truth about Talbot Street and all the other bombings will be revealed ... so that at last we can come to terms with the treatment we have received from the Irish Government.

BERNIE O'HANLON
... I was 16 years old. I worked in O'Neill's shoe shop in Talbot Street, Dublin. I was the junior assistant.... It was a lovely bright summer evening and I was in such a hurry to get out into the hustle and bustle I went down to get my bag at about 5.25 p.m. Two of the senior assistants ... sent me back upstairs to the shop floor.... A late shopper came in for sandals. Her size was not on the shelf so I was sent to the storeroom in the basement.... I ran down and as I entered the storeroom a very loud rumble stopped me in my tracks. 'That sounds like a bomb,' I thought but I dismissed that idea and decided it must be thunder. Very loud thunder.

I hurried back up the stairs with the sandals. In the hallway between the ladies' and gents' shops, Mr O'Neill, the shop owner, and May McKenna were standing. The big hall door that led onto Talbot Street was half open. They both had their hands on the door. Mr O'Neill was advising May to close it. She was disturbed by the loud rumble (it was the Parnell Street bomb). She [worked] in Clery's, O'Connell Street who were on strike so she was at home that evening (which was a flat over O'Neill's shop). As I got near them she turned and asked me, 'Did you hear a bomb going off?' 'Yes,' I said, with some hesitation, I still thought it was thunder.

I continued into the ladies' shop and before I could close the door a huge flash and another loud rumble threw me to the floor. The floor and building were shaking very violently and the shelves and ceiling were falling down and the big shop window exploded on top of the late shopper and me. As I lay on the floor I was very frightened and confused. I thought I had been hit by lightning. It felt like I was being electrocuted. While the building continued to vibrate I forced open my eyes to see what was happening but I couldn't see. Gradually the vibrating stopped and I was able to get onto my hands and knees. Then the sound of a woman moaning very weakly caught my attention. I grovelled around for her. I couldn't find her as she moaned louder. I said, 'I can't find you.' Then I realised I might be hurting her if she was under me. 'I'll get someone to help you,' I said and went back to where Mr O'Neill and May McKenna were standing, for help, but they were gone. I discovered later that May McKenna had been killed and Mr O'Neill was very seriously injured.

I realised at this stage I had no sight. 'Please God, don't let me be blind,' I said, and my sight returned to my left eye. From the ground up I couldn't believe the devastation before me. I walked through where the window had been into Talbot Street. The silence was sickening. The dust was thick and the street was desolate. I stood in the street in disbelief at what was before me. Then a Garda asked me who else was in the shop. I told him about the lady who was moaning weakly. I watched a fireman lifting a child from Guiney's window. I thought it was a mannequin. I realised years later it was a child. I was brought to Moran's Hotel to have my injuries seen to. Although there was a lot of blood on my clothes I didn't know I was injured. While walking the short distance to Moran's Hotel I saw an elderly lady with legs seriously injured and another person sprawled on the footpath. There was commotion on the corner at the bank but I was afraid to look.

Inside Moran's Hotel a doctor was attending to some of the injured people. He got sheets from the hotel and tore them to make bandages for my head wound. A man in a pin-stripe suit washed my hands and chatted to me for a while. Then someone told us there was a bus outside the bank for anyone who could walk to take to the hospital. Mr Kevin Roe was in town on that evening and came to help people in Talbot Street and as there were no ambulances available he took a bus from Busáras to get us to hospital (Thank You).

The bus was full of injured people. They were crying and moaning in shock and pain. I felt a terrible panic. There was a detective from Store Street on the bus who was standing up front with the driver. He was trying to encourage everyone and telling us to keep our chins up. But he was aggravating me. I wanted to get off that bus and run home. The bus pulled in to the hospital gates and as we were about to get off the bus an elderly lady was sitting with her back to the window, her legs draped over the adjoining seat and a newspaper was covering what was left of her right leg. It was gone from the shin down and she didn't know or seem to know she was injured. She just sat in silence. Two young nurses were standing at the doorway of the hospital. They told us to follow a coloured strip on the ceiling to get to casualty.

Casualty was already full with injured people. Róisín, a girl I worked with, and myself were told to wait in a small room. We waited for a long time. Doctors, nurses and journalists came in a steady stream for our names and addresses but no one saw to my injuries. Then I realised my Mam and Dad didn't know where I was. 'I better go home,' I said. Róisín agreed and we began to leave the hospital. A lady in the corridor asked us where we were going. 'Home,' I said. She brought us back to a room. Róisín went to ring my family and her husband. The lady doctor removed my clothes to look at my injuries. We had no privacy and it was embarrassing. A doctor began to stitch my hip and, while this was happening, my father arrived with my sister and brother. Then Mr John McDougall, an eye specialist, began to attend to my eye. He seemed very concerned. He wanted to get me to the Eye and Ear Hospital but there were no ambulances available and the doctor's car was blocked in so we all went in my father's car.

I was admitted to the Eye and Ear Hospital. I had surgery late that night to remove glass from my right eye and to stitch my head wound. I had further surgery a few weeks later and more complications. It was suggested I would have to have the eye removed. Mr McDougall fought very hard to save my eye. He knew I could not have faced any more trauma. I was discharged from hospital on 3 July 1974 and I held on to my blind and badly scarred eye for twenty-four years. This in itself caused other problems for me. Then, on 5 May 1998, the eye had to be removed. To this day I still attend hospital and need more surgery to correct the physical appearance.

I never understood what actually happened that day. Somewhere in my mind I believed it was an accident but as time unfolds — the terrible truth of that sad day as I remember the slaughter of the innocent — my blood runs cold. Thirty-three people murdered. Hundreds injured and still suffering today. Over thirty families still grieving for the loss of their husbands, wives, mothers, fathers, sons and daughters and the unborn.

I could never understand why no one was held responsible for the terrible atrocity.... Even at this late stage our Government still can help us find the truth. It should not be left up to us the victims, but it has been.

I think the Irish Government should leave no stone unturned until it finds the truth and justice we deserve. Then and only then can we heal.

JOE O'NEILL

On Friday, 17 May 1974, at about 5.25 p.m., I was in the office of Number 18A Talbot Street clearing the till at the end of the day's taking. Suddenly I heard a loud bang. Immediately I left the office and went out into the street and walked up to the corner of Talbot Street — junction of Gardiner Street. I spoke to Brendan who was selling papers and asked him if something happened in the car park in Gardiner Street. I had my car parked there. He said he thought it was further up the street. I went back to the shop and went into the ladies' department and spoke to one of my staff, Mary Higgins. Then I crossed over the shop to open the door to cross over the hallway which would bring me to the gents' department, number 18

Talbot Street, to collect the day's taking. Just as I put my hand on the knob of the door, Miss McKenna who lived upstairs had her hand at the other side, trying to push the door open — shouting what had happened. Just then there was a bright flash and very loud bang and the door went out of my hand into the hallway and the street came flying in. At that point Miss McKenna disappeared. I was thrown to the ground. When I got back on my feet I was in shoes up to my knees. I saw a piece of timber blazing. I thought the place was going on fire. I was very worried as the staff were down in the basement getting ready to go home. I pulled up my right foot to stamp on the timber and discovered I had no shoe on my right foot. I then used my left foot and put the flames out. Then I made my way out to the street. I'm still not sure how I got out to this day. All I wanted to do at this stage was to lie down. I decided to head towards the benches in Moran's Hotel. I could not see my way even though it was still only 5.30 p.m. (approx.) on a bright May evening — now as I am writing this account twenty-five years later the darkness is my most vivid memory. I thought a steam roller had come down the street and crushed all in front of it. I remember Joe O'Rourke, one of my staff, shouting and waving, trying to encourage me to come back towards the shop but I still continued to walk. When I reached the traffic light at the junction of Talbot Street/Gardiner Street I noticed the traffic was extremely heavy. I walked halfway across the street, at this stage I looked down and saw a big hole in the jacket of my suit. There seemed to be a yellow liquid flowing down my left side — at this stage I collapsed (semi-conscious). A man who worked further up the street opened his car door and lifted me into the back seat. He asked me where I wanted to go and I said to the nearest hospital. We went down the Quays to O'Connell Bridge and Lower O'Connell Street and into Abbey Street which was one-way in the opposite direction. He stopped the car for a while and I told him to continue and I would pay the fine if the Garda caught him. When we arrived at the big green doors of Jervis Street Hospital the porter wouldn't allow the car in. He came out to the car to have a look and when he noticed I was injured in the back seat the car was allowed in. I was lifted out and put on a stretcher and there was people all around asking me what happened. I remember a nun asking me was I in Parnell Street and I said 'No'. She asked me where I was from and I said Monaghan. I could hear them discuss that I was a northerner. I felt they were suspicious of me for something I couldn't quite understand. I was taken into the hospital and put into a lift with two men and two nurses. When I was wheeled out, more nurses and a nun said to make a place for me in St Laurence's ward. They were all asking me who I was and one nurse said, 'I think I know him or his friend.' I asked for a drink as there was hair falling into my mouth. They said I would have to wait until I came back from theatre. They kept asking me was my face and head sore and I told them my stomach was very painful. They then cut my clothes off with large scissors. They also kept asking for phone numbers of a friend. I was getting weaker and a doctor and nurse got oxygen for me. Later I opened my eyes and I saw three doctors or surgeons coming along a long corridor and one said, 'I will take him.' I was taken into the theatre. After this I don't remember anything until Sunday evening when I opened my eyes for a short while and went back to sleep. When I opened my eyes again on Monday mid-morning I thought I had lost one of my legs and my left arm would not move. After some time the nurses came and covered my face with gauze and cream and got a doctor to look at my eyes.

A few days after being discharged from hospital I had to return to casualty as I was unable to sleep the previous night with severe pain in my right foot. On examination the doctor discovered my foot was infected. He had to incise it and discovered a huge piece of glass embedded in it. I returned to work later in July. On Friday, 17 September 1974, I returned home from work complaining of abdominal pain. I went to bed and the pain got worse and I was violently sick. My wife contacted Jervis Street and an ambulance was sent immediately for me as they were aware I was a bomb victim.... My diagnosis was small-bowel obstruction due to the severe injuries the previous May. My stay in hospital was two weeks.

KEVIN ROE
On Friday, 17 May 1974, I was on duty at Busáras working on the 18.00 Dublin to Donegal Express when suddenly there was a loud bang. I said to my fellow workers that it must be a bomb. I ran around to Talbot Street to find the street covered in rubble and broken glass from the shop windows. I met people coming towards me, blood pouring from their injuries. I first walked into O'Neill's shoe shop which was completely destroyed. There were bodies lying on the floor and I lifted the injured, some of whom were on the shelves of the shop and took them to Moran's Hotel. I then returned to O'Neill's where I helped carry out the dead and put them at the corner of Talbot Street and Gardiner Street. You can imagine how the street must have looked. The Omagh bombing brought it all back to me. After some time I asked a garda why there were no ambulances at the scene. He told me that there were two other bombings, one in Parnell Street, and one in Leinster Street, and so the ambulances were all in use. I said, 'Give me five minutes and I will have a bus to take the injured to hospital.' I then went back to Busáras and drove the bus that I should have been driving to Donegal that day to Talbot Street. By that time members of the Emergency Services had arrived. We all helped take the injured from Moran's Hotel onto the bus. We took between thirty-five and forty injured people to Sir Patrick Dun's Hospital, with a Garda motorcycle escort. It took some time to get there as all roads were congested with traffic due to the bombing on the southside of the city. Also there were more cars on the road due

to the Dublin bus strike. Some of the people on the bus were very badly injured. When we got to the hospital it took some time for the doctors and nurses to take the injured off the bus. Because the bus seats were badly stained from the injuries I had to take it to the garage to be cleaned. I then returned to Busáras, got myself cleaned up and did a journey on the Navan service. When I finally arrived home that evening my family were worried about me because they had heard about the bombing, but because we had no phone at the time, I hadn't rung them to say that I was all right.

As you can imagine, I did not sleep too well that night and for many other nights after. Down the years I often wondered about how some of the people were that I carried in my bus and if they had survived....

It is now twenty-six years later and I have just attended an Ecumenical Service in St Macartan's Cathedral, Monaghan, on Sunday, 14 May. It was the first time I spoke to anyone connected with the bombing since that terrible evening of 17 May 1974. It was very moving at the wreath-laying service at the site of the bomb in Monaghan. Also at the Cathedral it all came back to me.

MARIE SHERRY

On the day of the bombings I was working in an office in Parnell Square. I left my office at 5.20 p.m. to head down to Busáras for the 6 p.m. bus to Tyrrellspass in County Westmeath. I was due to spend the weekend with my aunt.... I just remember an awful lot of people were in town on that day for some reason. I was at the junction of Marlborough Street and Talbot Street when the bomb went off in Parnell Street. At the time I didn't know it was a bomb. I continued on walking towards Busáras. I was walking down the north side of Talbot Street and crossed over to the other side. I was just passing Guiney's when the bomb went off in Talbot Street. The window of Guiney's came in on top of me. I suffered cuts and bruises.

For as long as I live I will never forget the aftermath. There was total chaos, there was debris everywhere, people running around screaming hysterically, children crying, police sirens going ... I just got up and my immediate reaction was to keep running. I remember running past Clery's in O'Connell Street and a lady grabbing me by the arm and asking me what was wrong, and was I all right. I could not talk to her and I just kept running. I decided I would head down to Liberty Hall because my sister worked there and somehow she would look after me. She arranged a lift home for me. The journey from Liberty Hall to Donnybrook took an hour and a half, traffic everywhere was at a standstill. There was a Dublin bus strike at the time.

An insurance collector who used to call to my parents' home each Friday, when he saw the state I was in, insisted upon my mother to make me go to the hospital for a check-up and he would bring me. He brought me down to what was then Baggot Street Hospital and they attended to my wounds. I can recall a plain-clothes detective from

Donnybrook Garda Station coming into the hospital to interview me to see if I had seen anything suspicious. I was not of any help to him. I did not recall seeing any other injured person in the hospital.

My injuries did not render it necessary for me to stay in overnight and I wouldn't have anyway. I was aware of my left ear being sore and there was a buzzing noise, which I just put down to the noise of the bomb exploding. It was a couple of days afterwards that I experienced discomfort and a lump under my ear. I had this investigated further, in, I think, the Eye and Ear Hospital, or it could have been Sir Patrick Dun's. It transpired that I had injured my ear and suffered a hearing loss as a result. I still suffer with this ear if I am in a noisy room or whenever I fly. I also had to have a head X-ray done and a hairline crack was discovered in my skull.

The injuries mentioned above were nothing compared to the mental turmoil I suffered for years and years following that awful day.... When all of my peers were going into town to the cinema, dancing or whatever, I refused to go most of the time, and if I did go, I would spend the night watching around for any suspicious behaviour. I left cinemas in the middle of films because someone got up to go to the loo; I would have myself convinced that they were up to no good. If I saw an English or Northern-Ireland-registered car parked on a street I would walk around the block sooner than pass it. It was really a nightmare, and as far as I am concerned, ruined my young years.

To this day, I have a fear of crowded places. I am always watching for suspicious behaviour. I cannot seem to relax totally and especially if I am in a city-centre venue.

The way the police and politicians have treated me, and, in particular, the way they have treated those families who have lost loved ones in this tragedy, is absolutely appalling. To think that the people who carried out this atrocity, and who apparently are known to the authorities, are walking around free while the families of those who died are not free — they are still grieving badly for their loved ones — is a disgrace. This is so clear to see at the meetings of the Justice for the Forgotten Campaign.

I want to see this matter closed once and for all. I want a public inquiry. I want to see people named and charged for these killings. I want to know why the politicians who were in power at that time did ... nothing about the matter. I want justice for the forgotten victims of this horrific crime.

South Leinster Street, Dublin

BERNADETTE BERGIN

On 17 May 1974 at 5.30 p.m. I was standing on the steps outside the offices of Bowmaker Finance Company in South Leinster Street, where I worked as the secretary to the Managing Director. I was waiting for my boyfriend to collect me in his car. He was late and most of my colleagues had gone. As I watched out for him I was aware of a car being hurriedly parked and a man running away from it. At this stage, I have no real recollection as to a description of this man. A few minutes later there was a huge explosion. I was thrown up into the air and seemed to float for a while before being smashed into a car which was parked on my side of the road. For some reason, perhaps purely reflexive, I managed to protect my face with my handbag so that when I landed in what appeared to be a sea of glass I did not sustain any injuries to my face. The plate-glass window of the office had been blown out behind me and I was very lucky not to have been decapitated.

There was an eerie silence for what seemed like ages and then all hell broke loose — the screaming, roaring and shouting was unbelievable. When I tried to get up I could not use my right leg — it had been shattered and from the look of it I thought that it was hanging off. Two men came to my assistance. One was the elderly porter from the company in which I worked and I really don't know who the second one was. They carried me into the offices of P.J. Matthews, Bathroom Fittings, which was a few doors away from Bowmaker. I refused to be brought back into Bowmaker offices because in all the mayhem I thought that another bomb might go off in there as it was an English company and we had been getting quite a lot of bomb threats. In any event, by not going into the office it caused a lot of confusion because nobody knew where I was. I was very anxious about my boyfriend and was convinced that he had been killed as I had seen a car the same as his in flames on the street. After some time I was put into an ambulance but then had to be transferred to another as the glass had punctured all the tyres on the first. There was one other person on a stretcher in this ambulance and it turned out to be the body of poor Anna Massey who had been killed. My handbag was on this other stretcher. I was then brought to the Richmond Hospital. Eventually at about 9 p.m. that night my parents and my boyfriend located me at the Richmond having been to Sir Patrick Dun's, Jervis Street and the Mater. At the Richmond they were initially led to believe that I had been killed, because of the confusion over the handbag.

When the doctor saw my leg I was told that there was a strong possibility that I might lose it. They operated on the leg and left it in an open cast for a week so that they could monitor any infection. I also had severe lacerations to my left leg and hands and also fragments of glass in my head, bits of which I was still removing many years later ... [M]y boyfriend was not in fact injured but I feel that he was also a victim as indeed were my parents and sister since they had to do the rounds of the streets and hospitals and see all the horrible sights, not knowing what was ahead of them when they eventually located me. At the end of the day my story turned out to be a happy one as we got engaged when I was in hospital and that helped me in a very big way not to dwell on what I had gone through but to think of the future.

I spent two weeks in hospital and the following six months on crutches, returning to the Richmond every few weeks to have more plaster put on the cast. After that I had a lot of physiotherapy. I did not return to work until November 1974. I received no counselling and, to my recollection, was never interviewed by the gardaí or anyone in authority as to my recollection of what occurred on that fateful day.

For a long time I found it impossible to venture into Dublin city centre and was very uncomfortable being back in South Leinster Street. One night John brought me into town, parked the car and insisted that I walk with him around the town. I was extremely nervous and was convinced that every car I saw parked anyway badly was about to blow up. Eventually, with the help of John, my family and my colleagues at work, I managed to get on with my life.

In 1983, we had the option of moving to Tralee and I jumped at the opportunity to leave Dublin. To this day I hate going to Dublin and am still very nervous in the shops. I only go when it's absolutely necessary — to visit my mother who still lives there. I rarely go into town when I'm there. I would not move back to Dublin even though the opportunity to do so has arisen during the course of John's work. This anxiety has even affected my two teenage daughters. All their lives I have not been able to play with them as a mother should because I was fearful of causing further aggravation to my leg which has constantly given me pain down through the years.....

In common with all the other victims I am still suffering. On 1 September 1999 I had a total knee replacement and am presently recovering from that. The surgeon has informed me that it will take up to two years for a complete recovery.

My thoughts as to how the other victims and I were treated are that we have been totally ignored.... For years, nobody wanted to know and they still don't. When I see how the victims of Omagh have been treated I find it very difficult to understand how so-called 'celebrities' from the south of Ireland who can't do enough for those unfortunate people are not interested even today in getting involved with the campaign for the 1974 victims. Under no circumstances am I saying that the Omagh victims do not deserve what they are getting. They certainly do ... but I feel that it is time for the people who suffered equal tragedy and pain in 1974 to receive due recognition and some answers.

After twenty-five years I would like the truth of what happened to be brought out into the public arena. It will not bring back all those who lost their lives or help to alleviate the pain, suffering and loss of the relatives and victims but it will answer the questions once and for all. Then maybe we can get on with our lives on this island in peace....

JOAN ANN HOURIGAN (USA)

Joan Ann Hourigan was seriously injured in the 1972 Dublin bombings which killed George Bradshaw and Tommy Duffy. Uniquely, on 17 May 1974, she was also injured in the South Leinster Street attack.

... [M]y girlfriend and I left our jobs probably five minutes before finishing time (at USIT on St Stephen's Green), as I wanted to catch the train from [Westland Row] to Raheny, where I was going to meet my boyfriend. We were to baby-sit for my sister Miriam McGowan. We were on Nassau Street at the time and I was having a hard time rushing for the train as I was wearing cork platform shoes and tweed trousers (all the fashion at the time). I was constantly stopping to pull the trouser leg out as it was slipping under the heel of my sandal. I stopped for the last time to do this on Nassau Street and when I took the next twenty steps approximately, the bomb exploded.... At first we thought it was the laboratory to the left of us (Trinity College) but soon we realised it was a bomb. I was struck by flying glass and bits of debris. It was not quite dark so everything was very visible, it looked like a war zone. I may have had a flashback or have gone into shock as I ran all the way to the train station. I boarded the train to Raheny. Someone on the train told me there was blood running down my leg, and when I looked I had a small gash in the back where a piece of metal or something was stuck. I did not feel any pain at the time.

I never felt so scared in all my life; as we were delayed on the tracks between Tara Street and Amiens Street for some time for clearance, someone told us a few more bombs had gone off.

When I got off the train in Raheny, my boyfriend was waiting for me and took me to his parents' house where his mother tried to calm me with sweet tea. We then made our way to my sister's house and my mom came and picked me up. I refused to go to hospital for a check-up as I was afraid of more bombs going off in Dublin. My mom took me immediately to our family doctor [in Coolock]. I went to his office where he treated my leg (not serious) and gave me some medication. I have no visible wounds to the leg, only horrible memories and nightmares of that night.

Also, within the next day or so, two detectives from Pearse Street station came to the house and questioned me. They also asked me for the pieces of metal or whatever it was that had gashed my leg. They took a statement, and I never heard from them or anyone again.

After this second incident I did not return to my job at USIT as I could not face going into town for the longest time. I was suspicious of every car with a Northern or English licence plate, every package left unattended put me in a cold sweat, and my quality of life went down the hill. I loved my job at the agency as it was my first job and leaving it was heartbreaking but I had no choice. Taking the bus to work brought me to the Quays where the first bomb had exploded in 1972 and taking the train to go down Nassau Street to where the second bomb exploded in 1974.

My sister got me a job in Technicon Ireland, Swords, Co. Dublin. I started on 17 June 1974.

People told me after the first bomb that I would forget, but no, I never did. People told me again after the second bomb that time is a great healer. But unfortunately these two incidents made a huge impact on my life and future. I put my family through hell, especially my parents, with my mood swings, and even though I come from a family of five sisters and three brothers, I now keep to myself a lot.

When I first came to the States I loved the freedom of going to the city, and seeing the shows on Broadway, but for the past few years I ... never feel comfortable going to public places thinking it would be a target for a bomb (since the bomb exploded in the Twin Towers NY, and the Embassy in Africa).... I am always thinking I will be in the wrong place at the wrong time again, except this time I will not be so lucky!

I have constant lower-back pain that is particularly related to these traumas. I have seen a chiropractor ... but the relief I get is temporary. I take over-the-counter medication for the pain a few times a week.

I never received counselling for any of this, except after the first bomb one of the doctors sent me to see someone. I was 17 years old at the time and scared. I had one session, and could not figure out why he wanted to know about my family and not what I had been through the last year or so. I never went back as I felt humiliated/guilty for talking about my parents and siblings. I now regret it, but years ago, no one encouraged you to seek help. I was afraid if I saw a psychiatrist, people would think I was mad! Plus I never got reimbursed for medical or out-of-pocket expenses for the second bombing. I have learned to live with this mental and physical pain. It's now part of my life.

Approximately in February 1975, I was awarded exactly £3,000 from a fund that was set up by some department of the Government, or Corporation. I think it was called the Malicious Damages Fund. That was all I ever received. Out of this I was expected to pay for all my medical and any out-of-pocket expenses.

I am now 43 years of age. I have arthritis to the right hand which is very bad. My fingers are slightly bent and I have constant pain in my shoulder, especially in the winter, or if I drive for a long time. I cannot watch violent movies, or tolerate loud noises, even thunder. I do not wear anything off the shoulder due to the width and length of the scar. I am very conscious of this. I have learned to cope with the fact that when shopping, there are only certain styles I may wear.

Since I wrote this in July/August 1999 I had to get help. I guess dealing with it directly was more than I could handle.

PHIL LAWLOR-WATSON
I can remember little before the loud explosion of the bomb in South Leinster Street. I assume that I was in great form as I always loved Fridays, the end of the week's work and two free days to enjoy.

I worked with Chubb Alarms and I remember there was a bus strike. The Chubb staff were lucky as the company owned a fleet of vans, and we got driven home in the event of a public transport problem.

I remember clearly getting into the back of a double-parked Chubb van. A colleague, Pat Ryan, who came from Limerick, sat beside me. The driver, Jack Meyler, another colleague, came last. He turned the key in the ignition. I still remember the sound of that ignition.

Simultaneously there was a very loud bang and our vehicle began to rock vigorously, to and fro. The windows came in on us in small pieces, and I remember covering my face with my hands, and waiting to feel my body being ripped open. Jack said, 'It's a bloody bomb,' and jumped out of the van. I saw a ball of fire to the left of the street, just a few yards away. Pat, not waiting to push forward the seat in front of her, dived, head first over it, and left the vehicle. She dropped her bag, a blue denim shoulder bag, on the pavement beside the van, and ran screaming down the street.

I continued to sit in my seat, the van stopped shaking, my hair stood straight up, my scalp had glass embedded in it, my ears were full of glass, one of my fingers was bleeding, there was a tiny slit in the red shirt I was wearing and a small wound on my left ribcage. I heard people screaming all around me. I looked to my left and saw a car burning. I continued to sit in the van and remember saying to myself, 'I'm not going to panic.'

Sometime later, I do not know how long, it could have been minutes, or hours as time seemed to stand still, Jack returned to me and pulled me out of the van, saying, 'There is going to be another bomb'. We both returned to the reception area; the glass front of what was a very high-security entrance was totally gone.

A young girl was lying on the floor and was being attended by first-aid men from Trinity College. Her lower body had been stripped of clothing; one of her legs had the back of it missing. One of her thumbs was injured. I remember, one of her sandals was still on her foot; it was a trendy sandal, with ankle strap, which was very fashionable at that time. I remember thinking this is a very young girl maybe only 19 or 20. She was conscious and asking for her mother and her boyfriend. I went to her, kneeling on the floor beside her and she asked me for a drink of water which I quickly got for her.

Minutes later the building was vacated and I had to leave this victim and go to Power's Hotel just down the street. By this time I felt extremely upset and shocked. I felt as if I was in a nightmare, everything seemed unreal. I kept thinking of the young victim back in our reception area. It could have been me and in a sense I felt guilty because this young girl was much younger than I. My finger was dressed by a first-aider and I spoke to an *Irish Times* reporter. Sometime after, I was driven to my home, a flat on Dufferin Avenue, by whom I have no idea, presumably a Chubb driver.

I went into my empty home and sat on the bed with my back to the wall and my knees up to my chin. I was very cold and felt sort of numb. I remember thinking I should do something but could not motivate myself to even move from that position. My hair still stood straight up, my face, I was told afterwards, was very dirty and grimy. My ears and scalp were full of glass. I felt, this is a nightmare — I will wake up soon.

Ultimately, and I have no idea how long later, my sister Josheen, who at that time lived in Carysfort, cycled across the city and came to me. She made me some tea, but I still felt unable to move. The phone, which had been ringing almost non-stop, became jammed. Later that evening my brother Denny and sister-in-law Elsie came up from Wexford to be with me.

I was worried then about my boyfriend who was sometimes in Trinity and who had not contacted me.... I was too shocked to realise that he could not phone me as the phone was jammed and that he had told me he was working out of town on Friday.

Later that evening, as I was still very shocked, someone took me to the Accident and Emergency Department of some hospital (I am still trying to find out which hospital was involved). I remember a nurse telling the doctor that there was a 'bomb victim' next door. This amused me as I did not see myself as a victim and thought to myself, the doctor is going to expect some horrific injuries. I was checked for injuries and the doctor talked to me about my experience. Eventually I was given medication and sent home....

Later that week I was told by my boss that the girl to whom I had given a drink of water had died just moments after I left her. It was this news that broke me. I burst into uncontrollable weeping for a long period — nothing could console me. That night my attempts to sleep became nightmares: fire, loud bangs, and the face of that young woman. For years after, that young woman was, for me, the Dublin/Monaghan bombs. (I discovered more recently that the young woman was, in fact, Bernie Bergin, and she had not died. Thankfully I have had the pleasure in meeting her through the Justice for the Forgotten Campaign).

Since I joined the Campaign I have come to realise the total devastation of so many people who lost loved ones. The victims who received serious and long-term injuries, physical and emotional, carry the pain for the rest of their lives; nothing could ever be the same again. In realising how lucky I have been, I also feel a sense of guilt that I survived and so many so much younger than I, even babies, lost their lives.

How am I now? I am still quite jumpy, and I still have nightmares. I still feel shaky in the city centre, and in large stores I am watching for anything or any person who is acting suspiciously. I have had therapy for panic attacks, as at one time, even years later, I could not go into crowded places.

There was no counselling then and though I am one of the least of the victims, receiving no serious injuries, I still suffer twenty-five years later. I am sure it would be different now and I would have had some counselling. My husband tells me I jump in my sleep.

It is only twenty-six years ago, much less than even half a lifetime, so to me it is incredible that so little was done to help to try to compensate victims, and it is incredible that the Government did so little to bring the perpetrators of such a heinous crime to justice.

I now want the truth. I want justice. I want to see the perpetrators brought to justice. I want, even at this late stage, some form of counselling to help me forget or come to grips with this appalling event. I want to see the victims, particularly those who lost loved ones, and those who survive but have horrific injuries, compensated, in some way for the pain. I want to see their pain recognised by this State.

CATHERINE MCLAUGHLIN (NÉE CLEVER) (USA)
It was Friday evening.... As any normal teenager, I had the weekend plans etched in my heart. The bus strike would not deter any of the planned events. I walked briskly to town where I had arranged a lift home to Fairview. I decided to buy a nice juicy apple. Upon exiting the shop ... I crossed over to South Leinster Street. I remember biting into the apple and admiring its sweetness. BOOM!

Flames engulfed me. I had no idea what was happening.... I was only aware that I couldn't see for the ball of flames surrounding me.

I recall putting my hands up to try to protect myself....

Then something triggered in my brain which said 'It's a BOMB.' With this thought I instinctively tried to run away from all the madness. As I attempted to run blindly, I felt that there was something wrong with my feet and legs. Once again my subconscious indicated, 'Don't look down. If your foot is missing, you will lose all courage in trying to escape this nightmare.'

... I felt someone throwing something over me. Later I realised it was my saviour, Charlie Coyle, in order to quench the flames of my leather coat.... Charlie led me across to Bowmaker's offices, where all the windows had been blown in, and laid me down on their floor of green carpet, as he supported my limp body. I have no recollection of him saying anything other than asking, 'What is this?' It was the face of my watch. I just asked that he place it in the pocket of my coat. My sight began to return as I lay in Charlie's arms observing this beautiful carpet absorbing the blood from my wounds. I was feeling absolutely lethargic.

As I became aware of all the commotion around me, I remember trying to get someone's attention and reiterating my parents' phone number. I wanted someone to please call them and let them know I was okay. By now I just wanted to be dunked in a bath of cold water so that this burning sensation might go away. Charlie Coyle, apparently, observing the anxiety creeping in on me began explaining that the ambulance would be here soon. We waited and waited for what seemed like an eternity.

Then they were there; I was placed in the left, another victim was placed to my right, and a body wrapped in a blanket was placed in the centre aisle. The ambulance attendant kept trying to give me something through a mask. I thought, 'No, they are not going to put me out. I may not gain consciousness again.' I just wanted to know what was going on.... I kept asking 'Are we there yet?' When we arrived at Jervis Street Hospital ... the attendant kept saying, 'Take her, take her, she is in a bad way.' I don't remember much upon entering the hospital except that there were stretchers with bodies everywhere, and the staff was running around doing their best....

I just recall awakening for brief moments from time to time over the next week or so and my family being around my bed.

Then comes D-Day. I must be transferred to the Burns Unit in Dr Steeven's Hospital ... the staff lined up at the door of the ward to wish me good luck. I remember feeling extremely emotional about that, as I had no real memory of the devoted attention they had given me.

... Seeing the distress in each one of my family's face as they visit is absolutely real.... I remember thinking 'I'm happy it's me' — not one of my family because I could not bear to see any one of them in this agony. I spent two months in the Intensive Care Unit, another month in a regular ward, followed by 18 months of physiotherapy.

Now, over 25 years later, I am more hurt and disappointed ... that despite both Governments having factual information on the terrorists, nothing has been done, to the point that it is too late.... I see no future for the victims of the '74 and '72 bombings and many other atrocities that have gone unresolved.

Monaghan Town

NORA FITZSIMMONS
I left Downpatrick that Friday evening. I was going to visit my mother in Monaghan.

I arrived at approximately 6.55 p.m. My son Jerome who was four years old asked me to stop in town because he wanted chips. I stopped the car beside the Court House and walked over to McGlone's Café.

I had ordered chips to take out and, before I received the chips, there was a loud bang which I thought was a gas explosion.

The next thing I knew was the café came down around me. As I turned around, I noticed a hole in the wall. I decided to push my son out and I followed. The place was in darkness. A man came along in a car and put us into the car with another boy who had been in a bus and took us to the hospital. All the time the man was calling out, 'A bomb in the town!'

We arrived at the hospital in a state of shock. Jerome was shaking and did not know where he was. The staff in the hospital settled us down in the children's ward because Jerome would not stay on his own.

We were treated for cuts to my neck and face. Jerome had cuts to his arm and head. We were in hospital for two days. We were traumatised for a long time after.

At 2 a.m. two detectives arrived in looking for details and taking my car away for tests on it. As it came from the North, we were under suspicion for some time. An hour later they arrived back, telling me the car was outside the hospital. They asked me if I had seen anything on my way coming to Monaghan which I did not notice. They seemed to think the car came in from the North that day. The next day two detectives came out to my mother and questioned me again. From that day we never heard a thing from Garda or politicians, which to me was a disgrace.... All I am asking for is the truth about what happened that day.

JOSIE MCCORMICK

I was working in Greacen's bar. I was serving customers that evening. It was a very busy bar. I think the bomb went off about 7 o'clock. I heard the explosion and I remember looking up at the TV. I thought something happened to the TV. I was knocked out. The next thing I remembered was Mrs Ward saying to me, 'Come on, Josie, till we get out of here.' I asked her what had happened and I recall seeing daylight at the back door. Mrs Ward pulled me by the hand. We both struggled out through the back door to Mill Street. There were people saying there was going to be another bomb. We didn't know what to do. The two of us were out of our mind what to do. We were hardly fit to walk. We met this man on our way up to the hospital. He walked back with us to the hospital. The staff took over after that. Everyone was running everywhere and shouting that night. Later, the woman that worked upstairs with us (Peggy White) was in so much pain and suffering I'll never forget it. I was knocked on the head and had to have stitches. People were coming later to see their friends, etc. The nurses and doctors were great. We were in hospital until the next day. I'll never forget that night in hospital wondering [about] all the people that we knew so well — how were they? Dead or alive? The next day we came down the town coming home. It was just terrible to see the extent of damage the bomb had done. We were so glad to get out of town. I was so nervous for months and months after. I was so glad to be alive, to get back to my husband and child. I felt so very sorry for the people who lost their loved ones.

My thoughts about the explosion — it was up to yourself to get back to normal as soon as you could. You would think you just had the flu. I done my best to get back to normal and, believe me it was not easy. It took a long time. I would rather not think or talk about it. I had a hip operation done at 49. I remember the doctor that took the X-ray saying to me, 'Woman dear, what happened to you?' I know this was years after. I had suffered years with the pain in my hip and leg and now I have to have another one done. I know people have hips done and they were not in a bomb. The bone man told me I was young to have a hip operation, that usually people are in their sixties. He said when you get it done at that age you abuse it more and it is much harder for them to do it and harder for the patient and I always feel afraid.

Chapter Three: The Dead

For those throughout the island who had family members working in Dublin, news of the bombings was followed by long hours of anxious waiting. There were no mobile phones and only the odd neighbour who had private telephones, so many anxious hours were spent hoping and praying for contact from loved ones.

In some instances, the news of the bombings brought a deep sense of foreboding. As loved ones failed to return home, there was real cause for concern. The *Evening Press* of 18 May 1974 described the scenes at the Dublin City Morgue, as over two hundred people turned up, throughout the night. Some left relieved, their worst fears unfounded; others were crushed with sorrow having viewed the mutilated bodies of loved ones. Some of the injuries were so bad that callers at the morgue were not automatically allowed to view the bodies laid out,

Gene McKenna, writing on the front page of the *Evening Press* on Monday, 20 May 1974, described the arrival of families for the removal of their loved ones. Throughout the day empty hearses arrived and departed with the remains of the murdered. Sorrowful cortèges made their way to churches throughout Dublin, Offaly, Waterford, Louth, Sligo, Wexford and Tipperary. From the mortuary of Monaghan General Hospital, the dead were collected and brought to their homes throughout the border county. Officials from the Italian and French Embassies worked with the Dublin Coroner's office and Irish Government officials to obtain the release of the remains of Antonio Magliocco and Simone Chetrit so that they could be returned to Italy and France for burial.

On Tuesday, 21 May, and Wednesday, 22 May, churches were packed with families, relatives, friends and dignitaries of Church and State. One of the most poignant requiems was held at Dublin's Pro-Cathedral for John Dargle, May McKenna and the entire O'Brien family. The back page of the *Irish Independent* on 22 May carried a photograph of two adult coffins flanking two small white caskets. It is the only family picture in existence of the entire O'Brien family.

The Archbishop of Dublin, Dr Dermot Ryan, was principal celebrant at the requiem mass. During the service he invoked prayers for peace in Ireland and 'for the strength to forgive'. Representatives of other Christian Churches were in attendance. A special service of Holy Communion was held in Dublin's Christ Church Cathedral in memory of those killed. The Church of Ireland Archbishop of Dublin,. Dr Alan Buchanan, was the chief celebrant.

As the graveyards emptied and the bereaved returned to their homes to cope with their loss, an invisible veil was being woven in the corridors of power. Within months of the bombings, as families struggled to recover and others faced the sudden and unexpected deaths of aging parents brought on by shock and heartbreak, the veil had descended across the land.

On 27 May 1974 the inquests into the deaths of the victims of the Dublin bombings were opened and adjourned at the Coroner's Court. The names and ages of the deceased were recorded, as relatives and friends made formal identification of the victims. Mr Peter Sutherland, acting for the State, applied to the court for an adjournment since the Garda investigation into the blasts had not been completed. The Coroner, Professor Bofin, agreeing to the adjournment, said he hoped the perpetrators of 'this obscene act' would be apprehended.

Over a quarter of a century later, the Garda investigation into the bombings has never been 'completed'. The Dublin inquests were never resumed.

Within a couple of years, the next-of-kin of the bereaved were paid derisory compensation. There were no major outpourings of public support. There were no visits from An Garda Síochána to inform the bereaved of progress in their murder hunt. There was no trauma or bereavement counselling. Apart from the honourable few, after the politicians had made their public appearances at the funerals, they were seldom seen again.

In the early 1990s, Denise and Angela O'Neill whose father, Eddie, died in Parnell Street, began to make contact with other relatives who had lost loved ones in the Dublin and Monaghan bombings. It was the beginning of the end of silence and acquiescence. The bereaved and wounded now stand as a formidable voice of conscience — a voice that can no longer be ignored.

What follows are the personal stories of the bereaved. Each one tells a traumatic story of struggle against forces of indifference, and captures the essence of those who were lost.

With the help of Margaret Urwin and John Scally, I managed to contact the next-of-kin of all of the victims of the bombings, with two exceptions: John Dargle and Elizabeth Fitzgerald.

John Dargle died in the Parnell Street blast. He was a pensioner, aged 80, living alone at Portland Row, Ballybough, Dublin. Neighbours told reporters at the time that they didn't know whether he had a family. He had served in the British Army and spent a number of years working at the Corporation Fruit Market in Dublin.

Elizabeth Fitzgerald, aged 59, was fatally injured in the Talbot Street explosion. She was married and living with her husband, Christopher, at 2 Phibsboro Place. Both were injured in the explosion. Elizabeth died on 19 May 1974, at St Laurence's Hospital, while her husband was recovering in the Mater Hospital. It is my understanding that they were childless. Phibsboro Place was demolished in the intervening years.

Parnell Street

MARIE BUTLER (REMEMBERED BY HER MOTHER)
Marie was born on 2 November 1952. She was an adorable lovely child and grew up to be a lovely girl. She attended Affane National School and later Saint Anne's Secondary School in Cappoquin. I remember bringing her to school in the mornings and collecting her in the afternoons.

She liked Saint Anne's Secondary School. My goodness, she used to be loaded with books. She did well in her Leaving Certificate too....

I remember a man came to her funeral and he told me he met her one evening walking home from school. 'My God,' he said, 'the amount of books she had. I don't know in the name of God how anyone could lift them. I put them up on the bike for her and I walked with her. When we parted I don't know how she brought them home.'

She loved the outdoor life especially on the farm. My late Uncle John idolised her. She used to be on the farm with him and on the tractor and loved the outdoor life of farming. His farm is only about two miles from where she's buried up the road.

I have many special memories of Marie. She loved the car and was learning to drive. She loved the dances and loved to pinch my clothes to go to them. I'd have to fix up a frock for her and that kind of thing. She loved the music of Brendan Bowyer.

She had a very special relationship with her grandmother. My mother idolised her. Anything she ever wanted she gave it to her. She had that love for her. The day she was killed my mother, in a way, actually died too. My mother died in 1991 but she remembered Marie every day — even when she was very ill and near her own end in hospital in Dungarvan....

Marie was a very gentle and generous person and she especially loved elderly people. She would cross the road to link them. She crossed the road to help carry their bags and whatever for them.

She wanted to be a nurse. She was going to Sir Patrick Dun's Hospital in Dublin and she was on a waiting list for it. In the meantime a job at Clery's turned up and she took that....

She was only about twelve months in Dublin when she was killed. She celebrated her twenty-first birthday on 2 November 1973.... I remember going up to Dublin for her twenty-first birthday party in her flat.... Marie was a quiet person but she was well liked. She had a boyfriend, Sean Henry, from Mayo. We met him at her twenty-first birthday party. He was down and he was at the funeral and stayed for the best part of a week afterwards with us.

I've never been back in Dublin since. I used to frequent Dublin a lot in my younger years before I was married.... But after what happened to Marie, I never intend going back. I am too frightened.

The reason why Marie was in Parnell Street was because, as well as there being a bus strike, there was also a strike in Clery's. She wasn't working that day and she went to Parnell Square to collect the money you get when you are on strike from her union. She had the money in her purse. If I'm not mistaken, it was a fiver only. She was with a few friends and they bade goodbye to her and they went down O'Connell Street and Marie walked up Parnell Street and shortly after they parted she just went right into the bomb.

I remember seeing the bombs in Dublin on the television and it was like a premonition. When she didn't return back to her flat her flatmates reported her missing. All through Friday evening and night I was very worried. I tried phoning her flat in Ranelagh. She stayed with three flatmates who were from Mayo and Galway. They said she hadn't returned. We knew it was something terrible then.

At that time we had no phone and it was a case of driving back and forth to the village to make phone calls from a public phone. We knew too that Marie would have known we would be worried and that she would have called if she was able to.

I feel very bad about the Irish State and how they dealt with us. It's the same with all the other victims. We had no dealings with them.... No one offered counselling. The guards never came to talk to us. We were abandoned.... I don't know what to make of the

Government. I feel a certain bitterness because of the way they treated us. There was a few telegrams that came from them at the time. That was all.

I feel horrible when I think of the people who killed her and, to be truthful, I sometimes feel bitter. If I had the opportunity to speak with them, I don't think I could....

There is something definitely not right about the whole thing. Someone was responsible and somebody knows. There is somebody holding back and not coming forth to tell....

PATRICK FAY (REMEMBERED BY HIS WIFE, MAURA, AND SON, PAT)

MF: Pat was a very quiet man. We were chalk and cheese because I was full of chat. He was very soft and never got angry with anyone. He loved children and he always had children around him. He was from County Louth and didn't drink or smoke. He was very involved in the church....

I will never forget the day he was killed. I was working in a shop at the time and Pat was due to collect me that night at twenty to twelve. I was a bit worried when he didn't come to collect me. I had heard the news about the bombing and I was starting to think he might have been caught up in the bombing. My boss, Sonny, tried to calm me down and he brought me home. I knew immediately as we drove up to the house that he was injured because the house was dark and the gate was open and his car wasn't there. I rushed inside and I saw his stew was there uneaten. I went into hysterics.... We went down to the garda station in Raheny and at half four [in the morning], I think, I learned he was dead. I couldn't believe it.

We went to the hospital but I fainted. I got an injection then and I was out until Monday evening. It was a friend who identified Pat in the hospital, though I didn't find that out until a few years later. I never saw Pat except in a closed coffin. He had been getting petrol for his new Volkswagen car when the bomb went off. He only had it for eight weeks.

Patrick had served twelve years in the army and he was a marksman. He then worked for the civil service with the Post and Telegraphs. Yet the government did nothing for me. Nobody did anything for me....

We had only one child, who was also called Pat after his father. He was in his twenties when his father died and was working and living in London.... He has done very well for himself in London and Patrick would have been very proud to have seen his son do so well.... I was so lucky to have such a good son. Otherwise I would never have got through it. There was a lot of tough times for me. I think that Christmas week was the toughest for me. A few weeks after the funeral we had tried to pay the funeral expenses but the funeral parlour wouldn't let us pay for it then. They said that the government would pay for it but they didn't.

That Christmas week, I was sick in bed. I had pneumonia. The Christmas cards were coming in the post, and Pat's nephew, Gerard, was reading them out to me. All of a sudden he came on this brown envelope ... it was from the funeral home and they were looking for their money for burying Pat. I remember falling back in the bed and getting weak at that news, but I paid it and I still have the receipt.

I can't forgive the people who planted the bomb nor the man who drove that car. I would love to come face to face and tell them exactly what I think of them. My life was never the same again. I lost the best husband a woman could have asked for. He was only 46 years of age and I've had twenty-five years of living on my own. The loneliness has been awful....

PF: I will never forget 17 May 1974. I was living in London. I heard on the news that parts of Dublin had been bombed. I ... started making calls to Ireland to find out what exactly had happened.

I was unable to contact my mam or dad but I rang around neighbours and relatives to see if anybody in the family was hurt or injured. I was told all was well. I could not speak directly with my mam or dad as they were not on the phone in those days but I kept contact via a neighbour and the news.

When it went past midnight I got a certain amount of relief because I felt if anything had happened to anyone in the family I would have heard by now.

The next morning, Saturday, 18 May, I went into my office as usual at 9 o'clock. My assistant said to me that Mrs Murphy (my mother-in-law) was on the telephone looking for me and would I ring back. I thought that was strange, and the next minute I was told there was a telephone call for me. Mrs Murphy was on the other end. 'Pat, I've got bad news for you — your father....' She did not have to say any more. I knew. Nature is strange. I just knew. I never had that feeling in my life. I don't remember a great deal what my actions were but I went straight home and told my wife and we both went straight to the airport. We both got the next plane to Dublin.

I was met at Dublin Airport and taken straight to the City Morgue. The morgue was in chaos. I introduced myself to the person in charge and was taken to see my father. I was told it was not pleasant what I was going to see inside and that I may get upset.... I really did not know what I was about to experience would stay with me for the next twenty-six years. There were bodies everywhere — some very badly mutilated. I was taken to where my father was laid out. I stopped a short distance away. I went numb.... I eventually backed off and the attendant took me to one side and said, 'He'll look better when he's fixed up and is laid out in the funeral parlour.'

I was led back out to the main reception where, by now, my grandparents and aunts and uncles had arrived. I approached them and the first thing they said was, 'How is he?' I replied, 'He's fine'. They asked me why they were not being allowed in to see him. I told them that this was due to the scale of the disaster and once the body was identified it was down to the funeral parlour after that.

My next stop was home to see my mother.... There were people everywhere.... I made my way towards my mother who was totally in a state of shock which I had never seen before. I put my arms around her and she was screaming and shaking. She would not let me go. I got her to sit down. She had been heavily sedated. Being an only child, I had to take on my father's role as my mother had to be heavily sedated daily. So I had to look after things for her.

I went to Jervis Street Hospital to collect my father's belongings, etc., and spoke to the nurse who remembered my father. When she was giving me his clothes, she said to me, 'We tried our best to save him but to no avail.' That really moved me. The tears started to run non-stop, holding his blood-stained clothes in a plastic bag in my arms, and even now, after twenty-six years, I still can't keep the tears back thinking of that moment.

I next went to the scene of the bomb in Parnell Street, hoping to collect my father's car. I did not believe my eyes. It was like something out of a war scene. I identified his car to the police, which I was not allowed to remove, so I returned home....

The Monday afternoon I went to the funeral parlour which I was asked to do. I met with the funeral director and he thought it best that I view the remains alone. There were three coffins — two closed and one open, which was my father's. I looked into the coffin at my father and broke down. It was not pretty. The funeral people consoled me; they were very good to me and suggested it would be best for everyone to remember him as he was before and for us to give permission to have the coffin closed, which I agreed. I then had to go out and tell the family. This was not easy because I knew I would be denying my mother the chance to see him and say her last goodbye. But I did not want anybody to see my father in the state he was but to remember him the way he was.

It has taken me twenty-six years to say this. I was never able to discuss it with anyone. I kept it to myself. I thought it was the best decision at the time. I returned to London, and after twenty-six years how I still miss him. He would have loved to see me back especially with his two grandchildren, Shaun and Tara. He loved children.

ANTONIO MAGLIOCCO (REMEMBERED BY HIS BROTHER, MARIO, AND SON, TOMMASSINO)
On 17 May 1974, 38-year-old Antonio Magliocco was visiting his brother Mario's fish-and-chip shop, the Venezian Café in Parnell Street, when the first of the three Dublin bombs exploded. He died instantly.

A week later, his brother, Mario, his sister, Savina Borza, and brother-in-law, Vittorio Borza, accompanied Antonio's remains back to Casalattico in the south-central Italian Apennine mountains, to inter his body alongside those whom he loved, surrounded by the sights and sounds of his childhood.

I interviewed Mario Magliocco and Antonio's eldest son, Tommassino, in 1998. On 13 February 1999, I travelled to Casalattico, to visit Tommassino and his mother, Anna. Earlier in the day we had met President Mary McAleese, on a state visit to Italy. It was the first time in almost twenty-five years that any official representative from Ireland had made time to listen to the pain and sorrow of these people. The President's sensitivity and compassion were greatly appreciated by Antonio Magliocco's family.

MM: Antonio came to Ireland first. He came in 1961 or '62. I came after him, in 1963. I opened my fish-and-chip shop, The Venezian, in Parnell Street, roughly between '64 and '65. I stayed there until the bomb happened in 1974. We did not open again after that.

We came from south of Rome, near Casino, a small village called Casalattico. We had relatives working here in Ireland. We liked Ireland and we mixed well with the Irish. Antonio liked Ireland.

I remember Antonio came to help me that day. We were working inside and he went to go for messages and was trying to find a place to park his car outside. He was standing beside the car and the next minute — BOOM! We didn't know what happened at first.

I was behind the counter which probably saved me. I was very shaken but I was worried because I knew that Antonio was outside looking for a parking space. I went outside but I couldn't see at first. Everything went blank. But then it was terrible to see people lying around the street. I was about 24 at the time and Antonio was 38. He was a hard-working person and very good-natured. In this business it's hard unless you have the time off.

We brought Antonio home to Casalattico to be buried. Everyone at home was shocked when it happened. What was really terrible was that Anna, his widow, received very little help from anyone, other than the family. We felt very alone, very abandoned. We had to struggle for ourselves but we built up our life again. But it was very hard because we were in debt.

Our mother was still alive when Antonio was killed, but she died just nine months later from the shock. Those responsible don't realise the terrible impact violence has.

We were not seriously injured but we were very traumatised. We did need help to cope but it never came. I have been to some meetings now and they are very interesting. Sometimes it is better to talk.

The Irish Government should have done something about it. They should have helped the people. I also think it is time for the British Government to tell the truth. I was talking to the other families who lost people and they say the same thing. They want justice. Mostly people just ask for justice. It is time for truth. Until the truth is told it remains an open wound.

TM: I was three years old when my father was killed. I had a younger brother, Corrado, aged nine months, and a younger sister, Marinella, aged two. I was very young, so I do not really remember a lot about what happened. I know that we stayed in Ireland for a good few years after. We went back to Italy in 1983 for good, to our original place.

My mother found it very difficult to go on. Even at this moment she has got no pension from either the Italian Government or the Irish Government. She has got nothing at all. She received very little help to raise three children on her own. She is coping now, but she seldom talks about the day my father died.

I have a feeling of betrayal and of being let down, knowing that, even now, after 25 years, nothing has been done to seriously bring out the truth. After 25 years it is time for truth. I also believe that something has to be done by the European Community and the Italian Government to help us find the truth.

I don't remember much of my father but I missed him a lot.

THE O'BRIEN FAMILY (REMEMBERED BY ANNA'S SISTER, ALICE DOYLE; JOHN'S SISTER, LINDA SUTHERLAND; AND ANNA'S FATHER, PADDY DOYLE)

AD: My sister and her husband and their two children were blown up in Parnell Street at half five. I was in work at the time and we just heard the bang in town from Finglas and we didn't know anybody was in the bombing until the next day. People started coming to the house at 4 o'clock in the afternoon and the telly was knocked off and things like that. It wasn't until a quarter to seven that the police came and the priest, and my father came back in a police car after being in the morgue identifying the bodies.

Anna was 21, and her two children — they were only four-and-a-half months and a year and four-and-a-half months. Her husband, John, was 23.... They were only three years married....

My father had to go in and identify the bodies. He said it was like a slaughterhouse in there....

One baby was thrown from her buggy. I'd say it was shock mainly that killed that child, but the other baby was burnt and she was blown into the cellar of the Welcome Inn pub.

When my mother found out, she never got over it. She died nine years later, but she might as well have died on the day it happened because she didn't want to live after that....

They died on the Friday evening and they didn't go to the church until the Tuesday, and they were buried then the following morning and, as far as I know, the graveyard was black with people. It was impossible to get in and out of the graveyard. Something happened to my mother in the graveyard and, as far as I know, my father and her were taken out to the railings and brought to hospital. They thought the two of them had a heart attack and they were in hospital but I couldn't really tell you what happened because everything was up in [the air].

It was very sad to see two little white coffins up there and the parents on either side of them, and for children to be so young to be blown up like that for no reason at all.... I often wondered what went into the coffins because if they were so badly burnt and their arms and legs blown off, how could they make up a body in the coffins?

We were very young then, but I realise now the impact of it on my mother and father.... It's only when you have children of your own ... you really know exactly how they must have felt.

The scars are still there because I have a brother and he never goes into town, and I have another brother and he doesn't want to talk about it.... He just wishes they would leave it and let it go but you can't — you have to find out the truth of the day.

We can't get any information out of any of the governments, even though I went over to Westminster to meet them and they didn't want to know either. The same way they don't want to know in Dublin. It doesn't matter what government got in or anything else, they still don't want to know up to today. We [have been] fighting to get the files released and have had to go to the High Court and the Supreme Court. They have never made it easy for us. We've had to fight every inch of the way.

Patricia McKenna and Trevor Sargent are really the only two politicians who will back us, and Tony Gregory....

Anna was a very good singer. She was mad about Tom Jones in 1974 and she used to sing all his songs.... I think of her all the time, just like on 2 January, it's the children's birthday — Ann Marie and Jacqueline, they were born on the same day. Anna's own birthday is on 18 March, the day after Saint Patrick's Day. Then her Wedding Anniversary is 30 December. They are special dates and you never forget....

LS: That Friday, my sister Eileen worked in Palm Grove, the ice-pop factory, and she let our brother, Johnny, off early to meet his wife, Anna, and take the kids into town. She feels so guilty that it's playing on her mind now that if she never let him off, would that have happened? This is why we're still pushing this.

It happened on the Friday and we didn't find out until the Saturday. My mother was in town on the Saturday and my little sister was making her First Holy Communion the following Saturday. She was in town collecting her clothes. Two detectives knocked on the door. I was there with my brother. They just said, 'We need to speak to your mother,' and I said, 'She's in town at the moment; what's the problem?' They said, 'We need to get your mother.'

But my mother heard the news in town, and she was taken home, and the doctor was called, and that's how we found out about it. We didn't find out until the Saturday. John was our eldest brother. Jacqueline and Anne Marie were her first two grandchildren. My younger sister could have also been killed because she was supposed to go with them. The only reason why she didn't go was because she had to go and collect her First Communion clothes.

As I've said, we've been pushing it this far and we'll never give up because somebody out there knows something ... we want to get on with our lives and let our dead rest. But I know my brother would want us to keep this up.... It's heartbreaking. My mother has never, never been the same. She'll never be the same. It just tore our whole family apart. The few days after, my mother was heavily sedated.

I used to always go into town with Johnny. He was out visiting us the Thursday night before with his little one. I used to stay with them and help mind their little ones. I was only 13 or so at the time.... My father died Christmas 1972 and they were killed 1974. He was 47. He died of cancer. It was a big blow to my mother. Two years later, a whole family just wiped out like that. It's something that haunts me.

I lived in England for a while, but I had to come home. I came home to carry this on because my mother is always saying, 'If anything happens to me, don't give up until you find out because I'll never rest until I know who done this.' I've had to move my family over here to carry on and to keep this going....

They think by putting that memorial stone down Talbot Street we'll go away. A stone won't bring them back, but the truth means that we can get on with our lives. The families are not looking for compensation. Money won't bring them back, but if they give us the truth about who done it and why it was done, that's all everybody wants to know. The truth will come out in the end. It might be another twenty-five years but we're getting closer....

Looking back, it was horrible. I mean, to see two little coffins. There was thousands of people there. There was flowers from everywhere. It was very sad. I looked at my mother, she had to be carried in. Two babies, one of them was just barely walking and the other was four-and-a half months old. It's just ripped us apart. I can't even say how I feel. I look at my own children and think my nieces could be there today. My kids never knew my brother.

Even my youngest brother was only a baby himself. He always says, 'Mam, what was he like?' ... I had a sister, Alma, she was making her First Communion the following week. She couldn't make her Communion ... it wasn't a day of celebration at all.

Christmas and May is a bad time for us because my mother was after buying Jacqueline, who had only started walking, a pair of shoes and I remember even seeing them in the *Sunday World* when the bomb went off.... It's just tragic, they were just here one minute and gone. I'll keep it up and I'll keep it up until we find out what happened. I owe it to them.

PD: I heard the news from my brother-in-law who came out from town and he said, 'You'd better come into town because you're wanted at Store Street.' That's beside the morgue. So I went down and there was an inspector there and he knew the brother-in-law well and said, 'Tom, bring him down there and give him a brandy.' So I went down and had a bottle of stout and I came back and I went into the morgue and, Jesus, when I looked ... all bodies ... just legs ... they weren't even their own legs ... they were just put together to make a complete body with a sheet over the centrepiece. The two grandkids, I seen them. They were in a small box, foot to foot, which I wouldn't say they were all there even, by the size of the box. Now I knew Johnny, but I couldn't identify the daughter. It was a sister-in-law of mine. She identified her through ear-rings that she was after giving her. And there was only a bit of her top left and she knew by that because she was after giving her that as well....

I think the Government are useless. We're after being years and years trying to get the files for our barristers and solicitors and the police commissioner [refused] to give them....

EDWARD O'NEILL (REMEMBERED BY HIS WIFE, MARTHA)
On 17 May 1974, Eddie was murdered. Billy and Angela were making their first Communion on 18 May, and their dad and I were just over the moon. Eddie was taking Billy to Berkeley Road Church and I was taking Angela to make hers in the Convent. She was picked out of the class to do a reading and I'll always remember — little things that you will never forget — the readings was from Saint Paul's Epistle to the Corinthians, and Angela was saying 'A reading from Saint Paul's pistols'.

Her dad and I lifted her up on the coffee table every night and she kept saying 'A reading from Saint Paul's pistols'. We were trying to help her teacher to get it into her head. On the Friday evening before he was killed he said to me after giving the children's bath, 'I'd love to be there to hear Angela saying the reading to see what way she's going to come out with this.'

On the day of the bombing, Eddie took Billy and Edward to the barber's in Parnell Street. Edward wasn't supposed to go but wanted to, so he was taken. Eddie had come home from work early to do this and I left for the hairdresser's with Angela.

My next-door neighbour, Mrs D'Arcy, offered to baby-sit the other children, Denise, Niall and, as I thought, Edward. I rang my husband Eddie from the hairdresser's and said, 'I'm going to be very late because the hairdresser's is packed.' ... I said, 'It won't be until about 7 o'clock before I get out of here. Will you feed the children?' He said he would....

They went into the Welcome Inn with Brian after he had brought Billy and Edward into the barber's shop, having left them in the safe-keeping of Liam Sullivan ... who was a personal friend of his.

My cousin [Brian] was sitting in the Welcome Inn, and Eddie went in to get the boys. Billy was just after getting his hair cut and he waited for Edward. Eddie had the boys into karate. Liam Sullivan the barber was in the same club and that's why he brought them to his barbershop. As they were leaving the barber's, Eddie spotted a picture of Bruce Lee on the back of the door and he called the boys back in to show them the picture. I sometimes wonder if he hadn't gone back to see the picture of Bruce Lee, he could have been in the Welcome Inn.

They were talking as they came back out of the barber's, and just then a button fell out of Eddie's coat. I didn't know this until about fifteen years after. I was sitting one day talking to Billy. I never talked to the boys about the bombing, but this day I said, 'Billy can you tell me something — what happened on that day?'

He told me that a button had fallen out of his dad's coat and he ran after the button. As soon as he went to pick the button up, the bomb went off. That's how Billy didn't get any facial injuries. Edward got the facial injuries and his daddy — I don't know what ever happened. I don't know the extent of my husband's injuries because I never saw him. They never opened the coffin. I don't know whether he died on the spot or whether he died in hospital. I know nothing....

Billy doesn't remember anything after that. All he remembers is picking up the button and the bomb going off. Edward was blown onto the middle of the road. When my cousin, Brian, came out of the Welcome Inn, all he could see was carnage everywhere. He said he'd never seen anything like it. He ran over to this rag doll thing he saw on the ground, and it was my [son] Edward. He had a piece of the car embedded into his face and into his head.

He stopped a car that was coming down and he said to the driver, 'Can you take him to the hospital?' Edward was the first to get to the hospital. Brian didn't know where Billy was and he couldn't find Eddie. I don't know what condition Eddie was in. As for Billy, I don't know where he was. I don't know whether he was under the car or whether he was blown through a window. But the injuries Billy sustained were to his legs, his feet, and his stomach was blown open. The only thing that wasn't injured on Billy was his face....

I was sitting in the hairdresser's with Angela. And a strange thing happened.... It was very warm and there wasn't a breeze in the world. I'm a great believer in Saint Martin de Porres. I called the boys Edward Martin Jude, Niall Martin Jude and William Martin Jude. The statue of Saint Martin fell down, rolled along the floor and stopped at my feet in the hairdresser's. I got this sensation through me, you know, I got this feeling something was wrong. Angela's hair was just finished. She looked great and I said, 'Come on'....

I had to go into the chemist to get her white clips for her veil and I was in the chemist on the corner of Dorset Street. The man in the chemist and another man were talking. I asked them what had happened. The man said, 'There's after being hundreds of people killed and injured in the bombs. We don't know how many are dead, so be careful going home.'

As I walked down the street, there was just silence. There wasn't a car, there was nothing. There was just people all gathered together in groups. I looked each side of the flats and people were all looking down at me and they were all talking. 'God!' I thought. I didn't notice Eddie's van. There were no cars at all around. I was trying to catch someone's attention but as soon as I'd look up, they'd turn away. They were looking at me but yet they couldn't tell me anything.

I was five or six months pregnant at the time. It wasn't until I was turning to go up the stairs of the flats that a friend of mine, Mavis O'Toole, came towards me and said, 'I've something to tell you.' She said, 'Eddie was in the bombing,' and with that I understood the feeling I had sensed from the time the statue come to my feet. I didn't know what it was I was feeling until the moment I was told. I became very upset and Mavis caught a hold of me. I asked, 'Is he alive?' She said, 'Yes, I'm after being talking to him'....

As I went into Jervis Street I will never forget the sight. It was like a war zone....

They brought me over to a waiting room. There were other relatives there. They had been there before I'd arrived. Everybody seemingly had known before I'd known. My sister-in-law was there. Eddie's brother was there, while I was sitting in the hairdresser's....

I went in and there was a list up of the injured and they were putting a list up of the dead. Eddie's friend was there — Con — I said to him, 'What's wrong, what's wrong? We don't know anything yet.' [Someone] roared out a list of the injured and I heard him say, 'Edward Junior'. Well, I nearly died. No, said I, 'it's a man!' 'No', said he, 'it's a boy. 'No,' said I, 'My husband is Edward O'Neill. 'No,' said he, 'it's Edward O'Neill Junior, a boy of eight.'

I couldn't believe what I was hearing and that's when I realised that my Edward was there. Edward had only forty-eight hours to live. It all depended on whether they could take a piece of shrapnel safely out of his face without him bleeding to death. And then they roared out from the list 'Edward Senior'. They got a priest from Dominick Street and he told me Eddie was dead. How he died I don't know. Where he died I don't know. Whether he died in hospital or whether he died on the street I haven't got a clue. These are things I would have liked to know.

Angela made her First Holy Communion the following day. Billy never got making his, of course, because he was in hospital. However, a few weeks later, he did. His school organised a special mass, and all his classmates dressed up in their good clothes just for the occasion. It was really lovely, and Billy, I always remember, looked beautiful in his new First Holy Communion clothes.

After more than twenty-five years what we as a family would like most at this point is to have the Garda files opened to a full public inquiry. We want recognition for the victims and their families, with a full state apology from the government of the day and every successive government since then....

I would like it to be in everybody's memory because when people's memories are jogged, everybody seems to know ... where it was that they heard the first of the Dublin bombings. In the light of the Omagh bombing, I think people should be aware that this also happened in our very own twenty-six counties....

I mean in Enniskillen they have had apologies; Warrington, they've had everything done, like Mary Robinson going over. That was brilliant. It shows people that we care, that we just don't accept what's happened. Omagh was absolutely dreadful. I've cried for the people of Omagh because I understand. I saw a poor woman on the news this morning. You should have seen her injuries: her face, her eyes, the whole lot. I was just thinking there was no camera there to see my son's face, to see his ear. They never even knew that he was deaf. They never even took an ear test and the child had a perforated eardrum from the whole lot and he was left with that until the school discovered it and he was only four when that happened. There was no one there to see Billy's feet: half of his toe gone and his kneecap practically blown off him....

I don't know what's so wrong about the Dublin and Monaghan bombings that they will not allow us a public inquiry....

I want to see justice before I die, I really really do.

BREDA TURNER (REMEMBERED BY HER PARENTS)
Like everyone else, we heard it first on the news. At first we weren't overly concerned because you didn't think there was anybody belonging to you involved. Shortly afterwards, perhaps an hour later, we started to become uneasy wondering was there any danger to Breda. We had a son in Dublin and we rang him. As far as he knew, she would at that time be on her way home from work and should have been clear of the area.

There was a bus strike on, so that's the reason why she was there at all. As far as we know, she had been speaking to someone and she was going into the cleaners to get something for a party that night. But funnily enough we had a premonition about it from the word go that she was in it.

A neighbour of ours came over to say that the guards had rang him and she was first on the list when it came out on the television at about 12 o'clock that night.... And her friend was killed as well....

Breda was in the income tax and she was just going for her examination for inspector of taxes and was doing very well for herself and she had just got engaged in the September. She was 21 and was to get married the following year at Easter. She was talking about the colours of the dresses and she was going to have three bridesmaids. Then this happened.

We never had a bit of trouble with her. She was into music and everything like that, and had a great sense of humour.

She was killed in Parnell Street. She was passing a garage and the car was outside and she was between the car and the garage and she was blown way up the garage, herself and the other girl with her, and she had multiple injuries — practically all her bones were broken — ribs, legs, arms, everything.

They had told me she wasn't badly disfigured but the sad part was we never got to see her. We just went up and that's the only thing we found very hard was you were in and out. There was no waiting or anything else, so we just went up to Dublin and brought her down here then. We always regretted that.

Our other girls were going to the school and, on account of that, all the schoolchildren were let off from school duties and they marched [at] the funeral. It was a great spectacle all right.

We have a tape that she made us at Christmas the year before. We haven't really played it fully yet. And to tell you the type of sense of humour she had, you know that ad that used to be out on the television about 'Do you like Daz?' or whatever it is. She and the boyfriend did a mock version of the ad, interviewing me. They taped it here. The funny thing about it was they used to tape over everything they taped and she said, 'No, that's one tape we'll never tape over'....

Her grave is just behind us here. We can just look out the window and see it — the upstairs window — and we keep it well.

We used to pick her up at the station here when she'd come down. She used to come on the half-past-five train and we would hear the train blowing from the station. For months after that it would make us very sad to hear that whistle.

We often said nothing would ever bring her back. But the pity of it is that she and the others were dead and buried and nobody was interested enough to do anything about it. And then, as we say, everybody has a mother and father, including those who did it. If their parents know what they did, they must be living in hell as well.

On the night Breda died I remember I was so upset the doctor came down and gave me a tablet and Jimmy said 'Look at it this way — we had her for twenty-one years'.

Talbot Street

JOSIE BRADLEY (REMEMBERED BY HER SISTER, SR CLAUDE, RSM)
Josie (Josephine Euphrasia) Bradley of Coolfin, Kilcormac, Birr, County Offaly was born at 3.20 p.m. on 5 December 1954. Marian, her twin sister, was born at 3.25 p.m. They were the third youngest of ten living children of May and Chris Bradley. The Bradley family had a strong farming background. Chris ran the family farm until his untimely death on 8 April 1959. May, our mother, then reared the family with great wisdom and courage. Her profound faith and deep hope in life and in her God certainly coloured the family development. Little did she think that she would bury one of her children fifteen years later beside her husband in the family plot in the graveyard close to home in Ballyboy.

Josie was a beautiful fair-skinned curly-haired girl with a quiet, jovial and gentle disposition. She had a natural positive outlook on life, and a great sense of humour. She no doubt inherited some of Mam's good looks. At four years of age Josie and Marian began their formal learning at Ballyboy National School. Some years later it was time to go to Scoil Mhuire Secondary in Kilcormac where, after three years, the Intermediate Certificate was sat. From 1971 to 1973 Josie went to St Joseph's Convent of Mercy boarding school, Tullamore. She attended the Sacred Heart secondary school from which she graduated with a fine Leaving Certificate. She pursued a clerical career and was accepted in the civil service where she worked until her untimely death....

Our family recall Josie's deep affiliation with nature. She had a special love for animals in particular. Her love for Patsy, the pet lamb with a crooked neck, will always be recalled. This left the lamb unable to puck as he played. He knew Josie's way so very well. When she arrived from school he was ready for fun and play. Hours were spent running by the big black gate and bounding down the steps at the little gate leading to the front garden. Once when they were playing, Josie fell. Patsy-lamb as he was fondly called stood by rather mute until help arrived....

One last fond memory of Josie was of the night before Sheila left to study for nursing in London. She had a lovely green coat which she had bought in America. She left the coat with Josie because she lacked space in her luggage and Josie showed a fondness for it. Josie got up the next morning and accompanied Sheila to the airport. This gave Sheila great comfort. She was lonely leaving. Their next meeting just three weeks later was Monday evening, 20 May, hours before Josie's death. Josie was wearing Sheila's green coat on that terrible Friday evening.

The nightmare story in our life with Josie began on Friday evening, 17 May 1974. At 5.30 p.m. a car bomb exploded in Talbot Street. Whenever you see TV coverage of this horrific event, you will notice Guiney's large shop sign. Very close to this sign Josie was seriously injured. Chaos followed. The family believed that Josie was safe. A family member phoned to be informed that 'Josie' who turned out to be another Josie was okay. The rosary was said in Coolfin that night in thanksgiving.

Next morning as Mam went milking, a garda called to the house to say Josie's bag had been found. Mam told her story of the previous night and didn't really hear the garda's story.... Marian, Josie's twin, had been contacted. She, all alone ... spent Saturday morning searching for Josie, her twin, in the morgues. Josie was not to be found. Marian then with a wee ray of hope proceeded to visit the hospitals. After much searching, she found Josie with the name Janice Bradley at the foot of her bed in Jervis Street Hospital. Josie was unable to respond but Marian felt her reflexes were good.

It was 11 a.m. [Pacific Standard Time] on Friday morning, 17 May, when another family member stood reading an airmail letter. It was from Josie. As it was read, news of a bomb blast in Dublin came across the local airwaves, in Costa Mesa, California. It was Sunday midday when the news came that Josie was seriously injured in the bomb blast. On boarding the plane in Los Angeles, one hoped against hope that Josie would be alive. Passing over New York, the witnessing of a glorious sunrise didn't go unnoticed. It was at this very time (11.30 p.m. Irish time, Monday 20 May) that Josie died. Each family member has vivid and horrific memories around those hours, hours that grew into days, then into months and into years....

Words and phrases that have been repeated in the family are: 'I felt so cold, so terribly cold.' ' It was like being in a deep dark hole forever,' and 'There seemed no way out for us.' Loneliness; aloneness, fear, unable to get up and go on with life; terrible shock that stayed, it seemed, forever were family experiences. Mam, while trying to keep the best side out, never got over Josie's death. It took her until 1979 to begin to come to grips with the whole experience. She never spoke much about Josie's death, and for years she seldom could speak about her life ... Josie had been home the weekend before her death. She brought home the tape 'Maggie' to Mam. This song had been sung at Mam's coming-home party after her wedding. For years none of the family could bear to play that song or hear it either.

As I write, a sense of numbness surrounds me. It is now clear to me that for all those years we had no support system whatever. I can understand our not having such in those early days. Yet I fail to understand why an event such as Josie's death in such cruel circumstances, our family trauma, and that of numerous families were never addressed either generally or personally by respective governments, Departments of Justice or, for that matter, by any body responsible for this violent act. I fail to understand that the group Justice for the Forgotten had to be set up to highlight and bring to the notice of public figures that nothing has been done.... It was no choice of ours to be marginalised, we have been thus for twenty-six years. That is a lifetime.

ANNE BYRNE (REMEMBERED BY HER DAUGHTER, MICHELLE O'BRIEN)
I remember it was a Friday and my mother went into town, shopping. She was 35 years of age. My brother, Trevor, was four on the day that she was actually buried. A neighbour who lives on the road and who was doing some work in our house said to my mother that afternoon: 'Leave the kids here and I'll take care of them.'

I remember hearing three loud bangs in Donaghmede and at that stage we didn't realise what those bangs were. That evening when my father came home from work the neighbours on the road just said to him, 'Michael, Anne hasn't come home.' He organised for us to be looked after by my mother's best friend and he went looking for her in the hospitals. I think then in the early hours of the morning he found her. She was in the morgue.

I remember years afterwards, when my Dad got remarried, I always expected my mother to come back. I recall thinking to myself 'He'll be in trouble because he got married again and my mother is going to come back.' But as you get older, you get more sense, and you cop on to the fact that she's not going to come back.

My only real memory about the weekend of the bombings would be the Saturday evening. My dad's only sister was out in the house and she sent me shopping. And, at eight years of age, to be trusted to go to the shop was a big thrill. At that stage I didn't realise what had actually happened and that day my mother's best friend's son, Mark, was making his Communion and we went visiting with them that day. I remember everybody was being really really nice — not that they weren't always nice to us but sort of that it was extra special....

Then that evening all my mother's family, who were living in Birmingham at the time ... started to arrive home and a bishop came to the house. I'd never seen a bishop before. One of the priests who later on became Bishop O'Mahony came to the house as well. He was a priest in our parish.... The Sunday I don't have any recollection of at all or the Monday.... the 21st [Tuesday]... was my brother's birthday, he was four and I remember he had three birthday parties that day. The neighbours on the road all gave him birthday parties and I remember standing in the sitting-room window of one of our neighbour's houses and seeing the coffin going down the road. You know the way they pass the house, because we were not allowed attend the funeral. I didn't realise at the time my mother actually was in it. It's only in later years ... that I realised this was actually my mother's coffin.

I regret that I was not allowed go the funeral but I suppose in 1974 it wasn't really the done thing to take a child to a funeral.... I think it was probably because we never got a chance to say goodbye.

My mother did everything for us. She liked fashion, she liked jewellery. The one thing I mainly remember about her was the fact that she was house-proud — not obsessed by house pride but, you know, they worked hard to get their house, and she loved her home and she only got to live in it for not even two years.....

My dad's mother moved out to live with us in Donaghmede, and my granddad and my uncle, and they lived with us for maybe over a year, but my granddad was 80-odd years of age and I was nine at that stage and Trevor was five and my granny was elderly as well. So it was very hard for them to cope looking after us. Then we went and stayed during the day with my mother's best friend, Maura White.... Trevor was only starting school at that stage but I was in school and I would go back to her house. Then my dad would collect me and we would go home then in the evening time.

I only started to become aware about the enormity of what actually happened at the seventeenth anniversary. There was a mass in the Pro-Cathedral and I met Denise and Angela O'Neill and Martha O'Neill and we got talking. I think the Corporation had laid on tea in the Gresham Hotel afterwards and we got talking and they were talking about the fact that they wrote to this minister and that minister and they wrote to the Taoiseach and all this, that and the other, and they were getting nowhere. It's only then that I realised how bad the actual atrocity was. It was the biggest atrocity that had ever happened and the fact that nobody was ever brought to justice and the fact that the Government just didn't seem to care and to this day still don't....

There were moments of sadness in the build-up to my wedding especially. I had my mother's wedding ring. That's the only reminder really of jewellery that I have belonging to her, and the night that my father gave it to me to go and get it cleaned before I wore it that day will always stick in my mind. It was just hard, especially the whole week coming up to it. And as it got nearer, it got harder, but my Dad got remarried and I still have two other sisters and two other brothers and my dad's second wife — she was there and she helped me out every step of the way through the whole lot of it.

Personally, I find it has helped me to talk about what happened and I find to talk to the other relatives — especially because they're the only other people who know what we're going through — it helps to be able to sit and to talk to them, and people I have met from the North as well, that have been through similar things. It helps you to get through from day to day to be able to sit and talk to these people.

I met Tony Blair and he was lovely. He actually sat and he listened to what we had to say and Mo Mowlan was there as well and she actually sat and she listened to what we had to say. To me it seemed as though the Blair Government cared more about the people that were killed in Dublin and Monaghan than the Irish Government did.

We want to know why this happened. We want to know why there wasn't more done.... We're going to go the Court of Human Rights if necessary to get answers. We hope Judge Hamilton's assessment of all the evidence will lead to a public tribunal of inquiry. It means it's going to drag on even longer ... but I hope to God they don't let it go on [too] long....

They'll have to release the files and give us the answers that we need so we can lay them to rest once and for all.

SIMONE CHETRIT (REMEMBERED BY HER HOSTESS AND FRIEND, HELENA GUNN, HER BROTHER, ELIE CHETRIT, SISTER-IN-LAW, CAROLE AND NIECE, SYLVIE)

In 1996 the Justice for the Forgotten campaign had begun in earnest to make contact with and involve the relatives of all those who had died. Contact with some, however, had been lost. The family of Simone Chetrit was one of these.

Simone had come to Ireland on 20 April 1974 to learn English. She was placed with a young couple in Raheny, Dublin, Helena and Eamonn Gunn. It was a two-week English course, but Simone and another French student, Dominique d'Amiens, had decided in advance to extend their stay for an extra couple of weeks. They both planned to return to Paris on 18 May 1974.

HG: She was lovely. The nicest student we ever kept. She blended in so well we treated her as one of the family. She loved to sit with Eamonn and [me] in the evenings by the fire. She seemed to love the sense of family. She was like a little urchin ... she was full of fun and devilment.... The one consolation I have is that I know Simone's last month on earth was very happy.

Dominique d'Amiens later told Helena Gunn that as she and Simone walked in the direction of Amiens Street (Connolly) Station, they heard the sound of the Parnell Street bomb. Simone recognised the sound immediately, perhaps because of time spent in Israel. She looked at Dominique and said something like, 'That's a bomb. People may need our help.' Just as she made towards where the sound had come from, the second bomb exploded close by, killing her and injuring Dominique.

Helena Gunn heard the bombs go off as she waited to be collected by Eamonn at her mother's home in Killester. News reports were coming through of several fatalities and scores of injuries. As the evening wore on and Simone did not return, they became increasingly worried. Shortly after 8 o'clock they called Jervis Street Hospital from a neighbour's house and were informed that Simone had been admitted but had been discharged. This confused and concerned them, and they phoned Betty Shortall, the person responsible for finding accommodation for the foreign students. She checked with Dominique's host family and learned that she had not returned home either.

At around 9 o'clock Betty's son, Tony Shortall, met the Gunns at Jervis Street Hospital. Tony had already been told that Dominique had been admitted and could be visited the following day. The hospital corridors were teeming with distraught relatives and friends of the dead and injured. The Gunns met a priest to whom they described Simone. He advised them to go to Store Street Garda Station. The station was next door to Dublin City Morgue, and Eamonn Gunn found himself called upon to identify the body of Simone Chetrit. Tony Shortall accompanied him. Eamonn recognised Simone immediately. Tony Shortall said she had an expression of surprise on her face. The Gunns were devastated.

On 21 May 1974, Eamonn and Helena Gunn were the chief mourners at a special service held at the Jewish cemetery in Dolphin's Barn, before Simone's removal to Paris the following day. The service was conducted by the Chief Rabbi in Ireland, Dr Isaac Cohen, and was attended by the French Ambassador, M. Emmanuel d'Harcourt.

Almost a quarter of a century later, the Gunns had lost contact with Simone's family. I began to search for them in January 1999.

On 2 October a young French lawyer, Aude Catala, accompanied me to my meeting with Simone's brother, Elie Chetrit, his wife, Carole, and children, Raphael and Jessica. It was twenty-five years since the horrific murder of Elie's youngest sister, and no one from Ireland had come to speak with them before. I could sense that the deep hurt of Simone's murder was an unresolved trauma.

Carole: We had contact with the Irish Government at the time through our lawyer, Maître Azencot. He was a friend of Yvette Chetrit, Elie's other sister. He still retains the files.... Through our lawyer the Irish Government sent some compensation to the family five years after Simone's death.

We received letters from the Gunn family, the Jewish community in Dublin and others. Dominique d'Amiens came to visit us in Paris a few months after what happened. We haven't got in contact with Dominique since then. We have her address but we don't know if she is still living there.

As a boy of nine or ten, Elie Chetrit had witnessed his maternal grandmother being arrested in Paris and deported to a concentration camp at the start of the Jewish Holocaust. Simone was born on 2 September 1943 while her mother was in a Catholic convent, hiding from the Nazis. Her older brothers and sisters were in hiding in Switzerland. Her father, Salomon Chetrit, had fled to Spain before Simone's birth, where he was arrested and spent some time in prison.

Several years after the war Salomon and Esther Chetrit moved to Israel and Simone went with them. The family always found it ironic, Carole told us, that while Simone lived for years in a country engulfed in a major war, it was in Dublin that she had to die the way she did.

Carole: We really felt abandoned because Simone was the only French fatality. We also missed having contact with the other grieving families.

We were surprised to be shown an official document from the Coroner's Court, Store Street, Dublin, written in French, which stated that 'Simone Chretrit [sic] est décédée de façon naturelle (died of natural causes).'

Given their experience during the Holocaust, the family were hurt to find the word 'deportation' used in the context of returning Simone's body to Paris. Although someone had put a line through it and written directly above 'le transport', Elie did not show either of the documents to the rest of the family, especially Simone's parents. 'We did not want these documents to be the memory of Simone,' he said. A further document stated that Simone had died 'par suite d'accident' (following an accident).

Elie: I think it's important to look for the truth but I don't think the truth will ever be discovered because of the political context between the two Irelands. I think it's in everybody's interest to bury this case. Silence is also a kind of truth.

I asked how they had learned of Simone's death.

Elie: We were away and when I came back, I had a message on my answering machine. In fact, my partner in the office had received a message from the Embassy. He left a note on my desk with a phone number.... We didn't have much contact with [the Irish Government]. We just got condolences....

Carole: We realised that despite our efforts, we wouldn't get the news we were looking for, so we just gave up and we didn't get any more news.

Elie Chetrit's daughter, Sylvie, was very close to Simone, who was like a big sister to her. They had lived together in Tours.

Sylvie: My father bought me a very nice white coat and Simone loved it. So, I gave her my white coat before she left to go to Ireland and she gave me her blue coat and I can't help thinking that she might have died with my white coat on. For years I kept her blue coat, thinking that I would never see my white coat again and that I would never see Simone again.

Sadly, Simone did die wearing Sylvie's white coat. Helena Gunn told me 'she lived in it' and was wearing it on the day of the bombs.

Simone's family told of a happy, cheerful young woman, who was curious about life. She was interested in everything and wanted to travel the world. She was also a very good artist. Elie remembers Simone as a sensitive and loving person who was particularly adored by her nieces and nephews. Simone had qualified as a make-up artist, but as she couldn't find a job, she had decided to become a secretary and wished to be bilingual. That was why she had decided to go to Ireland to learn English.

On 17 May 1974, Simone sent postcards to all the family. They arrived after news of her death. Sylvie still has her postcard. 'Everyone of us keeps our own memories,' she said.

Simone's mother is now close to 90 and living in Jerusalem. A year after Simone's burial in Paris, she was re-interred in Jerusalem to be buried close to her father, Salomon Chetrit.

Almost four years after Simone's murder, Helena Gunn's sister, Yvonne Kennedy, kept a promise she had made to Simone during her last month in Ireland. Yvonne had told her that she so loved the name Simone, that if she ever had a daughter she would name the baby after her. On 4 April 1978, Yvonne Kennedy gave birth to her first child, a baby girl. She named her Simone.

CONCEPTA DEMPSEY (REMEMBERED BY HER NIECE, GERTIE SHIELDS)
My aunt was my father's sister and she was born in Drogheda. They all lived in Laurence's Street for quite a good few years and then moved up to ... Drogheda. My father was married at about 25 years of age, and Cepta and his sister Eva would have been the two girls left

at home. They had a younger sister who died in the 1914–1918 flu.

Cepta and Eva were educated at the Sacred Heart Convent in Drogheda and, after my father's marriage, Cepta took up employment in Murphy and Healy's in Drogheda, which was a fairly well-known establishment. She was a bookkeeper there and she would have been the bread-earner. I think they were closing or selling out and Cepta took up employment in Guiney's in Dublin.

Eva kept house and we have great memories of visiting them. They had a lovely back garden that went right down with a view of the Boyne River in Drogheda, and they had a huge old collie dog called Rock, a great old pet. But Cepta travelled every day to Dublin from Drogheda, and was a very devout, good-living person....

The evening that she died, she apparently was outside the building or coming out of the building and forgot her headscarf, and those few seconds made the difference [of] life and death to her. She had just gone up to the second floor where she worked when the whole front of the building was blown in. She didn't die immediately. She was taken to the Mater Hospital with severe back injuries because part of a huge piping from the outside of the building had come in and done ferocious damage to her. But there were no signs of other injuries. Her face was untouched. She died some days later in the Mater Hospital. She was on a life-support machine when my family saw her. I did not go at that time because I had young children, but my sister Deirdre, my mother and Deirdre's husband went in. My sister told me that although she seemed to be totally unconscious, when she put her hand out to her, Auntie Cepta squeezed her hand. So there must have been some life there at that stage....

I would like to pay tribute to the people who kept the campaign alive, who kept the whole cause alive over those many years. I always really felt that it was disgraceful the way those people were treated because they were all totally innocent victims of a violence that was done to them — people going about their business. I think all of those people deserve justice. They deserve recognition and they are entitled to know who did this. Somebody must be held responsible for the whole shambles that actually has ensued over the years....

COLLETTE & BABY DOHERTY (REMEMBERED BY COLLETTE'S MOTHER, WINIFRED, AND SISTER, JACKIE MCCARTHY WADE)
WMcC: I remember the evening I was after coming in from work and I was washing my hair. My husband Mick and I were looking at the television and the other girls were out. My son worked down on the docks on a lorry and, when I saw the news, I said to Mick, 'Jesus, isn't that terrible?' We were looking at it and it was our son, Michael, we were worried about because he was down that direction. We never imagined Collette was in danger. We got word our son was all right and I said, 'Oh, thank God.' Then we heard that Collette had gone out and wasn't back. She went up Talbot Street, and I said, 'Oh my Jesus, Mary and Joseph, Mick, Collette is not back.'

After that some of the family went around all the hospitals and then they went to the morgue and then we were after hearing that Wendy was in the police station. Collette had Wendy in a buggy in Talbot Street.

Of course, when they went to the morgue, Collette was there, and it was devastating.... I'll really never forget it and I don't suppose any one else that had anybody hurt or murdered then will either.

Collette was a good girl, she was an ambitious girl, and she always wanted to get on. The mirror is still up there with Collette's name written on the top of it. We never took her name off it. As I say, it was devastating that time. It was really terrible, and to think, she was nine months pregnant at the time, so her little unborn baby was the thirty-fourth victim of the bombings.

JMcCW: I have to admit Tony Gregory and Patricia McKenna were the only politicians who really fought for our campaign. There were a few others too....

Fr Cleary, Lord rest him, he kicked it off, fair play to him. Fr Cleary had us, not long before he died ... on his radio show. Up to that it was very hard to get the attention of the media, very hard.... Now, one of our committee members on the twentieth or twenty-first anniversary rang up one of the country's top broadcasters. His attitude was 'Let sleeping dogs lie.' Now, there was an attitude of one of the biggest media commentators in the country. The whole episode was very much an embarrassment to the Irish establishment. They just wanted to keep it very quiet. I think it's dreadful.

Collette was so full of living, so full of life. None of us were ever the same after what happened. I don't think there is a day that goes by that we don't think about it.... And like that, when anniversaries come around, or a birthday ... you think, 'God, she would have been such and such an age.' The girl next-door was celebrating her twenty-first the day Collette was killed. They were not buddy-buddy but friendly enough with each other. Every time I see her, I often think of Collette and I wonder what she would have been like now....

BREDA GRACE (REMEMBERED BY HER HUSBAND, TIM)
My wife, Breda, was killed in Talbot Street. She was 34 years old and we had a baby son of twelve months. She had gone in to buy some things for the child and she had taken my car on the day. It was quite by chance that she was in Dublin because my car would not normally be there ... it was there on [that] Friday because the night before I had walked on a nail outside the door and punctured my foot.

[By] chance ... I was at home and she normally went into town when the car was available to her.... The baby was also a little bit difficult that day. He was teething and causing her a bit of bother so I said, 'I'm here, I'll look after the child.' I encouraged her to go in. I actually said, 'Go on into town — the car is there.'

My wife went into town and the bombs exploded at 5.30 and she must have been passing fairly close to the car in Talbot Street.

I went downstairs at 6 o'clock and I switched on the television and the next thing I heard the words 'bombs have gone off in Dublin'. Naturally I was very concerned at that and I tried to telephone ... a friend of mine who had a hotel in Gardiner Street ... but the telephone systems had totally jammed in Dublin.... So by about 7 o'clock I was watching outside the door for my wife and I decided to leave the child with next-door neighbours.

I borrowed [a] car and went into town and I first of all went to Gardiner Street where I knew she would normally park the car, not far from Talbot — a normal car park — and ours was the only one left. Dublin was in chaos at this stage....

[W]hen I saw the car, I knew my wife was involved ... and ... the only hope I had then was that maybe she had been somewhere close by when the thing had gone off and she got very nervous and had gone to some house and stayed there — something like that.

I knew she was involved, so I then went to look for her, and I got the help of the police to clear the road for me in one or two of the places. I went to the various hospitals and she wasn't on any of the lists in any of the hospitals....

There were no bodies in the Rotunda but there were injured lists, but she wasn't on that. Then I went from there to the main hospital, Jervis Street. So, when I got there — I have never seen such mayhem in all my life.... You'd nearly have to fight your way to get lists of the injured. People were in such a state. I understood that there were five or six bodies there but I didn't go to view those bodies. I went on to the other hospitals. I didn't start looking at corpses.... I kept hoping that maybe she was injured in one of the hospitals.

I went down to the Mater Hospital. There were two bodies there. Again I didn't go to the morgue but I knew eventually, after I'd checked all the hospitals, I'd have to go. At 10 o'clock I rang my brother and he joined me in town and I went to the morgue. They had no lists there. They didn't know. The chaos was unbelievable. It was indescribable....

I went home to Portmarnock. And obviously I couldn't sleep so I stayed up all night. I went in the next day. Eventually, I identified my wife's body at roughly 12.30 in the morgue. I had gone in, checked various things, and they brought me out a piece of the trousers she was wearing, so I knew then that that was it.

The state of her injuries was that she was very close to the explosion and she died instantly. She wasn't badly mutilated. But she died instantly....

She was a young woman; she was in excellent health and was most concerned, as most women would be of her age, about her figure. She wanted to walk miles — that's why she wouldn't have a car.

I was running a company at the time.... We had a very nice home and I was at the zenith of my career. I was at my very best.

I have lost seven or eight years of my life due to this. I was obviously shattered....

It got worse after six or eight months. I never was the type for depression or for psychiatrist stuff, but, in fact, I did go to a psychiatrist. I had two visits to one and I just forgot about him. Just as I did the week after I lost Breda. They gave me Valium on the day she was being buried, and, a couple of days after, I threw them down the toilet because they were just putting me to sleep. But I was totally shattered.

I didn't feel there was any point in achieving anything in life. What was the point in doing anything? The only thing that kept me going was that I had a boy twelve months old I had to bring up. He kept me going. I looked into my wife's grave and looked at her coffin and felt I'd just as well go down there. That was my feeling. But I couldn't go down there because I knew I had to bring this boy up....

I absorbed myself in my business and I worked twelve hours a day, which was great therapy. I felt at the time there was nothing done, and over the early years, the early two or three years, it was just forgotten. Never mentioned. And even still, they will mention Enniskillen; they will mention what happened in Warrington and Omagh. Terrible things. Don't misunderstand me. But there is never much reference to what happened in Dublin — the greatest atrocity of the whole lot. And even southern politicians never mention it. That hurts a lot of the people....

My son, Edward, fortunately was only twelve months old. He never remembers his mother. That was one good thing, it was a help to me, a consolation to me that he wasn't two, three, or four years old that he would have known, or maybe six or seven, which would have been worse.

MAY MCKENNA (REMEMBERED BY HER SISTER, MARGARET MCNICHOLL)
There was my sister, May, my mother, and myself in our family. My mother was from Monaghan so May lived a while in Monaghan, but she went up to Dublin and was working [there] most of her life, since she was a teenager. She loved Dublin. She wouldn't have lived anywhere else. She came up home, surely, to my mother, and the funny part of it is, after my mother died, there was no Troubles then, of course, after she died, I so often rang her and said, 'Why don't you come up for a holiday?' She wouldn't come over the border [Margaret had married and moved to Dungannon, County Tyrone]. She would say, 'I'd be too afraid.' And I couldn't get over this because then she was killed at her own door [in Dublin].

I got word about the bombing on Friday evening here — my family were young at the time and never watched the television a lot. But they gave out the word about a bomb in Dublin. Well, we had so many bombs that we thought nothing of it. You just say, 'Oh another bomb.' It was on Saturday I went into town and when I came home my husband said to me, 'You had better go over and make a phone call because they are after giving out that there is a May McKenna dead in Dublin.' I said, 'It couldn't be May,' because it was impossible. Well, he said, 'Go over anyway — the gardaí have given out a number you could ring.' So I went over to neighbours across the street and when I got through to the gardaí they asked me to describe her as best I could. Now, he said, 'It sounds very like her, she has been identified by a friend....' He told me then ... to come [to Dublin].... I couldn't get away until Sunday morning, as we had no car.

I had to go into the morgue and I had to walk through all those bodies. They were all laid out covered, as they were doing post mortems on them. It was terrible. I came out of that place and I screeched my head off. And the only thing I could think of at the time was if only they could get who done it and put them in there with the dead. Just put them in there. It was the only punishment I could think of at the time. To see what they had done....

Thank God, May was quite recognisable. The only thing I will always remember about her was that her hair was blew straight back on her head. I can always remember that. It must have been the blast.

She lived in 18 Talbot Street, just across from Guiney's, and the bomb was parked just outside her door.

She lived up on the second storey. Mr O'Neill in the shoe shop below told me that there was a bomb went off in Parnell Square before Talbot Street. He said he heard it and he said it suddenly dawned on him about the car sitting at his door. It had been there for some time. He said he heard May running down the stairs, and he went to the door to shout at May, 'Don't go out!' when the thing went up.

I suppose the most treasured memory I have of May was up in Dublin, you know, when I'd go up and see her in Dublin and she would take me out and we would go to different places, sitting and talking. I think the best ones I have of her were in Dublin. Of course, she came up home too. But us living in the country, well, we would go to a few places together but could never go awfully far. But I think my best memories are with her in Dublin.

I don't think I have ever accepted May's death, the way she died. No. I mean, I feel as if there has always been hatred there. One of those priests was saying to forgive the Omagh ones. No, I could never forgive them. I never accepted her death. I don't think she should have died the way she did. No. It has always been a sore point from that day to this. That they could do that in Talbot Street on a Friday evening, which, you know, was quite a busy street. No. Gradually I came to terms with it, of course. You do as time goes past, but it's always there with you.

I kept every cutting that came out, thinking that I would get one that would give us a bit of news, but to this day I don't know what happened or why. They won't release the files. And why are they not releasing the files? What is the reason? I don't think they'd get away with that up here in the north.

Another thing that bugs me is the gardaí's attitude. I can tell you that we drove straight into Dublin and I don't honestly remember that we were ever stopped over the border and the same coming back. So, it seemed to me they weren't looking for nobody. They had nobody out on the roads, although I suppose they were long gone. The gardaí didn't do enough. Did you see the way they were working in Omagh? In Talbot Street, that Sunday we were up, we only saw one or two gardaí.

I never got May's personal belongings — her handbag and her jewellery, or photographs, or things like that. I never got any of them. They were all gone....

The gardaí eventually let me into her flat. I don't know whether it was that week or the week after, but there was nothing.... What I'm trying to say is the gardaí should have had that completely sealed off and nobody could get in until everything was sorted out and cleaned up and you name it.

I was always waiting on them to get caught and I always promised myself I would go every day to that court-house, but they never were caught. And they will never be caught now....

ANNE MARREN (REMEMBERED BY HER SISTER, MARGARET O'CONNOR)
Anne was just twenty when she died. She was working in the Department of Posts and Telegraphs in Hawkins House, Dublin.

There were five of us in the family. She would have been the more serious type and would have gone home almost every weekend if she could. She was concerned because my mother had died when we were young, so she would be very attached to my father and concerned about him. That particular weekend she was going home as usual....

At this stage, I was in Scotland, doing midwifery, and I had been home the weekend before and had met her [in Dublin]. That's why I know she was going home that weekend. I was back in the hospital in Scotland that Friday and about to finish an evening shift. A girl from Ireland who was coming on night duty met me and told me about the awful bombs in Dublin. I just went pale and I asked, 'Where were they?' She answered, 'Talbot Street.' I said, 'Oh no! Anne was going home this evening — I bet she was there.' She saw the reaction on my face and said, 'No, it wasn't Talbot Street.'

I ran off duty and I turned on the television to see the news and I froze. I was afraid I'd see something that would tell me she was in it. I saw nothing but I had this awful feeling, so at about 10 o'clock that night I rang the flat in Dublin where she stayed for over two years with some cousins. I asked them, 'Did Anne go home?' and they told me she had. I then asked, 'Did she get home?' They didn't know. I left my telephone number in Scotland, just in case they might have cause to call me during the night. I went to bed but never slept.

In the meantime, they had gone to meet her at the train at Ballymote from home. She wasn't on the train, but then people on the train said some were turned back. So they went home and they tried to ring the flat in Dublin and they couldn't get through because the lines were jammed. Eventually they got through and asked the girls if

Anne had gone home. When they said she had and Anne wasn't at home, they said they would check the hospitals, which they did.

They were told there were many bodies in the mortuary that hadn't been identified so they went there and they identified her.... When she had been identified, the guards then contacted them at home in Sligo. They also contacted the police in Scotland. I can still remember hearing the night-sister coming from the hospital to the nursing home. I could hear her walking in the door and she didn't have to tell me. I just knew. My father then rang at the same time, so that's how I heard the news.

It was an awful shock, and still today it's like a dream. You wonder did it happen or did you dream it or whatever. It was total devastation. My mother was just thirteen years dead the same week. There were still two younger ones in the family. I had an older brother, I was the second eldest, and then my sister, Anne.

She didn't have any major hobbies. I'd say her main social scene would have been at home. I think when you are from the country, you tend to go home at weekends to go out. A lot of her secondary school class would have been in Dublin and would have visited each other at nights and met again when they would go home at the weekend.

My father, I suppose, had only got over my mother's death. We were all so young when she died, and at this stage we were all getting independent. I know he lived for almost twenty years after but he didn't live really, he only existed. It really broke his heart. My other sister was just about to do her Leaving Cert in June and it was very hard for her. My younger brother as well — he was 17. I suppose when there is no mother, an older sister really takes the place. Prior to that I had been in Dublin and I would have been going home. When the bombings happened, I was only three months in Scotland but I came home and stayed for a while and went back again after three months....

They were very good to me at the hospital. They had arranged the flight by morning and they drove me to Glasgow. I remember Dublin so clearly. Everything was deserted. It was like a bombed city. I met my father and older brother and it was a wild-goose chase because we couldn't get to the city morgue that particular Saturday. To add insult to injury, when we decided we had to come home again and we went to the station to get the train, there was a bomb scare. We were just about to board when we had to leave the station. We went in somewhere nearby to get a cup of tea, and they said they would alert us when the train was leaving, but they didn't. When we got back, the train was gone, so we had to get a taxi to Longford, and somebody came to meet us there.

There is very little about her funeral I can remember. I know we went up to collect Anne's remains in Dublin on Monday, but I can't remember travelling up. I can't remember anything about the mortuary. I can't remember seeing her. I know my father was upset until we got back home. I can remember the girls from the convent where she went to school had a guard of honour for her. But I can just remember the emptiness afterwards. The only thing I can really say is that the house was so full for so many days, I said one day, 'I wish everybody would clear out and let us be together ourselves.' But everybody was, in truth, so good and so nice....

On the Sunday after Anne was buried, we went to the grave, and it was covered in wreaths from the people of Derry. My father said people from Derry had actually called to the house to find out where the grave was. It was a nice gesture. They said that a lot of people from the south had gone up there after Bloody Sunday.

I can remember letters from everybody and anybody. But it was just the emptiness. What's strange is that while I can't even remember being at Anne's funeral, I can remember my mother's funeral, even though she was actually thirteen years dead at the time.

It was only when I went back to Scotland, the reality of what actually happened hit me. But time has passed since, and still when we get together and talk about it, it is like a dream. To look at photographs you sometimes wonder did she really exist, it's so long ago now....

Her colleagues at the Department of Posts and Telegraphs were very good. I can remember them coming down for the first anniversary, and for several anniversaries they actually arranged masses. Some came down to visit my father outside anniversary time. They were ever so good. I can remember that more than I can remember the funeral. I had come to terms with it a bit by then.

I only had the two sisters but I only have the one sister now. It's funny, when the children were born, I absolutely missed Anne, and it's strange, when I would speak to my other sister, it doesn't happen now, but up to some years ago, I would talk as if I was talking to Anne. I would be calling her Anne or say to my sister, 'I must tell Anne this' as if she was there somewhere....

It bothers me that no one was ever convicted for her murder. Even when I met my husband, Val, I would have told him the story and he would say, 'God, I can't understand.' You feel there was so many people just banished and nobody seems to be able to find anybody. But this case was just put under the carpet, for what or why, I don't know. I would like to see it resolved and I would like to see them remembered properly....

A proper memorial to me, and one I would be quite keen on, would be for the government to investigate this properly and let us know the whole truth.

DOROTHY MORRIS (REMEMBERED BY HER NEPHEW, MAURICE REDMOND)
Dorrie, as most people knew her, was the youngest of four sisters, in a family of six siblings. She was both my aunt and godmother. She lived all her life in No. 41 Larkfield Avenue, Kimmage, with her mother.... The family was well-known in the Kimmage area, as my

grandmother, Leah Morris, a qualified nurse and midwife, looked after all the ailments within the locality.

Also living in the house was another aunt, Georgina Morris, who had a small dressmaking business. Both Dorrie and Georgina were spinsters.

My own mother, Maud Redmond (née Morris), together with Dorrie and Georgina, became affectionately known among the family as the 'Three Lovely Lasses from Kimmage'. They did most things together, and when my father, Leo Redmond, died, my mother moved back to 41 Larkfield Avenue. This was in 1972.

Dorrie Morris was a petite, attractive and good-humoured lady, who took pride in her appearance. She enjoyed life to the full. She worked in Cadbury Ireland most of her adult life, first working in East Wall Road and then in Coolock. She was dedicated to her work and was very well-respected by her bosses and fellow-workers. She made some lifelong friends there. When Cadbury's moved to Coolock, she liked her job so much that every day she made the trip without ever complaining — sometimes even taking three buses. She then found that a work colleague, John Walshe, came from the same area and was able to organise a lift. It is so sad to realise that such a kind gesture resulted in the untimely deaths of two very fine people.

Some of my fondest memories of Dorrie are of when both she and Georgina would come to my family home in Landscape Road, and the 'Three Lovely Lasses' would go to the local lounge, where they would enjoy a cigarette and a drink, and catch up on all the gossip, and then return to the house, where my mother would prepare supper.

Dorrie was a very quiet and caring person, and it is sad to think that such a good person should meet with such a violent death. I only hope that her death was instant, and that she felt no pain. To this day, I find it difficult to come to terms with the horrific events of May 1974.

I will never forget the events of that traumatic day. Dorrie left for work as usual and, when she hadn't arrived home at her usual time, both my mother and Georgina became anxious and phoned me, as they had heard of the bombings on the evening news. It was approximately 9 p.m. that myself and my brother, Brendan, decided to go looking on the streets, and, when we spoke with the gardaí at one of the scenes of the bombing, they said we should go to Donnybrook Garda Station. This we did, only to be told that we should, in fact, visit the bomb-site in Talbot Street. When we got there, we spoke to a garda, and enquired if a car, which had been blown through Guiney's window, was a black Morris Minor. He confirmed this, and very kindly brought us down to the site. Other gardaí at the scene said that, unfortunately, they did not think that anyone could possibly survive such an impact, and that we should make our way to the City Morgue. This we duly did, and we came across the most horrific scenes I have ever encountered. There were literally bodies and limbs everywhere. We were informed that it would be impossible to make any positive identification at this stage, and that we should return on the Saturday morning. When we returned on the Saturday, the scene, while still horrific, at least had some semblance of order, and we were brought to a table where we formally identified our aunt. My aunt had been killed by a piece of shrapnel which had apparently pierced her heart. Apart from a slight mark on her right cheek, there were no visible signs of damage to her petite frame.

MARIE PHELAN (REMEMBERED BY HER FATHER)

It would be about half past five when we heard the news. I called that Friday night to the shop for a message or something. The girl told me there that there were a lot of people killed in a bombing in Dublin, and I just listened away to her and came home, and I said to myself I'd hear the 6 o'clock news. I done a few jobs first and I came in specially to hear the news. We saw the bomb and saw where the people got killed all about the place. My wife happened to say to me, 'That's not far away from where Marie is, you know.'

We wanted to find out more, but we never heard anything else until some time around 12 o'clock that night. I went to a pub down the road for a game of cards. But the news was on my mind all the time. There was something about it. About 10 o'clock that night there was a knock at the door of the pub, and it was a guard who wanted to see me. So I said to myself that was it. He told me that there had been people killed, and he didn't tell me that she was actually dead or anything, but he told me she was in an accident or something. It was some way like that he put it to me.

It was other guards who told us the news, and that was about half past twelve. That was the night it happened. The next day, of course, I went to identify her. Her only identification was a ring. She was very close to the car.

She was going to a twenty-first that evening, and her friend from work, they went into a place called Guiney's to get a present, and, coming outside, the car was directly across the road, so they got the full force of the blast. They were killed instantly in that respect.

We still today would very much like to know how it happened, why it happened and who was directly involved. Mostly, just to find out why people were never caught as such. I thought they might have done that little bit extra to try and find out who the culprits involved were. Why didn't they do that?

Marie took [an] interest in everything. She was great and a great worker. She had a great way about her. Anyone would take to her. We missed her terrible. She was a great sort. You'd always miss her. When she would be in the house after work, when she would come home from school, or anything, you'd know she would be around because you'd have noise.

Her mother hasn't been well for a lot of years because of what happened to Marie. We think of her every day. I suppose it was better for her to be killed outright than to be maimed for life in hospital in Dublin, and going up and looking at her and unable to do anything for her.

Her mother visits her grave every Saturday evening.

SIOBHÁN ROICE (REMEMBERED BY HER SISTER, LIZ GLEESON)
It appeared to be like an ordinary Friday in May. Of course, that was up until the fateful newsflash that evening. I can recall my father resting in bed, and both my mother and I listening intently to the news bulletins. Perhaps it was a mother-and-child bonding but immediately my mother felt that there was cause, serious cause, for concern....

I can recall the agony and mental torment during that dreadful night. It seemed as if our lives had just been taken out of our control. There was no direction, only complete despair and utter torment.

My father had just recently retired after seventeen years of work in England. We were a very close family. We had always experienced a great sense of togetherness. Our parents lived for their children. They were parents devoted to each other and to us.

Siobhán was always there. As far as I was concerned, during the years we were together, short as they were, she was an utmost caring person, far beyond her years.

That night was to be one which will always be embedded in my memory. I will never forget the deep sadness we all felt, even though, as yet, we had to learn the exact truth. But, as a family, we knew already Siobhán was gone. How? I don't know. Where and when it had happened, we still had to wait and see. What remained was one of the longest nights we ever experienced as a family. We knew that a precious treasure had been stolen from us.

Early on Saturday the 18th we embarked on what was to be the worst day of my life. We travelled to Dublin to investigate for ourselves. I can still to this day hear the mobile police units, alerting the public, to be aware and alert. We checked her flat, the hospitals and, eventually ... the City Morgue.

I recall the sad picture of my father, doing what must be the most difficult thing for any parent, having to identify the remains of a dead child. To be absolutely certain, my brother-in-law had to make a second identification.

One could go on forever about the injustice of parents robbed of their child. A brother who was at sea could not be home before her burial. Our mother was so overcome and grief-stricken, she could not be present at her child's funeral. Please tell me, where is there justice in that?

Politics means absolutely nothing in my vocabulary now. Once, perhaps, I had faith in politics. But, after our experience as a family, not any more. And, as for the people who perceive that murder and destruction is the direction they wish to take, then they are truly sad and misguided people....

We have now reached a new millennium and I often wonder what Siobhán would have been like. Would she have married or what course would her life have taken?

A lost child and sister, maybe, but never a lost memory. I had fourteen years with her, and I feel the void that we can never fill. But as we say, that is her — Siobhán's — space, and she is always with us.

I have now reached a point in my life where I can't help thinking what a sad reflection on our Government this whole sorry episode is. The fact that for twenty-six years, consecutive powers have denied what is truly ours — a just and final conclusion, and closure, to this long and sad story....

As a family brought up to respect the law of the land, we sometimes hold our hands up in despair and ask, 'Whom do we have faith in? Who do we trust?' The sad irony is, there is no answer. There is no trust.

MAUREEN SHIELDS (REMEMBERED BY HER DAUGHTER, FIONA RYAN)
Maureen Shields (née Caplis) was born in December 1927 at the foot of Piper Hill in the village of Hollyford, County Tipperary. The eldest of seven, she was always the guiding light in her family, the one to look up to, to turn to for advice or comfort for her younger brothers and sisters, and later for her own family.

After completing school, Maureen set out for Dublin to carve out a life for herself. She secured a job in the civil service and remained there until her marriage to Leo in 1953. They had three of a family — a son and two daughters.

Maureen was lively and vivacious, and her circle of friends ever-expanding. She was the centre of everything she touched — her family, her friends and her community. No amount of superlatives could describe her. Her greatest treasure was her family and her greatest gift to us was her love, which she wrapped us in each day....

Her tragic death was a blow to us that cut to the quick, the pain so severe that it was like an open wound.... Leo felt the pain of her passing intensely and died less than two years later, of a broken heart.

Her death was indeed heartbreaking for all her family. Even though we cannot see or hear her, and the scent of her perfume and sound of her voice are long since gone, we have always striven to keep her memory alive, and a sense of her presence with us. Maureen left her mark on all of us — the way we approach things, the way we do or say things. She is always a part of our everyday lives.

One of the greatest tragedies is that her grandchildren and great-grandchild didn't get to know her. They would have brought each other so much joy. Maureen was a lady and her untimely death will never be forgotten. There is no doubt that she is watching us from above. We have always been proud to say, 'We are Maureen Shields' family.'

Keep watching over us, Mammy.

JOHN WALSHE (REMEMBERED BY HIS NEPHEW, GAVIN CORBETT)
Like a mosquito trapped in amber, Uncle John, and everything I know of him, seems to belong to another era. I was born in 1976 and my uncle was killed in 1974. For someone who tends to mark time by major football tournaments instead of calendar years, that was seven World Cups ago, the golden age of Johann Cruyff and skin-tight jerseys and ridiculous sideburns; I can only remember as far back as

four World Cups. Even the few things I inherited from him are relics of a time gone by. There's that solid fibreglass fishing rod (they're all carbon fibre or kevlar these days), a couple of hardback books with picture-less, sun-bleached covers, and this chunky signet ring — the kind of gaudy accoutrement that simply *defined* the 1970s. But I love that ring and I cherish it and I always wear it, because my mum gave it to me for my twenty-first birthday, and it's the same ring Uncle John got as a present for *his* twenty-first birthday. I'm sorry that there aren't many other tangible memories of my uncle around, but then, in life, Uncle John was not noted as being a particularly materialistic person.

And yet, despite those one or two fossils to inform my image of my uncle, when I look at the photo of him on the piano, I can partly see what my mum means when she says that Uncle John is the family member I've inherited the most characteristics from. I understand now where the smile came from, and the eyes (and indeed the dodgy eyesight), and the cheeks and the slight frame. (I sometimes curse that I couldn't have made the best out of my frame as Uncle John made of his. At a stretch, I could muster enough co-ordination and athleticism to take part in a game of donkey, but Uncle John was a great little winger for Terenure College, a very good runner, and his enthusiasm for the round-ball game earned him the nickname of 'Soccer' at a rugby school.) Apparently, the similarities don't end with physical appearance. Whenever my mum tells me that a quip or a turn of phrase of mine reminds her for an instant of Uncle John's sense of humour, I regret that there isn't a kindred spirit in my small family to laugh along and save me from the ignominy of so many jokes that fall flat on their backsides around the Christmas dinner table.

Even after all these years (what is it, twenty-six now?) Uncle John still enters our conversations, and he is remembered with great fond-ness and fun, and, of course, sadness, by my mum and my aunt. Obviously, my cousins and my younger brother and I have no memory of him, and my older sisters only have vague but happy ones, but it hasn't prevented me, and (I think I can speak for other family members when I say this) my siblings and cousins, from thinking about him a lot, and Uncle John from having a more profound influence on our lives than could have been consciously conceived.

What we do share of Uncle John, we tend to keep to ourselves. Occasionally this has caused problems for researchers in the past. I noted that in that recently published book about the victims of the Troubles, *Lost Lives*, my uncle's memory was marked with the most minuscule of entries, and what *was* written was partly, and deeply, incorrect. They got his age right okay (27) and his faith (Catholic), but described him as 'married with children'. For the record, he wasn't married, but he had a long-term girlfriend with whom he'd just bought a house.

I suppose you can't blame a blip like that wholly on crass assumption. The researchers probably weren't helped by a dearth of information on my uncle in the public domain. But forgive us for merely wanting to keep Uncle John's memory within the family, and for fearing that it might be co-opted ... for God knows what end.

Whenever I see references to Uncle John in cold print in the context of what happened to him, it strikes me that he might be regarded as just another black-and-white statistic of a conflict in which he had no involvement. Is it possible to build a mental picture of someone from only the information that he was 27, Catholic, and the inheritor of a name ('John Walshe') that would rival 'Pat Murphy' for ordinariness? To fill out the picture would require a whole book in itself, but I hope I've done him some sort of justice in what I've written so far. And in the few lines I have left, might I add that I'm sorry I didn't inherit some other of his traits — his level-headed temperament and his magnanimity, something I suspect was passed down to him by my grandad, who astounded everyone with his complete absence of bitterness in the aftermath of his only son's death; his kindness; his fun-loving nature; his enviable ability to make friends. It's been churned out a million times about any young person that has died in the past, but then this cliché really was true about Uncle John: he was just a great guy, and I wish he'd been around to show me how to cast a bait properly on the end of a fishing rod, or to show me how to pass a rugby ball, or just to tell me a few jokes.

South Leinster Street

ANNA MASSEY (REMEMBERED BY HER FATHER, FRANK)
To us Anna was everything. She was the eldest [of eight girls]. She was a twin. She was 21 on the Sunday before she was killed. She was to be married.

We had presents. We had her wedding dress in the making, her wedding cake, and she was a very bright and intelligent girl. She was the leader of the family, you know.... I've heard since that, if there was a decision to be made, she was the one that made it....

She worked in Lisney's, the auctioneers, on St Stephen's Green. That's how she was coming down from Kildare Street to go for the train that night....

She didn't drink and she didn't smoke. She never gave us a minute's trouble; she was quite ordinary in a way, but still a great kid.

I knocked off work at 5 o'clock that day. I came home and had my dinner and was sitting down, and the woman from next-door came in and said, 'Did you hear about the horrible bombings?' I said, 'No.' I hadn't turned on the telly that evening.

Then there was no sign of Anna coming in and she was the type that, if she was going to be late, she would ring up or get in touch with you in some way. So coming on to 7 o'clock or half seven we went out to look for her.... Neighbour's children, friends of hers, got into cars and went in different directions.... We only got as far as Mount Street Bridge when we were stopped. We would not be allowed go any further. And a policeman said he was very sorry he couldn't let anyone in. So we traipsed around and we came back a different direction along the Stillorgan Road. We were coming back I suppose around 9 o'clock. Still no sign of her.

We went in and had a cup of tea, sitting down; about half ten there was a knock on the door. There were two policemen saying, 'You're wanted in Pearse Street Station.' So I asked the policeman, 'What is it?' He said, 'To be quite honest with you, I don't know.' I went out to the car, the missus was getting ready, putting on some clothes, and I said to the policeman, 'Is it the Dublin bombings?' He said, 'I don't know.' I said, 'You can tell me'. He said, 'Honestly, I don't know anything, but I guarantee you I'll get you into Pearse Street Station as fast as I can.'

We got into Pearse Street Station and the Superintendent said we were wanted in the hospital that closed over in Brunswick Street [the Richmond].... So we went in there, myself and the wife, and the head sister I think she was, or the matron, she said, 'I think you'd better sit down and have a cup of tea.' She came in with Anna's watch and a thing she had around her neck and I said, 'Yes that's Anna's. What is it?' So she said, 'I'm afraid she's dead and you have to go to the morgue.' We went over to the morgue, which was like a battlefield, and we had to identify her. So that's how I found out. All in all, it was about half past one in the morning before we really found out....

My wife is still on medication even though it's twenty-six years. To us, as a family, I think it only happened yesterday. People ask me, 'Why are you pursuing this business?' The answer is simple. I owe it to Anna to find out who murdered her and why. And I know a lot of the relatives are of that opinion too. I don't know how many times I've said to myself, 'Give it up,' but I don't know how many times I've woken up and something at the back of my head keeps telling me, 'No — keep pushing it.' And even some of my family has said, 'Ah, give up, Daddy.' But I can't.

This is the first time I've ever made this public but on the Sunday after the funeral, at mass with my family, when I was coming out, a man approached me and asked me was I Mr Massey. I said, 'Yes.' He said, 'There's a couple of people want to see you.' And I went over to a car and there were three people in it. They were northern people and they said to me, 'We're from the IRA and we just wanted to tell you that we did not do the bombings on Friday last and if there is anything we can do for you, we're quite willing.' I said, 'I don't want any help from you or anybody else so forget it. End of story.'

I did not like IRA, UVF, UDA. I did not like paramilitaries, to be quite honest with you. I did not like what they were doing. As a matter of fact, I hated what they were doing. I didn't hate the people, I never hated anybody. I hated what they were doing. And that's why I dismissed those people. I said, 'Forget it.'

However, for nearly three decades now, we've been treated like lepers by the Irish State. I want to find out why....

I'm not looking for compensation because if you put a million quid on the table this morning, it wouldn't bring back my daughter and it wouldn't compensate me. I'm looking for justice. They've tribunals set up all over the place investigating themselves, but they don't want to know about the Dublin and Monaghan bombings....

Our children and our grandchildren will continue until we achieve a public tribunal of inquiry which forces everyone to come clean.

CHRISTINE O'LOUGHLIN (REMEMBERED BY HER HUSBAND, KEVIN)
The day that it happened I was coming back from work at about 5.30 in the evening. I worked in Dundrum and I used to get a lift home. As I got out of the car, a friend said, 'The bastards are after doing it again.' I didn't know what he meant.

When I came home, my sister and her family, who live two doors away, were here and one of them said there had been an accident in Nassau Street. Chrissie didn't come in yet ... but as time went on there was no sign of her and my sister said, 'Something has happened her.' And I said, 'Nothing's happened.' As time went on, I decided I had better go and see if there was any word anywhere.

The first place I went to, Jervis Street Hospital, there were no reports of her there. Somebody suggested I should try the Mater, but there was no reports of her there too. I even went as far as the Richmond Hospital. It was nearly 10 o'clock that night when somebody said, 'Maybe you should try the morgue.' So I went down there and they asked me who I was looking for. They then asked me what Chrissie looked like, her age and a description of her clothing. They let me in and there she was. She looked as though she was asleep.

She worked in the Shelbourne Hotel as a polisher and was with Anna Massey when the bomb went off. They had become pals because her uncle worked in the Shelbourne Hotel too and she got to know them. And whatever happened, she just said, 'Hold on, I'll be down with you', and that was the last of her.

The only thing I was thankful for at that time was that the boys were grown up. One was born in 1959. He's in his forties now. The other chap was a year younger. The eldest was working and the other boy was in college at the time.

The shock lasted a long time afterwards. I was working away but shortly after I took a turn and was brought into Jervis Street with pneumonia. I was there for a while and then they discovered I had angina, and to this day I'm attending the hospital....

Sometimes when you hear certain music, you remember she used to sing that. Everywhere you go, if a particular song comes on, you think, 'Oh there's Chrissie's song.' It always brings back memories....

I think the families who lost loved ones have been very badly treated by the politicians. I attended meetings with people like Máire Geoghegan Quinn when she was Minister for Justice, but they never did anything for us.

When the door is shut, I suppose all is forgotten.

Monaghan

PATRICK ASKIN (REMEMBERED BY HIS WIFE, PATRICIA, AND CHILDREN, PATRICK, SONIA AND SHARON)

Patricia: My husband Paddy was killed in the bomb in Monaghan on Friday, 17 May, and it was an awful shock for us. A newsflash on the radio came on some time after seven o'clock. By then he should have been home from work so one of the neighbours drove me to the hospital in Monaghan because I knew something had happened when he wasn't home. When I reached the hospital, one of the porters said that Paddy was all right. I knew nothing until the surgeon took me to one side and said they had done all they could for Paddy.

His lungs were punctured and half of his face was off and they couldn't do anything more for him. I insisted on seeing him and they didn't want me to see him but they took me in and they had a sheet over him and they just put the sheet down, and a big ear, that was all I seen of him. I was in a bad state of shock. They wanted me to stay in the hospital overnight but then I had the four children to think of. The twin girls were two and the boys were six and seven.

We were a very, very close family. He took them for walks and played football with them. You know, the usual things a father does. They really missed him.

The next few days after the funeral was over we were just on our own. From then on there was just the five of us. Nobody came near us at all about anything. As soon as he was buried, people forgot about us.

I didn't get his due pay on the night he was killed and I didn't get his pay until three weeks after he died. It was very hard. I was living between my sister and sister-in-law, so I had no house to keep at that stage. I'd no home to go to.

I got £5,000 and the children got £1,000 each in compensation, and that was it, and the money would obviously have gone to buy a new house. I bought a house which hadn't been lived in for years for £2,750, and it took the rest of the money to bring it up to living standards. There was no water in it. There was no toilet, nothing in it.

It was very, very hard. Very hard and I was living on £25 a week for a number of years down south. To bring up four children on that, because that was all that was coming in.

A couple of years ago, my son Paul was getting married. It was a very happy day for our family. But I remember he cried because his father wouldn't be at the wedding. This kind of thing happens not just with Paul but also with the other children regularly. They miss him terrible. I still miss him. People talk about the passing of the years and time healing all the wounds but it hasn't healed my children's, or mine, definitely not.

Paddy was hard-working and very quiet. He minded his own business and he went about his own business because he was a family man.

Patrick: One of my memories of my dad is teaching my younger brother and myself how to ride a bicycle. He would sort of hold on to us and not let us fall off or anything like that. I was very close to him. I used to run down the lane and meet him coming home from work and things like that. I was almost seven when he died.

I can remember the day as if it was yesterday. I was standing beside my mother at the kitchen sink and I could see the windows shaking with the force of the blast even though we were a few miles from Monaghan Town. I think Mammy knew straight away because she dropped everything and said, 'Oh, your father!' So there was a panic to get up to Monaghan. My mother got going and when she came home she was in very bad shape.

It didn't really affect me until a while after. I really missed my father not coming in from work and not being there ... even now, my brother, he would think about him. You know, not being able to see him married or things like that.

I would like to see more publicity about the bombings, and hopefully have an outcome at the end. I would like to see a public inquiry into what happened.

I can remember a time I was messing about in a ... car and I accidentally let the handbrake off so it hit a wall but Ma was a bit mad and she spanked me, but Dad wouldn't have any of that so I got away with that. He was easygoing, that's how I remember him. It's very ironic that such an easygoing man would die in such a brutal way.

It definitely wasn't right. He was just a man going about his everyday business and he had gone to have a drink in the pub before he came home from work. He was a man who went to work, came home and looked after his family. Just an ordinary man and then — gone!

Sonia: What bothers me is that the two boys were six and seven, they had time with my father, but my sister and myself — we have no memories of him at all. We haven't even got any photographs of us with him. We've children of our own now and they're not going to have a grandfather and it's strange for them too when you're taking them down to visit the grave. You can't really explain to them why it happened because nobody actually knows why and that's hard.

The day of my wedding, my oldest brother, Patrick, gave me away. That was hard because I would have liked my father to have been there for it.

I think I was sad too having Conor because I would have liked my father to have known his grandchildren, and he has eight grandchildren and he's not going to know any of them, and that's hard, and Conor is the only grandson. The day of our First Communion it was hard. Occasions like that when you want your father to be with you. It is a major part of your life.

Because our father wasn't there, it was obviously hard for our mother keeping things together and making ends meet. I think it became more obvious when I got older, not so much when we were six or seven or that. I've never really wanted for anything, but now I know when I've children of my own how hard it was for my mother to actually manage the whole lot of us on her own. It took a lot of strength and it's even harder because at the time it wasn't talked about. Anniversaries and everything pass and the only ones that really remember are the actual people who lost anybody in the bombs. It's like nobody else cares. It doesn't seem to be part of the history of Ireland at all. It's just blanked.

In many ways we have been the forgotten victims of what happened....

Sharon: When we were going to school, you noticed everybody there had a mammy and a daddy. Especially where we lived in Glaslough it was a small village, and everybody knew everybody's business and you were in and out of everyone's house. Like, when you were going to school, you did notice, maybe the boys noticed it more because girls would naturally come to their mother, you know, the boys, they knew their father; we really have no real memories of him. But it was hard even when we got bigger, they'd be saying, 'Your daddy must have run away.' It was hard — I think more for the boys, they would have known him and it was hard knowing the fact that somebody went out to do it and it is always somebody's father, no matter what way you look at it. We never had the opportunity to know our father.

My children don't know their grandfather. I have two girls. One's eight and one's four, Caroline and Lisa. The oldest one sort of knows now, she notices now. When her granny, from her father's side, died, she said to me, 'Is my granny going where my grandad is, up to heaven where the angels are?'

My mother always tried to give us the best, and whatever we wanted, we got. She made sure we got it. She did her very best for us. She was brilliant, especially considering there was four of us and we were so young, and with twins it was twice as hard because you had to do everything double. For birthdays, it was double; for Christmas, it was double it all too. She did very well for us. Nearly too good. You'd wonder how she coped because she didn't get any help at all. They didn't even bring her a bag of coal, nothing; she wasn't offered any help for anything so she just had to do it herself. Seeing how begrudging they have been, it was probably the best way.

THOMAS CAMPBELL (REMEMBERED BY HIS SISTER, MARY)
Thomas lived at home with my late mother. At the time, I was working away and was only home at weekends. He was a very quiet man. He could say almost nothing for a whole night but he was still great company for my mother. He was very interested in football though he didn't play himself. He worked in agriculture and was very well known in the area. Among the people he would have known through his work was Thomas Croarkin who was also killed in the bombing. It was very common for him to be in Monaghan as he was that evening.

The news came as an awful shock to all of us, but especially to my mother. He also had two stepsisters in England, Mary and

Alice, who doted on him. My mother was too traumatised by the shock of Thomas's death to even attend his funeral. She never got over that shock and died six weeks later from a broken heart although she came from a family where everybody lived to a very old age. In a sense she too was yet another casualty of the Dublin/Monaghan bombings.

THOMAS CROARKIN (REMEMBERED BY HIS BROTHER, JIM)
I worked along with him in farming. We were very close, especially because the rest of the family, apart from one sister in Belfast, lived in England. He enjoyed a few drinks and the craic. He loved kids.

He had finished work and on every Friday evening he always went for a few drinks to the Ulster Arms and then went across the road for his tea. So that's why he was there that evening. We didn't hear about it until the next morning.

Thomas was taken to the Richmond Hospital in Dublin from Monaghan Hospital and we went up to see him. He was still in intensive care. He ... had one of his arms and legs amputated.

He was moved back to a normal ward after a few days. Money was tight then and we had to hire a car twice a week to go up to Dublin to see him. We got word on a Tuesday that he had died. It came as a bolt out of the blue. We were sure he was going to make it because he had lived that long. We had been to see him the previous weekend and he was in the best of form and was looking forward to getting transferred back to hospital in Monaghan and he was wondering about how he was going to get about and everything. We had to go up then and identify the body, which was very traumatic.

As he lived for nine weeks after the bombing, he was more or less forgotten, because no one really realised that he was in the Dublin/Monaghan bombings. He lived at home with my mother. She missed him big time. She always used to talk to him and she was 97 when she died. She came to Dublin every time we went to see him.

It wasn't like Omagh. There wasn't much compensation or help or anything. Somebody admitted what happened in Omagh but not in Dublin/Monaghan. I'd love to see the truth — without pushing it under the carpet. It seems like a cover-up to me. I'd say there was a lot of collusion, as the Ulster paramilitaries didn't have the technology nor the sophistication to do it on their own.

ARCHIE HARPER (REMEMBERED BY HIS DAUGHTER, IRIS)
That day I went with him into Monaghan to see a member of the family and had some business to attend to in the town. While I was visiting, a newsflash came on the television with news of bombs in Dublin. Just as I was leaving, the house shook. We wondered if it was a bomb but thought, 'There wouldn't be a bomb in our town.'

I ran in towards the centre of town but the police stopped people from getting through because they were very afraid there was going to be a second bomb. I suppose because there were three bombs in Dublin, they were being particularly careful. There was glass coming out of windows and so on. It was a frightening experience and I fainted with the shock.

When I came around, I asked about my father and was told that he had been taken to Monaghan Hospital in a car but not in an ambulance which appeared to suggest that his injuries were not as serious as they might have been. I got a lift to the hospital. It was in chaos. To make matters worse, there was a funeral leaving at the time. I've never seen anything like it. My father was taken to the operating theatre but I wasn't let near him.

Not knowing what was going on was really awful. A clergyman I knew went to check the exact situation for me. When he returned, he said, 'He's got bad head injuries but there's a lot worse.'

My father lay unconscious on Saturday and Sunday, but a change came in him on Monday, and he leaned forward to us. We took this as a sign he was getting better. Although he couldn't speak, we were told he could hear us. However, on Tuesday, we saw that, in fact, things had taken a turn for the worse and he died that night at 11.45.

Although he was 73, he had always been very active. His father had died when he was 14 so he had a lot of responsibility on him from a young age. He still ran the farm and family pub, though the farm was his first love. He enjoyed giving my mother a break from the pub in the evening and going behind the counter and having a chat with the farmers from around the area.

Although Archie was a Protestant, he was respected equally on both sides of the religious divide.

This was really brought home to me when I travelled up to Dublin for the unveiling of the monument to commemorate the people who died. A Sinn Féin councillor came up to me afterwards and said that he knew my father. When I asked him how, he explained that he often was thumbing lifts in Cootehill and my father, even though he knew exactly who this man was and his political leanings, would always give him a lift whenever he saw him on the road....

It was very tough for my mother. They were very close and she had always given him great support. It's not something that goes away. It just becomes part of your life. Neither Christmas nor living in Monaghan was ever the same after his death.

It concerns me that the media often neglect the Monaghan part of the story and seems to focus on the Dublin bombings. I also feel a sense of anger that twenty-six years on there are still so many unanswered questions about the bombs in Dublin and Monaghan.

My mother is in her late eighties now and I would love her to get the answers all of us have been waiting for for so long. Who planted the bomb and what were the reasons for it?

JACK TRAVERS (REMEMBERED BY HIS SISTER, EILEEN MCCAGUE)

We heard on the 6 o'clock news that there had been a bomb in Dublin. Jack's girlfriend, Frankie, worked in Dublin so he decided to go into town to telephone her and see if she was okay. He also wanted to go to Greacen's pub to cash a cheque. At about ten to seven he shouted up the stairs to ask if I wanted to accompany him. I told him that I wanted to watch a film on television.

At about three minutes to seven I heard a boom and I knew there was something wrong. We lived in Park Street, so we were less than half a mile away from the source of the noise. I ran down the stairs to my father and mother. The next thing, the neighbours were all out on the street. We could see the pall of smoke as we looked towards the centre of the town. The gardaí arrived within minutes and evacuated everyone from the street, as there was a car parked opposite the chapel and they were treating it as a suspect car bomb. Talking to neighbours, I said that there was something very wrong as I knew Jack would have returned immediately to let us know he was okay and to check if we were okay.

We went in the direction of the bomb but the gardaí had cordoned off the area so we headed for the General Hospital, but again the gardaí were stopping all but essential services. We got into a car and went back to the hospital. Don't ask me why I wanted to go to the hospital. I just had a horrible feeling.

When we got there, it was pandemonium. I remember running through wards and seeing different victims. I don't know how long I was there for. Time stood still at that stage. Then I saw my other brother, Jim, with Dr Eddie Duffy, and I said to him, 'How come you're here? Where's Jack?' He replied, 'Unfortunately he's in there,' pointing to the morgue. I said to Dr Duffy, 'That can't be true.' He answered, 'I'm sorry, Eileen, it is'.

We went back and at that stage my parents knew in their hearts and souls but waited on us to confirm their worst fears. My father took a slight turn at home. It was pure shock. The priests lived across the road from us and were in our house when we returned. It was bedlam with people coming and going. The doctor came to treat my parents for shock. He gave my father some medicine. My mother was in total shock. I don't think she spoke for two days. The next day the doctor gave her an injection, at our request. She always regretted it, as she never remembered anything, even the funeral. I think she couldn't believe it happened. She died exactly twenty years later and she never got over it. She aged overnight, and for years never went out unaccompanied. She never walked downtown past the bomb-site.

My father talked more about it and about Jack. Jack loved sports, especially Gaelic football. In his youth, he played with the CBS and later with Monaghan Harps. He also followed soccer and car rallying. My father shared his love of Gaelic football and missed his company. We were and still are heartbroken. We had to cope but we will never get over it. He was a good one.

THE PARNELL STREET VICTIMS

Marie Butler (21)

*Jacqueline O'Brien
(16 months)*

*Anne Marie O'Brien
(4 months)*

*John O'Brien (24) and Anna O'Brien (22)
Their two daughters were also killed in the bombing
(see above)*

Previous page*: A Dublin Fire Officer carries an injured woman from
the scene of the Talbot Street bomb.*

Partick Fay (47)

Antonio Magliocco (37)
from Italy

John Dargle (80)

Edward O'Neill (39)

Breda Turner (21)

Above: Aftermath — Dublin firemen search through the rubble of Parnell Street the morning after the explosion.

Below: The morning after — A Garda cordon limits access to Talbot Street where cars and commercial vehicles remain as they were at the time of the explosion.

Above: *Within minutes of the Talbot Street explosion ordinary citizens attend to the dead and wounded as they await the arrival of the ambulance service.*

Below: *The remains of the Parnell Street bomb car lie to the right of a badly damaged mini. On the right of the picture, Dr Conor Cruise O'Brien, Minister for Posts and Telegraphs, can be seen visiting the scene.*

THE TALBOT STREET VICTIMS

Josie Bradley (21)

Anne Byrne (35)

*Simone Chetrit (30)
from France*

Concepta Dempsey (65)

Collette Doherty (20)

Elizabeth Fitzgerald (59)

Breda Grace (34)   *May McKenna (55)*   *Anne Marren (20)*

Dorothy Morris (57)   *Marie Phelan (20)*

Siobhán Roice (19)   *Maureen Shields (46)*   *John Walsh (27)*

Following page: *An aerial photograph surveys the Parnell Street bombsite a few days after the explosion. The Department of Posts and Telegraphs towers above the scene on the left.*

PEGGY WHITE (REMEMBERED BY HER CHILDREN, MARIE, BRENDAN, ALAN AND MAURICE)

Our mum had a part-time job in the restaurant section of the pub that was blown up in the Monaghan bombing. When the bomb blast went off, the younger children did not initially realise it was a bomb. The oldest in the family, Marie, who had been watching the news of the Dublin bombing, knew almost immediately what it was. Living in Monaghan town, they could see the smoke rising from the bomb-site from their garden.

It took a while for the news about Mummy to filter through to us. Daddy was also in town that evening and he rushed to the scene. He came home distraught. We went to the hospital to find Mummy. Her injuries were severe and she was in a lot of pain. She died around 10 o'clock that night.

She was a kind, lively, outgoing woman. Her family was very important to her. She was a wonderful person in every way and everything a mother should be. Mummy had great faith. She brought us up to have great respect for the truth. The truth is important. A lot of the relatives need answers. That is the least they deserve. Twenty-six years later it should not be up to the families to look for those answers. That should have been given at the time. Maybe we were all too traumatised to even look for answers at that stage.

We have tried to cope with her loss in our own different ways, just like the relatives of all the other victims. One thing we'll always remember is the genuine concern and kindness of our friends and neighbours — not just in the following days and weeks, but long afterwards.

GEORGE WILLIAMSON (REMEMBERED BY HIS NEPHEW, THOMAS STEENSON, AND NIECE, MARGARET MCADAM)

TS: George was born in March 1901. He was survived by one sister, Mrs Margaret Steenson, Armagh City, and two brothers, Mr Isaiah and Mr Jesse Williamson, Guelph, Ontario, Canada. His sisters, Mrs Jane Carson and Anna Williamson, died in 1939 and 1927 respectively.

George was a farmer who lived on his own after his father's death, his mother having died some years previously. He liked field sports and was a good runner. On the day he was buried a commercial traveller (a school friend of his) told how he had watched George at a Castleshane picnic as a young man beat an all-Ireland champion. When the race was over, the champion said, 'No one has beaten me before,' and George replied, 'You'll not have that to say again.' That was Uncle George. He had a real dry wit. That was typical of the man. He liked everyone and everyone liked him. As was evident by the numbers from all walks of life who attended his funeral at First Monaghan Presbyterian Church on 22 May 1974.

His remains were interred in the surrounding churchyard in the family plot. Two nephews live in Canada: Alex Steenson, Guelph, Ontario, and myself, Thomas H. Steenson, in Richmond Hill, Ontario. His niece, Mrs Margaret J. McAdam, lives in Finaghy, Belfast.

MMcA: After the death of his parents, George didn't have the same interest in the farm anymore. He was more interested in doing anyone and everyone a good turn. He was such a good-natured person and a gentle soul who wouldn't do anyone any harm. Often when he came to Armagh he would be out buying shoes, which neighbours had asked him to get. My mother used to laugh sometimes and say of him, 'Your Uncle George needs a gentleman's gentleman to look after him.'

He spent six months in Canada once and returned to Monaghan. He laughed, saying, 'They make you work too hard over there.' He had a great sense of humour.

When his body was taken to the church from Monaghan Hospital, we were amazed at the crowds. There were so many people who wanted to carry his coffin that in the end it was decided to just let his cousins carry him a short distance, otherwise the minister would have been left waiting for a very long time. Protestants and Catholics alike stood together to mourn his passing.

Chapter Four: Government and Police Reaction

It was the biggest loss of life in one incident in Dublin since forty-three people had been killed on Dublin's North Strand, following a German bombing raid during the Second World War.

The Government faced an immediate challenge. In the first place, it was necessary to ensure an adequate security response to the atrocity. In the second place, there was the issue of managing the public response to the four no-warning bombs and their resultant carnage. The latter issue also included minimising public outrage at the Government's failure to provide adequate protection for its own citizens and for visitors to the country.

An emergency meeting of the Cabinet was immediately ordered and was underway within two hours of the blasts. A ministerial order was made to RTÉ to allow the Taoiseach, Liam Cosgrave, to address the nation on television and radio at 10 o'clock that evening.

The Cabinet Security Committee comprised the Taoiseach, the Minister for Justice (Patrick Cooney), the Minister for Defence (Patrick Donegan), the Minister for Posts and Telegraphs (Conor Cruise O'Brien) and the Minister for Local Government (Jim Tully). By the time the Minister for Justice met the press that evening and the Taoiseach addressed the nation on television, a line had been agreed. This line was often repeated in the days to follow, both in the press and within Dáil Éireann. In summary, it was a simple message: the ultimate blame lay with republicans and republican violence in Northern Ireland.

On Saturday, 18 May 1974, the *Irish Independent* reported:

> The Minister stressed that the danger would remain until the people completely and unequivocally accepted that the cult of violence must be removed, that they must turn in people who perpetrated or condoned violence.

Patrick Cooney also told reporters that the security forces 'had no indication from any source that such an attack had been planned'. This important revelation immediately calls into question the entire basis of the relationship between elements of An Garda Síochána and British Military Intelligence, dealt with in Chapter Eleven.

Within an hour of the explosion, the Minister for Justice had been informed that two of the cars used in the Dublin bombs had been hijacked in Belfast but didn't know in which part they had been taken. I have written to both An Garda Síochána and the RUC asking them to inform me as to the precise time this information was exchanged. Both refused to answer my question.

In his address on RTÉ, Mr Cosgrave sympathised with the bereaved and injured. He said that the security forces would give citizens all the protection that they could but called upon the public to be vigilant. He then commended the emergency services, and said that the 'evil deeds' would serve only 'to strengthen the resolve of those North and South working for peace'. Crucially he stated:

> The Government are as yet unaware of the identity of those responsible for these crimes but everyone who has practised violence, or preached violence, or condoned violence, must bear a share of responsibility for the outrages.

The Chief Minister of the power-sharing Executive at Stormont, Brian Faulkner, sent a message of sympathy to the Taoiseach, saying that it was with the deepest distress that he and his colleagues had learned of the outrage.

The Cabinet met again on Saturday morning to review the situation and to hear reports from the Minister for Justice and the Garda Commissioner. They also had reports on the bomb-sites from three Ministers, including the Minister for Foreign Affairs, Garret FitzGerald. A decision was made to request from the United Nations the release of 340 Irish soldiers serving in the Middle East, to help strengthen security at home. The Government also considered calling on the FCA to take over barrack responsibilities so that regular soldiers could be released for border duties.

Ministerial assurances that no money would be spared in ensuring that the security forces had the best possible equipment came too late for the bereaved and maimed.

The question of cross-border co-operation between the Garda and the RUC in identifying the culprits and bringing them to justice was also considered. The *Sunday Press* on 19 May 1974 stated that 'the RUC was in regular contact with the Gardaí throughout Friday night and Saturday with information on the stolen cars used in the bombings'. The Minister for Justice said that the RUC's co-operation was 'full and unequivocal' and that the two police forces were considering 'whether the flow of information in both directions might be improved.' While there is no doubt that the RUC co-operated in providing basic information, until the Garda files have been independently viewed, the degree of that co-operation cannot be assessed. There are questions concerning the hijacked and stolen cars used in the attack which call into question the Minister's assertions at this early juncture. Crucially, why did the RUC fail to launch a murder inquiry since there was evidence to suggest that a great deal of the plotting had been carried out in its jurisdiction?

By Monday, 20 May, three days after the atrocity, it was known by the authorities in the Republic that the cars used in the attack had been stolen and hijacked in loyalist areas — despite denials by the UVF and UDA. However, the first major security offensive in the wake of the attack saw huge army and police resources deployed in a nationwide raid on republican homes and premises. The question is, did these raids play into the hands of the perpetrators of the bombings? Loyalists planted the bombs, Republicans were being pursued by the State.

Despite the magnitude of the outrage, a decision was taken by the Government not to hold a national day of mourning, because, according to a spokesman from the Government Information Bureau, 'More than 1,000 people have now died in the current Troubles'. The national flag was flown at half-mast over public buildings in Dublin and Monaghan during the funerals but even this simple gesture seems to have caused political indigestion, as it had originally been reported in the *Evening Herald* of 20 May that this would not happen.

On 21 May, the Taoiseach told the Dáil about the messages of condolence received from the British Prime Minister and Leader of the Opposition, as well as from many other leaders of Church and State. He referred to the bombings as 'without exception, the worst single outrage in these islands ... caused deliberately by man against man since the end of the Second World War', and gave an impassioned speech about the futility of violence, the central thesis of which was that the blood of the innocent victims was 'on the hands of every man who has fired a gun or discharged a bomb in furtherance of the present campaign of violence in these islands — just as plainly as it is on the hands of those who parked the cars and set the charges last Friday'. Having promised 'all possible support' to the Garda in their efforts to apprehend those responsible for the bombings, Mr Cosgrave called on the House to rise to observe a minute's silence in sympathy with the victims. Former Taoiseach and Leader of the Opposition, Jack Lynch, joined with the Taoiseach in extending the sympathy of his party to the bereaved and echoed many of Mr Cosgrave's sentiments, including those regarding responsibility for the atrocity.

Deputy Neil Blaney (Independent Fianna Fáil) expressed his sympathy and that of his organisation, and called for an urgent debate on the question of security. The Taoiseach said he would consider the matter.

On 23 May 1974, the Minister for Justice, Patrick Cooney, gave details of the report of the Law Enforcement Commission, which had been set up following the Sunningdale Agreement. The Commission envisaged that, following the introduction of appropriate legislation 'courts in both parts of Ireland would be able to try certain specific crimes wherever in Ireland they were committed.' He said that the Irish and British governments had agreed that there would be 'the closest co-operation between the police forces in the investigation of offences', and that the Irish and British Attorney-Generals would co-operate closely. 'I shall be meeting Mr. Rees shortly', Mr Cooney stated, 'to discuss what can be done to improve further the existing co-operation between the security forces on both sides of the Border.'

Deputy Andrews questioned the timing of the Minister's announcement, suggesting that it might be 'a further attempt to appease the militant Loyalists'.

The Attorney-General, Mr Declan Costello, echoed the Government line in his condemnation of the attack. On 19 May he said that a 'very heavy burden of responsibility' for the bombings lay with the Provisional IRA, and described the Provisionals' condemnation of the bombings as hypocritical in the light of similar outrages carried out by themselves. He blamed all those who advocated, condoned or preached violence. The Attorney General ruled out the possibility of introducing internment and the use of military-type courts, saying that the law was sufficient and would be enforced to the full.

The Minister for Posts and Telegraphs, Conor Cruise O'Brien, who lost two employees of his Department, Pat Fay and Anne Marren, in the Parnell Street and Talbot Street bombs, addressed the annual conference dinner of the Post Office Engineering Union in Ennis, County Clare, on 22 May 1974. In his address he attacked those who condoned violence implicitly, whether 'by a facial expression, an inflection of the voice, by a smile or even by silence', especially those who condoned violence from their own community 'by dwelling exclusively on violence arising from another community'. His message was that people had no right to be angry at those responsible for the bombings unless part of that anger was directed towards republicans and the violence they condoned by their support for the IRA.

The overall effect of the State's approach was to sow confusion in the minds of the public. Instead of the type of response witnessed in the aftermath of the Omagh massacre, there appears to have been a collective stepping-back. This struck the Victims Commissioner and former Tánaiste, John Wilson, when he listened to the stories of the 1974 bomb victims. In his report, *A Place and a Name*, he writes:

> Another aspect of this tragedy which puzzles me ... is the inertia over the years of the citizens of Dublin. They are known as a generous people, having sent aid in human and material resources to every corner of the globe. Yet no citizens' committee was formed in Dublin in aid of these victims.... When the Dublin–Monaghan victims see (and they see with no begrudging eyes) what is happening elsewhere, they feel neglected. They think that somehow they are less important than others!

It is perhaps unfair to wonder only about the response of the citizens of Dublin. This was a national tragedy and called for a co-ordinated national response. The response did not happen simply because the encouragement and leadership were not given by the politicians of the day.

There were many citizens who were conscious of the need for financial support. The *Evening Herald* reported on 20 May 1974, that the Dublin City Commissioner, George Butler, had asked the Government to release funds immediately to aid the victims. The press does not report the Government's response.

The *Sunday World* of 26 May reported that some Dublin undertakers were prepared to await payment until such time as the bereaved received compensation.[1]

By the end of May, the Minister for Justice was being questioned in Dáil Éireann about the Garda investigation. In response to a question from Deputy Lemass on 30 May 1974, the Minister said that the investigations were continuing but that it would not be appropriate 'to speculate about the likelihood of early arrests in relation to these or, indeed, any other crimes'.

On 20 June, Deputy Des O'Malley asked the Minister for Justice if cars crossing the Border from the North on 17 May 1974 had been searched by gardaí or the Army. Mr Cooney replied that checkpoints had been in operation, 'some through-out the day and others at different times at various places all along the Border. At some of these points all the cars were searched and at others a proportion was searched.'

Deputy O'Malley's question concerning security alertness on the day of the bombings is important, given threats and overtures from loyalist paramilitaries and politicians in the days leading up to the bombings. It is particularly relevant

---

1   When eventually compensation was paid, the process of determining the 'value' of each victim appears to have been erratic and patently unfair. It is clear from speaking with the bereaved that those who could afford lawyers received more, while those who couldn't, received less. Without divulging personal and specific information I can, however, offer a few examples by way of illustration. The family of one unmarried daughter received approximately £1,900, while the family of another unmarried daughter received over £16,000. The latter starkly contrasts also with the compensation offered to widows with young dependants who received approximately £5,000 each.

when viewed alongside the testimony of a retired pharmacist, Mr John Burke, who approached *Ireland on Sunday* in April 2000 with information which he said had troubled him for over a quarter of a century.

According to Mr Burke, when he arrived at his pharmacy on Marlborough Street, situated close to the intersection of Talbot Street, shortly before 9 a.m. on 17 May 1974, he noticed a northern or UK-registered van parked outside his premises. He thinks that the van was a Morris 8 model. He says that he was 'bomb-conscious' because the 1972 bomb in Sackville Place had damaged his pharmacy extensively, heightening his sensitivity to Garda warnings.

John Burke reported the sighting to the gardaí, including the fact that he had noticed on the floor of the front passenger side, 'something about two feet square and over a foot high, covered by a sheet of tarpaulin from which protruded a piece of heavy-duty electric cable.' Uniformed gardaí arrived in a squad car over two hours later. John Burke says that one of the gardaí, 'a big heavy man emerged ... circled the van and tried unsuccessfully to open the doors.' He said the garda spent some time looking into the rear of the van then turned to him and said, 'There could be a hundredweight of stuff in that.' The garda reassured him that the matter would be taken care of 'without delay' and departed the scene.

Mr Burke says that he was not advised to evacuate his premises. He waited for the vehicle to be taken care of for the rest of the day. At 5.30 p.m. his pharmacy shook when the Talbot Street bomb exploded, killing fourteen of the twenty-six Dublin victims. He ran to the scene of the explosion and was deeply distressed by the enormity of the destruction and carnage. Upon returning to his pharmacy, he heard people shout, 'Keep away, keep back, there's another one here', indicating the van parked at his shop.

He says that he frantically phoned 999 again, and shouted his protests down the line, 'at the lack of follow-up to the morning's events.' Fifteen minutes later, he states, gardaí arrived, produced a loud hailer, and ordered people to leave the area at once. This part of Mr Burke's testimony is corroborated by eyewitness testimonies and by contemporary newspaper reports.

The following morning 'there was no sign of the van' outside his shop. He states that attempts by him to gain information from the Garda Síochána about the van 'were rebuffed'.

John Burke's allegations suggest an alarming laxity in security on the very day of the biggest mass murder in the history of the Republic of Ireland. Mr Burke has made a sworn affidavit to lawyers representing the families of those killed, a copy of which has been given to former Chief Justice Liam Hamilton.

These disturbing allegations must be investigated by Mr Justice Hamilton as part of his Independent Commission of Inquiry into the bombings. If substantiated, they carry very serious implications. There are several aspects of Mr Burke's testimony that can be easily and quickly checked, including the 999 emergency logs for the morning and early evening of 17 May 1974, which should record his phone calls.

On 26 June 1974, in Dáil Éireann, Deputy Neil Blaney pointed to the anomaly of the Republic's security forces being used as a protection buffer to Northern Ireland, with little regard to the obvious dangers to the citizens of the Republic, particularly from loyalists and British agents who had been active in the Republic from the beginning of the Troubles. The Deputy said that, crossing from Lifford to Strabane, cars were searched, but the same security concerns did not apply to vehicles crossing from Northern Ireland into the Republic.

Deputy Blaney's comments followed a heated debate on Northern Ireland and the collapse of the Sunningdale power-sharing Executive. In his remarks, the Minister for Justice again moved to focus some of the blame for the collapse on the violence of republicans and to offer reassurance to unionists and the British that a new get-tough policy was being implemented in the Republic. Without making specific reference to the 1970 Arms Crisis, he said that unionist doubts in its wake had to be removed and assuaged, and that unionists had to be reassured.

The Minister went on to demonstrate both the effectiveness of the Garda and the determination of the Government to get tough on terrorism, by listing a series of security force actions that had resulted in arrests and convictions. All of the cases he recited involved republicans. He made no mention of a determined effort to apprehend the murderers of the innocent victims of the Dublin and Monaghan atrocity just five weeks previously. Speaking of the 'mutual interest in defeating terrorism', he said, 'if there were any lingering doubts about that mutual interest down here ... they were removed by the tragedies of the bombings in this city.'

There was no question of contemplating the suspicion that the loyalists who delivered the bombs might have received outside help, although, by that time, some senior members of the Garda investigation team were of this opinion.

Deputy Neil Blaney said that he was appalled by the Minister's speech and asked why the organisations suspected of having carried out bombings in the Republic had not been proscribed under the Offences against the State (Amendment) Act. He also pointed out the infiltration of the Irish security forces by British Military intelligence and cited the case of British agent John Wyman who was discovered to be running a sergeant in the Garda Special Branch.

Deputy Vivion de Valera criticised the Government's apparent obsession with IRA violence as opposed to all violence, pointing out that, 'It was not the IRA who bombed Dublin'.

Deputy George Colley highlighted the Government's policy of alienating even elected representatives of the northern minority as a means of currying favour with Ulster Unionism and reassuring loyalists that the Republic posed no threat to their desire to remain part of the United Kingdom. He pointed to a discernible imbalance in the respective responses of the British and Irish Governments to the northern crisis.

Reference to the Dublin and Monaghan bombings became less frequent in the Dáil after June 1974. It was not until 21 May 1975 that the first direct question on the Garda investigation into the bombings was raised. Deputy Noel Davern asked the Minister for Justice what progress had been made by the Garda Síochána in their investigation into the May 1974 bombings. Mr T.J. Fitzpatrick, on behalf of the Minister, answered:

> I am informed by the Commissioner of the Garda Síochána that Garda investigations into these outrages continue although nobody has so far been made amenable for them.

Deputy Davern followed by asking the Minister if he was aware 'that it is a well-known fact that three people have been arrested, interned in Northern Ireland and released who, it is well-known, were responsible for this outrage?'

The Minister replied that he had no specific information about the arrests and that the Garda Síochána had 'not received evidence from the RUC that particular persons perpetrated these outrages'. Neither had the Garda any 'positive information with which to identify the people who committed these outrages'.

Deputy Davern asked why the information regarding the people responsible for the bombings had not been passed on to the Garda by the RUC. The Minister replied:

> I am not saying that. The fact that these people were interned might suggest — if they were interned — there was not sufficient evidence to sustain conviction. Even if these were the people who were guilty, the offence was committed here and, unless the reciprocal legislation which is now being sponsored here and in Britain were available, it would not be possible to bring these people to justice in Northern Ireland for crimes committed here.

On 20 November 1975, Deputy Lemass asked the Minister for Justice to make a statement on the line of inquiry being followed in the investigation into the bombings. The Minister referred to his statement of 21 May 1975 in which he had said that investigations continued although nobody had been made amenable for the outrage. He said that he could give no indications regarding the lines of inquiry, as such disclosures could benefit the perpetrators of the crimes.

When asked by Deputy John O'Connell whether he had been informed by the Secretary of State for Northern Ireland or his assistant, that those believed to have been involved in one outrage in Dublin were detained in Northern Ireland, the Minister replied that he had heard 'that rumour' but had no hard information on it.

On 19 May 1988, Deputy Michael D. Higgins questioned the then Minister for Justice, Gerry Collins, regarding investigations into the Dublin bombings in 1972. The Minister replied:

> ... No one has been made amenable for these outrages but the Deputy can take it that the Garda investigation into the incidents in question have not been closed.

The Minister's answer became the standard response of the Department of Justice for the next quarter of a century whenever the issue of the Dublin and Monaghan bombings was raised.

The Garda Investigation

The nature, extent and adequacy of the Garda investigation into the Dublin and Monaghan bombings are largely unknown. What we do know is that, within weeks of the explosions, the Garda Detective Branch and Special Branch had identified prime suspects, all from the Portadown/Lurgan area of County Armagh. All were known members of the mid-Ulster UVF Brigade. According to Yorkshire Television's *First Tuesday* documentary, *Hidden Hand — The Forgotten Massacre*, broadcast in 1993, and which is dealt with extensively in the next chapter, two of the suspects were identified in police photographs by three separate eyewitnesses as drivers of two of the four bomb cars.

These details are highly significant given that journalists from Yorkshire Television are the only people, outside political and police circles, who have been given limited access to the Garda files into the bombings. According to *First Tuesday*, the Garda extended their list of suspects with an additional twelve names, derived from intelligence sources in the North.

The Yorkshire documentary also reveals that the RUC had carried out an investigation into the bombings. A letter sent from the RUC to the solicitors representing the Dublin and Monaghan bereaved, dated 28 August 1996, states:

> ...(4a) ... a number of persons were arrested and interviewed in relation to the theft of the vehicles.
>
> (4b) A number of persons were arrested and interviewed in relation to these murders.
>
> (5) Details arising from the interviews... as well as other material, were passed to An Garda Síochána at various stages of its enquiry.

This assertion by the RUC is disputed by the *First Tuesday* programme, which states that in Garda Chief Superintendent John Joy's final report he wrote, 'Enquiries in regard to [suspects] are being made by the RUC and results of the investigation will be reported'. However, according to *First Tuesday*, 'There is no record on the Garda file that the RUC ever did report back.'

The urgency and determination of the Minister for Justice in assuring the nation of the RUC's co-operation introduced a false sense of confidence in the public mind that efforts were progressing towards apprehending the culprits. However, in analysing the

RUC's handling of information concerning the hijacked and stolen vehicles used in the bombings, it is difficult to be convinced that their co-operation was as the Minister wished the nation to believe.

I had hoped to clarify Patrick Cooney's motives in reassuring the public on this issue. However, in a letter dated 2 May 2000, he declined my request for an interview. He wrote:

> Having retired and closed the door, I am not keen on reopening it and trying to joggle memory. Regretfully therefore I have to decline your request. In any event it occurs to me that I would have nothing to add to whatever was said at the time by way of press release or in the Dáil.

I have in my possession a number of statements made to the RUC by the owners of the cars used in the bombings and which I know to be in the Garda files. The car used to carry the bomb which exploded in South Leinster Street was a lagoon-blue Austin 1800, registration number HOI 2487. It belonged to a Mr William Henry, now deceased, who worked for Ariel Taxis, which had an office on Agnes Street, in the Shankill area of Belfast. Chapter Two contains salient details of the hijacking of Mr Henry's taxi. However, it is the circumstances, timing and details of his release, which are of relevance here.

Henry told the RUC that he was held in a room by people involved in the hijacking of his vehicle until nearly 2 p.m., after which he was taken to a car which he describes as an 1100. While he had been hooded when taken into the building where he was held, he does not indicate if he was hooded when being taken out. As a taxi driver, he would have been familiar with the streets where he was detained.

Henry gave no details of the colour or registration of the vehicle he was placed in and doesn't appear to have been asked by the police officer taking the statement. He was, he states, driven to Boyd Street, Peters Hill, Belfast, where he was released. He said that one man drove off in the car and a second man followed him up the Shankill Road 'as I had been told not to go near my taxi firm and to go straight home until 3 p.m. and I was then to go to Tennent St. Police Station.' He concludes by stating that after 3 p.m. he came to Tennent Street RUC Station.

The statement was taken by Detective Constable Kennedy at 3.20 p.m. It was checked and certified a true copy of original by Detective Constable J.J. Woods.

There are several issues that immediately come to mind with regard to basic RUC detective work. Did the RUC follow up on the information supplied by William Henry? Did RUC detectives visit Mr Henry in the wake of the bombings to see if he could provide additional information? Did they ask him to attempt a better description of the 5' 4" hijacker who he said was around 30 years old and who wore a black jacket? Did they ask him to describe a second man who took part in the hijacking? Did they visit Ariel Taxis to enquire if anyone in the office at 9 a.m. on 17 May had seen the man whom their colleague William Henry agreed to take to Sandy Row? Did they check to see if anyone in the vicinity of the taxi office had seen the man standing outside?

Did Ariel Taxis report the disappearance of Mr Henry and his vehicle to the RUC when he failed to return to the taxi rank after a maximum 20-minute job? If so, when? Did the RUC do a house-to-house enquiry in Woburn Street to see if anyone had noticed men acting suspiciously or if anyone had witnessed Mr Henry being physically removed from the driver's seat and forced into the back of his taxi? While we know that these were exceptional times and the RUC were, no doubt, under stress, the above questions are reasonable, given the magnitude of the crime committed. They are also questions to which the families of the deceased and the maimed have a right to receive answers.

Some of the most vital information contained in William Henry's statement concerns the circumstances of his release. He was released at 2 p.m., while the bombing mission still had three-and-a-half hours to run. He was told not to go near his taxi firm but instead to go straight home, stay there until 3 p.m. and then report the hijacking to the RUC. (The bombing mission at this point still had two-and-a-half hours to run). He was specifically told to go to Tennent Street RUC Station.

It must be remembered that the bombers did not attempt to disguise the vehicles used in their mission, particularly by way of changing number plates — a somewhat cavalier approach to an operation executed with military precision and professionalism. And why was Henry not held until 7.30 p.m., when the mission had been completed and the bomb drivers were safe? Such questions lead to other questions. Did the organisers have inside information concerning RUC operational procedures?

By 10.30 a.m., the car used in the Talbot Street explosion had been reported stolen from Drumcrue Road, Belfast — a full seven hours before it was used to deliver such appalling carnage. Did the RUC alert the Garda Síochána that this car was missing? If so, when? If not, why not? Again, it is important to point out that no attempt was made to disguise the vehicle's registration. All four vehicles, therefore, were operational inside the Republic with apparently little concern that their details may have been passed on by the RUC to the Garda. This casts grave doubts on the accuracy of the Minister's assertion that the RUC were co-operating closely with the Garda.

On 8 December 1998, I wrote to the RUC Chief Constable, Ronnie Flanagan, requesting information on the RUC investigation into the Dublin and Monaghan bombings and the co-operation of the force with the Garda Síochána regarding the incidents. On 15 December 1998, the Chief Information Officer at the RUC Press Office, David M. Hanna, replied:

> ...As you will appreciate, our involvement was to assist in any way we could with the Northern Ireland end of the Garda Síochána's investigation into the terrible events of 1974. In the circumstances, I do not feel it would be appropriate to release material which might have formed part of their files.

On 26 January 1999 I wrote to Officer Hanna: 'Can you inform me as to what the operational reporting procedures were in the early 1970's between the RUC and An Garda Síochána with regard to stolen vehicles in their respective jurisdictions?'

On 3 February 1999, Inspector Fred Campbell, Staff Officer to the RUC Chief Information Officer replied:

> The operational reporting procedures between ourselves and the Garda Síochána in respect of stolen cars in the early 70s were pretty much as it is today. It took place on two levels:
> (a) At Headquarters level: stolen car lists were exchanged between the Forces by telex several times per day;
> (b) at local level: often on a more ad hoc basis but equally efficient. Stolen cars in border areas were notified by RUC to neighbouring Garda Stations by telephone and vice versa as and when appropriate.

On 23 February 1999, I requested specific information regarding the time at which the RUC had informed the Garda Síochána of the stolen cars used in the Dublin and Monaghan bombings.

Inspector Campbell replied, on 26 February 1999, that the RUC did not feel that 'it would be appropriate to release material which might have formed part of the Garda Síochána's files'.

On the same day that I wrote to the RUC Chief Constable (8 December 1998) I also wrote to the Garda Commissioner, requesting his assistance with my enquiries. On 17 December, a Garda Ronan Farrelly phoned me from the Garda Press Office. He informed me that as the High Court had already given a ruling that the Garda files could not be made available and as there were ongoing investigations, it would not be possible to help me. Garda Farrelly indicated that it was my reference to 'information on the Garda investigation at the time' that seemed to have caused a problem. I asked Garda Farrelly to respond to my letter in writing. On 18 December 1998, Superintendent John T. Farrelly from the Garda Public Relations Office wrote:

> Unfortunately, we are unable to discuss at this time any matter relating to the Dublin/Monaghan bombings in 1974. We can say however, that the investigation files relating to both incidents remain open and will remain that way.

Niggling questions remain. Why are the Garda being so defensive and circumspect? Why are they putting up so much resistance to the families in their legitimate quest to know the truth about the murder of their loved ones?

With the RUC making reference to the Garda files, it becomes increasingly clear that many, if not most, of the unanswered questions, lie hidden there. Within three months of the explosions, the Garda investigation was wound down. At one level, it would appear that the Garda had done all in their power to hunt down the killers, only to have their efforts frustrated by a sectarian police force north of the border. But such a conclusion is too simplistic. Proper procedures were, in many instances, not followed, and additional avenues of useful pressure appear not to have been explored.

While the families of the deceased are left with lingering doubts and open wounds, their dead will not rest in peace.

Chapter Five:
Hidden Hand: The Forgotten Massacre

To date the most extensive independent research to be undertaken by any body into the 1974 Dublin and Monaghan bombings is by Yorkshire Television. On 6 July 1993, as part of their *First Tuesday* series, Yorkshire Television broadcast a one-hour special, *Hidden Hand: The Forgotten Massacre*. The programme was to give a major impetus to the families who lost loved ones and to many of the wounded in their quest to find answers and achieve justice.

Following the broadcast, the families established a campaign demanding a public inquiry. The official reaction to the broadcast, almost two years later, was to shift the emphasis of the campaign profoundly. From wishing to pursue the perpetrators of the atrocity, the campaign began vigorously to demand transparent public accountability from the Irish Government and the Garda Síochána into their handling of the entire investigative process, including their reaction to the *First Tuesday* documentary.

With the announcement by the Irish Government, in December 1999, of its intention to establish an Independent Commission of Inquiry into the bombings, the families and wounded insisted that the issues raised by the *Hidden Hand* documentary should be examined. However, they have insisted that the Commission, headed by retired Chief Justice Liam Hamilton, should also examine the response of the Irish State and the Garda Síochána to the broadcast.

Since Mr Justice Hamilton has been asked, as part of his independent assessment of the bombings, to examine the contents of *Hidden Hand: The Forgotten Massacre*, including the Government and Garda's response to it, it is important that the public are conversant with the entire thrust of this ground-breaking Yorkshire Television documentary.

As stated, it remains the most thorough examination of the bombings to be undertaken to date. Yorkshire Television spent two years longer than the original Garda investigation in research-ing the programme and expended stg£400,000 in its making.

In the following pages, I have attempted to recreate on paper the entire Yorkshire Television documentary.

First Tuesday
Hidden Hand: The Forgotten Massacre

The programme opens with 24-year-old Edward O'Neill who, as a four-year-old child was seriously injured in the Parnell Street bomb which killed his father, Eddie, and also seriously wounded his seven-year-old brother, Billy. The wounds are clearly etched into his face. He says:

> Justice is all I want to see done. To have them brought back down to Dublin and to stand trial for what they did.

The voice of Olivia O'Leary speaks over images of devastation caused by the explosions:

> It was the biggest mass murder in Britain or Ireland, thirty-three people died; why has nobody ever been charged?

Paddy Doyle, who lost four members of his family in the Parnell Street explosion, says:

> They shouldn't be let off with it. This government definitely does know who done it.

Olivia O'Leary speaks to camera from a prepared script:

> Good evening. If you live in Dublin it's possible to forget that Belfast is only a hundred miles away. Daily life in the Republic is almost untouched by the terrorist violence which bedevils Northern Ireland, a fact that tourists are reassured about constantly.
>
> Ask about the Dublin and Monaghan bombs of May 1974 and the response will be hazy. It was the worst atrocity of the Troubles and yet it's almost been forgotten. No one was convicted, no one ever charged. There's been no public outcry. The grieving relatives

of those killed must ask why. Was it fatalism, a feeling that Dublin at some stage was bound to get its share of the north's misery? Or was there a more sinister reason for this long silence on both sides of the Irish border? That's what *First Tuesday*'s been investigating over many months in *Hidden Hand: the Forgotten Massacre*.

The interior of Dublin's Pro-Cathedral appears with scenes from the annual commemoration mass in 1992. Fr John Delany is the celebrant. He concludes the Eucharistic prayer:

Through Him, with Him, in Him, in the unity of the Holy Spirit, all glory and honour is yours, almighty Father, forever and ever.

It then cuts to part of his sermon:

For many of you, you come here in sadness and sorrow, as you remember the Dublin victims who have been bombed in 1974. It's a day of which memories and wounds will be reopened again as we think, and remember, and pray for those who have died. We are joined with you in offering this mass, that the Lord will give them eternal happiness and peace and that each of us may be....

The voice of narrator Philip Tibenham takes over:

Every year on May the seventeenth a memorial service is held to honour the victims of a terrorist atrocity, forgotten by most, yet unique in the history of the Anglo–Irish conflict. Nineteen years ago, Ireland's dignitaries filled Dublin's Pro-Cathedral to pay their respects to the victims of what remains the worst bomb outrage of the Troubles.

Images of a multiple funeral mass in the Pro-Cathedral in 1974 show former President Eamon de Valera, former Taoiseach Jack Lynch and members of Taoiseach Liam Cosgrave's cabinet. The church is packed. The black and white image fades to colour and viewers see the same church in 1992 — half-empty, for the anniversary mass. The narrator continues:

Today, only the relatives of the dead and injured attend the ceremony. But their prayers for the perpetrators to be brought to justice remain unanswered.

Edward O'Neill's mother, Martha, speaks with determination:

It's never too late. I would love to see justice being done and find out who bombed Dublin.

Edward O'Neill speaks again:

I'd like to see it exposed. I'd like to see the people who were involved in it. I'd like to see their names being brought out. Something has got to be done.

The narration continues over images of carnage and devastation:

> In 1974, the Troubles had barely touched the south. All eyes were on the latest wave of violence in the north. Then, suddenly, the bombs struck central Dublin on May the seventeenth 1974. It was rush hour on a Friday evening. There was no warning. The first bomb exploded in Talbot Street at 5.30 p.m. A second bomb detonated in Parnell Street.[1] A third in South Leinster Street. Within ninety seconds central Dublin had been devastated.

Contemporary black and white footage shows an interview with eyewitness Robert Whelan, standing in the midst of the Parnell Street devastation. He is in deep shock as he recounts:

> There was a man lying, his two legs were mutilated, the side of his head was literally cut off. There was a young baby, she was like a ragdoll, she was all torn to pieces.

Eyewitness Fr Tony Maher from an inner-city Dublin parish is interviewed amidst the devastation of Talbot Street:

> It was like a battlefield. The first thing I saw was two bodies mangled into each other. There was also a body there and it was decapitated. With a few of them you could just actually see the life going out of them.

Forbes McFaul, witness to the South Leinster Street carnage, says:

> I edged towards the car that was blazing and there behind it was the car which had in fact exploded and beside the car was a body decapitated and the only way in which you could possibly determine who it might have been were a couple of brown platform boots lying there. It had been a young girl.

The narrator gives the statistics:

> Twenty-six were killed in Dublin. Two hundred and fifty-three injured.

Edward O'Neill recalls:

> I just remember this big flash coming straight towards me. I remember lying on the ground. It will never leave me — never ever leave me.

His mother, Martha, recounts the trauma that befell her:

> They told me that it was Edward, and Edward only had twenty four hours to live, little Edward, and that my husband was dead.

---

1   It is clear from eyewitness statements reproduced in this book, especially those of people injured in Talbot Street, that the first bomb in fact exploded in Parnell Street.

And like I just ... I didn't even do what I'm doing now, crying ... I wasn't able to cry. I just went totally and utterly numb, like as if every living thing I had inside of me, everything I had for life, just drained out of me.

Tibenham tells us:

Edward O'Neill was five years old. The extent of his injuries shocked his surgeon.

Edward himself elaborates:

The shrapnel or metal was still sticking in my face. He said all he could see was just bare bone from right down here. He said my whole side of my face was just brought completely over. He said he could actually see the bridge of my nose and my ear was sort of like halfway across the back of my head. They thought I was going to die on them, on the table.

Paddy Doyle is introduced. His daughter, son-in-law and two baby granddaughters died instantly:

The kids were like two pieces of gold. I don't think I'm really the same ever since that. I think it was the scenery in the morgue. I think that really knocked a bit out of me, you know. It was like going into a slaughterhouse, bits of bodies everywhere. I identified the son-in-law and the two kids, but the daughter — I couldn't place her. But it was an awful sight to go in, when you went in you had to step over legs and arms, where they were putting legs and arms just to make up a body.

Tibenham takes us to Monaghan Town where we see images from outside Greacen's public house where the fourth bomb exploded:

Ninety minutes after the Dublin explosion, a fourth bomb went off in Monaghan, seventy miles to the north and just south of the border. By drawing security forces from the border, it allowed the Dublin bombers to escape north. Again, there was no warning. Seven more were killed here. In Dublin and Monaghan thirty-three lay dead, and nearly three hundred were injured. To this day, it remains the worst atrocity of the troubles.

A clip from the Taoiseach, Liam Cosgrave's address to the nation, on the evening of the bombings, follows:

To the evil men who have perpetrated these deeds we express the revulsion and condemnation which every decent person in this island feels at their unforgivable acts. The Government are as yet unaware of the identity of those responsible for these crimes....

Over images of the devastation and carnage, Tibenham sets the context for the Yorkshire Television investigation into the atrocity:

Nineteen years later none of those responsible has ever been convicted. No paramilitary group has ever claimed responsibility. Nobody has been arrested. But tonight *First Tuesday* reveals disturbing truths behind the Dublin and Monaghan bombings, a story that's been buried for nearly twenty years.

Over images of the Irish tricolour above Garda HQ, Garda files, forensic reports and official photographs, the narrator says:

The Irish police, the Garda Síochána, carried out the official investigation into the bombings, the biggest murder hunt in their history. Most unusually in a terrorist case, the Garda have formally co-operated in our investigation. In a series of briefings, the Garda revealed the contents of many classified files, eyewitness statements, forensic reports and released official photographs. We also interviewed retired senior police officers including three former commissioners. Those officers who did not wish to be identified allowed us to use their verbatim statements.

It's now clear that within weeks of the bombings, the Garda knew how they were carried out and the identities of the leading suspects, but were powerless to do anything about it.

A panoramic view of Belfast appears, followed by images of UVF murals in the Shankill district:

The bombing mission started in Belfast on May the seventeenth 1974. Two cars were hijacked in the Protestant Shankill area, and a third stolen. They were later identified as the three Dublin car-bomb wrecks.

A red line on a map indicates the movement of the cars:

The Belfast hijackers headed south out of the city. Their job was to deliver the cars to the bomb gangs. The rendezvous took place at an isolated farmhouse in South Armagh. The bombs themselves had been stored at the farmhouse and taken down separately to Dublin.

There is footage of a car travelling through secluded country roads and crossing a small stone bridge:

The Dublin bomb cars entered the Republic unchecked at an unapproved border crossing at Ball's Mill, an old smugglers' route. They crossed the River Boyne at Oldbridge, and continued south on the back roads.

There were detailed eyewitness accounts. All three cars were seen and remembered on their journey to Dublin, as the police files reveal. One eyewitness stated:

'I noticed another car coming towards me from the Sheephouse direction. It was a peculiar shade of blue, an Austin I think. I took the registration number as "HOI 2487".'

Just over one hour later the same witness saw another suspicious car in the area and took the number as 'DIA 4063'. He had seen the Parnell Street and South Leinster Street bomb cars hours before they blew up.

A map appears showing the red line making progress towards Dublin. Tibenham continues:

The bombers took minor roads past Drogheda towards Dublin Airport. By 4 p.m., all the vehicles had gathered in a car park on the outskirts of Dublin.

Viewers see footage of the imposing red-brick edifice of the Church of the Holy Child, Whitehall, situated in the northern suburbs of Dublin. Its expansive car park is shown. The narrator says that a Garda detective confirmed to Yorkshire Television that this was the rendezvous point. An Irish voice reads from a statement attributed to a senior policeman:

That's where they all met up. Civilian eyewitnesses who'd spotted their number plates put them on the spot. There were three or four cars met there to prime their bombs.

Footage shows a car driving into Parnell Street and pulling up outside the Welcome Inn pub. The narration continues:

The bombers now had to give themselves time to reach their target streets in the city centre. As the Parnell Street bomb car arrived at its destination, it was seen by an eyewitness parked outside the Welcome Inn.

An eyewitness statement given to the gardaí is read by a female voice:

There was a vehicle parking space behind our car but this man did not appear to want to use it. As we pulled away this car reversed into the space that we were leaving.

Tibenham continues:

It was 5.15. All three Dublin bomb cars were in place.

Pictures of West Street Car Park, Portadown, appear:

Meanwhile, the Monaghan bombers stole a Hillman Minx from this Portadown car park on the afternoon of the seventeenth of May. An hour earlier, a church minister spotted three men attempting to steal a car. He later picked them out from police mug shots. All three were prominent loyalist terrorists from Portadown.

A map traces the progress of this car from Portadown to a location just north of the border, close to Monaghan. The narration continues:

The car was driven from Portadown through Armagh city and stopped at a farmhouse at a small village just north of the border where the bomb was loaded and primed. The car slipped over the border at Ward's Cross, another unapproved crossing used by smugglers. A blue car, almost certainly the getaway vehicle, was seen following the bomb car in the town centre.

Footage of a car travelling along secluded roads and a shot of Tyholland Customs Post accompany the voice-over:

It left the Republic at the Tyholland customs post five minutes before the bomb exploded in Monaghan.

A graphic of a Garda file opens to reveal eight silhouettes:

Everyone who had seen the Dublin and Monaghan bomb cars was shown official police photos. The result was a list of suspects: Eight faces and eight names.

This was a significant early breakthrough for the Garda. All eight were members of the Ulster Volunteer Force, a loyalist terrorist group. And all eight were members of its mid-Ulster brigade based in Portadown, County Armagh.

Two of the silhouettes light up to mug-shots of named suspects.

All the eyewitnesses we contacted reaffirmed their original statements.

Two of the eight suspects they identified closely resembled bomb-car drivers. [Name withheld], for Dublin, and [name withheld] for Monaghan. In both cases, police had *three* separate eyewitnesses who identified them from photos as drivers of the bomb cars.

As a statement appears with an Irish voice-over:

Police confidence was high. Says one Garda officer who worked on the investigation:

'We had no doubts that these people at least had a case to answer. We could have taken them to court with such positive identification. It was more than just one person picking out a photo. It was good, strong evidence.'

There is footage of the Special Detective Unit at Harcourt Square, Dublin 2.[2] The narrator continues:

The Garda then extended their list of suspects with twelve further names based on their Intelligence sources north of the border.

---

2   In fact, in 1974, the headquarters of the Special Detective Unit were located in Dublin Castle.

Graphics of the Garda Suspect File reappear, with the silhouettes, again lighting up with photographs as the narrator names them:

Garda files named William 'Frenchie' Marchant, the leader of the Belfast hijackers, and Billy Fulton, the quartermaster who took charge of the explosives for Dublin and Monaghan. Also named were three leading loyalists as the planners of the bombings:

- Billy Hanna, the leader of the UVF in Portadown;

- Harris Boyle, his second-in-command, a UVF Major;

- and a loyalist killer known as The Jackal who we cannot name for legal reasons.

The Garda did not know that there may have been a fourth planner. *First Tuesday* has discovered evidence that he was Robert McConnell, a farmer from South Armagh. All four were former or serving members of the British Army's biggest regiment, the UDR.

Within weeks the Garda had a list of twenty suspects for the bombings.

Viewers see pictures of Garda Headquarters, RUC Headquarters and a focus on the RUC emblem:

In the early stages of the investigation, the Garda enjoyed good co-operation from the RUC. Armed with their list of suspects, a team of detectives headed north, hoping to interview them and have them arrested by the RUC. But at RUC headquarters in Belfast the trail ran cold.

The Garda were not able to interview the bomb suspects or the owners of the hijacked cars, even with the RUC present. All they could do was hand over their information and wait. They were to be disappointed.

A statement from a Garda officer, made to Yorkshire Television in the course of their investigation appears, with an Irish voice-over:

You were dealing with a Protestant force and there was definitely a lack of co-operation. Our investigation had to end because we couldn't get any further in the north. The well just ran dry.

A photograph of Chief Superintendent John Paul McMahon, who led the Monaghan murder hunt, appears, with a paragraph from his final report:

These investigations were greatly hampered by reason of the fact that no direct enquiries could be made in the area where the crime originated. There was no access to potential witnesses in Northern Ireland and there was also the disadvantage of not having been able to interrogate likely suspects and put them on identification parades.

A photograph of his Dublin counterpart, Chief Superintendent John Joy, appears with text from his final report in which he said:

> Enquiries in regard to [name withheld] and the others are being made by the RUC and results of the investigation will be reported.

Tibenham says:

> There is no record on the Garda file that the RUC ever *did* report back.

The programme then quotes from a statement made by a senior Garda officer:

> It's incredible that we don't have more details about what the RUC did in our files. Even in our final report, they list the suspects but don't say if they were questioned or arrested. That's astonishing.

A second Garda officer is quoted as having told YTV:

> We were in a position to bring them to court. On the life of my grandsons, I'm telling you — we could have had them.

Attention is focused again on RUC Headquarters, followed by shots of Belfast city traffic with the narration:

> In fact, the RUC *had* conducted their own inquiries north of the border. We have spoken to two of their Special Branch officers who were detailed to find out more about the bombings.
>
> They confirmed they had a list of UVF suspects which tallied with the Garda's. They reported their information to RUC headquarters but were never asked to interview or arrest any of the suspects.

Tibenham continues over footage of a vehicle returning to Garda Headquarters in the Phoenix Park, Dublin:

> Isolated in the north, the Garda team could only report back to their political masters in the hope that the Irish Government would take up the issue. The Garda investigation had nowhere else to go. After only three months it was quietly wound down.

Against the backdrop of more UVF wall murals, the narrator asserts:

> But our independent inquiries in loyalist circles produced a list of 20 UVF members suspected of taking part in the bombing. Their names appeared on the RUC and Garda suspect lists. And they confirmed that the bomb plot did indeed centre on Portadown — the same conclusion as the Garda and the RUC.

Pictures of Portadown, along with a detailed map focusing on Killycomaine Estate:

Portadown is and was in 1974 a haven for loyalist paramilitaries. Many acts of terrorism were planned in *this* network of streets by the mid-Ulster brigade of the UVF.

But did Portadown's loyalist paramilitaries really have the capability to bomb Dublin in 1974?

Tibenham introduces Captain Fred Holroyd who, he reports, spent 1974 in Portadown, working undercover for Army Intelligence and MI6. Viewers are told that Holroyd had personal contacts with many of the Portadown bomb suspects. Fred Holroyd says:

At the time the loyalist explosive capability was pretty limited. They mainly used Double Diamond kegs, beer kegs, filled with explosives with a black powder fuse on, and they'd light the black powder fuse, disappear and this thing would burn down. The detonator would go off, and the bomb would go off. They weren't as sophisticated as the IRA who had electrical detonators, trembler devices and all sorts of other very sophisticated bits of equipment, anti-handling devices. I mean they were pretty primitive basically.

The narrator continues over a map of Dublin showing the three locations where the bombs exploded:

But the Dublin operation was anything but primitive. It involved the use of sophisticated timing devices to detonate three car bombs within ninety seconds of each other.

So could the Portadown loyalists really have bombed Dublin? And if they did, where did they get their new-found expertise?

Viewers are told that Yorkshire Television's First Tuesday *commissioned two leading experts to examine all the technical evidence on the bombings, including the official forensic report, never previously released. Lieutenant Colonel George Styles is introduced. He was formerly head of the British Army's bomb-disposal network worldwide and served in Northern Ireland from 1969 to 1972. He says:*

To put one bomb on wheels together, you have to have a fair amount of training and expertise. To get three to go off all at the same time, you've got to have some pretty good technicians organising the timing mechanisms for instance.

The organisation of getting three cars into the centre of a city all going off roughly at the same time — that smacks of some pretty good administrative ability and whatever organisation therefore that was behind this outrage, you could say they were not low down on the learning curve — they were high up on it.

The narrator then introduces Commandant Patrick Trears who, we are told, was one of the Irish Army's top bomb-disposal officers, with wide experience of defusing terrorist devices. According to him:

It was a very sophisticated operation, very military-type operation. The terrorist group had to be well trained to carry out this smoothly and without a flaw.

We are told that the bombs contained 400lb of explosives which detonated so efficiently that there was no residue to trace back to source. Commandant Trears continues:

The fact that all the ingredients of the bombs exploded and were expended, indicating that the mix was consistent and that the expertise of the people that made up the mix — 'twas at a pretty sophisticated level. From a military point of view, it would have been considered a hundred per cent successful.

Tibenham says that, despite eyewitness and Intelligence evidence, these experts believe it highly unlikely that Portadown loyalists could have mounted so complex an attack. George Styles says:

I have no high regard of their skill in 1974. I don't think they were at a level that would equate to the sort of techniques that were used here in Dublin.

Producer Glyn Middleton, who is conducting the interview, based on a report produced by Styles, presses him on this point:

GM: What about the loyalist history of synchronised car bombing?

GS (chuckles): I don't think there was one. In my view, they had not done this sort of thing. This is, as I say, outside their field of technology.

GM: Have they done it since?

GS: I don't ... not to my knowledge.

The narrator informs viewers:

Lieutenant-Colonel Styles concluded that the bombings bore the hallmark of the IRA, but when he compiled his report, he did not have access to Garda files naming all the suspects as UVF men.

Commandant Patrick Trears supports Styles' assessment:

If the loyalists did it, from their own experience, I would find it hard to find they could do it without being assisted by some other experienced people, because I think that they did not have the experience to carry out such a sophisticated operation at that particular time.

A photograph appears of former Garda Commissioner Eamon Doherty. Tibenham informs us:

That's a view shared by former Garda Commissioner Eamon Doherty, one of the men who led the investigation into the bombings and told us [Yorkshire Television]:

'I didn't think at the time and I don't think now that any loyalist group could have done this on their own in 1974. I believe that if they did participate in this operation, they must have been helped.'

Part One concludes with images of workmen clearing debris from the streets of Dublin. The narrator poses a question based on the statement attributed to the former Commissioner:

But if so, who did help the Portadown loyalists and why has nobody been brought to account for the bombings?

Part Two opens with images of a multi-storey derelict building. The narrator continues:

Lurgan. The abandoned headquarters of the British Army in County Armagh. On the fourth floor — the Intelligence cell, the base in 1974 for Captain Fred Holroyd, Army Intelligence Officer for Portadown. The security forces infiltrated Portadown's loyalist terrorists to run them and their leaders as informers.

The Holroyd interview resumes:

FH: We knew who they were, I mean, there was no question about that and we knew what they were involved in.

GM: How well infiltrated were they?

FH: Well, I would say we ran them. I mean, if you really want the truth, we were running the organisation, hands off, because the leaders belonged to us.

Over images of UVF murals, the narrator states:

According to Holroyd, in return for information, the Protestant informants were allowed to continue their terrorist activities unchecked.

Holroyd continues:

Atrocities were allowed to be carried out by the Protestants. We knew who they were, we had information and no action was ever taken against them. And this caused a lot of disquiet, as you can imagine.

Over pictures of the devastation in Dublin, Tibenham says:

Captain Holroyd was surprised that he was not ordered to investigate the Dublin bombings, since he was the Military Intelligence Officer for Portadown, where the suspects were based.

Holroyd continues over images of traffic in Portadown town centre:

I mean, I was never asked once by anybody to question my sources or to try and find out any information about this whatsoever. At the time, and immediately afterwards, there was just no interest at all.

It was only quite some time after that my Special Branch colleague told me in fact who the Portadown men who were involved in this were and where the cars had come from.

Pictures of Garda Headquarters, Dublin, reappear followed by a photograph of Detective Garda Dan Murphy, and statements attributed to two Garda officers involved in the investigation. Tibenham continues his narration:

The Garda officers who went north had no doubt that their investigation had been blocked. Says one:

> 'Dan Murphy who was then head of the Garda murder squad told me in his opinion it was a deliberate policy by the RUC not to help the enquiry. But he said that someone was making the RUC act that way.'

Says another:

> 'Suppose some of the suspects were Intelligence sources for the RUC Special Branch or MI5 or the British Army. Would you sacrifice them for an investigation in the south? When you do have a source like that, you protect him, even if he's killed people.'

The notebooks of Captain Fred Holroyd appear with close-up shots of details to be highlighted by the narrator. Where his notes name Portadown loyalists, their photographs appear on screen:

In 1974 Captain Fred Holroyd kept an official diary and Intelligence notebooks.

They reveal that the Portadown loyalists had 124 members with 20 per cent active. And they were clearly being monitored.

They show that in the two months before Dublin, instructions in making bombs were given on Monday nights by William Hanna. William Hanna was on the list of suspects for Dublin of both the Garda and the RUC.

Billy Fulton is recorded in the notebooks as collecting illegal fertiliser for explosives in the very month of the Dublin bombings. Billy Fulton, again, was on the suspect lists for Dublin of both the Garda and the RUC.

The notebooks list six of the eight men identified by eye-witnesses — including [name withheld] and [name withheld] — as active paramilitaries known to Army Intelligence in 1974. Holroyd and other sources state that two of the eight were paid informants of the security forces at the time.

An aerial picture of British Army HQ, Lisburn, appears, followed by a black-and-white image of Colin Wallace, a military information officer. Tibenham introduces Colin Wallace:

Lisburn, headquarters of the British Army in Northern Ireland. In 1974, one of its senior information officers was Colin Wallace. He briefed the media on the Dublin and Monaghan bombings. Wallace, too, soon knew the names of the suspects.

Colin Wallace says:

The difficulty I think with the Dublin bombings is that there was really no follow-up, no major offensive, no major determination to find out whether these people had been responsible or not.

And it was the lack of interest I think that concerned us, that it was a departure from normal procedure because the outrageous nature of the bombing would have justified a greater interest and that just didn't seem to be present at that time.

A letter dated 14 August 1975, written by Wallace on official military notepaper appears on screen, with the camera scanning it and highlighting relevant sentences. The narrator continues:

Wallace says he knew, through Intelligence briefings, the names of the bomb suspects by September of 1974. One year later, he wrote to a former colleague, naming eight of them including [name withheld], Hanna and McConnell.

So, not only did the Garda and the RUC know who the suspects were in 1974, so did the British Army and MI6.

Both Holroyd's and Wallace's claims about undercover activities in Northern Ireland have attracted controversy. We have submitted Colin Wallace's letter and Captain Holroyd's notebook to a leading forensic analyst. Both documents are consistent with having been produced in 1974 and five.

Wallace's letter goes on to make an even more startling claim. He writes that some of the Dublin suspects 'were working closely with INT — Intelligence — at that time.'

Wallace elaborates on camera:

I believe that that is probably members of the special duties team, who were then linked to SAS personnel.

Footage of drumlins and woods appears, with a stately house emerging from amongst hills in County Armagh. Tibenham says:

That special duties team was based in the rolling countryside of County Armagh, at Castledillon, in the grounds of a stately home. The team was a group of SAS-trained undercover soldiers who formed the most secret unit of the British Army in Northern Ireland.

Fred Holroyd recalls:

A remarkable little place — I mean, set behind an ordinary regiment of engineers in a compound of its own, guarded by civilian MoD police and it was sort of made up of wooden huts and in there I was shown, for example, the locker with all their spare barrels so they could use weapons and then change the barrels and claim that they'd never shot people.

I was shown their communications equipment, which was quite separate, and I suspect went straight through to Hereford and to MoD. I was shown a number of things which meant that they were funded separately and they were supported separately from regular Army, uniformed Army people. Now, there are only one ... there is only one organisation who can sponsor anything like that and that's the SAS.

Tibenham continues over pictures of the Castledillon complex:

The team's cover name was Four Field Survey Troop. Officially, they were answerable to Army Headquarters in Lisburn. But routinely, they operated in virtual isolation. Ultimately, their chain of command led to MI5.

Lord Merlyn Rees who was Secretary of State for Northern Ireland at the time (March 1974–September 1976), is interviewed about Castledillon and the Special Duties team:

Here was a special duties unit that operated down there and I approved of that ... um ... I knew that it wasn't a large organisation and I know that it worked to Lisburn.

If you are going to have a force operating like that, then it's got to be given a great deal of freedom of movement anyway, that they couldn't have through the normal army arrangements.

Official House of Commons documents show the Government's response to a 1988 parliamentary question about this secret unit:

The role of a royal engineer field survey is to provide or process aerial photographs, ground surveys and mapping for the army.

Yorkshire Television has interviewed a former member of Four Field Survey Troop who painted a very different picture of its role in 1974. A graphic appears with the SAS symbol superimposed over Castledillon, and an English voice, saying:

We were a specialist unit with training in surveillance and anti-surveillance, silent weapons, breaking and entering. We were also trained in weapons for sabotage with explosives and assassination. We also crossed the Irish border with explosives to booby-trap arms dumps and for other missions.

Lord Merlyn Rees responds, in particular, to the point regarding the issue of incursions into the territory of the Republic of Ireland:

I would certainly not have worried too much if they found arms buried in the ground that they left them in a position that would cause harm to those who were going to pick them up ... you know ... one lives in a harsh world. But, as for crossing the border, they certainly had no permission for any of it from me and neither should they in general but if they were going to cross the border, they would have had to have had permission from the man in charge of security and that was me.

Tibenham informs viewers that in 1988 the Government stated that all records relating to this secret unit had been destroyed. Holroyd's intelligence notebooks reappear as the narrator continues:

In 1974 Four Field Survey Troop was led by two key officers: Captain Tony Bell, in command; and Lieutenant — later captain — Robert Nairac.

Nairac had already spent twelve months as an undercover specialist in Northern Ireland.

The former member of Four Field Survey Troop states:

'Nairac's job at Castledillon when I was there was as a source handler. He was getting Intelligence and had contact on both sides.'

The narrator continues over pictures of Castledillon, UVF murals, mug-shots of named suspects and a lingering photographic profile of Captain Robert Nairac:

We have evidence from police, military and loyalist sources which confirms the links between Nairac and the Portadown loyalist terrorists. And also that in May 1974, he was meeting with these paramilitaries, supplying them with arms and helping them plan acts of terrorism against republican targets.

In particular, that three prime Dublin suspects — Robert McConnell, Harris Boyle and the man called the Jackal [Robin Jackson] — were run *before* and *after* the Dublin bombing by Captain Nairac.

That three of the Dublin bomb suspects at the time of the outrage were run by Nairac has been confirmed to us by a series of security force sources from 1974. They include officers from the RUC Special Branch, CID and Special Patrol Group; officers from the Garda Special Branch.

And key senior loyalists who were in charge of the County Armagh paramilitaries of the day also confirm the Nairac connection.

But why should Nairac and Ball involve themselves with known loyalist terrorists?

The cover of a British Army manual appears on screen. The camera scans the title: Land Operations: Counter Revolutionary Operations, Part 1: Principles and General Aspects. *The narrator informs us that the Army's own secret training manual specifies this kind of role for SAS forces when it states that they:*

... are particularly suited to liaison with and organisation, training and control of friendly guerrilla forces operating against the common enemy.

Tibenham reminds viewers that:

The friendly guerrillas in Northern Ireland were loyalist terrorists.

A wedding photograph of Billy Hanna appears as Tibenham says:

A similar range of sources confirm that Billy Hanna, the most senior loyalist on the suspect list, was run separately as an agent by the British Army from Lisburn and Three Brigade Headquarters in Lurgan.

Colin Wallace elaborates on the relationship between loyalist paramilitaries and the British Security Forces:

Loyalist paramilitaries by and large worked willingly with the Intelligence community, ostensibly with the Army, because they felt that both they and the security force were doing the same job — defeating the IRA. So, in many ways, they would have been much easier to manipulate because any work or any task given to them by the Intelligence community they would have seen almost as an honour. That this would have been an extension of what they themselves were doing.

Tibenham continues:

The extraordinary concept that elements in the British security forces could be involved in acts of cross-border terrorism was not new.

Photographs of Keith and Kenneth Littlejohn appear over a map of Dublin, followed by a map of Counties Dublin and Louth. Pulses, simulating explosions, light up over Louth and Castlebellingham. The narration continues:

In 1972, two English brothers, Keith and Kenneth Littlejohn, were arrested for robbing a Dublin bank. Their campaign included firebombing Irish police stations and blaming the IRA, to provoke tougher Irish Government action against them.

The Littlejohns maintained that they were MI6 agents acting under orders. The British Ministry of Defence later confirmed the Littlejohn connection to MI6.

Viewers see the devastation in Dublin following two explosions.

Then in December 1972, two car bombs exploded in Dublin, killing two people as the Irish Parliament was debating new anti-terrorist laws. The Irish opposition was against the measures but now voted for them believing the IRA had planted the bombs.

Yet within weeks, rumours that the British were responsible were rife. Even Jack Lynch, the Irish Prime Minister at the time of the bombs, suspected British involvement.

Archive footage of an interview with Jack Lynch in 1973 follows:

Well, my suspicions naturally are aroused more, we have no, as I said, indication who was responsible and as it is now well known a lot of people in Ireland believe that many of these unexplained activities and actions could well be related to British Intelligence or other activities of that nature.

The camera scans the front page of the Evening Herald *of Tuesday, 21 August 1973. The narrator informs us:*

Two days after Mr Lynch's statement, the Garda leaked a file on the 1972 bombings to the Dublin *Evening Herald*. The file's conclusion: that the car bombs were the work of the British Army's SAS.

A voice speaks words attributed to a senior Garda officer:

The 1972 Dublin bombing was the work of the SAS — there's no doubt about it. They were such convenient bombs with the Dáil debate going on. That's probably why the article appeared.

There was a lot of frustration about the SAS role and our inability to do anything about it.

Pictures of devastation following the 1974 bombings appear, followed by snapshots of the report prepared for First Tuesday *by Lieutenant-Colonel George Styles. Tibenham says:*

In his report for *First Tuesday* on the *1974* car bombings of Dublin and Monaghan, Lieutenant-Colonel George Styles, the head of the Army Bomb Disposal in Northern Ireland in 1972, said, 'It could be a covert military operation by UK Armed Forces.' But added, 'In my view — which is based on experience of such operations — [this] is extremely unlikely.'

YTV's Glyn Middleton questions Lieutenant Colonel Styles:

GM: But did 'such operations' mean the British Army covertly detonated their own bombs?

GS: I don't think without breaking the Official Secrets Act, or getting somebody to break it, you're ever going to get any information about every operation that goes on covertly, whether it involves setting a bomb off, or whether it doesn't.

GM: I understand that, but you see where it says here: 'It would be unthinkable for a covert operation such as this to use other than captured IRA materials.' That suggests to me that the military were undertaking covert operations using captured IRA explosives.

GS: No, I would ... I think I would say if somebody said to me ... if somebody said to me, 'We want you to set off a bang tonight so that we can go and have a look at whatever,' and because the bang would be allied to an IRA explosion and therefore wouldn't be other than a normal occurrence, it would be unthinkable to an operation such as that, to use other than captured IRA materials.

GM: But for us to set off a bang, we're still setting explosives?

GS: Yes.

GM: So the British military were carrying out explosions?

GS: Well, they could have been — no reason why they shouldn't, if that was a way of getting information.

Tibenham continues over pictures of bomb explosions:

So, according to Lieutenant-Colonel Styles, in the early 1970s the British Army in Northern Ireland was planting and exploding bombs in populated areas, so that soldiers could search evacuated premises for information. These bombs were then blamed on terrorist groups.

Lord Merlyn Rees responds to a question on this issue:

I don't believe that it was difficult under the law to go into areas to search if they had reason to believe that there were arms or bomb kits to be found. I don't believe that one needed a bomb that, I presume, was going to be set not to kill anybody, to go in ... um ... and for whatever reason, I believe it is a grave mistake for that to be done.

Over a picture of Lieutenant-Colonel Styles speaking with Queen Elizabeth II outside Buckingham Palace, Tibenham says:

George Styles left Northern Ireland in 1972 having received the George Cross for heroism. There is no suggestion that he or his team had anything to do with cross-border bombs. Lieutenant-Colonel Styles discounts the possibility that the 1974 bombing of Dublin and Monaghan was a covert British military operation.

Lieutenant-Colonel Styles says:

Oh, certainly it wasn't, I can't see that happening at all — you see if you're talking about 1974, I can say definitely that it wasn't or certainly it wasn't carried out by the part of the organisation that I represented.

Over pictures of devastation following the 1974 Dublin bombings, Tibenham tells viewers:

That some elements of the British security forces had been involved in the Dublin atrocity is maintained by a senior source in the RUC Special Branch, by five senior Portadown paramilitaries and by Captain Holroyd and Colin Wallace.

Colin Wallace says:

The belief, certainly by certain people at Army Headquarters in Lisburn, was that some of the explosive used in the Dublin bombings had been provided from security force sources — and that was security forces in the wider sense, which could mean from the RUC, from the UDR or from the Army, it wasn't specific, but it was a genuinely-held belief that that had been the case and that the planning and some of the organising of that operation had been done with the assistance of people who were working within the security community.

Over pictures of bomb devastation, Tibenham asks:

But why should even the most extreme elements in the British security forces want to play a role in bombing the south?

Loyalist paramilitaries are shown marching in Belfast, followed by pictures of newly elected British Prime Minister Harold Wilson entering 10 Downing Street. The narrator continues:

In December 1973 the Sunningdale Agreement was signed. It established power-sharing in the north and gave Dublin its first political role in Northern Ireland.

The Protestants rebelled. Loyalist paramilitaries stepped up their campaign of sectarian killing.

Then, in February 1974, Harold Wilson's minority government came to power. Some feared that Labour would move towards a United Ireland and go soft on the IRA. According to Wallace, this alarmed elements in British Intelligence, fearing that their war against the IRA would be undermined.

Colin Wallace says:

I suppose they regarded the election of a Labour government as a major threat to the Irish situation. The Army seemed, in the early days, much less involved; but I think they became increasingly concerned by statements made by senior Labour people about possible withdrawal from Northern Ireland.

Over footage of buses burning, cars being hijacked and loyalist paramilitaries patrolling the streets, while the British Army look on, Tibenham continues:

By April, Merlyn Rees, the Northern Ireland Secretary, was still promoting Sunningdale, planning to phase out internment, cut troop numbers and hand over the Army's security control to the police.

Merlyn Rees believes his 1974 policies were being undermined by a subversive faction in Army Intelligence.

Merlyn Rees says:

It was a unit — a section — out of control. There's no doubt it reflected the views of a number of soldiers — let's go in and fix this lot, and so on.

But that it went on, and that it went on from Lisburn and it went on from the Army Information Service and those associated with it, I have no doubt at all.

Pictures of loyalist paramilitaries lining streets, marching and manning roadblocks, precede footage of the devastation in Dublin following the bombings. The narrator continues:

On May fifteenth, loyalist resentment boiled over. The Ulster Workers' Strike brought the Province to a standstill. On the strike's third day the Dublin and Monaghan bombs exploded.

For those who opposed the Republic's new role in the north and saw the south as a safe haven for the IRA, the bombs gave Dublin and its politicians a taste of the carnage already suffered in Northern Ireland for five years.

Within two weeks the loyalists had destroyed much of the political will in Dublin and London. Sunningdale was dead.

Eight photographs and twelve silhouettes appear:

Nevertheless, in three months, the Irish police had the names of twenty prime suspects — eight of whom were identified by eye-witnesses.

The camera scans a Dáil transcript, dated 21 May 1975, in which Tom J. Fitzpatrick (standing in for the Minister for Justice, Mr Cooney) replies to a question from Noel Davern (Fianna Fáil), as follows: 'As far as the Garda Síochána are concerned, they have not received evidence from the RUC that particular persons perpetrated these outrages. They have no positive information or evidence that would identify the culprits'. *Tibenham states:*

Yet a year later, the Irish Government told its parliament that the Garda had *no* positive information with which to identify the bombers.

Today, all the ministers on the Irish Government's Security Committee interviewed by *First Tuesday*, say they were never told the Garda *had* any suspects for the bombings.

An extract from Liam Cosgrave's address to the nation on the evening of the Dublin and Monaghan bombings follows:

While our society is menaced by men who perpetrate cowardly acts of violence, the gardaí and the Army will give the citizens all the protection they can.

Over a letter from the former Taoiseach, Tibenham says:

We asked former Irish Prime Minister Cosgrave what pressure he'd put on the British authorities to trace the bombers and if *he* knew his police force had a list of suspects.

He declined to answer any questions about the bombings. Cosgrave's letter, dated 3 April 1993, reads:

Dear Mr. Middleton,

Thank you for your letter of 19 March 1993.

This is to confirm that I will not give an interview or answer questions.

Yours sincerely,

Liam Cosgrave

Mug-shots of the prime suspects reappear as the narrator says:

- Suspect William Fulton, the UVF's Portadown quartermaster, was captured one month after the Dublin bombings. He was imprisoned in Scotland for carrying explosives, but was never arrested for Dublin and died in 1989.

- Suspect William 'Frenchie' Marchant, the man named in the Garda files as the leader of the car hijackers, was assassinated by the IRA in 1987, and given a full UVF paramilitary funeral.

- Suspect Harris Boyle died a year after the Dublin bombings, killed at the Miami Showband Massacre by his own bomb. He too received a UVF military send-off.

- Suspect Billy Hanna, who won the Military Medal with the British Army in Korea, was shot dead in 1975 by fellow loyalists, suspected of leaking UVF information to a rival section of British Intelligence.

- Suspect Robert McConnell was shot dead by the IRA in April 1976, while serving as a Corporal in the Ulster Defence Regiment. At his funeral, he was described as a man who worked 'ceaselessly for peace.'

- Suspect [name withheld] is serving life for a sectarian murder, and fourteen years for arms possession.

Other Dublin suspects remain free. There's no record of any being arrested or charged with the greatest massacre of the Troubles.

- Suspect [name withheld] left Portadown in 1975. He's now believed to be living somewhere in England.

And the man known as the Jackal was left free to carry out some of the worst atrocities of the Troubles.

*When informed that the names of prime suspects were known to
the British and Irish security forces shortly after the bombings, the
Secretary of State at the time, Merlyn Rees, tells* First Tuesday:

> I am absolutely astonished to hear that such ... there was detailed
> information about those who had been involved in Dublin.
> Certainly it wasn't notified to me. And if it had, to hell with any
> problems that there might be with the Garda — suspicion of the
> south you know, and all that. If names were given and the names
> were in the north, it would be my job, without ever interfering in
> day-to-day security matters, to make clear that something's got to
> be done within the rule of law — that these people should be
> questioned and, if needs be, dealt with by the full process of law.

*Footage is shown of people gathered around a small memorial
stone at the Garden of Remembrance in Dublin. Uniformed gardaí
are in attendance. So too, sitting in a light blue unmarked car, are
members of the Garda Special Branch. The narrator says:*

> Each year a memorial service is held in Dublin on May the
> seventeenth to honour the victims of the bombing. Their relatives
> are joined by uniform and Special Branch officers, who monitor
> the gathering.
>   Says Paddy Doyle who lost four members of his family:

> *PD:* It's like taking a big lump of your life away, isn't it? Especially
> your first grandchildren, you know.

> *GM:* How do you feel about the people who inflicted this on your
> family?

A wedding photo of Paddy's daughter and son-in-law appears:

> *PD:* Well, I don't know how they sleep in the night, but they were
> only carrying out orders, but they were very bad orders to carry out.
>   I'd feel a hundred per cent better if this Government done
> something and get these fellas on trial and let them get ... serve
> their sentence. And that would make me happy, 'cos they be
> killing a hell of a lot of people and they shouldn't be let off with it.
> And this Government definitely does know who done it.

*Martha O'Neill speaks as her husband's photograph and grave
appear on screen:*

> When I go to the cemetery and I visit that grave, how can I not feel
> for that man that's in that? How can I not feel for the five children
> that were left behind and the baby that was stillborn after it?
>   If they are listening to this programme and they know they're
> responsible, and they have a family, I hope and I pray that God
> will keep them together, that they will not ... their families will
> not go through what our families up here went through.

Her son, Edward, says:

> For nineteen years I've lived just referring to these bombers as
> bombers. I've never seen a face. I can't understand why any
> human being would go out and inflict so much destruction and
> death on his fellow human being. I mean, my father was an
> innocent man, so were a lot, the rest of the people who died.
> Justice is all I want to see done for them, to have ... to be brought
> back down to Dublin and to stand trial for what they did.

Over pictures of Castledillon in County Armagh, the narrator says:

> Robert Nairac continued to serve in Northern Ireland, maintain-
> ing his contacts with loyalist paramilitaries. He was murdered by
> the IRA in 1977, while on an undercover mission and post-
> humously awarded the George Cross.
>
> His commanding officer at Castledillon, Tony Ball, was awarded
> the Military Cross for his undercover work. He died in 1981.
>
> The Castledillon base was closed down in 1975, but the Special
> Duties Team — which now goes under the name of Fourteenth
> Intelligence — lives on in Northern Ireland, the most secret unit
> of the British Army based there.

*The camera scans a press cutting with five photographs and five
names and the heading 'The Victims of Sunday's Slaughter'.[3] The
narrator says:*

> Today, the Jackal is still one of the UVF's most active gunmen. He
> is said to have killed at least thirty people.
>
> In one murder case, he was named in court as the actual
> killer, but the RUC had never interviewed him about the crime.
> During the trial, an RUC superintendent was asked why. The
> officer replied: it was a 'matter of operational strategy'.

*Narrator Philip Tibenham concludes his commentary as the
blindfolded statue of the Goddess of Justice, holding scales over
Belfast Crown Court, is pulled into sharp relief through a mesh of
barbed wire:*

---

3   The names are: John Martin Reavey (24) and Brian Reavey (22), shot
during a gun attack on their home at Greyhillan, Whitecross, County
Armagh on 4 January 1976, and Joseph O'Dowd (61), Barry O'Dowd (24)
and Declan O'Dowd (19), shot during a gun attack on their home at
Ballydougan, County Down, on the same day. All were Catholics. A sixth
victim, Anthony Reavey (17) died from gunshot wounds twenty-six days
later. The following day, 5 January 1976, a group calling itself the
Republican Action Force, a *nom de guerre* for the Provisional IRA,
stopped a minibus at Kingsmills, Bessbrook, County Armagh, and shot
dead ten Protestant workmen in retaliation.

Many believe the Jackal was not charged with this and many other killings because he was — and is — protected by the security forces of Northern Ireland.

The Yorkshire Television First Tuesday *broadcast is concluded by presenter Olivia O'Leary:*

The RUC did not want to take part in our programme. A spokesman said they had provided factual evidence and Intelligence to the Garda.

The relatives of the dead and injured are now calling for an enquiry and *First Tuesday* will co-operate with any properly constituted public inquiry.

Chapter Six:
The Media Response to *Hidden Hand: The Forgotten Massacre*

The Irish Times, Sunday Business Post, Sunday Press **and** *Sunday Independent*

The media response the day after the broadcast was disturbingly quiet and muted. There had been considerable pre-publicity about the Yorkshire Television documentary in the week leading up to its screening. Several national newspapers were predicting that the prime suspects in the bombings would be named. The day after the broadcast, however, there were no editorials in any of the national newspapers. In fact, the only national editorial devoted to it was in the *Sunday Business Post* on 11 July 1993.

The only serious controversy regarding the documentary was created when journalist Tom McGurk took issue, in his *Sunday Business Post* column of 11 July, with an article written by *The Irish Times* Security Correspondent, Jim Cusack, on 8 July.

McGurk first compares the reaction to the *First Tuesday* documentary with the reaction to Granada TV's exposé on the Irish beef industry two years previously, which had led to enormous pressure being put on the Haughey government to establish a sworn public inquiry. He then refers to what he sees as 'a determined attempt by *The Irish Times* to undermine the credibility of the programme' and raises some perplexing issues concerning the national response to the documentary:

> Has anyone attempted to interview either Liam Cosgrave or Paddy Cooney, who were in charge at this time? ... the reaction to this film here has been a deafening silence. Heads have gone

down, phones have gone off the hook, the survivors are still out in the cold.

McGurk's reference to 'a determined attempt by *The Irish Times* to undermine the credibility of the programme' relates to journalist Jim Cusack's article of 8 July. The whole thrust and tenor of the article appears to be aimed at damaging the credibility of the programme. In his opening paragraphs Cusack raises the issue of the Garda files containing the names of twenty loyalist suspects. He writes that the actual Garda file does contain names but not the number referred to in the programme. He continues:

> ... according to a senior Garda source yesterday who saw the programme, it did not contain a 'shred of evidence' that could further the investigation.

Programme producer Glyn Middleton states categorically that Yorkshire Television has the names of twenty suspects in their transcripts, as read directly from the Garda files. In an e-mail to me, dated 14 March 2000, Middleton writes:

> It is ridiculous to suggest that a retired Garda officer gave us the 'confidential' files ... this information came from our official contact with the force....
> The number of suspects we referred to in the film came specifically from the names suggested on the files, which named them all, either by eyewitness identification, or Intelligence....

What is of importance is that the names on the Garda files were simply a corroboration of names which Yorkshire Television had already gathered from their enquiries north of the border from former Army Intelligence, RUC and loyalist sources. The programme also interviewed retired senior police officers whose statements raise disturbing questions concerning the quality of co-operation the Garda Síochána received from their RUC counterparts.

Responding to the assertion of no new evidence by a Garda source referred to in Cusack's article, Middleton says:

> [The] Garda officer quoted in the article... when he says the film didn't contain any new information ... is clearly missing the point — which is that enough information existed on the file to further the investigation at the time, yet nothing was done to establish the truth of the presence of those identified by eye-witnesses.

The concluding paragraph of *The Irish Times* article asserts:

> The UVF had been involved in a substantial bombing campaign since 1969 and had bombing skills more advanced than those of the IRA at that time.

Glyn Middleton's response to Cusack's assertion is blunt: 'Prove it,' he says. Moreover, experts interviewed in the programme, who were not the subject of 'controversy', had serious doubts as to whether the loyalist suspects acted alone. Former Garda Commissioner Eamonn Doherty, who worked on the original investigation also stated:

> I didn't think at the time and I don't think now that any loyalist group could have done this on their own in 1974. I believe that if they did participate in this operation, they must have been helped.

The day after the broadcast of *Hidden Hand: The Forgotten Massacre*, the *Belfast Telegraph* quoted Ulster Unionist MP, David Trimble's reaction to the programme. In 1974, Trimble was a Lecturer in Law at Queen's University Belfast and Chairman of North Down Vanguard Party. He was also believed to be legal advisor to the UWC. The article concluded:

> ... Ulster Unionist Upper Bann MP, David Trimble, said he was extremely skeptical about claims of British Intelligence involvement.
>
> 'I must question why the Irish authorities now want to blacken the name of [Robert] Nairac. It is remarkably convenient that all those named are dead', he said.

Responding to his comments, Mark Ackerman, a co-producer of the programme, faxed a letter to the Editor of the *Belfast Telegraph*. It was published in the edition of 24 July 1993:

> In your edition of July 7, you published a quote from Ulster Unionist MP David Trimble in which he stated that it was 'remarkably convenient' that all those named in our 'First Tuesday' documentary on the bombing of Dublin and Monaghan were dead.
>
> This is incorrect in that we named two men in the programme as bomb suspects who are still alive. I should also point out that the UVF have since confirmed they carried out the attacks and have not denied the involvement of any of the suspected bombers we named.

One of those named in the programme was [name withheld]. He spoke to me by telephone from his home on 2 July 2000. After he

had categorically denied involvement in the bombings, I asked
Mr _____ why he did not sue Yorkshire Television for
naming him. He replied that he wanted to sue the company but
his solicitor could not get him legal aid.

On 4 July 1993 — the Sunday before the broadcast of *Hidden
Hand: The Forgotten Massacre* — the *Sunday Independent*
published a front-page story written by an Irish researcher, Joe
Tiernan, who had been employed by the British company.
Tiernan's article outlined many of the elements dealt with in
Hidden Hand. In it, he claims that research found the following:

- The Garda Síochána knew the names and addresses of most
  of the bombers.

- Billy Hanna was the person who masterminded the atrocity,
  and, from 1972 until his death in July 1975, he had worked
  as an agent for the British Army's Three Brigade in Lurgan.

- Some County Armagh RUC members knew a number of days
  beforehand about the plans to bomb Monaghan, but did
  nothing to prevent it.

- The Monaghan bomb had been manufactured in Portadown
  by a British Army unit, and an RUC file confirmed this.

He wrote that the head of the murder squad, the late Dan
Murphy, held up a photograph of a man who had been identified
by three witnesses as having driven the Parnell Street bomb
car, and said, 'This [is] the bastard we are looking for.'

According to Tiernan:

> Garda say they are satisfied the bombers went home in two
> separate teams. They say Hanna and 'some helpers' travelled
> home across the border as early as 5 p.m.

The latter statement by Tiernan is crucial as it implies that the
Garda knew that Hanna was in the Republic on 17 May 1974,
and suspected his involvement.

Tiernan finishes his article by saying that the Garda
authorities had no comment to make, and that the Minister for
Justice at the time of the bombings, Paddy Cooney, said: 'The
RUC and the gardaí may well have been discussing names, but
nothing came before me.'

Such an admission by Mr Cooney is surely a damning indictment of the political and security handling of the investigation

into the bombings. It is disturbing that the Garda Síochána, apparently, did not inform the Minister for Justice about the details of the biggest mass-murder case in the history of the Irish Republic. But, equally disturbing is the fact that the Minister for Justice, apparently, took such a hands-off approach to the investigation. Neither position makes sense.

On 11 July 1993, the *Sunday Independent* carried a second article by Joe Tiernan, listing copious murders in which the notorious loyalist serial killer, 'The Jackal', was involved.[1] The Jackal, who died with cancer on 2 June 1998, aged 49, was Robin Jackson. Former RUC Officer, John Weir, whose evidence and statements are examined later in the book, estimated that Jackson was, in fact, responsible for almost a hundred sectarian and politically motivated murders.

One of the most alarming statements written by Joe Tiernan is his preamble to Robin Jackson's murder list:

> The ... list of murders attributed to the Jackal have [*sic*] been collated by the RUC Serious Crime Squad and checked with former UVF colleagues who operated with the Jackal....

Why then was he allowed such freedom to murder? Is it the case that the RUC were not able to build up a credible case against the Jackal? Did he cover his tracks so expertly that RUC detectives were unable to nail him? It has long been suspected that Jackson was, like Hanna, being run by both military Intelligence and the RUC. The murder of William Strathearn is a clear demonstration of collusion between members of the force and loyalist paramilitaries. The fact that Jackson was never questioned about his involvement in that murder, for 'operational reasons', is an indictment of the criminal justice system of Northern Ireland. More especially, it is an indictment of the failure of successive British governments to ensure the

---

1   Patrick Campbell (October 1973), Dublin bombings (May 1974), Eugene Doyle and Arthur Mulholland (February 1975), John Francis Green (February 1975), Michael Feeney, Brendan O'Hara and Joe Toman (April 1975), Francis Rice (May 1975), Billy Hanna (July 1975), Fran O'Toole, Brian McCoy and Anthony Geraghty, Miami Showband (July 1975), Sammy Neill (January 1976), three members each of the O'Dowd and Reavy families (January 1976), Catholic RUC Sergeant Joe Campbell (February 1977), William Strathearn (April 1977) and Adrian Carroll (November 1983).

highest levels of impartiality, underpinned by the principles of truth and justice, in the day-to-day affairs of Northern Ireland.

Also in the *Sunday Independent* of 11 July, Dr Conor Cruise O'Brien, a columnist with the newspaper, launched a scathing attack on the Yorkshire Television documentary, in which he showed himself to be either unaware of, or unimpressed by, Tiernan's exposé in the same edition of the newspaper. He wrote that *First Tuesday* had 'scraped up a few ... inconsequential makeweights, like the stuff about the anonymous 'Jackal'.

With regard to *First Tuesday*'s assertion that British Military Intelligence were involved in the bombings, he writes:

> There is nothing implausible about these allegations, which have been going around for years, but neither is there coercive evidence in their support.

These are the words of a former Irish government minister who served in a cabinet 'Security Committee' at the time of the bombings. They are also the words of a distinguished academic and United Nations diplomat.

The fact that the former minister saw 'nothing implausible' in the idea that British Intelligence personnel could have been involved is deeply disturbing. He states that while there is no 'coercive evidence' in support of such allegations, they have, nonetheless, 'been going around for years'. While there may not have been 'coercive evidence', the fact that those suspicions were held and, indeed, had been articulated the previous year by former Taoiseach Jack Lynch, regarding other bombings and 'unexplained happenings', surely warranted investigation.

In December 1999 I interviewed the former Northern Ireland Secretary, Merlyn Rees, about the bombings. He consistently asserted that no one in the Irish Government had raised the issue of the Dublin and Monaghan bombings with him during his term of office. The very fact that the security forces of an EEC neighbour were suspected of involvement surely merited, at the very least, the matter being raised with the Northern Ireland Secretary.

Cruise O'Brien takes issue with what he believed to be the programme's implication that the Garda Síochána had been unable to act because they did not have the support of the government of the day. He admits to listening to these words 'with a kind of sick horror'. He continues:

The clear implication is that the Coalition Government of 1974 knew from the Gardaí who the perpetrators of those bombings were, but failed to take any action to bring them to justice, thereby acquiescing in the murder of some of those citizens whose protection is the first duty of any Government.

As a member of that Government, I was outraged by that monstrous and utterly unfounded innuendo....

Yorkshire Television, quite reasonably, questioned why a promising Garda investigation into such a serious crime, had failed. The programme asked why there appeared not to be a co-ordinated approach from the Garda and the Government, given the cross-jurisdictional nature of the crime. And it asked why the Garda, apparently, had failed to seek Government help in forcing co-operation from the northern police force.

Furthermore, as circumstances had it, Yorkshire Television had not been the first to break the story. Much of what Dr Cruise O'Brien criticises about the documentary had been contained in Joe Tiernan's article published by the *Sunday Independent* the previous Sunday. Dr Cruise O'Brien does not take issue with the paper for which he himself was a columnist.

Chapter Seven:
The Political Response to *Hidden Hand: The Forgotten Massacre*

On the day following the broadcast of *Hidden Hand: The Forgotten Massacre*, the Fine Gael leader, John Bruton, asked the Taoiseach, Albert Reynolds, to make a statement on the bombings. Mr Reynolds declined to make a statement 'at this stage'. Deputy Austin Currie pressed the Taoiseach further, suggesting that he, the Minister for Justice or some other minister should make a statement. The Taoiseach replied that he did not propose to make any statement at that stage, but said that the Department of Justice and the Garda Síochána were 'examining all the allegations made.'

At Dáil Question Time, the Minister for Justice, Máire Geoghegan-Quinn, responded to Deputy Ivor Callely, saying that it had never been the practice to report to the House on the progress or findings of an ongoing Garda investigation. But, she said, 'I can say that I have been assured by the Garda authorities that the files on these cases remain open.'

The Minister informed the house that the Garda were considering the contents of the documentary with a view to assessing whether there were any matters which required further investigation. She welcomed the assurance at the conclusion of the programme that Yorkshire Television would co-operate with any properly constituted inquiry.

Prior to the broadcast of the documentary, the families had called upon the Minister for Justice to establish a public tribunal of inquiry 'irrespective of the content of [the] TV documentary.' Ms Geoghegan-Quinn told the House:

The proper and most appropriate form of inquiry in this instance is the police investigation which is already in being.... Suspicions, however strongly held they may be, do not secure criminal convictions. I can assure the House that the Gardaí have my full support in their ongoing investigation into these horrendous crimes against the people of Dublin and Monaghan.

The Minister's speech ignored the fact that Yorkshire Television had produced a version of events and evidence which were stronger than 'suspicion'. It also ignored serious issues concerning the nature of the original Garda inquiry and how a promising investigation had ended just as it appeared to be taking off.

In the Dáil Adjournment Debate of the same day, the issue of evidence in the Yorkshire Television programme was raised by Deputies Eamon Gilmore (Democratic Left) and Tony Gregory (Independent). The many questions they raised within the confines of Dáil Éireann and in the presence of the Minister for Justice, Máire Geoghegan-Quinn, are as pertinent today as they were in 1993. They are also questions which the Garda investigation into the programme failed to address. Why was the Garda investigation frustrated by the RUC? Why were the suspects never interviewed? Why were the Garda never permitted to pursue their investigation? Was there a massive cover-up? Did the Garda report on this to the then Government? What action was taken to obtain clearance from the British to continue with the investigation? Was British Intelligence involved in the bombings?

Deputy Gilmore suggested that the matter be taken up 'at the highest level' with Britain and that an immediate investigation should be carried out by an independent international force. He called on the Minister for Justice to spearhead such an investigation and to comply with the demands of the relatives of persons killed and injured in their request for a full judicial inquiry.

Deputy Tony Gregory followed Deputy Gilmore, echoing some of the questions Deputy Gilmore had asked, and adding a few of his own. Would the matter of the Jackal be addressed urgently? Would the Minister seek to establish from the British Government why none of the suspects had been arrested, charged or even questioned by the RUC? What type of inquiry would be considered? Would the matter be referred to a Select Committee of the Dáil or a sub-committee of a Select Committee on Legislation and Security?

The Minister, in her reply, largely repeated what she had said during Dáil Question Time. Certain key sentences in her statement found their way, almost verbatim, into the statement issued by the Department of Justice on 17 May 1995, following the internal Garda investigation, by which time, a change of Government had occurred and Nora Owen had succeeded her. The following are the key sentences:

- 'The appalling events in Dublin and Monaghan on 17th May 1974 stand out not only among the most tragic events of those years but in the history of this State. Thirty-three innocent people were slaughtered and a great many more lives, of the injured, their friends and relatives, were scarred....'

- '... the bombings in Dublin and Monaghan in 1974 were the subject of an intensive Garda investigation over a protracted period of time during which all relevant leads were pursued. Unfortunately, despite those intensive inquiries, no charges have, so far, been brought in connection with the bombings.'

- '... the Garda files remain open and any and every lead will be followed to bring the culprits to justice.'

Ken Livingstone MP, supported by MPs Frank Cook, Lynne Jones, Dr Norman Godman, John Gunnell and Bob Cryer, tabled two motions in the House of Commons, Westminster, on 22 July 1993. The motions, numbers 2369 and 2370, and titled *Dublin and Monaghan Bombings (Nos. 1 and 2)* highlight the important issues and allegations arising out of the *Hidden Hand* documentary, and call on the British Government to establish a full public investigation into the allegations.

In the weeks immediately following the broadcast, the Minister for Justice did meet, on separate occasions, with two groups of families who, unfortunately, were split at this crucial time. Both groups, however, were united in their demand for a public inquiry. On 27 July 1993 the Minister met with the group calling itself the 'Dublin and Monaghan Relatives'. Minutes concerning that meeting contain the seeds of exasperation:

> [We] were kept waiting 40 minutes... The Minister interrupted three times to receive telephone calls. The relatives were very unhappy with the meeting and felt that the Minister wasn't really interested. They were informed that a Garda investigation would take place.

The Minister emphasised the Government's desire to see a properly conducted investigation by the Garda Síochána, into the allegations made in the broadcast. She informed the families that a senior Garda officer was to travel to England 'within a week' to interview the programme-makers. According to Frank Massey, whose daughter, Anna, died in the South Leinster Street bomb, Ms Geoghegan-Quinn also promised to keep the families informed of progress.

By late August, however, the families were beginning to express acute public disquiet at the apparent lack of urgency in official follow-up. Frank Massey informed media sources that 'to date the programme-makers have not had a telephone call from the Gardaí.' Speaking to journalist Colm Keena of the *Irish Press* (30 August 1993), he said:

> You can only take their word for what they are saying. If responsible people like the Minister for Justice are leading you up the garden path then what can you do? We are only ordinary people whose relatives were killed 20 years ago. I would have thought the investigation would have been carried out by now. I am disappointed. She gave the impression she was 100 per cent behind us. I put a lot of faith in what she said.

Despite difficulties and disagreements amongst some of the families, they had managed to build up a considerable head of steam in the wake of the documentary. When the Dáil reconvened after the summer recess, the campaign presented a petition signed by 45,000 people, including over 2,000 from New York.[1] The petition was addressed to the Taoiseach, Mr Reynolds, and demanded the establishment of a public inquiry 'into the failure to bring to justice those responsible for the Dublin and Monaghan bombings of 1974, particularly in view of the findings of the Yorkshire Television programme....'

However, on 27 September, the Minister for Justice, formally ruled out a public inquiry into the bombings.

Following enquiries by the relatives as to why the Garda had not been in contact with Yorkshire Television, J. O'Dwyer, Private Secretary at the Office of the Minister for Justice, wrote on 13 October 1993:

---

1   These had been organised by Catherine Clever, who had been wounded in the bombings and was now living in the Bronx.

The Garda authorities report that a senior Garda officer has been in contact with the programme makers and that the Garda assessment of the contents of the programme is still in progress. The Minister will be in touch in due course about arrangements for a further meeting with you and your colleagues.

The relatives then wrote to the Garda Commissioner, on 22 October 1993, asking for an update on 'the present state of your investigation'. On 4 November 1993, Superintendent John V. Kennedy, private secretary to the Commissioner, replied:

The matters you refer to are still being enquired into by the Gardaí and on conclusion a report will be furnished to the Department of Justice.

On 28 January 1994, O'Dwyer wrote to the relatives, stating:

... the Minister is still awaiting the Garda assessment of the contents of the Yorkshire Television programme on the bombings and will be in touch with you and your colleagues about a further meeting when this comes to hand.

The growing frustration among the families of the bereaved and wounded, and their gradual loss of faith in the Department of Justice and the Garda Síochána's investigation, culminated in their decision, announced in a press release of 25 January 1994, to set up their own inquiry 'to expose and compile all available evidence relating to the massacre'. The date set for their inquiry was 14–15 May 1994, the eve of the twentieth anniversary.[2] The Dublin and Monaghan Inquiry came to naught, however, as it lacked public or private funding.

On 19 April 1994, Deputy Trevor Sargent of the Green Party received a written parliamentary answer to a question regarding the Garda Report which the Minister had had since December 1993.

The Minister replied that the report was confidential and that she was seeking 'additional information and advice" prior

---

2   It was hoped to model the inquiry on a very successful unofficial public inquiry into the controversial killing by British Royal Marines of Fergal Caraher (20) and the serious wounding of his brother Micheál on 30 December 1990, at Cullyhanna, Co. Armagh. The Cullyhanna Inquiry, which sat over two days in June 1991, was chaired by the eminent British barrister Michael Mansfield and included judges and senior attorneys from the US, France and Germany. Testimonies were heard from members of the local community who had witnessed Mr Caraher's murder.

to making a statement. The nature of the 'additional information and advice' is not known. A further thirteen months were to pass before such a statement was issued.

In late spring 1994 a letter was sent to the Taoiseach, Albert Reynolds, seeking his support for an official commemoration to mark the tragedy. The relatives had seen the Irish political establishment participate in various commemorations marking, amongst others, the IRA bombings of Enniskillen, Birmingham and, as recently as the previous month, Warrington.

Deputy Tony Gregory had raised the same issue with the Taoiseach in a Dáil Question on 29 June 1993. On that occasion, Mr Reynolds had replied that it would be 'invidious' to single out individual events for special official commemoration. A heated debate ensued between Deputy Gregory and the Taoiseach in which the former declared it 'a matter of great shame ... that no member of Government attends the relatives' memorial service.'

The debate concluded with the Taoiseach repeating the standard words: 'the Garda ... files remain open ... any new information which becomes available will be thoroughly investigated.'

On 11 April 1994, Deputy Eamon Gilmore asked the Minister for Justice if she had any plans to commemorate the twentieth anniversary of the Dublin and Monaghan bombings. She referred the Deputy to the Taoiseach's reply to Deputy Tony Gregory on 29 June 1993.

Responding to the request from the relatives for an official commemoration on the twentieth anniversary of the bombings, Brendan Boylan, Private Secretary to the Taoiseach wrote in a letter dated 22 April 1994:

> The Taoiseach would be concerned, with deepest respect for those who reflect at this time on their lost family members as a consequence of the Dublin and Monaghan bombings in 1974, not to give an impression that any among the thousands of lives lost was more particularly regretted by the Government. Every death arising from the unresolved conflict on this island is equally deserving of our notice and regret, just as every murderous assault deserves our condemnation regardless of place or victims.
>
> The Taoiseach believes that the most fitting tribute which he can make to the memory of the Dublin and Monaghan bomb victims is to strive towards the realisation of lasting peace in Ireland. You can be assured that his efforts in this regard will continue with all the urgency and resources which this tragic conflict demands.

While it must be acknowledged that Mr Reynolds was indeed engaged at that time in historic efforts to bring about peace throughout Ireland, the reality for the families was that after the funerals in 1974, whatever the political climate or historic moment, no Taoiseach had taken time to stand with the families in their grief or in their efforts to achieve truth and justice.

The twentieth anniversary arrived. There was no official commemoration. However, it was, as *Irish Times* journalist Edward O'Loughlin reported on 18 May 1994:

> ... the first time the bereaved and the scarred were joined by the official representatives of their fellow citizens.

Present at the anniversary mass in the Dublin's Pro-Cathedral were: the President, Mrs Robinson; the Lord Mayor of Dublin, Mr Tomás MacGiolla; the Minister for Finance, Bertie Ahern; the Minister for Enterprise and Employment, Ruairí Quinn; Ministers of State, Eithne Fitzgerald and Tom Kitt; the US ambassador, Jean Kennedy Smith; and the British ambassador, Mr David Blatherwick.

Also in attendance were TDs John Bruton (Fine Gael leader), Mary Harney (Progressive Democrats leader), Liz O'Donnell (Progressive Democrats), and Austin Currie (Fine Gael). TDs Tony Gregory, Joe Costello and Seán Haughey were present with a group of city councillors in their ceremonial robes.

During his address Archbishop Connell appealed for those involved in the bombings to admit responsibility and end the agony of the victims' families. An editorial in the *Irish Press* of 18 May 1994 described his appeal as 'well meant ... but not likely to happen.' It continued:

> But what the families of those who died are entitled to demand from Government is the truth about the Garda investigation into the atrocity, and why no one has been brought to justice.

The editorial went on to discuss the promised investigation and report by the Minister for Justice. It said that the relatives were 'both hurt and suspicious about these lengthy delays', and suggested that while the findings of the report might be embarrassing — given the sensitivity of inter-governmental and Garda/RUC relationships at the time — this was no reason to deny the relatives 'the fullest possible information'. The leader writer concludes: 'they are at least entitled to the truth.'

The report would take another year before its contents were revealed and would ignore the crucial questions, which were being raised in the intervening period by a small number of concerned deputies — Trevor Sargent, Eamon Gilmore, Jim Higgins, Austin Currie, Bobby Molloy, Gay Mitchell, and Ivor Callely.

A new year dawned and with it came a new coalition government under Taoiseach John Bruton. There was still no sign of the long-awaited report surfacing and so, during Dáil Questions on 8 February 1995, several matters were raised with the new Minister for Justice, Nora Owen, by TDs Bobby Molloy, Trevor Sargent, Tony Gregory, Dermot Ahern and Tony Killeen.

The Minister responded by saying that she was aware that the relatives and victims had been awaiting a statement for eighteen months, and that it was her intention that the matter be brought to a conclusion and a statement made 'as quickly as possible'. She did not commit herself on the question of a public inquiry but said that she would give it careful consideration. However, she expressed reservations, as she said that her 'preliminary view' on the matter was that 'it would not assist in any way in identifying and convicting the perpetrators', and 'a public inquiry could damage rather than assist the criminal investigation'.

The latter point has been considered by three senior British lawyers in a joint opinion for Amnesty International, regarding the murder of Human Rights lawyer, Pat Finucane. Given the historic ties between the British and Irish legal systems and the fact that the 1921 British and Irish Tribunal of Enquiry Acts are the same — their establishment having predated partition — the points argued by the lawyers are relevant in this instance. Robert Owen, QC, Ben Emerson and Tim Otty, in their paper 'The Murder of Patrick Finucane and the Case for a Public Inquiry', dated 29 October 1999, write:

> 26. The Government has also expressed concern as to the possibility that an inquiry would compromise criminal prosecutions in relation to Mr Finucane's death. We consider that on a proper analysis this concern is wholly unfounded....

> 28. (a) As Lord Salmon and the Royal Commission indicated the procedure of an inquiry is just as valuable for clearing away unfounded suspicion as for unearthing misconduct and,

accordingly, the establishment of an inquiry should not, as a matter of logic, have any material impact on or implications for the conduct of the criminal proceedings;

The lawyers go on to list three examples where a decision to hold a public or judicial inquiry ran parallel with criminal investigations into the same or related subject-matter. The most well-known of the three examples cited was the Lawrence Inquiry, established in June 1997 by the British Home Secretary, Jack Straw, into the conduct of the Metropolitan Police investigation following the murder of a black teenager in June 1993.

The argument employed by the Minister for Justice had a hollow resonance to the ears of the bereaved.

Less than a week later, on 14 February 1995, Deputy Tony Gregory asked the Minister if she would recommend that the report of the Garda investigation into the Dublin and Monaghan bombings be referred to the Select Committee on Legislation and Security. Minister Owen replied that this would not be appropriate as the report was 'a confidential Garda document which forms part of the investigation file.'

On 26 April 1995, Deputy Michael McDowell (Progressive Democrats) asked the Minister for Justice to explain the delay in issuing a statement and to say when she would be meeting the families and victims. The Minister replied that she would meet the families 'as quickly as possible' and that she hoped 'to be in a position to fulfil this commitment shortly'.

The Department of Justice Statement

The long-awaited meeting with the families happened on the twenty-first anniversary — 17 May 1995. Unfortunately, at this crucial time, the families were still split and the Minister met the two 'camps' at separate meetings. Margaret Urwin, Secretary to the now-united 'Justice for the Forgotten' campaign, gave me the following report on the meeting she attended:

> The Minister stated that she greatly regretted that she was unable to report a successful outcome to the investigation, alleging that no new evidence had come to hand to enable any person to be charged. She said that the DPP had confirmed this. In reply to a direct question as to whether she would be prepared to hold a public inquiry into the bombings she was emphatic in her refusal, stating that it would serve no useful

purpose and might, in fact, prejudice the case. We informed her that we intended holding our own unofficial public inquiry. She said that whatever suspicions people had about the involvement of the British, there wasn't a shred of evidence to back this up. She was asked about whether the RUC co-operated with the gardaí or not. She stressed that they had co-operated. I personally asked her about the allegation made in the programme relating to the fact that Superintendent John Paul McMahon had stated that they were unable to question suspects in the North. She dismissed this by saying that, of course, suspects in one jurisdiction cannot be questioned by the police forces of another. She said that YTV had no concrete evidence to substantiate the claims made in the programme.... Just as we were leaving she stressed that the Garda file remained open and suggested that if we found any new evidence we should bring it to her and it would be thoroughly investigated.

Copies of the statement issued by the Department of Justice and dated 17 May 1995 — the date of the meeting — were posted to the families. It was by now twenty-two months since the screening of *Hidden Hand: The Forgotten Massacre*. The statement, issued by the Government Information Services on behalf of the Department of Justice, follows:

Dublin and Monaghan Bombings 1974

The Minister for Justice, Nora Owen, T.D., today (17 May) met with members of the families of the victims of the Dublin and Monaghan bombings of 1974. She expressed her sympathy and that of the Government to the families on the occasion of the twenty-first anniversary of the bombings in the course of lengthy meetings which took place in Leinster House. The Minister advised the families of the victims that the outcome of the latest Garda investigation into the atrocities had produced no evidence that would enable any person to be charged. She stressed that the Garda investigation files remain open and that any new evidence, which would enable the culprits to be brought to justice, would be rigorously pursued.

Following those meetings, the Minister has issued the following statement in regard to the Garda investigation.

17 May 1995.

Dublin and Monaghan Bombings 1974
Background

1.   The bombings which took place in Dublin and Monaghan on Friday 17 May, 1974 were among the most appalling outrages in the history of this island. Three car bombs exploded without prior warning within a few minutes of each other at around 5.30 p.m. in the centre of Dublin. The bombs, which had been placed in Parnell

Street, Talbot Street, and South Leinster Street, resulted in 26 persons being killed. Later at 6.58 p.m., a fourth no-warning car bomb exploded outside Greacen's Pub on the North Road in Monaghan Town resulting in a further 7 persons being killed. More than 240 persons required hospital treatment as a result of the four bombs. Not only did the bombings result in thirty-three lives being lost but a great many more lives — of the injured, of friends and of relatives — were scarred forever.

2.   The bombings were the subject of an intensive Garda investigation over a protracted period of time. Those investigations involved extensive interviewing of potential witnesses, forensic examination of the scenes of the explosions and of items recovered, and contact with the RUC. Confidential information available to the Gardaí at the time also led the investigation team to examine evidence against a number of loyalist suspects. Unfortunately, despite those intensive inquiries, it was not possible to bring charges against any person at that time, or subsequently, due to lack of sufficient evidence to bring the matter to court.

The 'First Tuesday' Programme

3.   On 6 July, 1993 a 'First Tuesday' television documentary on the bombings, prepared by Yorkshire Television, was broadcast which purported amongst other things to identify the culprits.

4.   The 'First Tuesday' documentary contained a large number of assertions and allegations in relation to the events leading up to and following the Dublin and Monaghan bombings. The more significant of those assertions and allegations related to events which took place preparatory to the bombings, the subsequent Garda actions and investigation into the bombings, the identification of suspects, allegations of a lack of co-operation on the part of the RUC and security force collusion with loyalist paramilitary groups. Moreover those assertions and allegations were presented in a manner intended to suggest that the programme makers had access to evidence to back them up.

Garda Inquiry following the 'First Tuesday' Broadcast

5.   A review of the investigation carried out in 1974 was undertaken as part of new Garda inquiries into the events of May 1974 following the broadcast of the 'First Tuesday' programme. Those inquiries also involved interviewing the programme makers, persons who appeared on the programme and other persons who the Gardaí believed might be able to assist with the new investigation with the assistance of police forces in other jurisdictions where necessary.

6.   The co-operation of the programme makers was sought as part of that investigation because the documentary makers had indicated in the broadcast itself that 'First Tuesday' would cooperate with any properly constituted public inquiry. The researcher on the programme and the co-producers were therefore

interviewed as part of the Garda investigation. The interviewing Garda officer stated that the programme makers did not provide any evidence of those who committed the crimes and they did not indicate any persons who could provide evidence or information which would lead to a breakthrough in the investigation. The overall outcome of the interviews therefore was that no new evidence came to light and no information was received which would lead to any person being made amenable for the crimes in question despite the tenor of the assertions made on the programme.

7.   Also interviewed as part of the Garda investigation were persons who had appeared on the programme. Mr. F. Holroyd was interviewed and questioned closely on the comments made by him during the course of the 'First Tuesday' programme insinuating that security force personnel were in some way involved in the bombings. Mr. Holroyd informed the Gardaí conducting the interview that he did not have any facts or evidence to support the matters alleged by him during the course of his TV interview and declined to produce note books which had been relied on in the programme.

8.   Mr. C. Wallace was also interviewed but declined to make a written statement concerning his comments on the TV programme. Details of his TV interview were, however, discussed with him. Mr. Wallace stated that any matter mentioned by him on the programme was based on personal belief, suspicion and innuendo by other Army officers. He was not in possession of any facts or evidence which could substantiate the matters alleged, i.e., involvement of security force personnel in the bombings.

9.   Interviews were conducted with other persons who the Garda authorities believed might be able to assist with the new investigation. They likewise revealed no new evidence which would enable the perpetrators to be brought to justice.

Reference of Files to the Director of Public Prosecutions

10.   The views of the Director of Public Prosecutions, whose function it would be to institute criminal proceedings and who is independent in the discharge of those functions, were also sought on the case in the course of the new investigation by the Garda authorities. The Director, having fully considered the file relating to that investigation, stated that there was not then or at any other time any evidence available upon which a criminal prosecution could be initiated against any person. He further stated, in response to a specific query, that there was no further line of enquiry which occurred to him which might alter that situation.

The Garda Commissioner's Conclusions

11.   The Garda Commissioner is satisfied that the new Garda investigation has been extensive and exhaustive. He stated that the conclusions were as follows:

— interviews with the programme makers and others, including participants in the programme and suspects, did not indicate any persons who could provide evidence, or information, which would lead to the closing of the investigation;

— investigations carried out in 1974 were pursued as far as was then possible;

— there was no lack of co-operation between the police forces involved;

— on the balance of probability, the bombings were the work of loyalists from Northern Ireland but there was not sufficient evidence at the time to bring anyone before the courts, and no new evidence has materialised.

12.   The Commissioner added that the programme makers failed to substantiate any of the assumptions or conclusions which had been included in the programme. He is satisfied that the matter has been taken as far as it could go and that no useful purpose could be served by any further enquiries.

13.   The Commissioner has also indicated that the crimes will, of course, remain an open case subject at any time to re-activation if any realistic developments occur.

Final Comments

14.   The 'First Tuesday' programme contained very serious allegations and presented these allegations in such a manner that members of the public could reasonably assume that the programme makers had access to evidence to back up their assertions. The Garda authorities are satisfied that neither the programme makers nor those interviewed on the programme were in a position to furnish any evidence which would further the Garda investigation.

15.   The decision to issue this statement — which goes further than would be usual in such matters — has been prompted by the desire to ensure that the continuing suffering of the victims of the 1974 outrages and their families might in some way be lessened and the public disquiet created by the broadcast of the 'First Tuesday' programme.

16.   The Garda files on these murders remain open, and if any lead should emerge which might bring the culprits to justice, it will be pursued rigorously.

17 May, 1995

The statement is clearly a co-ordinated response, delivered by the Minister for Justice, on behalf of her department, and the Garda Síochána. It therefore deserves careful and detailed examination. The reader should be aware that my commentary is not that of a trained lawyer but of a concerned citizen.

However, as a lay person, I believe that the statement fails in its stated desire '... to ensure that the continuing suffering of the victims of the 1974 outrages and their families might in some way be lessened and the public disquiet created by the broadcast of the 'First Tuesday' programme [be also lessened].' (Para. 15).

In fact, it succeeded in achieving quite the opposite. Whether intentionally or not, its effect has been to prolong and intensify, not lessen, 'the suffering of the victims of the 1974 outrages.'

Analysis of the Statement

The statement opens by acknowledging that lives have been scarred forever by the bombings. The Irish Government and the Garda, however, must now accept that their failure, for over a quarter of a century, to deal honestly and openly with the grievances of the victims of the bombings has compounded the pain and suffering of the bereaved and maimed. In describing the response of Irish officialdom to their plight in the course of interviews for this book, the word 'abandoned' was continually used. Frank Massey speaks with consummate anger and bitterness when describing his experience. 'We've been treated like lepers,' he told me during my first visit to his home in Sallynoggin, County Dublin. 'Instead of being innocent victims, we've been treated as though we are the guilty'.

In over a quarter of a century following the bombs, the Garda Síochána failed to visit any of the families who lost their loved ones to discuss their ongoing investigations, as is normal procedure in an open murder case. For several years, victims support has been a core value in Garda training and practice. This has been singularly lacking in their dealings with the victims of the Dublin and Monaghan bombings. Indeed, until recently, the only time the families had contact with the gardaí in connection with the bombings, was when plain-clothed Special Branch men turned up to observe their poorly attended commemorations. Why?

The assertion in the Department of Justice statement that 'the bombings were the subject of an intensive Garda investigation over a protracted period of time' is debatable. There is no doubt that the initial Garda investigation was both 'intensive' and promising. However, what became of that investigation after only three months, should now be the subject of a public tribunal of inquiry.

THE SOUTH LEINSTER STREET VICTIMS

Anna Massey (21)

Christine O'Loughlin (51)

Below: *Dublin Firemen survey the aftermath of the South Leinster Street explosion the morning after. In the distance can be seen the Lough Swilly bus whose driver had eye-to-eye contact with the bomb-car driver shortly before the explosion.*

Previous page: *Smoke billows from the burning wreckage of the South Leinster Street bomb-car, which was parked next to the railings of Trinity College Dublin.*

Opposite page: *An aerial photograph of the South Leinster Street bombsite. To the right are the grounds of Trinity College. On the extreme left are the grounds of Leinster House, seat of Dáil Éireann.*

Above: McGlone's Café, Monaghan Town, is engulfed in flames in the immediate aftermath of the Monaghan bomb.

Below: Aftermath — the following day Monaghan citizens look at the wreckage caused by the explosion which killed seven people.

Above: *Masked UVF members pose for a gun salute in honour of Frenchie Marchant who was suspected of involvement in the Dublin and Monaghan bombings. In the immediate aftermath of the bombings, the UVF denied responsibility. In 1993 the UVF stated that it had carried out the mission, completely unaided.*

Below: *Aftermath at Monaghan — locals survey the scene outside Greacen's Pub where the car bomb exploded.*

THE
MONAGHAN
VICTIMS

Paddy Askin (52)

Thomas Campbell (52)

Thomas Croarkin (36)

Archie Harper (73)

Peggy White (44)

Jack Travers (28)

George Williamson (72)

Following page: *An aerial photograph surveys the scene of the bombsite around the Monaghan Town monument. To the top right of the picture lies the hinterland of County Armagh from where the attack originated.*

There is no doubt that 'potential witnesses' were interviewed. How extensive those interviews were needs to be
assessed in the wake of growing public disquiet. What is meant
by 'potential' also needs clarification, and why 'potential
witnesses' were never allowed to become actual witnesses.

Witnesses to whom I have spoken, some of whose testimonies
appear in this book, and witnesses interviewed by Yorkshire
Television, raise serious questions regarding police follow-up
and the determination of the authorities to bring the perpetrators to justice.

With regard to 'forensic examination of the scenes of the
explosions and of items recovered', information has come into
the public domain in the years following the publication of this
statement which gives grave cause for concern. These issues are
dealt with in Chapter Ten of this book.

We read in the statement of 'contact with the RUC' and that
an investigation, based on 'confidential information available to
the Gardaí at the time', led to the examination of 'evidence
against a number of loyalist suspects.' From my own enquiries,
it appears that none of the civilian eyewitnesses, who were in a
position to help the gardaí to identify positively or to eliminate
suspects in 1974 were revisited as part of this 'new investigation'. The assertion, therefore, that 'despite those intensive
inquiries, it was not possible to bring charges against any
person at that time, or subsequently, due to lack of sufficient
evidence' or 'to bring the matter to court', is not convincing.

The fact that a 'review of the investigation carried out in
1974 was undertaken' provided little comfort to the families.
These are decent, law-abiding Irish citizens who previously held
their police force in great respect. That respect has been
damaged by the events of the intervening years. The idea,
therefore, of the force investigating itself is disquieting.

Paragraph 3 of the statement opens the Department of
Justice and the Garda Síochána's joint critique of the Yorkshire
Television documentary. It begins by making a false assertion
about the programme — that it 'purported amongst other things
to identify the culprits' — and proceeds to undermine the programme's integrity based on that assertion.

On 25 November 1999, Glyn Middleton, a co-producer of the
documentary, testified before a Joint Oireachtas Committee on

Justice, Equality, Defence and Women's Rights. There were several aspects of his unscripted testimony which were disconcerting and which will be dealt with in subsequent paragraphs. On this assertion he was very specific:

> I am ... annoyed about the press release in 1995 from the Department of Justice saying that our programme purported to identify the culprits. It did not; it purported to identify the suspects. I do not need to point out to the Department of Justice the difference between suspects and culprits.

The Department of Justice statement makes a number of assertions, which give the impression that the promised co-operation was not forthcoming from the programme-makers, by way of evidence which could help to advance the investigations.

In the first place, this was not the 'properly constituted public inquiry' with which Yorkshire Television remains committed to co-operating. Nor was the long delay before the Garda contacted YTV helpful in developing the necessary trust. Glyn Middleton told the Joint Oireachtas Committee on 25 November 1999:

> ... after the film was screened, there was an investigation by the Garda Síochána.... I was informed of this by the Irish media. No one else informed me of this. I was told by the Irish media that Special Branch officers would be coming to see me any day, but that day never came. It got to the stage where I rang the Department of Justice and asked them if anyone was coming to see me. Eventually they came to Leeds and I was in the rather strange situation of being interviewed by a senior police officer about the contents of his own files....

Furthermore, from the moment the Garda made contact with Yorkshire Television, the programme-makers were suspicious of their approach. Middleton told the Oireachtas Committee:

> It is important for me to stress that the film did not claim to identify the bombers. It never claimed that new evidence had been gathered by which the bombers could be identified. All the film ever claimed to do was to identify the suspects. It was a film about an investigation which, clearly from the files and the memories of retired police officers, had been blocked in some way. The film was not specific on who carried out this blocking but there was certainly a feeling that the RUC did not co-operate fully and properly and that that hampered the investigation.

After his submission, members of the Committee questioned Glyn Middleton. During the course of his questioning by Charles

Flanagan TD, it came to light that Middleton had not received a copy of the Department's statement on its release in 1995, and had seen it for the first time only when I sent him a copy in 1999.

It is alarming to discover that some of the principals named in the Department of Justice statement were never given the courtesy of a copy of the statement. Deputy Flanagan clearly thought that this would have happened as a matter of course. A potential controversy would undoubtedly have arisen had the principals seen the document on its release.

According to the statement, the gardaí interviewed 'persons who had appeared on the programme', including Captain Fred Holroyd. The statement says:

> Mr. Holroyd informed the Gardaí conducting the interview that he did not have any facts or evidence to support the matters alleged by him during the course of his TV interview and declined to produce note books which had been relied on in the programme.

Brendan O'Brien brought paragraph 7 of the Department of Justice statement to the attention of Fred Holroyd prior to the *Prime Time* broadcast the day after its publication. On 18 May 1995, Holroyd read a statement, which O'Brien noted as follows:

> I was visited by 2 Gardaí and a Scotland Yard Officer — home in Shrewburyness [sic] (lasted two-and-a-half hours)....
>
> During the whole interview I kept offering them evidence kept in my home. They were not interested in it — only wanting to see my police notebooks which were at that time in the possession of a T.V. Company.
>
> I offered them access to the notebooks when they were returned to me but they showed no further interest....

The original notebooks, referred to above, were then, and, at the time of writing, are, in the safe keeping of Yorkshire Television. On 29 May 2000, Glyn Middleton informed me that Yorkshire Television received no request from the gardaí to see the notebooks.

Speaking to me on 29 May 2000, Fred Holroyd informed me that the two interviewing gardaí did not take a statement.

Paragraph 8 of the Department of Justice statement asserts that Mr Colin Wallace was also interviewed but declined to make a written statement concerning his comments on the Yorkshire Television programme.

On 1 March 2000, in reply to questions concerning the Garda interview, Colin Wallace wrote:

The interview was very informal and no formal statement was taken.... There was no solicitor present.... This is not a criticism of the officers involved — they were very polite and cheerful — but it was clear that most of my information regarding links between the UVF team, who were responsible for the bombings, and members of the Security Forces, was outside the scope of their enquiries.

The thrust of my evidence is that we (the Army) knew the identities of those responsible within 48 hours of the bombing and that the UVF team responsible for the outrages had been heavily infiltrated by the Intelligence Services, to the extent that we should have known about their plans or, at least, been in a position to detain suspects for questioning.

I have not seen the statement issued by the Irish Department of Justice on 17 May 1995.

On 22 May 2000, more than five years after the Department of Justice statement was issued, I sent Colin Wallace a copy of the statement, drawing his attention to paragraph 8. It was the first time he had seen it. I e-mailed on 25 May 2000, asking him whether he would have been prepared to make a formal written statement, had he been requested to do so. He responded:

Of course I would have made a formal statement to the Garda had I been asked to do so. I would still be willing to make a statement to the Garda — or to any other police force — in connection with the background to this matter.

Paragraph 9 states that, 'interviews were conducted with other persons who the Garda authorities believed might be able to assist with the new investigation.' Who these 'other persons' are or why they were selected for interview, and on what basis, is not clear. However, according to the statement, 'they likewise revealed no new evidence which would enable the perpetrators to be brought to justice.'

Retired Commandant Patrick Trears, who featured on the programme as a bomb-disposal expert, told me on 27 May 2000:

I can categorically state that An Garda Síochána did not interview me about my contribution to the Yorkshire Television documentary.

He has since confirmed this to me in writing.

Why was Trears not interviewed? His expert opinion was that he had never come across loyalist bombs with the synchronised sophistication apparent in the Dublin attack. He is not alone in this opinion. The documentary also included an interview with Lieutenant-Colonel George Styles, one of the British Army's most senior bomb-disposal experts. Styles said that he was not aware either of a loyalist history of synchronised car bombing.

On 30 May 2000, I spoke by telephone with former Lieutenant-Colonel Styles. He was adamant that the Garda 'certainly did not come' to interview him.

The omission of Trears and Styles from any Garda follow-up inquiry raises further questions. How extensive was this investigation? Who established its terms of reference? To whom was it accountable?

Paragraph 10 of the document states that the views of the Director of Public Prosecutions were sought. It is unclear from the statement what Garda files are being referred to, on which the DPP based his conclusion 'that there was not then or at any other time any evidence available upon which a criminal prosecution could be initiated against any person.' What specific query elicited the response 'that there was no further line of enquiry which occurred to him which might alter that situation'? On what basis was it formulated? Why were legal representatives of the bomb victims excluded from this entire process?

Moving towards its climax, the statement presents the Garda Commissioner's conclusions, based on the 'new Garda investigation'. The Commissioner at the time was Patrick Culligan who received his appointment on 5 January 1991.

In the first conclusion of paragraph 11 is a crucial reference to the fact that 'suspects' from the programme were interviewed. We need to know if these 'suspects' were interviewed on the basis of having featured on the Yorkshire documentary or because they are named in the Garda files. We also have the right to know, if indeed suspects were interviewed, why it took twenty years to interview them. What was the content and basis of the interviews? How were the interviews conducted? Where did they take place? Was it in a police station, a solicitor's office, their private homes or a neutral venue? Did the 'suspects' have legal representation during the interviews? Who facilitated the interviews as, presumably, none of the suspects travelled to the Republic of Ireland? Were the police forces of other jurisdictions present during the interviews? These are questions to which Mr Justice Hamilton and Dáil Éireann must seek answers.

Michael Mansfield, QC, gave me the following opinion:

> Police in England are not permitted to interview unless there is
> consent. Obviously if they have enough material to raise a
> reasonable suspicion of criminal activity, they may arrest and
> then interview per PACE (Police and Criminal Evidence Act).
> They cannot arrest for the purpose of interview only. All this
> plainly applies to any foreign police force such that they may
> interview if consent is given. If not they must begin the extra-
> dition process by requesting an arrest by the British Police, etc.

Yorkshire Television took legal advice as to whether or not they
should furnish the Irish police with information on the
whereabouts of surviving suspects. The programme-makers
concluded that they were obliged to do so in the interests of the
families who had lost loved ones in the bombings.

Glyn Middleton wrote to me on 24 May 2000:

> ... much of the material used in the film came from the Garda
> Síochána's own files, and was supplied with the knowledge and
> authority of senior officers. Our extensive co-operation with the
> Garda was not contested or challenged by them.
>
> We pointed out that the names of suspects came pre-
> dominantly — though not exclusively — from the Garda files....
>
> We had already drawn up a list of seven suspects — named
> in the Garda's files — for whom we had recent addresses. This
> list was handed to [Detective Garda] Sean O'Mahony on
> 15/9/93....
>
> The Jackal was not on this list. This was because we were
> primarily concentrating on those picked out by eyewitness
> evidence, and wanted to give the Gardai information about
> their whereabouts, in case they wanted to interview them 17
> years on.
>
> However, we did tell them that a variety of RUC and Garda
> sources suggested he was involved in planning the Dublin &
> Monaghan operation — and many other terrorist attacks....
>
> We supplied information we had about the South Armagh
> farmhouse....
>
> In addition, we told them a little more about the border
> crossings (based largely on eyewitness evidence in the files), about
> the use of the Whitehall car park as a rendezvous point, about
> Robert McConnell and about the priming of the Monaghan bomb.

In the absence of transparency, clarification is required regarding the Commissioner's conclusion that the 'investigations carried
out in 1974 were pursued as far as was then possible'. What
does 'as far as was then possible' mean? To many observers the
1974 investigation was very promising at the beginning and

went 'as far as was then possible' until halted by RUC stonewalling. Furthermore, the fact that political pressure was, apparently, not sought in 1974 to help break the logjam, renders the Commissioner's conclusion unacceptable. It is also interesting to note that the entire statement avoids the vexed question of the role of politicians at the time.

Some members of the force who were involved in the original investigation contradict the Commissioner's conclusion that 'there was no lack of co-operation between the police forces involved,' Again, in the absence of transparent public accountability, this conclusion is unconvincing.

His conclusion that 'on the balance of probability, the bombings were the work of loyalists from Northern Ireland but there was not sufficient evidence at the time to bring anyone before the courts, and no new evidence has materialized' is not acceptable given the handling of crucial eyewitnesses in the immediate aftermath of the bombs. It also fails to take into account the Garda's relationship with British military Intelligence throughout the period in question. Given the infiltration of loyalist paramilitary organisations in 1974 by British Intelligence, questions remain as to how Intelligence sources failed either to halt the attack or, at the very least, inform their Garda counterparts that an attack was imminent. The statement continued:

> The Garda authorities are satisfied that neither the programme makers nor those interviewed on the programme were in a position to furnish any evidence which would further the Garda investigation.

The Yorkshire Television documentary was principally about why, given the accumulation of corroborative information, such a promising investigation failed to build on basic police work.

The conclusion to the Department of Justice statement is that the Garda files on the Dublin and Monaghan murders remain open, 'and if any lead should emerge which might bring the culprits to justice, it will be pursued rigorously.'

The penultimate paragraph, however, states that the reason for issuing the statement is 'the desire to ensure that the continuing suffering of the victims of the 1974 outrages and their families might in some way be lessened' and also to lessen 'public disquiet created by the broadcast of the "First Tuesday" programme'.

In the interests of lessening 'public disquiet', one might have hoped that the Department of Justice and the Garda Síochána would have had a well-briefed team of public relations personnel working to ensure that the statement achieved maximum publicity. This does not appear to have been the case.

Why was the detailed text of the statement not published in the media? From beginning to end, it is less than 1,500 words. It is disappointing that the print media showed little interest. Given that the statement was issued on the twenty-first anniversary of the bombings, from a media point of view, the subject matter was relevant and topical. One or more of the national dailies could have been asked to run the entire statement.

An examination of Irish national newspapers around 17 May 1995 reveals sparse coverage, with only short commentaries and little analysis. The full four-page statement was issued at 20.03 on 17 May 1995 to Brendan O'Brien of RTÉ's *Prime Time*. *Prime Time* had requested an interview with the Minister for Justice, Nora Owen, for inclusion in its documentary about the bombings (See Chapter Nine). The Minister declined the invitation, stating:

> ... I believe that it would be generally recognised that it would be unwise in the extreme for any Minister for Justice to provide immediate reaction in relation to matters that may be raised on a programme of this kind. There is a real risk that instant reaction might hinder rather than assist the investigative process which is the last thing that any responsible person would wish to do.

It should be noted that no Minister for Justice has been available for a detailed discussion with the media on the subject of the Dublin and Monaghan bombings investigations. Given that the RTÉ *Prime Time* documentary was dealing with much of the subject-matter the new Garda inquiry had examined, that the stated aim of that inquiry was to 'lessen public disquiet' created by the 1993 broadcast, and that the occasion of the issuing of the statement coincided with the twenty-first anniversary of the bombings, this would seem to have been the ideal moment.

Whatever hopes the Department of Justice and the Garda Síochána had of lessening 'public disquiet' were short-lived.

RTÉ's *Prime Time* documentary *Friendly Forces*, broadcast the day after the statement was issued, once again raised the temperature.

The relatives and wounded have insisted that the 'Independent Commission of Inquiry', headed by Mr Justice Hamilton, should also examine the response of the Irish State and the Garda Síochána to the Yorkshire Television broadcast. It is absolutely imperative — in the interests of justice, humanity and the democratic mandate of this State — that it do so.

Chapter Eight: UVF —
Ourselves Alone

The strongest reaction to Yorkshire Television's *First Tuesday* was a statement issued by the Ulster Volunteer Force on 15 July 1993. The unsigned, typed statement was issued to Ulster Television who had broadcast the documentary nine days previously. It read:

> Following the sinister allegations of collusion, mischievously constructed by the presenters of the recent 'First Tuesday' programme, which supposedly investigated the 1974 Dublin and Monaghan bombings, the UVF avails itself of this opportunity to state clearly and without reservation that the entire operation was, from its conception to its successful conclusion, planned and carried out by our volunteers, aided by no outside bodies.
>
> In contrast to the scenario painted by the programme, it would have been unnecessary and, indeed undesirable, to compromise our volunteers' anonymity by using clandestine security force personnel, British or otherwise, to achieve an objective well within our capabilities.
>
> The operation while requiring a fair degree of preparation and not a little courage did not, as was suggested by the so-called 'experts', require a great deal of technical expertise.
>
> The comments made by some of those interviewed were at best naïve, if not deliberately misleading, given the backdrop of what was taking place in Northern Ireland, when the UVF was bombing Republican targets at will.
>
> Either the researchers decided to take poetic licence to the limit, or the truth was being twisted by knaves to make a trap for the fools.
>
> The minimum of scrutiny should have revealed that the structure of the bombs placed in Dublin and Monaghan were [sic] similar, if not identical, to those being placed in Northern Ireland on an almost daily basis.
>
> The type of explosives, timing and detonating methods all bore the hallmark of the UVF. It is incredulous [sic] that these points were lost on the 'Walter Mittys' who conjured up this programme.

> To suggest that the UVF were not, or are not, capable of
> operating in the manner outlined in the programme, is tempting
> fate to a dangerous degree.

It is important to note that the statement does not attempt to
dichotomise the Dublin and Monaghan attack. Both incidents are
presented as a centralised and co-ordinated attack, emanating
from the same command structure. This lends weight to the suspicion that the function of the Monaghan attack was to act as a
decoy to enable the Dublin bombers to escape back across the
border.

The question is, who took the lead role in the operation —
the mid-Ulster or Belfast Brigade of the UVF — if, indeed, the
UVF acted entirely alone?

Reaction

Reaction to the statement from relatives who lost loved ones
was sceptical. Terry Massey, who lost her sister, Anna, in South
Leinster Street, is quoted in the *Irish Press* of 16 July 1993:

> It's very odd that this is coming out 19 years later. Are they
> being pressurised? Do they want the British and Irish
> governments not to have to answer questions?

Jackie Wade, whose nine-months-pregnant sister, Collette
Doherty, died in the Talbot Street bomb, commented to Tom
Reidy in the *Evening Herald,* 'This is too much of a coincidence,
who is pulling the strings?'

The Irish Independent reported the following day that
Monaghan County Council had decided unanimously to ask the
Minister for Justice to undertake a further investigation into the
atrocities if fresh Garda evidence became available. Councillors
rejected the UVF denial of British security forces involvement.

On 16 July 1993 it was reported in *The Irish Times* that Joe
Tiernan, researcher on the programme, had 'confirmed ... that
he had further proof about the bombings which had not been
used in the documentary' and that he would release this evidence 'in due course'. The *Irish Independent* had the same story
on 17 July, with the additional information that the evidence
was on tape and would be passed on to the Minister for Justice.

What this 'further proof' is has not yet been established.
Mr Tiernan concluded his contract with Yorkshire Television

some three weeks before the broadcast, so presumably the evidence came about through research he carried out himself subsequent to his work for the programme.

Writing in the *Sunday Independent* on 16 May 1999, Joe Tiernan states that the attacks on Dublin in 1972, 1973 and Dublin and Monaghan in 1974 were carried out 'by the UVF with, by and large, the same personnel involved'. He goes on to name a Lisburn loyalist, Jim Hanna, as the leader of the 1972 and 1973 attacks and an Armagh loyalist, Billy Hanna, as the leader of the 1974 attacks. Tiernan reports that Billy Hanna was 'friendly' with British Army officers from Three Brigade, and that, between 1972 and 1974, these officers 'visited Hanna's home on a regular basis giving advice on the running of his terrorist campaign'. Tiernan even goes so far as to claim that the Dublin and Monaghan bombings were planned during fishing trips undertaken by the British Army officers and Hanna on Tarbot Lake in Banbridge in early 1974. He claims to have tapes of interviews with former associates of Hanna, which contain the names of the officers involved. He also claims that the *Sunday Independent* has the names of the drivers of the cars used in the attacks.

Based on the above, Mr Justice Hamilton and the Joint Oireachtas Committee who will consider the report of his Independent Commission of Inquiry into the bombings will, no doubt, seek the full co-operation of both the *Sunday Independent* and Joe Tiernan.

1974 Denials

In the immediate aftermath of the 1974 bombings, both the UVF and the UDA publicly denied responsibility. To do otherwise would have been political suicide for the Ulster Workers' Council and its strike committee, with whom loyalist paramilitaries were working closely. Furthermore, the newly appointed Secretary of State for Northern Ireland, Merlyn Rees, had de-proscribed the UVF on 14 May 1974, and admission of involvement in Dublin and Monaghan would have forced an immediate reversal of this decision. It would also have wrong-footed the security forces and intelligence services who were fostering an increasingly unhealthy alliance with loyalist paramilitary organisations in their war against the IRA. The nineteen-year silence maintained by the UVF is, however, extraordinary.

Did the UVF Act Alone?

While it does take 'not a little courage' to make, carry and deliver bombs deep into 'enemy' territory, to plan and execute the no-warning random killing of born and unborn babies, of infants, mothers, fathers, daughters, sons, sisters and brothers, is an act of supreme cowardice, whoever is responsible.

There is no doubt that the UVF was deeply involved and that Garda, RUC and British Intelligence sources on both sides of the border had, within a very short space of time, identified prime suspects from primarily the mid-Ulster UVF, supported by, amongst others, the UVF's Belfast Brigade. The mid-Ulster UVF was one of the most ruthless battalions operating in the 1970s. Security forces were aware of an ever-increasing murder triangle, which roughly encompassed an area around Lough Neagh — taking in Markethill, County Armagh; Dungannon, County Tyrone; Toomebridge, County Derry; Antrim/Aghalee, County Antrim; and Lurgan/Portadown, County Armagh — within which Catholic civilians, estimated to be in the hundreds, were murdered throughout the period of the conflict.

In their book *UVF* (Poolbeg Press, 1997), journalists Jim Cusack and Henry McDonald claim that 'The Dublin operation was largely the work of the Belfast UVF ... the Monaghan bombing was the work of the Armagh and mid-Ulster UVF.' As evidence of their assertion, they use the fact that the three cars which exploded in Dublin had been hijacked and stolen in Belfast, while that which was used in Monaghan had been stolen in Portadown. They go on to say that the UVF leadership still refuses to reveal further details about the bombings because they fear prosecution.

Writing in the *Observer* on Sunday, 7 August 1999, McDonald argues that what he terms a 'central ideological assumption of Republicanism' — namely that Ulster loyalists 'do not and cannot operate independently of the British state' — is a false premise. However, inherent in McDonald's argument is the implication that everyone who expresses concern about loyalist paramilitary collusion with the British security forces is wedded to Irish republican goals. This is clearly not the case.

It is an established and incontrovertible fact that collusion between loyalists and the security forces did take place throughout the period of the 'Troubles'. Both the Yorkshire Television documentary and the 1995 RTÉ *Prime Time* programme about the bombings drew attention to the adopted military strategy of General Frank Kitson, which encouraged security-force liaison with, and organising of, 'friendly guerrilla forces' against a common enemy. Numerous political commentators, former loyalist paramilitaries, retired British officers and intelligence operatives, acknowledge that such liaison was commonplace. The Secretary of State at the time, Merlyn Rees, admitted to me that he actually went out on patrols with the army and engaged in friendly chats with loyalist paramilitaries patrolling Belfast streets. Contact of this kind was endemic, emanating from operational strategy. It is not an assumption of the collective republican or even nationalist ideological mindset.

On 30 May 2000 I spoke to the former head of the British Army's bomb disposal operations in the early 1970s, Lieutenant Colonel George Styles GC, who had featured in Yorkshire Television's *First Tuesday* documentary. He had not seen the UVF statement following the broadcast. When I read parts of it to him, he responded, 'No matter what flag a terrorist flies, you don't believe a bloody word he says.' I later sent him a copy of the UVF statement, asking him for his opinion.

On 4 June 2000, retired Lieutenant-Colonel Styles replied:

> ... Motive would be the question I would ask the UVF; if they were bombing targets in the Republic 'at will', as they now claim, why did they not continue to do so?

Henry McDonald's *Observer* article of 7 August 1999 refers to 'conspiracy theorists' who 'conveniently ignore ... that the UVF were placing bombs in Dublin and killing civilians long before the 1974 atrocity'. However, while it is accepted that the UVF were indeed planting bombs prior to 1974, what Mr McDonald fails to address is the issue of the capability of the UVF, acting alone, to achieve the level of sophistication and military precision, evident in the 1974 Dublin bombings.

Furthermore, a Garda file, leaked to journalist Jim Cantwell in August 1973, suggests that the RUC helped to establish a

British military connection with regard to the 1972 Dublin bombing to which McDonald refers. The two bomb cars used in that attack were hired by an agent under the bogus name of 'Joseph Fleming'. Fleming shared a Belfast flat with a Mr Thompson. The British Army paid for the rent of the flat. RUC officers on a joint patrol with the British Army observed a car being stopped on the night of the explosions, having crossed from the Republic into Northern Ireland. Fleming and Thompson were two of four people in the car. RUC officers observed the occupants of the car being driven away by British Army units after a friendly chat. Subsequent enquiries made by the RUC were, apparently, 'ignored' by the Army. It is difficult to accept the suggestion that this attack was carried out by the UVF alone. Indeed, there is evidence to suggest that the UDA was involved in it.

Mid-Ulster Loyalist Source and Colin Wallace

I asked a loyalist source in mid-Ulster for his opinion on the Cusack and McDonald view that Dublin was bombed by the Belfast UVF and Monaghan by the mid-Ulster UVF. He responded:

> Personally I don't agree with the total argument ... regarding the roles played by Belfast and mid-Ulster. Certainly the Monaghan attack was mounted by mid-Ulster alone..... However, there was co-ordination between the two units operating in the Republic on May 17th. The commander of the Monaghan attack was one of two Portadown brothers heavily involved with the UVF at that time. He now lives in Scotland. Dublin was also commanded by a mid-Ulster UVF member. He is now dead.
>
> I don't agree with Cusack and McDonald's analysis as I believe it came from one source within the Belfast Brigade staff of the UVF. The identity of the source is known to me....
>
> Mid-Ulster always had the reputation of being the UVF's most effective and 'professional' unit up until it was stood down in 1996. There has always been a certain degree of personal jealousy between senior figures in this area and the Belfast command....
>
> Yes, the Dublin cars were stolen in Belfast. However, consider where they were taken prior to the attack ... [a]n area totally alien to the Belfast brigade....
>
> ... I believe that 3 individuals from mid-Ulster, i.e., Robin Jackson, Billy Hanna and Robert McConnell [a serving UDR corporal] were heavily involved in the Dublin attack....
>
> .... I also think it highly unlikely that if we accept the Belfast argument that no one else was involved, including security forces, they would be prepared to travel from Belfast to South Armagh carrying explosives and then on to Dublin....

On 23 February 2000, Colin Wallace sent the following opinion:

> I disagree entirely with Jim Cusack's view that the UVF 'had
> bombing skills more advanced than those of the IRA at that
> time'.... Two of the Mid Ulster UVF's 'bomb makers' blew them-
> selves up just prior to the Dublin Bombings — one in November
> 1973 and one in April 1974. As a result the UVF doing the
> Dublin and Monaghan bombs were believed to have used mainly
> or entirely commercial explosive (gelignite) — stolen from a
> quarry near Portadown. Unlike the IRA the UVF did not make
> use of light-sensitive devices, sophisticated anti-handling devices
> or precision timers. This was largely because, unlike the IRA,
> they were not trying to kill Army bomb disposal personnel. It is
> true that their bombs were often 'effective', but they were very
> basic in comparison with the IRA. I feel that a proper forensic
> examination of the debris from the Dublin and Monaghan
> bombs might have shown a different type of manufacture from
> previous UVF devices.... The year after the Dublin/Monaghan
> bombs a UVF bomb exploded prematurely [in] the Miami
> Showband [incident, killing two of the suspects]. Bearing in
> mind that the attack on the band was carried out by the same
> group who were responsible for the Dublin/Monaghan attack,
> what became of their expertise?

Yorkshire Television

On 19 April 2000, I challenged Glyn Middleton of Yorkshire
Television to defend the findings of his researchers. In his
response of 11 May 2000, he wrote:

> If someone can provide hard evidence that all our information
> was false and misleading — and that we were duped by
> hundreds of different interviewees, from loyalist groups, RUC,
> Garda Síochána, British Army. etc., etc., I will be the first to
> hold my hand up and say we were wrong (that would also mean
> ... that the whole Garda Síochána investigation was similarly
> wrong).
>   If the type of explosives, timing and detonating methods all
> bore the hallmarks of the UVF, why is it impossible to find an
> identical operation to Dublin & Monaghan?
>   ... Our information that the Dublin operation was principally
> the work of the Mid-Ulster UVF was based on information not
> only from those active in loyalist circles at the time, but many
> other sources, including key RUC officers....
>   We were told that apart from the hijacking of the cars, at
> least two Belfast figures were at the farmhouse the night before
> the Dublin bombings. That suggests a reasonable input, though
> our information was consistently that Mid-Ulster was leading
> the operation.

Former British Intelligence Officer

In May 2000, I spoke with a former British Intelligence Officer who operated in mid-Ulster during the period in question. He said:

> Personally, I do not believe the operation was planned and carried out by the UVF unaided. The complex nature of both operations and the intelligence required to carry them out would, I believe, have been totally beyond the capabilities of the UVF military personnel in 1974. Even the most cursory examination of the logistics required to mount such a complex and detailed attack clearly indicates that some form of outside assistance was available to those involved.

When asked if he knew of any similarities between the type of synchronised attack evidenced in Dublin and any other attack the UVF carried out at that time, he replied:

> There is no history of the UVF having carried out a similar co-ordinated attack involving such detailed planning and preparation at any time during the Troubles. The overall bombing capability of loyalist paramilitaries was nothing near that of republicans.

Finally, I asked him if he believed that the attack 'bore the hallmark of the UVF'. He replied:

> The make-up, timing devices and detonation techniques used in Dublin and Monaghan were totally different to any previous UVF bombings. They had no history of a co-ordinated series of attacks carried out within a short time scale. Nor had they a history of manufacturing an explosive device which, on detonation left little or no residue for forensic analysis.[1]

The Minimum of Scrutiny

To help evaluate the UVF claim regarding the 'minimum of scrutiny' required to reveal the similarity of the bombs used in Dublin and Monaghan to other UVF bombs, I wrote to the RUC,

---

1   On 28 December 1972, the UVF detonated three no-warning car bombs in Belturbet, County Cavan, Clones, County Monaghan, and Pettigo, County Donegal. The Belturbet bomb killed two teenagers, Geraldine O'Reilly (15) and Patrick Stanley (17). According to *The Irish Times* (29 December 1972), the Belturbet bomb exploded at 11 p.m. and the Clones bomb exploded at approximately 10 p.m. No time is given for the Pettigo explosion. It appears that these three no-warning car bombs did not have the synchronised consistency evident in the three no-warning bombs which exploded in Dublin on 17 May 1974. They were, however, delivered with the same deadly intent.

the British Army and An Garda Síochána. I asked each to provide me with the following information: a list of all loyalist bombings in Northern Ireland/the Republic of Ireland, from the start of 1969 to the end of 1975, including bombings where no fatalities occurred; a breakdown per year; a breakdown of types of explosions — car bombs/grenades, etc.; and a breakdown of those thought to be responsible — UVF/UFF/UDA/LOY, etc.

The RUC were unable to provide the required information 'in the format requested'. Instead, they sent a table of 'Security Situation Statistics', which combined loyalist and republican bombings and was of no use in analysing trends and capabilities of specific groups. I wrote again, seeking clarification. They replied:

> Your request was for information for the years 1969 to 1975 and unfortunately the information you require was not compiled for these dates.

The people I spoke to at the British Army's Northern Ireland Headquarters at Lisburn referred me back to the RUC. My e-mail to An Garda Síochána was not acknowledged. The only other option that occurred to me was to create a list of all loyalist explosions that had resulted in fatalities.

While not providing definitive answers, the list[2] does give a snapshot of UVF and loyalist bombing capabilities in the early- to mid-1970s. While the list does confirm a ruthless bomb-making capability, including the use of no-warning car bombs, there is little in this 'minimum of scrutiny' to reveal 'that the structure of the bombs placed in Dublin [in particular] [was] similar, if not identical, to those being placed in Northern Ireland on an almost daily basis' as the UVF statement of admission asserts. The question of the organisation's having received additional support and professional expertise from other sources remains a distinct possibility if not probability.

Was the UDA involved?

Quite apart from the many questions regarding the high degree of military professionalism evident in the multiple bomb attack

2   The main sources for this information are Malcolm Sutton's *Index of Deaths from the Conflict in Ireland 1969–1993* (Beyond the Pale Publications, 1994) and *Lost Lives* by David McKittrick, Seamus Kelters, Brian Feeney and Chris Thornton (Mainstream, 1999).

on Dublin on 17 May 1974, there are other questions that require attention. Should we accept without question the UVF statement that its members acted entirely alone? What of the UVF's more senior partner in the UWC strike, the Ulster Defence Association?

In their book, *UVF*, Cusack and McDonald state that 'The UDA did not have the materials or skills to carry out such an attack but it suited them to have people believe it had.'

Experts in the field of bomb disposal have argued the same regarding the UVF. The 'minimum of scrutiny' of the list of fatalities caused by loyalist bombs reveals that the UDA certainly did have bomb-making capabilities; their attacks included car bombings. As in the case of the UVF, however, there is no evidence that the UDA would have been able to mount such a synchronised bomb attack.

Given the political climate at the time, it is not beyond the bounds of possibility that both organisations co-operated in the bombing mission. In his book *The SAS in Ireland* (Mercier Press, 1990), Raymond Murray states that at the time of the Dublin and Monaghan bombings 'UVF/UDA paramilitaries in the Portadown area were quite interchangeable'.

In many respects, utterances from the UDA and their political associates were equally, if not more, hard-line than those of their UVF counterparts. William Craig was the leader of the Vanguard Unionist Progressive Party. On the eve of the bombings, interviewed on BBC Northern Ireland's *Scene around Six* news programme, Craig, who had never been shy of hinting at the need for force in achieving political ends, warned:

> The British government will have to recognise that it cannot ratify the Sunningdale Agreement or implement it in any way. If they do there will be further actions taken against the Irish Republic and those who attempt to implement it.

With the ominous threat of 'further actions' against the Republic of Ireland, the scene was set for the carnage in Dublin and Monaghan the following day.

In the immediate aftermath of the bombings, both the UVF and the UDA were suspected. Indeed, a survey of the newspapers indicates that the Ulster Defence Association was considered to have played an active role in the attack.

On 6 December 1987, the *Sunday World* published a statement from former Captain Fred Holroyd. For legal reasons it did not reveal the names that Holroyd had supplied in full. Part of the statement read:

> ... to my certain knowledge Sergeant X of the R.U.C. special branch was controlling key members of the U.D.A. and U.V.F....
>
> On one occasion while on duty with Sergeant X during a surveillance operation, he confided in me that the Portadown U.D.A./U.V.F. were responsible for the car bombs that detonated in Dublin and Monaghan.

Holroyd went on to say that three key loyalists whom he named in the statement 'were aware that their terrorist operations were being influenced by the security forces'.

The Holroyd notebooks, which are considered in Chapter Twelve, certainly indicate cross-fertilisation between the two organisations. The notebooks also state that the Garda had circumstantial evidence linking a senior northwest figure, associated with the UDA, to an earlier bomb attack on Dublin.

Albert Walker Baker

On 4 January 1986, journalist Frank Doherty wrote an exclusive article in the *Sunday World* pertaining to Albert Walker Baker, a Belfast man who was sentenced to life imprisonment in October 1973 for his involvement in the 'romper room' murder of four Catholics.

Immediately after the trial, Baker was flown to England to serve his sentence and his family too were spirited away to begin a new life across the Irish Sea. Frank Doherty tracked them down at their home near Blackpool, and the Baker family spoke openly with him. Without prompting, Doherty told me, they began to talk about the 1972 Dublin bombings. In his *Sunday World* article, Doherty quotes Baker as claiming that the cars for the 1972 Dublin bombings 'were driven from Belfast by UDA men but that the explosives and cars were supplied by a leading member of the UDA in Derry who also provided weapons and explosives for operations in Monaghan and Donegal'. Moreover, 'one of the Dublin bombers was a member of the UDA Inner Council.'

An article by journalist Brian Trench (*Hibernia*, 15 April 1977) states that, while the UDA and UVF denied responsibility for the 1974 Dublin bombings, 'a number of women, convicted for a romper room killing were later able to pressure the UDA into supporting their demand for political status by threatening to reveal the names of those involved in the Southern bomb actions'. Trench also adds weight to the UDA and north-west connection, when he claims that the bombs were 'manufactured by a Portadown man and carried by U.D.A. members from Belfast and Derry'.

The Derry Connection

On 1 October 1998 I spoke with a driver employed in 1974 by the Lough Swilly Bus Company. He had been assigned to take a group of about fifty students and teachers from the Creggan Estate in Derry, on a get-away-from-the-troubles weekend to Dublin. The group was staying at Power's Hotel on the corner of Kildare Street and Nassau Street — close to where the South Leinster Street bomb exploded.

On 17 May, the driver was sitting in the bus at 5.15 p.m., waiting to take the children swimming, when he observed a green-coloured car drive into a space on the far side of the road by the railings of Trinity College. He said he saw the driver working at something inside. Less than a minute later he got out of the car and, very carefully and gently, closed the door but didn't lock it. He looked up and down the street before making his way along South Leinster Street in the direction of the bus. As he drew level with the bus, he crossed the street, and passed directly below the window of the driver. As he did so, he glanced up and the bus driver made eye contact with him. The car driver continued to walk in the direction of Grafton Street. Minutes later, the green car exploded. The bus driver was fortunate to escape serious injury.

The bus driver gave a full statement that same evening to Garda Detective Sergeant Michael Cawley, in which he provided a detailed description of the bomber. He also assisted the gardaí in developing an identikit picture of the bomber.[3]

During my conversation with the bus driver he told me he had spotted the car bomber in Derry on two separate occasions

---

3   In researching this book, no trace could be found of that identikit picture in the papers of the time. None of the bereaved and wounded with whom I spoke could recall ever having seen such a picture either. If, as it appears, it was never released or published, the Garda Síochána must explain why such a crucial piece of evidence was withheld.

afterwards. He said that on one occasion he had seen him in a barber's shop in the Waterside district of the city. He expressed absolute confidence that the person he saw in Derry was the same person who left the bomb car on South Leinster Street on 17 May 1974. He reported the sightings to the gardaí.[4]

After the second sighting in Derry, the bus driver left the region with his family and took up residence elsewhere.

British Intelligence and the RUC

While interviewing the British Intelligence officer who operated in the mid-Ulster region in the 1970s, I asked him about possible UDA involvement in the Dublin and Monaghan mission. He spoke of 'a traditional overlap of UDA/UVF membership' in mid-Ulster and said that both groups 'joined in carrying out attacks in the infamous "murder triangle" area'. He was not aware of the same degree of overlap in the Belfast area, and thought a Derry connection unlikely.

However, just before our interview ended, the former Intelligence Officer told me about a former RUC Special Branch officer, who was based in Portadown at the time of the Dublin and Monaghan bombings and was 'running a number of the players "hands-on".' This RUC officer was 'linked to Captain Robert Nairac', again raising the spectre of security force collusion in the bombings.

Captain Robert Nairac

Nel Lister first met Robert Nairac in 1973. She had an affair with him from 1975 until his disappearance in 1977. I met her in London on 25 February 2000 where I recorded an interview.

According to Lister, Nairac unburdened himself to her when they were together. She admits to not understanding much of what she was being told at the time. Following his mysterious disappearance, however, she began a personal crusade to discover exactly what had happened to the man she claims is the father of her youngest child. Her journey of discovery has

---

4   What action the gardaí took is not known. If the South Leinster Street bomber was from Derry, there is still a reasonable chance that the Derry public might be able to identify the person in the identikit picture, which, presumably, is still in the Garda files.

caused more than a few headaches for the godfathers of British espionage. On one occasion she was beaten almost to the point of death and warned to back off. She refused.

According to Lister, the Dublin and Monaghan bombings were a very central area of concern to Robert Nairac because 'it was coming from Army Intelligence and had a political agenda'. She says that he was not involved in the bombings but that the unit to which he was attached, 14th Intelligence, was. She maintains that those involved included the OC of the 14th Intelligence unit, based at Castledillon, County Armagh, SAS Captain Tony Ball, and SAS Major Andy Nightingale. Ball and Nightingale died in an 'accident' in Oman in 1981. Lister also named Craig Smellie, the head of MI6's Northern Ireland operations between 1973 and 1975, who had a deep knowledge of cross-border activities and talked at length with Nairac, Ball and others throughout that period. Smellie, she informed me, 'met with a sudden and mysterious end in Athens in the early 1980s.' Lister later sent me documents which list one of the prime Dublin suspects, Robin 'The Jackal' Jackson, as working with the British Army's Military Reaction Force (MRF) and Ball's 14th Intelligence Unit.

All of the above is, of course, hearsay, and all of the principals named are now dead. Nevertheless, Lister's testimony is further corroboration of claims of British military involvement in the bombings. Of particular importance is her claim that Nairac led her to believe that British security force personnel were involved in the murder and mutilation of fellow European citizens on 17 May 1974.

RUC Involvement with Loyalist Paramilitaries

The second US edition of Sean McPhilemy's book *The Committee* (Roberts Rinehart, 1999) contains a signed affidavit from former RUC Sergeant, John Weir, in which he states that he was a member of the RUC prior to his conviction for the murder of William Streathearn. He says that, during his time in the RUC, he served in a specialist anti-terrorist unit. He states that many members of his unit had loyalist connections and supported the activities of loyalist paramilitaries. He says that, during the UWC strike in 1974, all members of his unit fully supported the loyalist efforts to bring down the power-sharing executive. Weir's affidavit states that he gradually realised 'that the security forces were involved in Loyalist terrorism'. He himself had several encounters with Robin 'The Jackal' Jackson. When he was transferred to another unit in Castlereagh, contact with his former colleagues was maintained. Weir states that on one occasion in 1975 he was told that 'the time had come to take direct action against not merely known Republicans or IRA activists but against the Catholic population in general'. Weir alleges that at a meeting to discuss such direct action, six RUC members were in attendance. Two of these explained in detail past activities of the group so that he fully understood the nature of the sub-group he was joining. According to Weir, one of the men, Officer A, told him about 'a farmhouse at [_____, Co. Armagh] from which they had already carried out several operations' but that the group might need to find another base as 'police officers, who were unaware that the group's activities had been authorised at a higher level, knew that the farmhouse had been used in connection with the Dublin and Monaghan bombings in 1974'. Weir further states that this man told him that the explosives for both Dublin and Monaghan 'had been provided by [name withheld], an Intelligence captain in the Ulster Defence Regiment'. Weir states that the man also confirmed the following points, some of which have also been stated by other sources:

- Billy Hanna was the main organiser of both attacks.
- The bombs were assembled at the farmhouse in Armagh owned by RUC officer _____.[5]
- Billy Hanna took part in the Dublin attack. Weir also mentions another person, who cannot be named for legal reasons.
- _____ led the attack on Monaghan.
- The Monaghan bomb-car was originally supposed to be parked outside a different pub.
- Those responsible were never questioned by the RUC.

---

5   I spoke to this man on the telephone on 2 July 2000. When I questioned him about the Dublin and Monaghan bombings, he hung up the phone.

- As the UDR Captain belonged to Army Intelligence, it is possible that both Army Intelligence and the RUC knew about the attacks in advance.

Weir claims that Officer A also told him of several other fatal attacks in which the subgroup was involved. Unedited and signed copies of Weir's statement have been made available to the Taoiseach's Department and the Garda Commissioner, Patrick Byrne.

On 12 November 1999 I met John Weir in London along with lawyers Greg O'Neill and Cormac Ó Dulacháin. While he reiterated much of what is contained in his affidavit, he also emphasised that RUC Officer A had not been directly involved in the Dublin and Monaghan bombings. Officer A was involved in other criminal activities but not directly in this operation. It was, nonetheless, Officer A who told him the details of the Dublin and Monaghan bombings which formed part of his statement.

Weir was not himself involved in the bombings and his information, therefore, is hearsay. However, he is able to impart so much detailed knowledge about personal experience of actual incidents involving collusion between known loyalist paramilitaries and serving members of the northern security sources, that it is difficult to dismiss what he says. For example, Weir told us that he himself was present at the farmyard on at least one occasion when the UDR captain brought explosives for a specific terrorist operation. If Weir was a witness to an Army Intelligence officer and UDR captain bringing explosives for a bombing mission, this in itself has huge implications. It also strengthens Weir's information, which, he says, RUC Officer A told him about the UDR captain's involvement in the Dublin and Monaghan bombings.

If, as Weir thinks possible, Army Intelligence and elements of the RUC knew in advance of the impending attacks on the Republic of Ireland, the implications are colossal and can no longer be ignored by either the British or Irish Governments.

Ourselves Alone?

As part of my research I made contact with the political representatives of the UVF in the hope of arranging a meeting with someone from the organisation. A meeting, unfortunately, did not materialise. I have been told that the UVF considers the suggestion that it needed assistance to carry out the attack as racist and sectarian. Today, the Belfast Brigade is adamant that the organisation carried out the attack completely unaided.

One leading loyalist, not associated with the UVF, but very active in 1974, spoke to me by telephone from his home on 28 June 2000. He said that it was his belief that the attack on Dublin and Monaghan had no connection with the UWC and that not a lot of thought had been put into the bombings. According to this one-time leading figure in Ulster loyalism, 'The stuff had been lying around prepared for some time on a farm belonging to an ex-B Special.' He said that the owner of the farm was worried lest the security forces would raid his farm, so the Belfast UVF agreed to remove it. In the end it was the mid-Ulster UVF who carried out the attack with no involvement from the UDA.

Whoever was responsible for the bombing, what is of far greater importance to the bereaved and wounded is transparent accountability from those whose duty it was to uphold their right to truth and justice.

The Irish Government has a duty to protect the lives of its citizens and any foreign visitors to our country. Having failed to do this, and having failed to bring the perpetrators to justice, it has a responsibility to scrutinise the reasons for those failures. In particular, it must examine the nature, extent and constitutionality of the known relationship between British Intelligence and An Garda Síochána, and must establish whether this relationship resulted in justice being compromised. It must provide an answer as to whether the right to truth of the Dublin and Monaghan bereaved and wounded suffered as a result of that relationship. The full co-operation of the British Government must be sought in examining the role of British Intelligence services in clandestine operations within the Republic of Ireland, and their collusion with known terrorists in the murder and mutilation of Irish, French and Italian citizens.

Chapter Nine: RTÉ *Prime Time*

Much to the disappointment of the Dublin and Monaghan rela-
tives, the Yorkshire documentary was never broadcast by RTÉ.
However, the contribution of RTÉ's *Prime Time* documentary,
Friendly Forces?, was crucial in applying further pressure on
the authorities to heed the call of the families for a public
Tribunal of Inquiry. The timing of the broadcast, the day after the
Department of Justice's statement outlining the Garda
Commissioner's conclusions on the Yorkshire programme, was
significant.

Just over twenty-four hours after the statement had been
faxed to RTÉ, the station's premier current affairs programme
placed the involvement of elements of British Intelligence and
the British security forces back on centre stage.

Friendly Forces?

Friendly Forces?, presented and narrated by Brendan O'Brien,
contains interviews in which official reluctance to question
loyalist suspects is alleged, and details are given of secret SAS-
type units during the 1970s. The programme, according to its
presenter, charts 'the dangerous strategy by British Intelligence
to work in conjunction with so-called loyalist "Friendly Forces"'.

The RUC turned down an invitation to appear on the *Prime
Time* documentary but issued a statement 'stressing total co-
operation with the Gardaí, impartiality and determination to
seek the culprits'.

Colonel Mike Dewar was a British Army major in Northern
Ireland in 1973 and 1974. Questioned on the programme about
the possibility of British military involvement in bombings, with

a political intent, he admits that 'on an ad hoc basis, people at a lower level might have launched attacks'. He says that, while he doesn't believe the bombings were 'crucial in altering the direction of the political process', he does think it 'conceivable they were making a political statement'. Dewar also has tough things to say about elements in the RUC Special Branch, saying that there is evidence that 'they may have even lent weapons' to loyalist paramilitaries over the years.

O'Brien gives viewers the background to the setting-up of a separate Army Intelligence system for Northern Ireland, making the British Army less reliant on RUC Special Branch. However, the Army also had 'undisciplined sections'.

Colonel Dewar discusses the 'tremendous pressure' under which the security forces in Northern Ireland were operating during the 1970s, and admits that the Army would have found assistance and information from loyalist paramilitary sources 'extremely helpful'. Brendan O'Brien comments that this has 'dangerous implications:

> With the IRA killing more and more soldiers and policemen other aspects got little attention, aspects that today raise compelling questions.

The RTÉ documentary gives details of unlawful activities concentrated on a particular Armagh farm and continues with a litany of details regarding known links between loyalist paramilitaries and the Northern Ireland security forces, all of which can be taken as evidence of 'a disturbing pattern of activities around the time of the bombs'.

O'Brien speaks of former intelligence operatives who described:

> ... a worrying pattern of activity, individual British military and RUC combining with Loyalist paramilitaries targeting IRA people but also trying to change the political agenda.

However, he admits that there is 'no proven link between that and the bombs in Dublin and Monaghan', telling viewers that men in the British military establishment are dubious of such allegations. These include Colonel Dewar who 'cannot conceive of any official sanction being given to any sort of operation like this', although he does concede the possibility 'that certain individuals might have worked independently along with renegade RUC Special Branch people in providing this sort of useful information'.

A former British secret operative in Northern Ireland was fearful of appearing on the programme but was willing to put on paper his knowledge of five secret units operating from Belfast, Newry, Derry, Castledillon in Armagh and, surprisingly, Dublin. 'Those units', the man told *Prime Time*, 'were jokingly called surveillance units. Their real job was assassination.'

As for the bombs in Dublin and Monaghan, this man told *Prime Time* that the talk among senior section leaders at British Army HQ in Northern Ireland was that it 'was done by us and carried out in conjunction with us'.

The man included in his written submission information on Derry's first specialist undercover unit, which 'took part in cross-Border events where civilian members lost their lives', and on similar units in Newry and Dublin. '*Prime Time*,' O'Brien informs viewers, 'is satisfied about the man's credentials', and the man has said that 'he would co-operate with a serious investigation by the Irish authorities.'

Castledillon in County Armagh was home to 14th Intelligence Company, which, according to *Prime Time*, has 'been associated with questionable activities involving untraceable guns and undercover operatives.' Brendan O'Brien interviews a former UDR officer whose identity is disguised. This officer claims that a man introduced to him as a military liaison officer at Castledillon, was, in fact, Captain Robert Nairac. The officer believes that Nairac was involved in 'some kind of specialist unit ... operating in the 3 Brigade area', and that the unit was 'running the Loyalist paramilitaries in mid-Ulster'. When shown a list of names, the officer says that he recognises them as those of 'the persons who were allegedly involved in the Dublin and Monaghan bombings'. He says that 'within a few weeks' of the bombings, these names were 'bandied about' in the company to which he was attached, and that, as far as he knows, none of these people were questioned in connection with the bombings. He comments on the 'minimal' reaction to the bombings, a reaction he finds 'strange'.

O'Brien reports the man as saying that he had received information on 'a named house in Portadown where the Monaghan bomb was said to have been prepared' and that the details 'were contained on an RUC file'.

In an interview with Captain Fred Holroyd, the former intelligence officer claims that a few months after the bombings, 'a Special Branch sergeant from Portadown' told him that the perpetrators of the atrocity were 'Portadown Protestants'. The sergeant went on to provide names of the people involved and details of the car they used. Holroyd's memory of the reaction in Portadown to the bombings is that 'there was no activity going on to indicate that anybody was very concerned about finding out who had done it'. When shown the list of suspects, Holroyd tells Brendan O'Brien that he recognises the names 'as those the Special Branch officer mentioned', and says that some of those named 'were very thick with the police and the SAS'. He says that since leaving Northern Ireland he has learned that some of those on the list were 'virtually controlled by us'.

Major [X]

Prime Time focuses on a bomb intelligence officer, identified only as Major [X], who is 'said to have masterminded the derailing of a train at Portadown in November 1974 as part of a pattern of explosives operations aimed at undermining the I.R.A.' This man is believed to have been connected with the Monaghan bomb, an allegation which Captain Holroyd accepts as tying in with his own experience of 'the closeness between Special Branch, S.A.S. undercover people and Protestants'. When shown Major [X]'s name, Holroyd confirms that the man named was a bomb expert who may have helped loyalists to make the Monaghan bomb.

The interview with the former UDR officer adds weight to this assertion. The officer claims to have been told that the intelligence officer named 'had been involved in other events, which had resulted in the death and mutilation of other individuals'.

While *Prime Time* admits that this does not amount to proof 'that Major [X] was involved in the Monaghan or Dublin bombs', it does connect him with 'a disturbing pattern of lethal activities at the time'. Moreover, he 'is known to have come South to make contacts.'

When invited by *Prime Time* to respond to the allegations regarding Robert Nairac and Major [X], the British Ministry of Defence described them as 'well-worn allegations, without truth, which had been thoroughly investigated'.

Brian Nelson

The *Friendly Forces?* programme goes on to show how the 'patterns of the 1970s [of co-operation between the Northern Ireland security forces and loyalist paramilitaries] continued into the 1980s'. Brian Nelson was placed by British military intelligence in the heartland of the loyalist UDA. His diary, quoted on the RTÉ documentary, contains shocking claims.

According to Nelson, he was told by 'the boss' that the UDA 'should think about carrying out a bombing campaign down South', which would put a strain on the economy of the Republic of Ireland and would 'cause the Eire Government to have a rethink about their extradition policy'. An oil refinery outside Cork was suggested as a possible target. The diary also confirms details of Nelson's part in obtaining South African arms for loyalist groups in 1987. O'Brien says: 'These arms greatly enhanced loyalist firepower.'

Prime Time connects these arms with the 1988 attack by loyalist Michael Stone on mourners at the funeral of three IRA members shot dead by the SAS in Gibraltar. Three people were killed and fifty wounded in the attack.

In his diary, Nelson claimed that one South African arms shipment was let through for his protection, 'because of the deep suspicion a seizure would have aroused'.

O'Brien informs viewers that the British Ministry of Defence denied authorising Nelson to do more than gather information for terrorist convictions. 'They made no mention of the question put about South African arms.'

The Holroyd Saga

In his interview with *Prime Time,* Fred Holroyd refers to 'an infrastructure here [in the Republic of Ireland] composed of people within the military, the police and the Government that were quite happy to have British military operatives working in the South against the I.R.A.' He says that they 'were actively helping these people who identified the targets by passing information to Commissioner Garvey, through me, back to M16'.

O'Brien informs viewers that one of Captain Holroyd's contacts was a Monaghan garda, codenamed 'The Badger'. This Garda admitted to O'Brien that he had been in contact 'with

Holroyd and five other British military operatives from 1972 to 1980'. Holroyd claims that the gardaí used to 'freeze' areas in the Republic 'so we could go in and kidnap people'. His meetings with the Badger took place 'in country lanes on the Border and ... Monaghan police station'.

Captain Holroyd feels that the evidence he gave to the Garda inquiry into the Yorkshire Television documentary was 'not taken seriously'.

Prime Time requested an interview with the Garda Commissioner about the Dublin and Monaghan bombing investigation and about Holroyd's claims. The request was turned down.

Referring to the Department of Justice statement the day before the *Prime Time* broadcast, O'Brien says:

> The Minister for Justice, in her statement yesterday, said that the Gardaí had found Holroyd's claims to be without fact. In a statement to *Prime Time* Holroyd emphatically refuted that claim.

Agent Thomas Doheny

Prime Time conducted an interview with a man who worked for the British Army in the Republic of Ireland. The man was known as Thomas Doheny, and, according to the RTÉ programme 'was reporting to Col. Williams in Northern Ireland, one of the leading intelligence officers killed in the Chinook crash off Scotland [2 June 1994]'. Doheny claims in the interview to have been 'part of a long-term covert operation'. He says that he had contact with gardaí who provided him with information, which he passed on to British Military Intelligence in Northern Ireland. Doheny, who says that some gardaí were paid for information, admits his role was to try to identify weaknesses within the Irish Army and the Garda Síochána.

When questioned by Brendan O'Brien as to the purpose of his activities, Doheny replies that the purpose was 'to abuse that system to the advantage of the security of the UK.' He says that the Irish Army officers and gardaí with whom he dealt were in no doubt as to who he was, but assisted him 'because they are very anti-IRA'. Doheny confirms that the gardaí with whom he had contact were based in border areas, specifically Monaghan.

O'Brien informs viewers:

> In a statement the British Ministry of Defence confirmed a
> relationship with Thomas Doheny but they said it was ended in
> June 1992 and that he had proved unsuitable for the role of agent.

When questioned about this, Doheny insists that anything he
did, he 'was tasked to do ... by the Intelligence Corps'. When
questioned about the attitudes of his British military handlers
in Northern Ireland and in Ashford, Kent, Doheny says that
they were 'dead-set against' the Anglo–Irish Agreement and
that they 'don't believe in the [current peace] process'. He
continues: 'I would say they would do everything in their power
to destroy it.'

Brendan O'Brien states that these claims 'must be taken
with caution but must also be tested', but says that the British
Embassy 'confirmed cross-Border activities by Doheny'.
However, he continues:

> The British authorities have decided that Doheny's story must
> not be heard in the UK. They have taken steps to ensure that
> this is not done.

Concluding the programme, reference is made to the statement
by the Minister for Justice, in which she stated that the Garda
Commissioner has decided that 'no useful purpose could be
served by any further enquiries into the Dublin and Monaghan
bombs'. Brendan O'Brien says: 'But if any of the claims in this
programme are to be truly investigated, it is a matter for the
British Government and the heads of its military agencies.'

Media Reaction

There was a dearth of media reaction to the broadcast of
Friendly Forces? Unlike with Yorkshire Television's *First Tuesday*,
no great passions were aroused.

Political Reaction

In the Dáil, no reference was made to the *Prime Time*
documentary until 8 June 1995, when Tony Gregory asked the
Minister for Justice for her response, if any, to the claims made
in the programme. Nora Owen replied that, as she had
previously stated, the files on the bombings remained open and

any leads would be 'pursued vigorously'. With regard to the *Prime Time* programme, the Minister said that the Garda authorities were 'examining' it, and that when they had concluded their examination and assessed the significance of the programme she would be in touch with the families and would report back to the TDs who had tabled the questions.

The *Prime Time* documentary was not raised again until after the summer recess. The Minister referred Deputy Ivor Callely, who had raised the issue, to her previous statements on the matter and said that the Garda examination of the programme was 'still ongoing', but that from what she had heard to date, it did not seem as if the programme had uncovered 'new evidence which could provide the basis for a criminal prosecution'.

On 29 February 1996, in a letter to Alice O'Brien, a member of the relatives committee, J. O'Dwyer, Private Secretary to the Minister for Justice, wrote:

> The Minister has now been informed by the Garda authorities that they are satisfied from their assessment of the contents of the broadcast that no new evidence or witness has been identified which would provide a basis for further Garda investigation. The Minister has asked me to express her regret that she is unable to convey a more positive outcome to the Garda assessment. She has asked me to again assure you that the Garda investigation file remains open and that any new leads will be actively pursued.

In the Dáil Debates of 15 May 1996, almost a year after the *Prime Time* broadcast, the programme was raised again, this time by Deputies Mary Harney and Michael McDowell, who requested the Minister to make a statement on the programme, the Garda investigation and whether the matter was now closed.

The Minister for Justice replied that a letter had been written to the relatives of victims and to other members of the House. She then outlined the main content of the letter received by Alice O'Brien in February, and repeated that the files remained open.

There was no reference to the serious issue of the claims of cross-border covert operations by British Military Intelligence and the threat that such operations might potentially pose to the political development of the Anglo–Irish Agreement and the emerging peace process. Serious issues of national security, territorial integrity and unconstitutional activities of State forces had been raised in both the RTÉ *Prime Time* programme and Yorkshire Television's *First Tuesday* programme, yet the response from Dáil Éireann was muted, minimal and, by and large, worryingly disinterested.

Statement of Former British Secret Operative

Prime Time made available to me a copy of a statement of a former British Secret Operative which was written for inclusion in the *Friendly Forces?* documentary. Of particular note are the following points from the statement:

- A nine-member unit of SAS operatives was sent to Derry in early 1974; it also 'took part in several cross-border events'.

- In early 1974, a similar unit was sent to Dublin. The Dublin unit, he states, consisted of twelve men, with an unknown back-up, reduced to nine men a year later.

- The statement alleges that, on at least one specific occasion, the Dublin unit, together with other similar units, 'reported back direct to Whitehall, without intermediate contact.'

- The Dublin unit was uncapped. 'They were allegedly always armed with their own issue equipment.

- The former British Secret Operative named a British Army officer, who was located on the first floor in Lisburn [NIHQ] and 'was responsible for co-ordinating some of the cross-border operations. Believed to be involved directly in Dublin operations....'

According to RTÉ's *Prime Time*, the man has stated that he would be willing to 'co-operate with a serious investigation by the Irish authorities'. The implications of his statement, if true, are serious and worrying.

The statement indicates that at the time of the Dublin and Monaghan bombings, a fully armed plain-clothes unit of trained SAS soldiers was operating in Ireland's capital city. The Irish people, through their government, have the right to demand an explanation from the British Government. Who sanctioned this SAS unit? What was its function? Specifically, what were its tasks and movements prior to 17 May 1974, and immediately after the multiple bomb attack in Dublin and Monaghan? What was its relationship with the British Embassy in Dublin? Were members of the British Diplomatic Corps part of its back-up? It must be noted that the secret operative states that on at least one occasion this unit reported directly to Whitehall.

If the Irish Government seriously intends to assist its own citizens in finding the truth about the unsolved murder of their loved ones, it will require the assistance of the British Government. There are enough well-founded suspicions of involvement by British military operatives in the 1972, 1973 and 1974 Dublin bombings, amongst others, to warrant an official request for assistance.

Chapter Ten: Forensics

The manner in which the bomb debris from all four bomb-sites was handled is disturbing. Based on the lack of information I have received from the Garda Commissioner, it is difficult not to suspect that the debris can no longer be located, in which case the Garda authorities will need to have a very good explanation.

In 1999, there was much consternation at the revelation that the British Army had systematically destroyed several weapons used in the Bloody Sunday massacre. The possible disposal of the bomb debris from the Dublin and Monaghan bombings must be viewed in an equally serious light. The disposal, or loss, of this crucial evidence adds weight to the cry for a public tribunal of inquiry into the Irish State's handling of the entire investigation.

On the Sunday following the broadcast of Yorkshire Television's *Hidden Hand: The Forgotten Massacre*, journalist Frank Doherty reported in the *Sunday Business Post* (11 July 1993) that former Garda Commissioner Edmund Garvey had instructed that the forensic evidence relating to the Dublin and Monaghan bombings be 'handed over to the British officers who are now suspected of planning the bombs.' He cited a retired 'senior Irish military intelligence officer' and a serving Garda detective superintendent as sources for the information.

Doherty goes on to say that informed sources had told him that the Garda information on the bombings was given in good faith to a British intelligence officer who helped mastermind the bomb plot. 'The officer,' writes Doherty, 'who is still serving in the British army at very high rank, is known to the Gardaí and to Irish army intelligence.' He went on to say that the officer, who had since been decorated, had visited the Republic 'in plain clothes but bearing arms, and attempted to recruit at least one member of the Irish security forces to work for British intelligence'.

On 4 April 1999, in a follow-up article in the *Sunday Business Post*, Doherty writes that new information from reliable sources in Britain and Ireland indicated that crucial scenes-of-crime forensic material was given to RUC Special Branch officers by garda detectives acting on orders from a high level in Dublin. Doherty also states that the RUC Special Branch gave the material to a British Military Intelligence man later identified by G2 (Irish Military Intelligence) officers as the man thought to have planned the attacks. Crucially, Doherty states, 'He had control of the evidence for a number of days.'

This raises not only the question of the present whereabouts of the bomb debris, but also the issue of a chain of custody from the time of the explosions to the present day — in particular, a chain of custody for the period between the time the selected samples of debris left Dublin and the time they arrived at the Northern Ireland Department of Industrial and Forensic Science for analysis by Dr R.A. Hall. The debris was not delivered until 28 May, a full eleven days after the explosions, a fact of which Dr Hall is critical in his report.

Doherty claims that the forensic material from Dublin was sent initially to a secret intelligence facility at Sprucefield near Lisburn. 'It was here that the man believed to be the mastermind behind the bombings had control of it.'

Towards the end of 1998, when I obtained forensic documents related to the explosions, including Dr Hall's report, I discovered that samples of bomb debris from all four bomb sites (Parnell Street, Talbot Street, South Leinster Street and Monaghan Town) were delivered to Belfast by the Garda Síochána, but only some fragments of the Parnell Street explosion were taken to the Irish State Laboratory in Dublin, to be analysed by Dr James Donovan.

Dr James Donovan and the Irish State Laboratory

On 28 January 1999, I interviewed a retired Garda who was a senior officer-in-charge in 1974. I was curious as to why crucial criminal evidence was allowed to leave this jurisdiction. I asked him specifically why the forensic evidence had been sent to

Belfast. While this officer was not involved in the decision to send the material to Belfast, his assumption was as follows:

> Dr Donovan was an excellent forensic scientist. He may have decided to do so for a couple of reasons: for double confirmation or because the RUC had specialised equipment.

This assumption was in my head when I interviewed Dr Donovan, now Director of the Garda's Forensic Laboratory, at Garda Headquarters, on 24 March 1999. (An edited transcript of that interview, which I recorded, is included in Appendix 1.) I was taken aback when Dr Donovan informed me that he had not been consulted about sending the debris to Belfast and that the decision had been taken independently of him.

According to Dr Donovan, he believed that the State Laboratory was competent and experienced enough to do the analysis and admitted to having felt 'shunned in that there we were able to do something and that something was whipped away from us to another jurisdiction'. He agreed that he found it strange that the debris had been sent north, and he wondered why it had been.

I then questioned Dr Donovan regarding alternatives to the Belfast Laboratory, given the natural distrust which may have existed. His response was quite unequivocal:

> Look, it happened here in our jurisdiction. There is no reason whatsoever for it to go anywhere else other than to stay in this jurisdiction. We can do it and we have done it in the past.

He insisted that the State Laboratory could have carried out a competent analysis in 1974.

Having discussed briefly the small particles of bomb debris which he received from the Parnell Street explosion, Dr Donovan revealed that he knew 'nothing whatsoever about what was sent to Belfast' and that he had never received a copy of Dr Hall's report. When I expressed surprise and amazement at this, Dr Donovan said that for him to have received a copy of the report and for his opinion to have been sought 'would be the normal thing.... Anybody reasonable would think that that should be done'.

On 30 March 1999, I delivered a copy of Dr Hall's forensic report on the bomb debris from the Dublin and Monaghan bombings to Dr James Donovan at Garda Headquarters. In an interview with RTÉ radio, around the time of the twenty-fifth anniversary of the bombings, Dr Donovan confirmed that I had given Dr Hall's report to him, and that it was the first time, in almost twenty-five years, that he had actually seen it.

Dr Donovan's Forensic Report

On 20 May 1974, Dr James Donovan received from Detective Garda Ted Jones (Garda Ballistic Squad) at the State Laboratory in Dublin, 'samples connected with the explosion at Parnell Street Upper'.

These samples were: 'Polythene bag containing five pieces of foam rubber; burned and charred white leatherette-piece; and scrapings from car used to contain bomb.' In his report, dated 23 May 1974, he states that he detected traces of ammonium, sodium nitrate and nitroglycerine. Microscopic examination of the car scrapings revealed 'the presence of two blackened prilles of ammonium nitrate'. Dr Donovan concluded: 'The results suggest the use of gelignite/dynamite as the explosive substance.'

On 23 May, Detective Garda Jones again visited Dr Donovan and brought him further samples 'connected with the explosion'. These samples were: 'Pieces of foam rubber; Pieces of jute carpeting; Pieces of tyre and scrapings from car used to contain bomb.' Dr Donovan produced a second report based on his analysis of this debris, dated 28 May 1974. He detected in the foam rubber 'a positive reaction for chemicals normally found in gelignite'; in the pieces of tyre 'very faint traces of ammonium nitrate and sodium nitrate'; and in the car scrapings 'sodium carbonate, nitrate and ammonium'. He found that the pieces of carpeting were 'too dirty to give any type of reliable results'. He noted that the chemicals detected 'are normally found in high explosives'.

Mr R.A. Hall's Forensic Report

On 28 May 1974, the date when Dr Donovan had concluded his second report, the Department of Industrial and Forensic Science, Belfast, received, in total, six bomb debris items connected with the Dublin and Monaghan bombings. The items of debris were analysed by Mr R.A. Hall, whose report is dated 5 June 1974. The report names a Detective Garda as having been involved in their delivery. It is my understanding that this garda denies any such involvement.

Dr Hall's report notes delivery of the following: Talbot Street: 1 item; Parnell Street: 1 item; South Leinster Street: 1 item; Monaghan Town: 3 items.

The Talbot Street 'item' consisted of the following: '... a number of twisted and torn fragments of sheet metal; part of a door lock and a suspension unit.' The Parnell Street 'item' consisted of '... a number of twisted and torn fragments of sheet steel ... and several fragments of foam rubber.' The South Leinster Street 'item' consisted of '... a number of twisted and torn fragments of sheet steel painted metallic blue.' And the 'items' from Monaghan consisted of 'Item 1: a number of twisted and torn fragments of sheet steel ... and a green painted headlamp rim.... Item 2: several fragments of foam rubber.... Item 3: seven fragments of twisted and torn aluminium and part of a clock cog wheel....'

Dr Hall's three-page report criticises the eleven-day time lapse between the explosions and delivery of the bomb debris to his laboratory for analysis. He writes in his conclusion:

> It has been my experience that identification of the explosive used ... can be achieved in the majority of instances providing the correct samples are received for laboratory examination within 6 hours.... [R]apid analysis ... is essential if the more volatile organic explosive components such as nitrobenzene and the nitrate esters are to be detected.... In the case of inorganic components speed is not so necessary, however items should be analysed within a few days if success is to be assured.... The results of the laboratory examination of the items from Detective Garda Jones must be viewed with these points in mind.

Dr Hall's reason for considering it necessary to make this statement must be the fact that his analysis rendered little by way of additional forensic evidence. His report is useful primarily because it raises questions regarding the competence and decision-making mechanisms within An Garda Síochána at the time, in particular, the Garda Ballistic Squad. Indeed, it is perhaps significant that Dr Hall thought it necessary to outline in his report to the gardaí what correct bomb debris samples are: '...[1] fragments of the bomb container or closely associated articles, [2] non-porous surfaces in direct line with the explosion or [3] debris from an explosion crater'.

Results of his laboratory analysis on the items allegedly supplied by the Garda Síochána are as follows:

Talbot Street: 'Examination for nitroglycerine ethylene glycer dinitrate, nitre arematics, ammonium, nitrate, nitrite, chlorate, chlorite, chloride and sugar all proved negative. The presence of oily deposits on the fragments made the examination for fuel oil invalid.'

Parnell Street: 'Examination of the sheet steel revealed no explosive residues. The only significant feature in the foam rubber was the presence of small quantities of nitrite.'

South Leinster Street: 'Examination revealed the presence of a discrete area on which sodium, ammonium, nitrate, and nitrate ions were detected and the presence of sugar strongly indicated but not confirmed. No other explosive residues were detected.'

Monaghan: 'Item 1 ... A similar examination to [the Talbot Street debris] was carried out with similar results. Item 2 ... no explosive residues were detected.... Item 3 ... No explosive residues were detected....'

Crater Analysis

Commandant Denis Boyle of the Irish Army's Explosives Ordnance Disposal (EOD) carried out crater analysis, but no debris from the bomb craters was supplied to either Dr Donovan or Mr Hall for forensic analysis. Why this was so requires an explanation.

Yorkshire Television's summary notes of their forensic investigation states:

> Commandant Boyle did the 'crater analysis' at the request of the Garda after the bombings.
>
> He visited the scenes of all three car bombs in Dublin and estimated that 150lb of explosives were used in the Talbot Street blast, 100lb in Parnell Street and 50lb in South Leinster Street. He also went to Monaghan and estimated that 150lb were used in that bomb.
>
> In a memo to the Garda, he said he was satisfied that the explosive used in each case was of a 'high-velocity detonating type, based on nitroglycerine and not ammonium nitrate'. In all probability, he said, it was a commercial explosive used for blasting. The possibility of plastic explosives could not be ruled out, though it was unlikely [since] this would not be readily available because of military protection.
>
> Commandant Boyle summarized the bombs as below:
>
> South Leinster Street — 50lb of explosives, mainly commercial in nature.

Crater size in South Leinster Street was 6ft x 3ft, 2 inches deep.

Parnell Street — 100 lbs, with a crater 6ft x 3ft, 2 inches deep. A shop 10ft away was virtually demolished. Glass was smashed 250 yards around.

Talbot Street — 150 lbs, with a crater 8ft x 4ft, 9 inches deep. Glass broken 250 yards around.

Commandant Boyle said he believed gelignite was the likeliest component, 'and probably the only component'. He does not attempt to dissect the various chemical components.

... according to the Department of Defence ... there was a 'complete detonation of all the constituents of the bombs. Very little was left, which was unusual because bombs that are made up by amateurs would normally have bits and pieces left behind'.

New York Bomb Squad

On 1 December 1998, I met with Ken Dudonis, a former member of the New York Police Department's bomb squad. We discussed Dr Hall's forensic report (I didn't have Dr Donovan's at that point) and Yorkshire Television's forensic summary. As a former police officer who understood the importance of securing and preserving the integrity of criminal evidence, Dudonis advised me to seek clarification from An Garda Síochána concerning the physical evidence from the 1974 explosions. He also recommended that I ask if they could establish a chain of custody for the evidence.

Significantly, near the end of our meeting, having pondered the details before him, Dudonis made an off-the-cuff remark which I believe to be insightful. He said, 'You really need to speak with a military bomb expert.' It was clear to the former NYPD bomb squad member that the Dublin bombings in particular were the work not of amateurs, but of highly trained tacticians, skilled in both preparing explosives and working with sensitive synchronised timing mechanisms. He said he would give me the name of a military bomb expert.

I wrote to Garda Headquarters on 26 January 1999 asking the following questions:

— Can you confirm that the bomb debris evidence of the Dublin/Monaghan bombs which was sent to Belfast for forensic analysis is still in the possession of the Irish security forces?

— Is it possible to establish a chain of custody of that evidence from the time of the explosions until the present day?

On 16 February, Inspector Simon O'Connor of the Garda Press Office called to say that the man dealing with Dublin/Monaghan was away for several weeks in Australia. He said that as soon as he came back he would discuss my letter with him and reply. It was not until 21 April, after several follow-up phone calls that I received an answer to my questions.

On 18 April 1999, I was pondering how other police forces would deal with bomb debris. I called the New York Police Department's bomb squad and asked Sergeant Jack Lanagan whether the NYPD would keep bomb debris for twenty-five years. He asked whether there had been injuries or fatalities in the case to which I was referring. I replied that there had been. He asked had anyone been apprehended or convicted. I replied in the negative. 'So it's still an open murder inquiry?' he asked. I replied that it was. 'You keep the evidence!' was his definitive response.

Sergeant Lanagan also informed me that the NYPD now have what they call a 'Cold Case Squad', assigned the task of going back over old unsolved cases, with the benefit of today's advances in scientific technology.

I had been continuing to call the Garda Press Office for an answer on the issue of the whereabouts of the bomb debris and a chain of custody. On 20 April 1999, I spoke with Inspector Simon O'Connor, who apologised profusely, saying he had been away. I told him that I had checked with another police force who had assured me that the debris would be kept in the case of an open murder investigation. He agreed. I asked him whether the Garda had the debris and he promised to get back to me within twenty-four hours.

True to his word, the following afternoon, Inspector Simon O'Connor called me on behalf of the Commissioner, Patrick Byrne, with an answer to my questions. It was as follows:

> In the Supreme Court Judgement (*Patrick Doyle v. the Commissioner*) 1998, it was held that it was of paramount importance that the information gathered by An Garda Síochána in the course of a criminal investigation should remain confidential. So, therefore, the information cannot be released.

All that I had asked of An Garda Síochána was: 'Do you have the debris and can you establish a chain of custody?' The simple and reassuring answer 'Yes' would surely not prejudice any case the Garda might be establishing. I could only conclude that the Garda did not have the debris.

I asked Dr James Donovan whether he knew if the bomb debris was in the custody of the Irish authorities. He said he didn't know, but assumed that it was still in Belfast. When I asked him why, he replied that it would be 'the norm' that the Northern Irish authorities 'would retain custody of anything that came into their possession'. The discussion continued:

DM: But it is the property of the Irish State.

JD: Is it?

DM: It should be.

JD: The Irish State hasn't taken too much interest in it.

In response to a UK Parliamentary Question (953) raised by Kevin McNamara, MP, concerning the whereabouts of the bomb debris related to the Dublin and Monaghan Bombings, Mr R W Adams of the Forensic Science Agency of Northern Ireland wrote to him on 19 October 1999 as follows:

> Items relating to the above incidents were received from the Garda Síochána at the laboratory in Belfast on 28 May 1974. No weight was recorded for them.
> There are no records available in the laboratory in relation to the internal continuity of the items or to their ultimate fate. The presumption is that they were returned to the Garda in line with normal practice for items received from the police.

A real and serious mystery surrounds the ultimate fate of crucial evidence relating to the biggest mass-murder case in the history of the Republic of Ireland, a case still unsolved. Where is the forensic evidence? If it is nowhere to be found, who got rid of it and why?

The Irish Times

The *Irish Times* Security Correspondent, Jim Cusack, stated in an article on 26 June 1999:

> *The Irish Times* has learned ... that key forensic evidence relating to the timing mechanisms used in the bombs links them

directly to dozens of other identical bombs used by loyalists in the 1970s.

Cusack goes on to say that 'no official forensic evidence has ever emerged about the timing and detonating mechanisms' used in the Dublin and Monaghan bombings. Crucially, he continues:

> ... both police and loyalist sources have confirmed that the timing mechanisms in the Dublin and Monaghan bombs were identical to those used in many other bombings carried out by loyalists in Northern Ireland.

If the 'key forensic evidence' to which Cusack refers exists, why was it not forwarded in 1974 to the Irish State Laboratory and the Department of Industrial and Forensic Science, Belfast, for analysis? If, on the other hand, the evidence does not exist, on what basis can 'police sources', in particular, confirm anything? The fact that 'no official forensic evidence has ever emerged' would seem to point to the non-existence or removal of such evidence.

It would appear that some evidence produced from the Monaghan explosion is being construed to suggest that the make-up of all four bombs and timing mechanisms were one and the same. Aluminium, consistent with explosives having been packed into a milk churn or beer keg, and a clock cog wheel were, allegedly, recovered from the scene of the Monaghan bombing. Despite their close proximity to the explosion, neither the aluminium nor the cog wheel revealed any evidence of explosive residue.

No torn or twisted pieces of aluminium nor any piece of a timing mechanism were made available for forensic analysis from any of the three Dublin bomb-sites. It seems reasonable to conclude, therefore, that these bombs may have been prepared and constructed differently. The 1993 UVF statement of admission clearly links Dublin and Monaghan as part of a centralised operation. While it has been assumed that Monaghan was a diversionary attack to facilitate the safe return to Northern Ireland of the Dublin bombers, it might also have served a second purpose — to contribute to the assumption that the three Dublin explosions were similar in design and construction. It would be a mistake to jump to that conclusion, especially since the available evidence does not support it.

Furthermore, those responsible for the forensic integrity of the respective bomb-sites must also explain why three items from the Monaghan bomb-site were sent to Belfast for analysis, while only one item from each of the Dublin bomb-sites was sent. Who made this decision and on what basis was it arrived at? People were likely to conclude that in their construction and detonation, the three Dublin bombs were similar, if not identical, to the Monaghan bomb which (based on the aluminium and part of a clock wheel allegedly recovered) did resemble a typical loyalist bomb of the period. But the Dublin bombs did not. Surely they required equal if not more serious analysis?

Jock Clocks

The *Irish Times* journalist describes the mechanisms allegedly used. He quotes 'sources close to the UVF leadership at the time' as providing information on the timer, which, he says, was an alarm clock with 'the brand name "Jock Clock"'. I consulted with various sources including watchmakers in Ireland and Scotland. None had ever heard of such a brand name. I also checked with former bomb-disposal experts who operated in the early 1970s. They too had never heard of a 'Jock Clock'. Commandant Patrick Trears suggested that it might be a name given to a device made by a particular individual. My loyalist source in the mid-Ulster region finally confirmed that a 'Jock Clock' was a name given to a mechanism devised by a Scottish loyalist with bomb-making skills.

I was informed that the so-called 'jock-clock' is a basic clock mechanism complete with face and hands. A cardboard disc, with a hole punched through it, is placed over the dial and secured. A match with a metal foil head is placed through the hole and secured to the minute hand on the clock face. The other components — battery/batteries, wire and metal contact — are taped to the timing device itself. The time-scale for the device is a maximum of 60 minutes to 24 hours, depending on which hand is used. My contact described it as 'a very simple and crude device with very dangerous possibilities for those individuals handling it.' He continued:

> I have grave reservations as to its potential to carry out effectively and efficiently the operation which we are currently discussing.

In the course of my research of 'Jock Clocks', I had been consulting with bomb-disposal expert Ken Dudonis in New York. On 1 March 2000, I e-mailed him:

> I've tried to find information on the website you suggested regarding Jock Clocks and cannot find them.
>
> In your last e-mail you made reference to 'Pieces that should have been found would be the main spring which has great resiliency and easily identified in post blast examination'. Does it surprise you that in all three cases, no such piece was found?

Dudonis responded that evening:

> I would think that for an examination of all scenes to turn up no timing devices — unless a 'Jock-clock' is a small wristwatch type time mechanism — is sort of odd.

Mechanisms used in Loyalist Bombs

Jim Cusack describes in detail the mechanism usually used in loyalist bombs of the period, explaining that in the case of the Dublin bombs the wire comprising the detonating circuit was probably attached to the minute hand of the clock face, as this would give the bombers time to get back across the border. According to Cusack's UVF source, the 'usual' UVF bombs of this time contained identical detonating and timing mechanisms. He says that the only difference between the bombs used in Dublin and Monaghan and those used in UVF bomb attacks in Northern Ireland was that they 'contained a much higher level of commercial explosives because this ... was a "special" job.' The UVF tended to use fertiliser mixes in bombs because 'commercial explosive was almost always in short supply'.

It is also the case, however, that Irish and British ordnance officers, active on both sides of the Irish border in the 1970s, had stated clearly and independently that the multiple bomb attack on Dublin on 17 May 1974 was far from 'usual' or 'familiar' to them. The synchronised timing devices and the efficiency of the detonations bore the hallmark of a level of professionalism they were unfamiliar with in the 'usual' UVF bombs.

Dr James Donovan

As already stated, I met Dr James Donovan on 24 March 1999, in his office at the Forensic Science Laboratory, run by the

Department of Justice, Equality and Law Reform, located in the grounds of Garda Headquarters, Phoenix Park, Dublin.

Dr Donovan has been a faithful servant of the Irish State over a long and distinguished career. He has survived two attempts on his life by one of Dublin's criminal underworld gangs led by the late Martin Cahill, known as 'The General'. He was lucky to survive the second attack in January 1982. Despite intense pain in the immediate aftermath of the attack, which has continued throughout the intervening years, Dr Donovan returned to the forensic laboratory, where the level of professionalism now apparent owes much to his vision.

In my interview with him (see Appendix 1), Dr Donovan was forthright and compellingly honest. Regarding the Belfast Forensic Report and the Garda investigation into the Dublin and Monaghan bombings he expressed surprise at never having been given a copy of the Belfast Forensic Report or consulted about its contents. He said that throughout the twenty-five years he has felt that he must have found something which nobody else wanted to hear. He 'assumed that somewhere there was an investigation' into the bombings, yet he was never interviewed or questioned, although his forensic analysis did find something. He said that for a scientist to be left out of the equation entirely was very strange. According to Dr Donovan, on one occasion he attempted to raise the Dublin and Monaghan bombings with Dr Hall — who did the forensic analysis of the bomb debris in Belfast, and with whom he was well acquainted — but was, he says, 'rebuffed'.

Concerning the vexed issued of the bomb debris, Dr Donovan said that it was his opinion that the State Laboratory could have adequately carried out the forensic analysis in 1974. However, he believes that there were members of An Garda Síochána who lacked faith in the emerging abilities of their own forensic scientists. He was aware of a disagreement within An Garda Síochána about where to send the bomb debris from the bombings. Dr Donovan considered the delay in getting debris from the bomb-sites to the Belfast Laboratory to be 'strange', given the close contact between the gardaí and 'the people in Northern Ireland'. He was critical of the Irish State which had shown little interest in this crucial criminal evidence.

Dr Donovan was scathing in his criticism of forensic evidence being sent outside the jurisdiction of the Republic, and reveals having had to resist persistent efforts by the Northern Ireland forensic laboratory to obtain the forensic evidence from several crimes in the Republic, the most notable being Lord Mountbatten's murder in 1979. He said that his resistance had led to complaints being made to the Department of Justice.

He referred to the relationship between the Garda Síochána and the RUC as being 'quite unique'. It was his belief that the RUC had a regular tactic of bringing gardaí north to get them drunk, in order to get information from them. He described being taken on one occasion by gardaí to a 'semi-military' firearms place where 'everyone was great friends'. He said that a member of An Garda Síochána told him that the technical know-how of a particular UVF bomb group came from a recently discharged member of the British Army, whom the garda named.

Legal Opinion

I asked a US lawyer, Arthur J. McCabe, to read Dr Donovan's interview and give me his observations regarding the content of what the encounter reveals. He responded as follows:

> In the case of a bombing at single or multiple sites, the single most important factor involved is getting control of, and restricting access to, the crime scene. This is to minimize or eliminate the possibility of contamination or deterioration of evidence.... It does not appear that any ... uniform crime scene security measures were employed in the aftermath of the 1974 bombings.... The next most critical element in an investigatory procedure is preserving the chain of custody of evidence gathered and the preservation of the evidence once within the chain. Defence attorneys can easily discredit even the best technical evidence if the integrity of control of the evidence cannot be established without doubt during the investigatory process.
>
> In this case, it would appear that there was no one office or individual responsible for assembling and inventorying all of the evidence and directing its evaluation. Accordingly, different pieces of evidence, some of which may have come from the same crime scene, were sent to different places to be evaluated by different people pursuant to different procedures. This ruins the sanctity of the chain of custody and significantly taints any investigation.... [T]o the extent external help was required ... it should have included direct Garda participation so that the level of in-house expertise and experience was enhanced for the future. In this case, it appears that significant portions of the control and direction of the investigation and, in fact, critical

pieces of evidence were unilaterally turned over to the British....
[G]iven the political situation at the time, there was obviously
an apparent political bias which would be subject to attack in
any criminal prosecution.

Furthermore, it does not appear in this case that the British
were in any way held accountable or responsible for the evidence
turned over to them, nor were proper follow-up reports received....
[T]here should have been a procedure by which a core team of
investigators with complementary skills and experience was
established as part of the investigation process. This would ...
provide a mechanism for insuring uniformity of investigatory
procedure, and awareness of that procedure by team members....

Finally, the inter-departmental and inter-agency competitive
spirit reflected in the communication between the Garda and
security forces in the North are unfortunately typical of police and
security forces all over the world.... However, given the political
environment in Ireland and Britain in 1974, it is inconceivable to
me that the Irish government had not established and strictly
enforced guidelines as to how and when even social encounters
between departments and agencies would occur. Such un-
monitored fraternization, as reflected in Dr. Donovan's interview,
so compromised the integrity and professionalism of the Gardai
that breaches ... should have been dealt with as a disciplinary
matter.... Not only did such fraternization seriously impair the
integrity of the investigation with regard to the hope for eventual
prosecution of the perpetrators, it also tainted the entire political
process and independence of the Irish state.

Sergeant Major Ed Komac, US Army (Retired)

The former NYPD Bomb Squad detective, Ken Dudonis,
recommended that I meet with Ed Komac, a retired US Army
sergeant major, who had served in the military from 1955 to
1986, including terms in Vietnam, Laos and Cambodia. From
1972 to 1986 Komac, a highly trained explosives expert, worked
in Explosive Ordnance Disposal (EOD). Since his retirement
from the military, he has worked as a civilian EOD expert.

When he examined Dr Hall's forensic report, Sergeant Major
Komac asked, 'Is this all the bomb debris that was collected?
Did they only find one clock cog wheel?' Having considered
various aspects of the incident, he commented:

> To get three bombs to detonate inside 90 seconds is either very
> lucky or very professional. To get three bombs to detonate with
> 100 per cent efficiency is either very lucky or very professional.
> To get three bombs to go off inside 90 seconds and detonate with

maximum efficiency, you would be measuring luck in the realms of the lottery.

On 17 February 2000, I sent Komac a collection of documents for an opinion.[1] I requested his independent assessment. On 15 May 2000, he sent the following response:

Type and Quantity of Bomb Debris Delivered for Analysis

When I received the information on the bombings the first thing I noticed was the lack of forensic evidence that was recovered and forwarded for analysis. I would have thought that with all the bombings that were taking place in the north and the south since 1969 that by 1974 a firm system for search and recovery of forensic evidence would have been developed.

It seems that from the four bombs that were detonated the only 'hard' forensic evidence recovered 'consisted of seven fragments of twisted and torn aluminum and part of a clock cog wheel' (Item 3 from the Monaghan Town bomb, which was separate from the other three bombs). It can be assumed someone else was in charge of collecting forensic evidence from this bombsite, but the amount of debris delivered for forensic analysis, even from this site, leaves much to be desired in the amount recovered.

I was involved in an investigation following a detonation that killed three people in the Kansas City Army Ammunition Plant that was manufacturing a submunition for our company. The complete submunition detonated. We recovered enough of the fuse components, mainly the arming stem to be able to tell what caused the detonation. This was just from one item. I find it puzzling that with the three Dublin car bombs, no forensic evidence was found of any timing devices.

Delay in Delivering the Bomb Debris for Forensic Analysis

I have no idea on how the Irish system works regarding the forwarding of forensic evidence for analysis. In my opinion the delay in delivering the evidence would allow some person or

---

1   These documents included: Forensic Reports of Dr James Donovan (23/28 May 1974); Forensic Report of R.A. Hall (5 June 1974); summary notes of Yorkshire TV forensic investigation (1993); transcript of YTV *Hidden Hand: The Forgotten Massacre*, dealing with forensic aspects of explosions (broadcast 6 July 1993); Jim Cusack and Henry McDonald, *UVF*, pp. 132–136 (Poolbeg Press, 1997); extract from Don Mullan, 'Endgame?', *Magill*, May 1999, dealing with forensics and interview with Dr James Donovan; Jim Cusack, 'Evidence links timers to bombs used by loyalists', *The Irish Times*, 26 June 1999; and Frank Doherty, 'Dublin bombings: new revelations', *Sunday Business Post*, 4 April 1999.

persons to sterilize (remove) any evidence of timing devices that could be traced to a certain group or faction.

You state that the Irish police have refused to inform you whether or not they can establish a chain of custody from the time of the explosions to this day. If there is no chain of custody, this bolsters my theory that someone could have sterilized the evidence.

With all the attention that would be focused on something of this nature, I would have thought that there would be a sense of urgency to find out who was involved and there would not be an eleven-day period before the evidence would be forwarded for analysis. Once again, this time delay would facilitate the removing of any evidence that would incriminate a certain group or faction.

Dublin Bombs

The impression being put forth concerning the Dublin bombs is that these were standard Improvised Explosive Devices (IED) with the tried and true timing devices, off the shelf clocks. I will go along with the idea that the explosives used were improvised, the reason for this assumption is because if you are going to place blame on one group or another, why not use something that has been used time and again by either group.

What I find very hard to believe is that the three bombs all detonated within 90 seconds by using the so-called 'Jock Clock'. There are just too many variables in mechanical timers. If these bombs were set off using 'Jock Clocks' how come not one piece of them was found at any of the three sites? Did a trained bomb disposal officer oversee the collection of forensic evidence? If one did, I find it hard to believe that he would overlook parts of a timing device at all three sites.

There are a variety of specialized timing devices that could have been used to set off the bombs in Dublin within 90 seconds and not leave any evidence. The main source of these devices anywhere in the world is the military.

Monaghan Town Bomb

This was a diversionary bomb. It was set to draw attention to the site, which would allow people who wanted to cross the border to do so. What is remarkable is that no explosive residues were detected from the evidence that was turned in for forensic analysis, even from the parts of the clock cog wheel recovered.

Most timing devices are placed in close proximity of the explosives or right on them and would show some evidence of explosive residue. The cogwheel could have come from a secondary source — the site itself and not from a timing device, since no explosive residue was found. This could give credence to my theory of a military type firing device which would be destroyed in the detonation. This device may have been set off by remote control.

A Military Operation

Having considered the documentation you forwarded to me, I have formed the opinion that this operation appears to be a military organized one.

I am of the opinion that an operation of this nature would require 20 men to carry it out. The reasons why I believe this was a military run operation are as follows:

- The organization and planning of the operation; the expertise evident in the building and detonation of the bombs; the delivery of the devices to each location (it takes a lot of nerve to drive around with over a hundred pounds of improvised explosives).

- With regard to the arming of the timing devices, you may be able to find one or two individuals who have enough nerve to arm a clockwork-timing device. However, to find three people to put their trust in arming clockwork-timing devices I find hard to believe. Think about it: you are parked on a street with over a hundred pounds of improvised explosives with people walking by. There are at a minimum a couple of connections you must make to arm the bomb.

- I understand that the eyewitness to the South Leinster Street bomb car has said the driver exited the car in less than a minute. This is one of the reasons why I do not believe the bombs were detonated by a clockwork-firing device.

- If you were arming a clockwork device that is supposed to go off within 30 seconds before or after two other bombs, how much faith would you place in the other people doing the arming of their bombs? However, with the military firing devices available, their reliability, and the ease in arming them, again points to a military operation.

- It is a known fact that people will talk. One side or the other has infiltrated all of these organizations. From the information available to me, it appears that no one involved in the operation has talked about it. I still haven't talked about some of the operational missions I did in Laos, since it is still classified over thirty years later. Military personnel that undertake operations of this nature are the types who do not talk. Of course, there are exceptions to the rule.

Former Sergeant Major Ed Komac has assembled a team of bomb experts who are prepared to fly to Ireland at their own expense to examine the bomb debris, if it still exists, as independent assessors. It is the wish of the families and wounded, represented by the Justice for the Forgotten Campaign,

and their lawyers, that the Irish Government give Sergeant
Major Komac's team clearance to do so.

Questions

The Irish State laboratory was given bomb debris samples from
Parnell Street only — three days and six days after the
explosion. It got no debris from Talbot Street, South Leinster
Street or Monaghan town.

Debris samples from all four bomb sites were sent to a
Northern Ireland forensic laboratory in Belfast.

It took eleven days for debris samples from all four sites to
be delivered to Belfast.

It would be interesting to know the bases for selection of the
debris samples chosen. One must presume that the necessary
technical and professional resources and expertise was readily
available.

To date, An Garda Síochána has failed to provide me with an
assurance that it can establish a chain of custody for the bomb
debris from 17 May 1974 to delivery to the laboratories and on
to the present day.

Crucially, where is the bomb debris today?

The authorities have demonstrated a marked reluctance to
give the lawyers representing the victims access to the Garda
files. I believe that this can be explained only by a fear on the
part of the authorities regarding the questions that will
naturally follow examination of each document. The moral
question, however, is whether state authorities, who have a
responsibility to uphold the rule of law and to protect their own
citizens, are willing to confront unpalatable shortcomings which
have prevented the families of the dead and wounded from
finding closure after a quarter of a century.

Chapter Eleven: The Garda Síochána and British Intelligence

Suspicions about British Military Intelligence contact with An Garda Síochána surfaced in the early 1970s when a member of the force, Special Branch Sergeant Patrick Crinnion, was arrested in Dublin for passing classified documents to an MI6 agent, John 'Douglas Smythe' Wyman. Concern about the extent to which the Garda Síochána had been infiltrated and compromised by British Military Intelligence increased in 1984, after a former British Army Intelligence operative, Captain Fred Holroyd, who worked to MI6, stated during a British television interview that he had had extensive undercover contacts with members of the force during his term of duty in the period 1973–75.

Holroyd was stationed in Portadown and Army HQ in Lisburn. In 1975 he was acrimoniously removed from Northern Ireland and forced out of military service the same year. He has since caused more than a few headaches for his former political and military masters with his revelations of security-force 'dirty tricks' in Northern Ireland.

When he left Ireland, Fred Holroyd was committed for a period to a psychiatric hospital run by the British Ministry of Defence at Netley, near Southampton. This Intelligence tactic is aimed at branding potential troublemakers as unstable, thus diminishing the value of what they might say. Holroyd has, none-theless, consistently stated his belief that loyalists did not carry out the 1974 attack on Dublin and Monaghan unaided.

During his 1984 TV interview, Mr Holroyd caused serious trouble for An Garda Síochána when he talked openly about his undercover contacts with members of the Republic's police force.

This prompted the first of three internal Garda inquiries into his allegations. Chief Superintendent Dan Murphy headed the initial inquiry.

The Holroyd Inquiries

Chief Superintendent Murphy's inquiry failed to interview the former Military Intelligence officer who had been attached to 3 Brigade, Portadown, and who was reporting to Craig Smellie, head of MI6 Northern Ireland. The findings of the inquiry were not made public.

Rumours began to circulate as to the identity of Mr Holroyd's Garda contacts. The temperature started to rise in August 1986 when the Director of Irish Army Intelligence, Colonel Desmond Swan, presented a report to Garda Commissioner Laurence Wren, detailing known Garda links with British Army personnel. The report was based on Irish Military Intelligence (G2) files, one of which gave details of a 1974 visit to the private home of an Irish Army officer in Dublin. The visit was made by a serving detective Garda and a British Army officer, Peter Maynard.

On 20 January 1987 the *Irish Independent* carried an interview by journalist Brendan O'Brien with a serving detective garda whom British undercover had codenamed 'The Badger'. It was a scoop for O'Brien but a calculated decision by the Garda detective who was clearly feeling the heat following the G2 disclosures. In the interview, the Badger gave tantalising details of his long-established 'double' career. O'Brien's article is dealt with more extensively later in the chapter.

On 3 May 1987 the Badger went public again in the *Sunday World*. On this occasion, his full identity was revealed. He was named as Detective Garda John McCoy, stationed at Monaghan Garda Station. In an interview with journalist Liam Clarke, the Badger went further, 'claiming that he was only one of a string of Gardaí who did the same thing....' In an interview I conducted with Fred Holroyd at his home on 15 December 1998, he told me that the Badger was 'only the tip of the iceberg'.

Seán Flynn, an *Irish Times* Security Correspondent, wrote on 18 May 1987:

> In Garda circles, the interview is seen as a signal to more senior officers that Detective Garda McCoy may be prepared to disclose

further details of Garda liaison with the British Army at that time, if any disciplinary action is taken against him.

Detective Garda McCoy's interviews with O'Brien and Clarke must be seen in the context of two internal Garda inquiries conducted in the first half of 1987 into the Irish Military Intelligence file, detailing known Garda links with British Intelligence, and Holroyd's 1984 allegations.

The first 1987 inquiry was led by Detective Superintendent Hubert Reynolds and Detective Inspector Jack Hennessy, who completed their report in April. While this inquiry did interview a former Garda Commissioner, Edmund Garvey, it did not interview serving officers above the rank of superintendent. Colonel Desmond Swan of Irish Military Intelligence was interviewed about the August 1986 report he had given to Commissioner Wren. Holroyd, who had stated his willingness to co-operate with the Reynolds/Hennessy investigation, was not interviewed. He says that he complained to the Irish Ambassador in London, Noel Dorr. A third 'Holroyd Inquiry' was held in May 1987, under Chief Superintendent Tom Kelly.

Fred Holroyd was secretly brought to Dublin by the Garda Síochána, under a false name, to testify at the new inquiry. He has retained the air ticket as proof. On 11–12 May 1987, he gave a detailed statement to the Garda Síochána, which, he says, was taken down not in pen, but in pencil. It ran to over thirty pages, giving copious details of his and other British Intelligence officers' dealings with several gardaí at various ranks. Holroyd says that the Garda failed to give him a copy of his statement before he left Dublin and have ignored his requests for one since.

As with the initial 1984 internal inquiry conducted by Chief Superintendent Dan Murphy, neither the findings of the 1987 Reynolds/Hennessy Inquiry nor those of the Kelly Inquiry into Garda links with British Intelligence were ever made public.

There are serious implications in all of this for the Garda authorities, especially regarding the force's known contact with British Intelligence in the early 1970s. According to McCoy in his interview with Brendan O'Brien, the relationship established in 1972 between the Garda and British Army undercover was on the basis of shared intelligence. This was the year of Bloody Sunday and the Widgery Tribunal. The burning of the British Embassy in Dublin in the aftermath of the Derry massacre and

the rising tide of sympathetic support for militant republicanism was causing concern in the corridors of both Westminster and
Leinster House.

1972 Dublin Bombings

On 1 December 1972 the Irish Parliament was due to debate the
Offences Against the State (Amendment) Bill, which proposed to
secure convictions of IRA membership on the sworn testimony of
a Garda superintendent. Defenders of civil liberties expressed
disquiet about the Bill and the Fine Gael party was unsure. The
scenario was being closely monitored by Britain, anxious to see
the anti-republican 'terrorist' legislation passed in the Republic.
Numbers, however, were crucial. With Fine Gael wavering, and
Labour set to vote against, the minority Fianna-Fáil-sponsored
Bill seemed destined for defeat.

Shortly before the Bill was due to be voted on, bombs exploded
at Liberty Hall and Sackville Place, killing two CIE workers and
injuring 127 civilians. As word reached the Dáil Chambers it
was assumed that the IRA was responsible. Consequently,
Fine Gael abstained, and the Bill was carried by 69 votes to 22.

Both factions of the IRA immediately denied responsibility.
There was no logic in their assisting the passage of such
legislation. Within days, the fact of the explosions occurring so
close to the Dáil vote had raised suspicions that their objective
had been to influence the voting intentions of Dáil deputies.

During Dáil Questions just four days later, an extraordinary
exchange occurred between Deputies Michael O'Leary and
Dr John O'Connell and the Minister for Justice, Des O'Malley.
Deputy O'Leary asked the Minister whether there had been any
progress in the investigation into a previous bombing at the
International Cinema in Dublin, on 25 November 1972, in which
thirty people had been injured. Deputy O'Connell asked the
Minister whether the investigation was yet completed into the
bombings and if he would make a statement on the matter.

The Minister responded:

> It is totally unrealistic to expect me to make statements in this
> House about events which obviously are still the subject of
> Garda investigations. I have repeatedly said that it is not open
> to me to make such statements and indeed I regard questions of
> this kind as an abuse of the processes of this House.

In August 1973, shortly after the trial of brothers Keith and Kenneth Littlejohn who claimed to be operating in the Republic as British MI6 agents, former Taoiseach Jack Lynch publicly stated that both he and his Cabinet had 'suspicions' that the 1972 bombs and other 'unexplained happenings in the Republic' had been the work of British Intelligence. They had good reason to be suspicious, especially with the revelations by journalist Jim Cantwell of a leaked Garda Special Branch file on the December 1972 Dublin bombings. The story was given front-page coverage in the *Evening Herald* on 21 August 1973.

Cantwell wrote that the Irish Government had been given evidence by the Special Branch, 'connecting the ... S.A.S. ... with the bomb blasts at Liberty Hall and Sackville Place, Dublin, on December 1 in which two busmen died.' He continued:

> It contains information that two of four men working under the code names of Fleming and Thompson, who stayed in the Belgravia Hotel in Belfast were, in fact, members of the Special Air Services section of the British Army. They are wanted here in connection with the bombings.

The two cars used in the bombing mission were hired by 'Fleming' from Avis Rent-a-Car at Aldergrove Airport, and Moley Hire Service, Victoria Square, Belfast, on 30 November 1972, the day before the explosions. It also emerged that the driving licence used to hire the cars was either forged or stolen, and that the real Mr Fleming, who lived in Derby, England, 'was an absolutely innocent party and had no knowledge that his name was being used by the S.A.S.'

Cantwell's report said that the Irish Government had no choice but to accept the words of their British counterparts that they did not sanction the bombing:

> If it did not accept Mr. Heath's word there would be little point in continuing normal diplomatic relations with Britain.

However, Cantwell said that, given official British connections with the Littlejohns, the Irish Government had to be aware that British agents could have been involved in the bombings. The Taoiseach, Liam Cosgrave, had protested to the British Prime Minister, Edward Heath about spying activities and the issue had also been raised by the Irish Ambassador with British Foreign Office officials.

Three decades later, satisfactory assurances are still awaited and British Army operatives Fleming and Thompson are still wanted in the Republic of Ireland in connection with the bombings in which George Bradshaw and Thomas Duffy were murdered and 127 Irish citizens were injured. The political will to pursue them, however, has been singularly lacking.

Official British denials of involvement in the politically motivated 1972 bomb attack are not surprising. However, they could not deny involvement in two other disturbing incidents from this period.

The Littlejohn/Wyman Saga

Kenneth Littlejohn was born in 1941 and joined the British Parachute Regiment on leaving school. However, in 1959 he was court-martialled and discharged for robbery. A known petty criminal, he subsequently served several short prison sentences. In August 1970, he left the UK, having taken part in a £38,000 Midland Bank robbery. His name and picture were distributed to police stations throughout the UK.

A short time later he appeared in Dublin, masquerading as the director of a lingerie company. The following year, his name disappeared from the UK wanted list. During his time in Ireland, Kenneth Littlejohn and his younger brother, Keith, engaged in subversive operations including kidnapping, bank robberies, fire-bombing, sending letter bombs, attacks on Garda stations, and intelligence gathering on the republican movement in the Louth border area. Their confessed aim was to engage in criminal activities for which the republican movement would be blamed. It was hoped that this, in turn, would lead to stronger anti-terrorist legislation in the Republic of Ireland, and a public backlash against the IRA.

Their cover was blown following a bank robbery on the Allied Irish Bank, in Grafton Street, Dublin, on 12 October 1972, during which the bank manager's family was held hostage and £67,000 was stolen. The gardaí were led to the Littlejohns' Dublin flat by an electricity bill found in the getaway car.

The brothers fled Ireland when they realised that the gardaí were closing in on them. When their Dublin flat was raided, police recovered £11,000 from the robbery, five guns, and false beards. The brothers were tracked down in England and held at Brixton Prison while extradition proceedings were launched from Dublin. Their lawyers opposed the extradition order on the basis that their criminal activities in Ireland were politically motivated. In a letter to Lord Carrington, the British Defence Secretary, dated 20 December 1972, the Littlejohns' lawyer (Mr Hughman) described his clients as 'British Intelligence agents'. Kenneth Littlejohn identified a John 'Douglas Smythe' Wyman as his Secret Intelligence Service (SIS) handler. Wyman was a man with several undercover identities.

Two days prior to Hughman's letter, gardaí had arrested John (Douglas Smythe) Wyman, in the car park of the West County Hotel, Chapelizod, Dublin. Wyman had previously made a phone-call to Garda Headquarters intended for Sergeant Patrick Crinnion, but another garda had taken the call and become suspicious. A surveillance operation was put in place. After his arrest, gardaí discovered that Wyman had been staying in Room 411 at the Burlington Hotel, Dublin.

Garda Special Branch Sergeant Patrick Crinnion was arrested in the Burlington Hotel car park, in the act of trying to escape from a member of the Garda Síochána the day after Wyman's arrest. Crinnion had earlier knocked at Room 411. Detective Sergeant Culhan opened the door. Crinnion asked for 'John'. The plainclothes garda asked 'John who?' and Crinnion replied, 'John Wyman.'

Crinnion's car was found in the hotel car park, and a search revealed ten documents taken from C3 section of Garda HQ, which had access to all classified information on the republican movement. It later emerged that Wyman was an MI6 handler who also ran the Littlejohns and other agents in the Republic.

Sergeant Crinnion had been caught in the act of treason against his nation. However, instead of being put away for a long time, as might have been expected, he and Wyman were given very lenient sentences of just three months' imprisonment. On 13 February 1973, they were released on good behaviour, and thereafter left Ireland. It was the quid pro quo for the extradition of the Littlejohn brothers.

On 19 March 1973, the Littlejohns were escorted to a plane and flown to Dublin. They subsequently revealed much to the press, candidly stating that they had been specifically recruited by the British secret services to carry out illegal activities in the

Republic of Ireland, the aim of which was to discredit the republican movement,

The Littlejohn trial opened on 1 February 1973 at the Special Criminal Court, Dublin, under Mr Justice O'Keeffe. An application from the UK Government to have a diplomatic officer present at the trial was turned down. Sixteen charges were brought against the brothers. However, several of the charges were heard in camera. The accused were ultimately acquitted of all charges heard in camera but were found guilty of all charges heard in open court.

On 6 August 1973, during their trial, Kenneth Littlejohn claimed he was working in the Republic as an MI6 agent.

Following the Littlejohns' disclosures, the British Ministry of Defence issued a statement, admitting that Kenneth and Keith Littlejohn had had official contact with 'the appropriate authorities'. The 'appropriate authorities' referred to none other than their Secret Intelligence Service controller, Douglas Smythe (alias John Wyman), arrested in Dublin in December 1972 along with Garda Special Branch Detective Patrick Crinnion.

The Littlejohns were convicted under the Offences Against the State (Amendment) Act — the Act whose passage had been assisted by the 1972 Dublin bombs.

Garda Agents

The extent of British Intelligence influence on — and infiltration of — An Garda Síochána is, obviously, not known. However, Richard Deacon, biographer of Sir Maurice Oldfield (head of MI6, 1965–77), gives an insight into the successful penetration of the force. Shortly after Oldfield's death in 1980, Deacon, who was himself a member of the secret services, wrote:

> ... MI6's main success was in establishing agents inside the Garda, the Irish army and government departments. One of the most vital informants was a senior Garda officer who (up to 1981 at least) was still in that force. He had not only provided information on the PIRA, but on the activities of the former Irish premier, Mr Haughey, and other prominent political figures.

In his book *The Stalker Affair* (Mercier Press, 1986) Frank Doherty provides disturbing insights into the British espionage network in Ireland and the potential for compromise which existed within the Garda Síochána throughout the period in question. According to Doherty:

> The primary task of the Garda Síochána Special Branch is to guard against internal subversion, the main threat of which comes from the IRA or other Republican groups. External subversion has never been considered a primary area of interest. The small section of C3 Detective Branch at garda national headquarters which deals with external threats to state security and activities by foreign espionage agencies concerns itself largely with Communist and Arab countries. In its prime task of guarding against the IRA, and in its surveillance of likely Arab or Communist agents, C3 relies on British, American and Israeli intelligence, to which it is linked through the 'Kilowatt' intelligence exchange network.

Doherty goes on to say that as British Intelligence and the Garda Síochána have common opponents, the Garda Síochána might be inclined to turn a blind eye to British Intelligence work in the Republic of Ireland, and be less likely to follow up on any allegations or claims regarding them. However, he argues, it is also possible that the inaction of the Garda Síochána could result from the infiltration and effective control by British Intelligence of the security sections of the force. He says: 'At least four former British intelligence men have made such claims to me quite separately.' This is alarming, especially in the wake of assertions by a former Irish Army commandant, Patrick Trears.

Commandant Trears has consistently stated that, on 30 July 1974 (ten weeks after the bombings), he was approached at his home in Castleknock, Dublin, by a British Army officer, Peter Maynard. Commandant Trears says that Detective John McCoy accompanied Major Maynard. He further asserts that both men informed him that their superiors were aware of their contact with him. Maynard was a bomb expert and intelligence officer (MI5), stationed at Mahon Barracks, Portadown, the heartland of the mid-Ulster UVF.

The level of intercourse between elements of the force and British Intelligence seems to have been intense throughout the 1970s. Against this background, neither the Government nor the Garda authorities can lightly dismiss the information presented by YTV's *Hidden Hand: The Forgotten Massacre* and later by RTÉ's *Prime Time* documentary, *Friendly Forces?*, both of which establish strong arguments in support of the very real suspicion that British Military Intelligence was involved in the 1974 bombing of Dublin and Monaghan. The reluctance of the authorities even to consider this possibility is disquieting.

In the absence of political backing to force British co-operation with their enquiries, any Garda investigations have been, and will continue to be, seriously impaired. However, whether or not the gardaí want or wanted political help is another matter.

It might have been expected that the suspicions voiced about British Intelligence by former Taoiseach Jack Lynch shortly after he left office in 1973 would have put Detective Garda McCoy and his superiors on guard concerning the quality of intelligence they were receiving. This does not appear to have been the case. Given the preparations required to mount an attack of the magnitude of the Dublin and Monaghan bombings, how could British Intelligence, who knew all of the loyalists suspects, fail either to stop the attack or, at the very least, to alert their Garda counterparts in advance?

Legal advice I have received has led me to understand that the Garda Siochána is entitled to deal directly with a foreign police force but not with a foreign military force. To do so, they would have to have government approval, sanctioned at cabinet level. If gardaí were engaged in cross-border contact with British Military Intelligence without government sanction, they were acting beyond their authority.

British Confirmation

A significant and unexpected development occurred following the publication of two articles I wrote for the UK-based *Irish Post* (5 June 1999) and *Ireland on Sunday* (20 June 1999). The articles reported on the unsolicited visit to Commandant Trears' home in Dublin by Garda McCoy and Major Maynard.

Following publication of the articles, Kevin McNamara, MP, tabled a question in the House of Commons, requesting the Secretary of State for Defence to make a statement on the matter of the 1974 visit.

The following reply was published in Hansard on 19 July 1999:

Mr. Doug Henderson: An informal meeting was held with a view to the possibility of exchanging technical information between Irish and British explosives experts which would have been of benefit to both sides. No action was taken as a result of the meeting.

Official British confirmation of this meeting has created major headaches for authorities in the Republic, most particularly the Garda authorities. Speaking to me on 27 April 1999, former Detective McCoy denied categorically that he was present at the meeting. This denial contradicts a report by journalist Liam Clarke in the *Sunday World* on 3 May 1987. In that article former Detective McCoy is reported as saying, 'I left the two of them [Maynard and Trears] talking and they seemed to be getting on well.'

Commandant Trears is adamant that Detective McCoy accompanied Major Maynard. He says that he reported the contact immediately to his superiors and was interviewed a few days later by Irish Military Intelligence officers.

It is imperative that the Irish Government confirm officially whether or not Detective McCoy was present, at what level within An Garda Síochána the meeting was authorised, and whether or not it had Government approval. This is vital, given that Trears has accused the retired Garda detective of assisting Major Maynard in his irregular approach to him.

Reacting to the British MoD's response to Kevin McNamara's question, Commandant Trears told me:

> Contrary to what the British Government has stated, there was nothing 'informal' about this meeting. If they wished to exchange technical information, the correct procedure was through the Irish Government and my Irish Army superiors. I have no doubt that the meeting was an attempt to subvert me. I have no doubt that Major Maynard was accompanied by Detective John McCoy and I have no doubt that McCoy was aware [what] the purpose of the visit was.... Furthermore, I have no doubt that McCoy's visit with a serving officer of a foreign army must have been [known to someone in authority], as he stated to me. The question is why? I also wish to reaffirm that Major Maynard was armed when he came to my home in Dublin. This too has serious implications.

He added:

> The reason why no action was taken by the British, following the meeting, was simply because I refused to co-operate and reported the visit of Maynard and McCoy to my superiors.

In the wake of the MoD's response to Kevin McNamara's question, I wrote to the Garda Síochána and the Irish Army seeking clarification on the visit. I attached a copy of an article published in *Ireland on Sunday* (8 August 1999), reporting the MoD response to Mr McNamara, MP. Extracts from the correspondence follow.

Correspondence with An Garda Síochána

17 August 1999 (Don Mullan to Commissioner Pat Byrne)

Attached is an article I published recently in *Ireland on Sunday*.

As you will see, the British MoD have officially confirmed that Major Peter Maynard visited Commandant Patrick Trears at his home on 30 July 1974. Comdt Trears has consistently stated that the visit was uninvited, that Major Maynard was accompanied by Garda Detective John McCoy and that both men informed him they were visiting him with the full knowledge of [text deleted. Ed]

1.   Can you confirm that Detective Garda John McCoy accompanied Major Maynard to Comdt Trears' home on 30 July 1974?

2.   Can you confirm that Detective McCoy was there with the knowledge of [text deleted. Ed]?

3.   Can you offer an explanation as to why such a visit was authorized by An Garda Síochána since Comdt Trears' Irish Army superiors were, apparently, unaware that such a meeting was taking place?

4.   Can you confirm that a report made by Comdt Trears to his superiors and to Irish Army Intelligence about the uninvited contact formed part of a file presented to Commissioner Wren by Colonel Desmond Swan in 1986?

20 August 1999 (Chief Superintendent Michael J. Carty, PA to Commissioner, to Don Mullan)

I am directed by the Commissioner to acknowledge receipt of your letter dated 17th August 1999, together with enclosure.

27 September 1999 (Don Mullan to Commissioner Byrne)

Attached is a copy of my letter to you dated 17 August 1999. ...

I would be grateful if you would respond to the letter and the four questions therein.

24 November 1999 (Chief Superintendent Carty to Don Mullan)

The Commissioner has directed me to refer to yours of 27th September 1999, concerning queries received arising from an article published in Ireland on Sunday and to enquire from you the context in which you require this information and the intended purpose of its use.

14 December 1999 (Don Mullan to Chief Superintendent Carty)

... The context is clear. The British MoD has confirmed that a British Army Officer visited the private home of a serving Irish Army Commandant on 30 July 1974.... Commandant Trears has also alleged that the Officer, Major Peter Maynard, was accompanied by a serving member of An Garda Síochána, Detective John McCoy, of Monaghan Garda Station....

The four questions, therefore, which I submitted to Commissioner Byrne on 17 August 1999 remain relevant and his response is eagerly awaited.

The purpose of my enquiry is for legitimate journalistic research in accordance with the standards of the National Union of Journalists to which I am an accredited member.

4 January 2000 (Chief Superintendent Carty to Don Mullan)

I have been directed by the Commissioner to ... advise you that, despite enquiries and research, the alleged activities forming the basis of your questions to him, as outlined in your communications of 17th August 1999, cannot be confirmed.

29 January 2000 (Don Mullan to Chief Superintendent Carty)

... I write to seek clarification concerning your letter....

Are you informing me that enquiries were made ... regarding the alleged visit by Detective John McCoy and British Officer Peter Maynard to the home of Irish Army Commandant Patrick Trears on 30 July 1974? Furthermore ... are you truthfully telling me that no such records or knowledge exists within the force to concretely establish the veracity or otherwise of Commandant Trears' very serious allegations? ... [I]s the Commissioner telling me that no records of Commandant Trears' assertions are contained in the file presented to Commissioner Wren by Colonel Desmond Swan in 1986? ....

29 February 2000 (Chief Superintendent Carty to Don Mullan)

I have been directed by the Commissioner ... to inform you, that for the purpose of facilitating a reply to your original letter of the 17th August, 1999, certain enquiries and research were, of course, carried out.

In light of the unambiguous nature of my letter dated the 4th of January, 2000, it is difficult to understand why you now seek further clarification, and therefore, any further correspondence in this regard will only be considered in the context of the public interest.

3 March 2000 (Don Mullan to Chief Superintendent Carty)

... I note your comments regarding the 'unambiguous' letter you sent to me on 4 of January 2000, to which I sought clarification. I note from that letter that the Commissioner was unable to confirm after 'enquiries and research' that retired Garda Detective John McCoy accompanied British Officer, Peter Maynard, to the private home of former Irish Army Commandant, Patrick Trears, on 30 July 1974.

I also note that while the Commissioner was unable to 'confirm' the above, he did not deny it.

With respect, I would have thought that given the very serious implications inherent in Commandant Trears' allegations, it is in the interest of the public, in the national interest, and in the interest of An Garda Síochána, to establish the truth about this matter.

Correspondence with the Irish Army

17 August 1999 (Don Mullan to Commandant Eoghan Ó Neachtain, Defence Forces Press Office)

Attached is an article I published recently in *Ireland on Sunday*....

I would be grateful if you could furnish me with answers to the following questions:

1.   Can you confirm that Comdt Trears reported the visit by Major Maynard and Detective McCoy to his Irish Army superiors on or near 30 July 1974?

2.   Can you confirm that he was visited by Irish Army Intelligence officers for the purpose of making a full statement as to the nature and content of the visit?

3.   Can you confirm that Comdt Trears' report to his superiors and the Irish Army Intelligence report formed part of a file presented to Commissioner Wren by Colonel Desmond Swan in 1986?

19 August 1999 (Commandant Ó Neachtain to Don Mullan)

... I passed your letter on to the relevant section,[1] who have now informed me that the answer to the three questions you asked, is no.

The Defence Forces are not able to confirm any of the matters you raised.

I regret therefore that I cannot be of any assistance to you.

---

1   In a telephone conversation (3.45 p.m., 19 August 1999), Comdt Ó Neachtain told me the 'relevant section' was Army Intelligence.

19 August 1999 (Don Mullan to Commandant Ó Neachtain)

... I would be grateful if you would clarify in writing, without ambiguity, the meaning of the answers you have sent in relation to my letter of 17 August 1999.

Does 'no' mean that 'the relevant section' are unable to confirm that the meeting between Comdt Trears and Major Maynard took place because they have no record of it, including the two reports on the meeting which Comdt Trears says he made to his superiors and Irish Army Intelligence. Or, does it mean they will not 'confirm' that the said meeting took place, which the British MoD have officially confirmed did, indeed, take place?

26 August 1999 (Commandant Ó Neachtain to Don Mullan)

... The relevant sections within the Defence Forces have found no contemporaneous reports which indicate that such a meeting took place.

Therefore, we cannot confirm or deny the incident as outlined by Comdt Trears (retd).

31 August 1999 (Don Mullan to Commandant Ó Neachtain)

... How is one to read your statement 'The relevant section within the Defence Forces have found no contemporaneous reports which indicate that such a meeting took place'?

Is Comdt Trears (retd) lying to the media and, more importantly, to the Irish public? Or, given the serious nature of Comdt Trears' statements, are we to view our State Forces as incompetent, negligent and indifferent? Surely Comdt Trears' report of an unsolicited visit by a serving major of a foreign army (given the implications of what he has stated took place) was reported to the Minister for Defence at the time? If not, why not? Again, I must emphasise, the British Ministry of Defence have officially acknowledged that Major Maynard did indeed visit Comdt Trears in Dublin. Are we to conclude, therefore, that the Irish Defence Forces are less rigorous in keeping records of potentially dangerous and damaging approaches to serving Irish officers by foreign military personnel who may wish to compromise their loyalty to this State? ....

A reply is still awaited from both An Garda Síochána and the Irish Army.

Peter Maynard

At the end of 1974, the year of the Dublin and Monaghan bombings, Her Majesty, Queen Elizabeth II, awarded an MBE to Peter Maynard.

In 1991, as Lieutenant-Colonel Maynard, he was awarded an OBE.

Peter Maynard is still serving in the British Army. The appointments section of the September 1999 edition of *Soldier Magazine* contains the following information:

P.C. Maynard to be Colonel of Special Projects DI (ST), July 5 — 3 year posting.

Interviewing 'The Badger'

J McC: I knew who the Badger was but ... I'm not saying it.

DM: Everybody thinks it's you.

J McC: I know that.

DM: And you're saying it's not you.

J McC: Definitely not!

Thus began my interview with former Garda Detective, John McCoy, at his home in County Monaghan, on 27 April 1999. Mr McCoy had long been suspected of being a key link between An Garda Síochána and British Military Intelligence. I had written to him on 26 January 1999, requesting an interview, but had received no reply. In April, I decided to travel to Monaghan and arrive unannounced.

In preparation for the visit, I studied two newspaper articles in particular. The first appeared in the *Irish Independent*, on 20 January 1987. It was written by RTÉ's Brendan O'Brien and reported an interview by O'Brien with the Badger. Although the identity of the Badger was obviously known to O'Brien, he did not name him in the article. A further report based on an interview with the Badger appeared in the *Sunday World* of 3 May 1987. It was written by Liam Clarke, who named the Badger as Detective Garda John McCoy.

The details of both articles are important as background to the interview I conducted with Mr McCoy in April 1999.

Irish Independent *Article, 20 January 1987*

According to Brendan O'Brien's article, the Badger 'worked directly to British Army Intelligence officers who, in turn, reported direct to the heads of MI6 and later MI5 in the North.' Fred Holroyd was named as one of his controllers.

In the interview the Badger tells of how he was recruited by the British Army in 1972 to get information for them on 'terrorists' in the Republic. He made frequent contact with a man named 'Bunny Dearsley'. The Badger provided information on IRA and later INLA members and activities. In return, he received information on loyalist paramilitaries and good-quality maps of border areas — far better than any available to the Garda at the time. He declined the one offer of money made to him.

According to the article, the Badger claimed not to know that the six British Army men with whom he made contact over eleven years were working for British Military Intelligence, and 'probably wouldn't have done it if he had known'. O'Brien asked the Badger if he knew for what purpose the information he supplied was being used. The Badger is quoted as replying 'I wouldn't lose any sleep over retaliation or tit-for-tat in some cases, but I would if innocent people get killed'.

O'Brien goes on to mention the fate of Seamus Grew, one of the INLA men about whom the Badger admitted to having given information. Grew was shot dead in Armagh by an RUC Special Mobile Support Unit.

O'Brien reports that the Badger recognised Fred Holroyd from a photograph, and recalled meeting him. He never knew that he himself was codenamed 'The Badger', and he had never been questioned by Garda authorities regarding his activities. He recalled 'a lot of "unofficial" goings on across the Border'.

One incident concerned a foiled attack by three loyalists on Seamus Grew and Paddy Loughlin. The loyalists were spotted crossing the border, arrested and sentenced to seven years' imprisonment but, O'Brien's report continues:

> [T]he three told the Gardaí they were to be paid between £100 and £500 by the British Security Forces to kidnap Grew and Loughlin.

Asked by O'Brien when his contacts had ceased, the Badger replied that 'his contacts finally ceased when each side had little new information to give'.

In the same issue of the *Irish Independent* (20 January 1987), O'Brien writes of an interview with Fred Holroyd. He quotes Holroyd as saying that the Badger was regarded by British Intelligence 'as a first class source', from whom they got 'a lot of good stuff', at meetings held 'about once a month.' Holroyd also mentioned 'two other Special Branch Gardaí whose information was passed through "The Badger".' Any information Holroyd got was 'delivered personally to MI6's Craig Smellie and other chiefs in "the secret corridor" at Army HQ in Lisburn.' The information then filtered down to the RUC special branch.

In the article Holroyd describes how men pinpointed by the Badger would be 'kidnapped and dropped north of the Border and lo and behold an Army man would come along'. O'Brien reports further statements by Holroyd, which 'if true, suggest that more than just 'The Badger' was involved in the Republic':

> Firstly, he says, an area would be frozen. This would mean both Gardaí and Irish Army staying out of it so as to allow kidnaps to take place.
>
> Secondly, that he often drove through Garda checkpoints while crossing the Border, showing his Army identity card:
>
>> 'We'd say we were going to Monaghan police station and we'd pass right through.'

Sunday World *Article, 3 May 1987*

Liam Clarke's interview echoes Brendan O'Brien's in many respects. However, Clarke goes further. He gives the identity of the Badger and reports that 'senior officers' knew of his activities and awarded him the Scott silver medal for Gallantry 'when he risked his life to disarm a deranged gunman intent on murdering republicans'. Clarke quotes John McCoy, the Badger, as saying that he regarded passing on information to British Intelligence as 'part of his normal duties':

> There was nothing unusual about it — it was normal procedure, I suppose we were gullible enough to believe these fellows when they said they were seconded to the RUC.

According to Clarke, Garda McCoy believed himself to be 'only one of a string of Gardaí who did the same thing and never thought twice about it.' He says that Garda McCoy recalls meetings with 'Drew Coid of the RUC Special Branch, Peter Maynard of MI5, Bernard "Bunny" Dearsley of MI6, P. David Delius of MI5 and a number of unnamed men with English accents who were introduced to him by his contacts.'

Clarke reports that Captain Peter Maynard took over most of Fred Holroyd's sources, when Holroyd left Ireland 'after a row between MI5 and MI6'. He writes that it was John McCoy who introduced Maynard to Commandant Patrick Trears of the Irish Army's bomb disposal team, and continues:

> Although Commandant Trears later reported the meeting to a superior officer and a file on the incident was forwarded to the Gardaí, Det. McCoy says: 'I left the two of them talking and they seemed to be getting on well'.

In his interview with Clarke, John McCoy denies that the Garda ever agreed 'to "freeze" areas to allow kidnap or assassination teams to enter the Republic in search of republicans', saying: 'so far as I know anyone who came in for kidnaps in this area was caught and jailed'.

Clarke writes: 'Since the 'Badger' reports started appearing in the papers ... [t]hinly veiled threats have appeared in *Republican News* referring to an incident in which he was convicted of assaulting IRA man John Milne at Monaghan Garda station.' He has also received anonymous threats. According to Clarke, Detective McCoy insists that he has 'always tried to enforce the law impartially'.

Liam Clarke, like Brendan O'Brien, went to Fred Holroyd to supplement his article. He reports that Holroyd's and McCoy's recollections 'differ on some points', but both agree that 'there were far more senior officers involved in secret contacts with British intelligence'.

Clarke reports Holroyd as recalling a meeting with members of the Garda Síochána, including Assistant Garda Commissioner Ned Garvey. Clarke writes: 'Mr. Garvey, however, does not recall any such meeting with Capt. Holroyd.'

He continues that Holroyd has 'written to the Irish Embassy on four occasions ... to ask to be interviewed in connection with any enquiry into British intelligence operations in Ireland'. His letters have been acknowledged but have received no reply. The *Sunday World* article quotes Holroyd's reaction to this:

> In view of the fact that my allegations are supposed to be the basis for this enquiry and that there have been questions in the Dáil demanding that I be extradited to give evidence, I find it extraordinary that my offer has not been taken up.

Interview, 27 April 1999

Having prepared several questions to put to John McCoy, if given the opportunity, I eventually found my way to his home, rang the doorbell, and asked to speak with him. A short time later a tall gentleman appeared. He acknowledged having received my letter in January. I asked if I could speak with him and he invited me in.

During the interview, which he allowed me to record, John McCoy retracted and denied several key elements of the Brendan O'Brien and Liam Clarke interviews, both of which have been in the public domain since 1987. The following are among the important points arising out of my interview:

- He denied that he was 'The Badger'.

- He confirmed that he spoke with journalists Brendan O'Brien and Liam Clarke.

- He said that RTÉ journalist Brendan O'Brien had taken what he said 'out of context'.

- He said that he knew of other guards who were talking to Holroyd and that his [McCoy's] name was being used by another member of the force who has since retired.

- He said that a senior officer had named a deceased garda detective, Liam McQuaid, as 'the real Badger'.

- He said there was another member of the force, of the same rank as himself, 'whose name never came up', who was also suspected of being the Badger.

- He said that he did have contact with the RUC and people 'seconded to the RUC' but had no direct dealings with British Army Intelligence. However, he said that he had his 'suspicions' about guards being involved with British Intelligence.

- He said he didn't like the idea of such contact.

- He denied ever having met 'Bunny' Dearsley or Captain Fred Holroyd and denied having received calls from Holroyd at his home.

- He revealed that he had been interviewed by Chief Superintendent Tom Kelly who conducted the third 'Holroyd Inquiry' in May 1987.

- He revealed that Chief Superintendent Kelly had a long statement taken from Holroyd.

- He said that a garda at a 'much higher rank' — not, he said, John Paul McMahon or his boss — had told him who Holroyd was describing.

- He revealed that Holroyd's statement had named two other members of the Garda as contacts. 'But,' he said, 'the other one I know now, wasn't mentioned.'

- He displayed, on occasions, considerable anxiety when speaking about Fred Holroyd.

- He denied several key pieces of information reported by Brendan O'Brien.

- He denied involvement in 'freezing' areas but said that a chief superintendent could, and admitted that it was possible that areas were being frozen.

- He was unclear when asked how British Intelligence had failed to alert the gardaí about the attack on Dublin and Monaghan, given their surveillance and knowledge of all the main suspects.

- He confirmed that he knew Commandant Patrick Trears.

- He denied visiting Trears' private residence in July 1974, with Major Peter Maynard.

- He confirmed that the visit to Trears' home was raised by Chief Superintendent Kelly during his 1987 investigation.

- He said, 'the Garda authorities investigated the thing and they cleared me.'

- When asked why neither he nor his Garda superiors had refuted or legally challenged the content of various articles over the years, in particular the O'Brien and Clarke articles, he replied, 'I should have.'

Edited extracts of the interview I conducted with former Detective Garda John McCoy are contained in Appendix 2.

Reaction to the 1999 McCoy Interview

Responding to John McCoy's denial of having visited his home in Dublin, on 30 July 1974, with Peter Maynard, former Irish Army Commandant Patrick Trears said:

I knew McCoy personally from the Courts. He was definitely the guy who was in my home with Major Maynard. I also reported the visit of Detective McCoy and Maynard to my superiors at the time.

When asked about the possibility that the person visiting with Maynard could have been using Detective McCoy's name as a cover, Commandant Trears emphatically repeated, 'I knew McCoy from the Courts. It was McCoy!'

Journalist Brendan O'Brien, when asked for his reaction to McCoy's interview, wrote to me on 29 May 2000:

I have read the [interview] as presented. I have also re-read my notes of the time and the *Irish Independent* article.

The article is an accurate account of my conversation with John McCoy, on 7 Jan '87, 5pm at his house. The notes run to twelve and a half pages and our conversation was detailed and serious, as well as friendly.

All I can say about his denial of contacts with Bunny Dearsley and his apparent denial of contacts with Fred Holroyd is that this directly contradicts the information he freely gave to me. I should stress that I did not name John McCoy in the article and have never since done so (a point I would appreciate you making) but he has himself chosen to confirm our conversation now.

He makes some play of the follow-up Garda 'investigation'. I was also questioned by senior Garda officers at the time, following my article and my subsequent reports in the *Irish Independent* relating to the activities of Fred Holroyd and his Garda contacts. The questioning I got from the investigating officers was superficial in the extreme ... along the lines of 'I suppose you're not going to tell us very much ... but we have to ask anyway....'

When I told Fred Holroyd that former Detective Garda McCoy had denied ever having contact with him he responded, 'Rubbish! What a scoundrel.'

Fred Holroyd reiterated that he had telephoned John McCoy at his home on a number of occasions, and said that he has the number written in his official police notebooks of the period. He said that he met John McCoy on at least six occasions, some of which lasted for several hours. He said that when he was interviewed for the internal Garda investigation in 1987 into the force's contact with British Military Intelligence, he was told that McCoy had admitted to meeting him only once. When asked if it might be possible that the man he had met was falsely using the name John McCoy he responded: 'Absolutely not. It was John McCoy.'

Fred Holroyd says that he has never heard of Detective Liam McQuaid.

Conclusion

The role of British Intelligence in liaising directly with (and, on occasion, subverting and attempting to subvert) members of An Garda Síochána and the Irish security forces in the 1970s, is disquieting. It requires a detailed and determined review by the Oireachtas. Of particular concern is the possible impact irregular and unauthorised contact of this nature may have had on criminal and murder investigations in the Republic of Ireland where the involvement of British Military Intelligence has long been suspected. The 1974 Dublin and Monaghan bombings constitute but one such case. These are not the fanciful imaginings of conspiracy theorists. We must constantly recall the public statement made by former Taoiseach Jack Lynch in 1973, when he expressed the suspicions of his Government that the 1972 Dublin bombings and other 'unexplained happenings' were the work of British Intelligence.

Was the contact between elements of An Garda Síochána and British Intelligence sanctioned by the Government? Were gardaí acting beyond their authority? Given the suspicions of British involvement in the bombings, why were the Garda Síochána, apparently, intensifying their relationship with British Military Intelligence, when, clearly, the latter, which was monitoring the prime suspects, failed to alert the Garda to the imminent attack? Credibility can surely be given to the idea of Northern Ireland security force and British Intelligence involvement.

There may be perfectly reasonable and legitimate explanations of all of the above. However, the public, and particularly the victims of these atrocities, have the right to transparent accountability.

Chapter Twelve: The Holroyd Notebooks

On 25 February 2000, I was given four copies of former British Army Captain Fred Holroyd's police notebooks. The notebooks, now in the safekeeping of a solicitor, contain intelligence information based on personal surveillance of loyalist and republican activists, as well as information provided by, amongst others, informants, RUC Special Branch Officers, Scottish Special Branch and, very likely, Holroyd's Garda contacts. They are filled with names, dates of birth, addresses and car registration numbers, along with various other notations. In most instances, specific dates are not given, but, from the information recorded, it is clear that it relates to the period when Captain Holroyd was active in Ireland on behalf of British Military Intelligence, 1973–75. Two of the four notebooks contain a detailed list of names and telephone numbers of Army Intelligence, RUC and Garda contacts.

According to Holroyd:

> We made reports, usually after an incident was over, when we finished and got back to the office.... Sometimes we made a report out for the colonel, sometimes just the MI6 guy; sometimes, if it was forensic, we would make one out for the colonel, the MI6 guy and it [depended] on what the distribution [needs were].

Holroyd wrote monthly reports which he submitted to his superiors. For all reports he drew extensively on the intelligence recorded in the notebooks. The notebooks were also occasionally used for the purpose of writing 'intelligence summaries'.

Holroyd is just one of many Intelligence officers operating in Ireland at the time. Extensive documentation concerning many of these matters should exist in various official archives. In the case of Holroyd, additional written sources should include the reports written by his superiors, and his own monthly reports and intelligence summaries. For this reason, among many others, the British Government's co-operation in a cross-jurisdictional Tribunal of Inquiry into the bombings is essential.

The original notebooks were made available to Yorkshire Television during their research for their documentary. Yorkshire Television had them forensically examined and authenticated as having been produced in the early 1970s.

The notebooks do not appear to follow a chronological order and at times require considerable effort to work out specific dates. Numbers were allocated to them by the RUC in the 1980s when Holroyd agreed to co-operate with an internal investigation on security-force dirty tricks and corruption. When interviewed for this book on 18 March 2000, Fred Holroyd said that, during the investigation, the RUC had removed a number of key pages from these notebooks, some of which referred to the Dublin and Monaghan bombings.

For the purpose of this book, I have confined myself to an analysis of information specifically relevant to the Dublin and Monaghan bombings. This includes:

- Surveillance notes on the mid-Ulster UVF/UDA, including surveillance on some of the main suspects in the bombings, and their associates;

- Intelligence information which makes specific reference to the Dublin and Monaghan attack and other Dublin bombing incidents;

- Holroyd's references to cross-border activities and his contact with An Garda Síochána, including his intelligence contact list on which the names and telephone numbers of three members of the Republic's civilian police force appear.

Surveillance of Mid-Ulster UVF/UDA

Even a cursory examination of the notebooks establishes that Holroyd and the Northern Ireland security forces were carefully monitoring the mid-Ulster UVF/UDA and several of the prime suspects for the Dublin and Monaghan Bombings, and their associates.

Police Notebook 11:

On page 19 of Notebook 11, Holroyd records:

Inf (information) on Chalet 17 Dec. B II

A 100 lb bomb — double diamond container is in Edgarstown. ____ ordered ____ to plant it in Chalet Bar on Mon 16th night, ____ refused, another man was detailed — he has left the area. ____ and ____ were then told by N to do it themselves if they were brave enough, they carried out an extensive recce of Chalet on Tues 17th.

On page 20, he records observing Harris Boyle driving from ____ Farm at 12.15 [am]. A line connects Boyle's name with a red Ford Escort, registration number UWM (or W) 496M. He also observed a Hillman, registration number 4862 XZ nearby.

At 12.30 a.m., he notes six further registrations. A meeting of sorts at ____ farm seems to be breaking up. He observes ____ in the red Ford Escort with Boyle.

On page 22 of Notebook 11 four names, including that of Harris Boyle are listed, with the reference UDA/UVF alongside. The location, 'bottom of Scotch Street, White Heather — Dungannon,' is given with the notation 'Sat [Saturday] night drinking spot. About 20 arrive.'

On page 26 he records that the Stranraer Special Branch has interviewed ____ who left on the twelfth and returned on the sixteenth on the 1900 hrs Larne Ferry.

Page 32 records the following:

J.F. Green
In rear seat/back of Volks beetle — 1 sten, 1 X .22 and ammo. check all VWs

This is a reference to John Francis Green, an IRA staff captain from Lurgan, shot dead in controversial circumstances at a farmyard near Castleblayney while an IRA ceasefire was being observed.

Page 54 notes extensive surveillance on ____. It records 'Queen's Bar 5pm each night. Assoc. [Names withheld], ____, ____.'

Police Notebook 12

Page 30 of Notebook 12 records four names, connected with the words 'Burkes Bar' written alongside. This is followed by:

to collect a bomb for South — more likely Chalet bar.
1st UVF Job for ____ who joined after UWC Strike.

Page 44 notes a Scottish address for ____, including the name of his father-in-law. It appears he has moved there but is still under surveillance.

Page 74 carries a startling note:

> Billie Fulton going to Monaghan this weekend to collect 1 ton of illegal fertilizer: furniture van of ... (parked outside Ballylum Park/Garvaghy Road) He went last week — no fertilizer so money went back to UDA.

Thus Fulton's previous visit was known about, as was the fact that another collection of illegal fertiliser was imminent. If the source of this information was not Holroyd's Garda contacts, did he or any other member of the British security forces, including the RUC, inform the Garda Síochána? Were gardaí, particularly in the Monaghan/Castleblayney division, aware of the existence of a supplier of illegal bomb-making ingredients to mid-Ulster UVF/UDA paramilitaries? The implications of this information are extremely serious and must be addressed.

Police Notebook 14

On page 3 of Holroyd's Notebook 14, the following is recorded:

> From 3 Inf [Infantry] Bde [Brigade]
> Instruction in making of bombs at _____ Street Portadown on Mon nights by William Hanna, 45, Houston Park Lurgan.

According to Yorkshire Television, these meetings took place in the two months leading up to the Dublin and Monaghan bombings. It appears that the security forces knew that classes in bomb-making were going on for at least two months in advance of the bombings, yet nothing was done to stop them. It also lends weight to the suspicion that even if the UVF carried out the attack alone, the security forces knew about it in advance, and, by their actions or omissions, were complicit.

On page 14 of Notebook 14 Holroyd records:

> B3 from HQ 3 Bde [Brigade]
> McGurk's bar explosion on 6.0.72 ____ [full name and address given] claimed he made bomb to others in discussion
> In similar discussions with other members of UDA

____ [full name and address given] Portadown admitted taking part and that ____ was the man who escaped on the bonnet of the car.

B2 Portadown UDA consists of 124 members on paper. Only 20% active
P'Down UDA house to house raffles funds healthy approx £800 mini bus £600.

There follows a list of names and addresses of people Holroyd describes as 'Active pers':

____, UDA inner council
____, Area Commander, Union Street,
____, Comdr Edgarstown
____, Mil Comdr — usually direct to ____
____, Trg Officer,
William Fulton, Comdr Bocombra,
____, (ht)
____, (Sgt)
____, (Sgt) (incendiary devices)
____, Paymaster
____, (Pte) Bocombra
____, (Pte) Bocombra
____, P'Down.

Page 36 of this notebook gives details of an explosion in which Joey Neill died.[1] Holroyd has notes from a 'reliable informant' ten minutes after the bang. The notes record other bombings and shooting incidents in which Joseph Neill had, allegedly, been involved. The names of two associates are recorded, one of whom is a suspect in the Dublin and Monaghan bombings:

____, ____.

UDA leaders — Lonsdale.

This note is crossed out with two large Xs.

Page 55 carries other interesting notes, also crossed out:

---

1   Joey Neill (25), a UVF lieutenant, was killed in a bomb explosion in a house in Union Street, Portadown on 16 April 1974. There are two theories concerning his death. One is that his own bomb killed him; the other that he was killed in a UVF/UDA feud. A detective at his inquest stated that he found 2lb of gelignite under a settee in the living-room of the wrecked house, the following day. If Neill died in a premature explosion, it adds to legitimate doubts concerning the UVF's ability to mount a highly professional and synchronised bomb attack on Dublin just over one month later

> UDA activity on decline, hard liners in nick lost public spt.
> [support]
> criminal activities murder of George Hyde
> present activities production of feeble propaganda mags
>
> UVF/UFF same org here still active — bombing one per fortnight
> capable of soft tgts, still in close contact with Belfast UVF.

From this it is clear that British Intelligence knew that the mid-Ulster UVF was carrying out approximately one bombing every two weeks. However, it is equally clear that British Intelligence had little regard for the bombing capabilities of the Portadown UVF, believing them capable of attacking only 'soft' targets.

References to the Republic

Page 14 of Police Notebook 11 has a note '3 miles from Monaghan on Cavan Road'.

On page 21 of the same notebook Holroyd has written:

> From Ray to Ian
>   Address on envelope
>   — Castleblaney

Page 51 in Notebook 12 carries a note under the name and home address of Bunny Dearsley, which reads, 'Meeting places badger with Code names.'

On page 73 of the same notebook, the name of a Garda Detective (not McCoy) is written. The same name appears on the page before the note relating to Billie Fulton (see p. 274). Whether these are of any significance, we do not know.

On the back page of Notebook 12 is written 'EIRE Border Code' with an arrow linking it to 'LIMA 29'.

In Notebook 13 is written:

> Gosforth [*sic*] Castle. 'Badger'.   Ops 55.
>   — 429.

Holroyd was unsure what the above note related to. It may have referred to a meeting place; Gosford Forest Park and Castle, Lough Gilly, is located seven miles from Newry on the Armagh Road. The castle was used by the British Army in the 1970s.

'OP 55' is written on the front of Notebook 14.

According to Holroyd, wherever names appear related to the Garda Síochána, it means he was 'active' with them at that time.

Reference to Dublin and Monaghan Bombings

According to Fred Holroyd, the RUC removed a number of key pages from his notebooks when he made them available for their internal investigation in the 1980s. He told me:

> My own view is that ... what those pages cover, [is] the liaison between the Garda and [intelligence services in] the north and ... the second bombing of Dublin [1974] ... those are the two areas that they really are very worried about and with good reason.

Pages 62 and 63 of Police Notebook 11 contain carefully recorded notes in a very neat handwriting, unlike many of Holroyd's other notes. According to Holroyd it is information he received from an RUC Special Branch officer. A careful reading of the information would suggest that at least some of the intelligence came from a Garda source. In total there are ten points, though not all are relevant to the Dublin and Monaghan bombings.

John Francis Green

The second and third points refer to the shooting of John Francis Green on 10 January 1975 (see p. 273 above). Point 2 states:

> 2.   JF Greens younger brother arrived in Monaghan — day before yesterday to ask Garda what calibre weapons were used on his brother.

I wrote to Laurence Green, brother of John Francis, on 3 March 2000, to establish the date of the reference. He replied that the visits to Castleblayney Garda Station occurred some time between 17 January and the end of February 1975. These notes, therefore, were recorded some time during that time frame. Given that the information is so fresh ('the day before yesterday'), the original source might be a garda stationed in Monaghan.

1972 Dublin Bombing

The fourth point appears to refer to the bombings on 1 December 1972 which killed George Bradshaw and Tommy Duffy, while Dáil Éireann was debating the Offences Against the State (Amendment) Act. It clearly identifies a former leading member of Ulster Vanguard who had UDA associations:

> ____ was involved in first Dublin bombings — he was in a shoe shop 1 day before 100 ft from the scene and his name is on the

sales docket. The manageress later identified him on Tele and informed the Garda.

There is nothing to suggest that this information was ever acted upon, or that this particular well-known figure was questioned concerning this information, either in Northern Ireland or during subsequent visits to the Republic. Yet it is recorded in the official notebook of a member of British Military Intelligence seconded to the RUC, who received it from an RUC Special Branch officer. It is quite probable that the RUC officer received it from a member of the Garda. Several paper trails must exist which would substantiate the accuracy of this recording, and help to increase confidence in the accuracy of other information contained in this series of entries.

Given the named person's close ties to a politician who was openly making war overtures towards the Republic of Ireland at the time, it is reasonable to wonder why this person was in Dublin at that particular time. There may well be a perfectly legitimate explanation, but the recording in Captain Holroyd's official notebook makes a very clear and unambiguous statement concerning his involvement.

The man's presence in the capital the day before one of the explosions and his close proximity to the scene was suspicious enough in itself to warrant an investigative follow-through. Almost thirty years later the questions to be answered are whether An Garda Síochána still have the 'evidence' upon which this statement appears to be based, and what they did about it at the time.

1974 Suspected Bomber Identified

The fifth point records the following:

> [Name withheld] was identified at the bombing of Belfast [*sic*] when the Monaghan bomb went off at the same time.

In points 5 and 9 Holroyd writes 'Belfast' when he means Dublin. He clarified this point when I met him in London, and in an edited copy of his notebooks I had in my possession he corrected both with a blue pen by writing 'for Belfast read Dublin'. He initialled both corrections and dated them 18/3/00.

This important information is in the possession of the RUC, British Military Intelligence and, according to Yorkshire Television, An Garda Síochána. If [name withheld] was identified at the bombing of Dublin, the same day as the Monaghan bomb, why wasn't he detained, questioned and put on an identity parade so that the accuracy of the eyewitnesses could be tested?

The Garda Síochána and the Irish Army

The sixth point gives an intriguing insight into the view of Irish Army Intelligence held by An Garda Síochána. It states:

> Eire Army intelligence is not trusted by any branch of Garda. Army regarded as eedjits and criminals.

From whom did the RUC Special Branch officer who passed on this information to Holroyd get this impression?

A decision was made at a senior level in the Irish Army to submit a file from the Army's Intelligence section, detailing known contacts between the Garda and British Intelligence. This move was significant on several counts. To begin with, it suggests that gardaí were operating in a manner which gave cause for concern in terms of national security requirements. It also suggests a disturbing distrust between the Army and An Garda Síochána. It could also suggest that the Garda Síochána, or elements of the force, were acting outside their lawful remit.

Political Instructions

According to point 9 of page 62 of Holroyd's notebook:

> BA [British Army] were involved in first [Dublin] bombings.

However, Holroyd has crossed out some words which are still readable. The sentence as first written states:

> SAS were responsible for first [Dublin] bombings.

When asked for clarification of 'first Dublin bombings', Holroyd said it was probably a reference to the 1972 bombings.

The second part of point 9, if true, has serious implications for the Irish State. It states:

> Political instrs (instructions) were given to Garda to stop investigations.

It is probable that the note is pertinent to both the 1972 and 1974 bombings since Holroyd uses the plural 'investigations' which, in the context of this overall entry, would make sense. Both attacks were clearly discussed during his encounter with the RUC Special Branch officer.

A reliable and credible source has informed me that around July 1974 a meeting took place which involved members of the Garda team investigating the 1974 bombings, senior civil servants, and possibly a politician. The team was commended on its work. However, following a summary of the overall investigation, a view was expressed that it was unlikely the investigation could go much further, and the gardaí were instructed to wind it down.

According to my source, a number of gardaí present strongly objected to ending their enquiries.

The Garda Síochána and Cross-Border Activities

The first page of Notebook 11 and the last page of Notebook 12 contain names and telephone numbers of Holroyd's contacts. The final three names belong to serving members of An Garda Síochána. For legal reasons, I am unable to publish two of the names but they have been passed for consideration to Mr Justice Hamilton's 'Independent Commission of Inquiry'. There are four telephone numbers listed which I have designated 1X1, 2X2, 3X3 and 4X4.

In Notebook 12, next to one of the Garda names, Holroyd has added a note which reads 'Bunny's mate'. This is a reference to Sergeant Bernard 'Bunny' Dearsley of MI6. According to Holroyd:

> Bunny used to go down there [to Castleblayney] and stay over the other side with him. I think he knew the family. I never knew the family and he was very close with [the named garda], much closer than I was.

The telephone number Castleblayney 1X1 is written opposite the name of this garda in both Notebook 11 and Notebook 12.

The name of a second serving garda officer is written beside the name John 'Badger' on the list in Notebook 11. A scribble links them to two telephone numbers, Monaghan 2X2 and Monaghan 3X3. Page 79 of Notebook 12 contains these same numbers.

Two of the numbers listed in Holroyd's notebooks were 1974 numbers for Monaghan Garda Station.

I did not find the number 3X3 in the directory. However, in Notebook 12, it occurs again, along with another number, Monaghan 4X4. The latter number is opposite the words 'Garda Station'. Crucially, Monaghan 3X3 crops up again on page 66 of Notebook 12. However, whereas in Holroyd's contact lists it is given opposite the names John Badger and Badger John respectively, in this instance it is written underneath the name and home address of John McCoy. One can only conclude that despite McCoy's denials to me in April 1999, John 'Badger' and John McCoy are one and the same.

In this entry, directly underneath McCoy's name, address and telephone numbers are the words:

(all garage expression)
        two plugs etc.
   Bunny — petrol man.

These are codenames used in telephoned conversations to conceal identities and to prevent IRA interceptions. When Holroyd was shown this entry, he said, 'And this is the guy I had nothing to do with, never saw him, didn't exist.'

Thus, it would appear that former Garda Detective John McCoy was, indeed, involved with members of British Military Intelligence, including 'Bunny' Dearsley and Fred Holroyd. British Intelligence gave the codename 'The Badger' to John McCoy — and not to former (and now deceased) Garda Detective Liam McQuaid, despite what McCoy told me.

It is clear from Holroyd's notes that McCoy was not acting alone; two other members of the force are named, one of whom was friendly with a member of MI6.

It would be unfair to allow former Garda McCoy to be used as a scapegoat. It is essential, however, that he account in public for his actions, and that he explain the nature of his relationship with Captain Holroyd of MI6 and Major Maynard of MI5. In particular, who sanctioned his visit with Major Maynard in July 1974 to the private home of former Commandant Patrick Trears in Dublin?

No further internal Garda investigations into these matters can be acceptable. What is called for is a transparent public investigation into how our civilian police force dealt with these serious issues.

Contact

When solicitor Greg O'Neill and I met Holroyd in London to discuss his notebooks, he gave us an example of his contact with the Badger. He said that one night he and Bunny Dearsley received a call to cross the Border to meet the Badger. According to Holroyd, when they met the Badger he explained that each morning an armoured car went along a certain road north of the Border at about nine o'clock. The Badger had apparently received a tip-off that the armoured car was going to be fired on at a certain point. Holroyd said that the Badger didn't want to arrest the people concerned but neither did he want anyone to get killed; he suggested to Holroyd and Dearsley that they get the patrol called off for at least ten days. Holroyd and Dearsley then drove back to Armagh, where they awoke the colonel of the Royal Scots in the early hours of the morning. When they explained to him the nature of the intelligence they had just received, the patrol was called off.

When asked about meeting former Commissioner Ned Garvey, Holroyd recalled being asked to come and visit an arms factory which gardaí had uncovered in April 1975 at Donabate in County Dublin. Garvey was then Assistant Commissioner and later denied having met Holroyd. According to Holroyd, he travelled to Dublin with Frank Murray, an RUC CID officer, in a joint Irish Army and Garda escort. Having met Garvey at Garda Head-quarters in the Phoenix Park, Holroyd and Murray were taken to a forensic laboratory to examine the equipment and arms that had been seized. He told us that Garvey asked him to make a note of all the machinery numbers and try to trace where it came from, but to keep what he was doing secret from a certain member of staff who wasn't 'one of us'. Holroyd continued:

> It was a posh portakabin type building ... I don't know where it was. I was told if I was introduced to him not to speak ... just to let Frank Murray do the talking. Now, the irony was, when we got down there, and we walked in, Frank Murray grabbed hold of me and said, 'For Christ's sake, there's one of our blokes here ... one of our bloody RUC men, he must be working undercover.' And he was. Frank didn't even know this....

According to Holroyd, one of the things Garvey said to him was, 'It's incredible, isn't it, Fred, here you and I are, exchanging this information and working to beat terrorism and we're more frightened of our own bloody masters than we are about the enemy.' He says that he didn't meet Garvey again although Garvey sent his regards through ____.

Holroyd had the impression that Garvey was acting under instructions from somebody senior — a political somebody:

> Now whether that was a legitimate part of the government, whether that was the Prime Minister or the Opposition, I don't know, but he was acting under instructions to co-operate fully with us and that's what he was doing.

Holroyd told us that after the visit to the lab and the arms factory they returned to Garda Headquarters where Garvey gave them 'a whole load of stuff' to bring back north. This included a large amount of photographic material. There was another person present during the handover of this material — 'an oldish bloke who looked as through he was a senior detective or a sergeant or inspector type. He didn't look to have much authority.'

According to Holroyd the material was given to him as opposed to Frank Murray, the RUC officer present. He says that Murray told Garvey that Holroyd was MI6, introducing him as Major. Later, when Holroyd protested at being elevated to the rank of major, Murray said, 'No, no, Fred, it goes down better if they think you're a major.'

'Social' Contact

Holroyd also spoke to solicitor Greg O'Neill and me about another encounter between members of An Garda Síochána, the RUC and the British Army. The following is an edited extract of our discussion in London:

> *FH:* There's no doubt that there was liaison between our police station and the gardaí because we had them up for parties, porno parties and things like that.
>
> *DM:* Porno parties?
>
> *FH:* Yeah. Well they came to the Army camp for that.... They just came up, they got free booze, about three minibus loads — about 25 or 30 policemen in civvies ... the Army would take them out, lots of booze, show them around the place and then sit down and watch porno films....
>
> *DM:* Was there something more sinister about that? Was it intelligence gathering as well? You bring them up and you get them drunk...
>
> *FH:* Well, the idea was that, if anybody was ever caught over the other side, these guys would be more amenable.... It's just smoothing the waters, I think.
>
> *DM:* Was the Badger among that group?
>
> *FM:* He was there that day, yeah. The Badger didn't drink and he was a devout Catholic.... He went off with Drew Coid. In fact, it was interesting that day, looking back on it.... Drew Coid never made anything of the fact that he knew who the Badger was. I mean he didn't know that Bunny and I were running him as a source but he knew the Badger separately at policeman-to-policeman level.

... I think the whole of the _____ _____ were very pro-RUC and had their contacts within the RUC on their level. It's a way of checking.... Everybody tries to achieve that — to have two or three sources you can go back on to make sure you're not being taken to the cleaners. But they were taken to the cleaners, weren't they? They were taken to the cleaners when the bombs went off in Dublin.... I don't think the Garda had any idea that that was going to happen.

The above makes uncomfortable reading. The Garda authorities will probably deny it, but it does echo aspects of my interview with Dr James Donovan, who described what might be termed an unhealthy level of familiarity between elements of the Garda Síochána and the British security forces.

Inherent in such a relationship is the risk of police officers being personally compromised, and thus potentially compromising the course of justice. While alleged drinking or porno-movie sessions cannot on their own be held responsible for compromising the biggest unsolved murder case in the history of the Republic of Ireland, the totality of what this former British Army captain and MI6 operative has to say about the level of intercourse between the Irish police force and British Military Intelligence cannot be dismissed lightly.

Dublin and Monaghan

I asked Fred Holroyd why, when he seemed to have such a remarkable memory for detail, he was quite vague when it came to Dublin and Monaghan. He replied:

Because there was nothing said, it's quite simple ... there was no reaction to that at all. As Sherlock Holmes said: 'The dog didn't bark'... That was the amazing thing about that.... It wasn't until [_____ _____] told me, when we were waiting for the Prods to turn up for that bomb. It wasn't until he mentioned that the car had come from Portadown and that our people were involved, that I ever gave it any thought. I mean, looking back on it, it was remarkable that nobody said anything.

However, when asked about the possibility that the UVF carried out the Dublin and Monaghan bombings on their own, Holroyd responded:

I don't think anybody with military knowledge ... will subscribe to the idea that that was the case.

Chapter Thirteen: The Victims' Commission Report

The sudden downgrading of the Garda murder hunt less than three months after the bombings is disturbing. The 'new Garda investigation' into the 1993 Yorkshire Television documentary, *Hidden Hand: The Forgotten Massacre*, is intriguing. The main thrust of the documentary was to ask why a promising investigation had petered out so quickly and unsuccessfully. It is a question which the Garda and successive Irish administrations have failed to answer convincingly.

For over twenty-five years the bereaved and wounded have had to battle for official recognition. Their struggle reached new heights in 1997 and 1998 when the Garda Commissioner fought them in the High Court and Supreme Court, in a determined and successful effort to prevent the European Court of Human Rights from seeing the Garda files. The families believe that these files contain crucial material concerning actions and omissions surrounding the case.

The Good Friday Agreement, reached on 10 April 1998 and ratified by referendum in the Republic of Ireland and Northern Ireland on 22 May 1998, included a section on Rights, Safeguards and Equality of Opportunity. Paragraphs 11 and 12 deal specifically with the plight of victims:

11. ... it is essential to acknowledge and address the suffering of the victims of violence as a necessary element of reconciliation....

12. ... The achievement of a peaceful and just society would be the true memorial to the victims of violence....

The Good Friday Agreement, therefore, offered an added dimension of hope to the bereaved and wounded of the Dublin and

Monaghan bombings, and to many other victims of 'unexplained happenings' in the Republic during the thirty-year conflict. It held out the hope of an official acknowledgement not only of their loss, but also of the suffering inflicted on them by years of official neglect. Furthermore, the Agreement held out the prospect of a 'true memorial' to their lost ones — the memorial of peace and justice. In the case of Dublin and Monaghan, such a memorial necessarily requires transparency, openness and accountability, founded on truth.

On 21 May 1998, the eve of the Good Friday Agreement referendum, the Minister for Justice, Equality and Law Reform, John O'Donoghue, issued a press release announcing Government approval for the establishment of a victims' commissioner in the Republic. The Minister said that he was glad to announce that former Tánaiste John Wilson had accepted his invitation 'to carry out this important task on behalf of the Government.'

On 25 September 1998 I attended a meeting between the Victims' Commissioner and a large gathering of the bereaved and wounded. I was impressed by the sensitivity with which he listened and responded to various contributions, many of which were punctuated with expressions of deeply suppressed anger. This was the first time in almost a quarter of a century that a representative of official Ireland had sat and listened to their story.

Great hopes and expectations were riding, therefore, on Mr Wilson's report. There was much to commend the report which was published on 5 August 1999. Of the Dublin and Monaghan Bombings (3.5.3), Mr Wilson wrote:

> ... there is a widespread demand to find the truth about individual cases. The most prominent of these is the case of the Dublin Monaghan bombings of 17th May, 1974. A quarter of a century later this is still the greatest atrocity of the Troubles. No one has ever been made amenable. This is obviously felt deeply by the relatives of those killed and by those injured. Little information has been given from official sources as to who may have committed the crime or why. My information on what happened comes, in the main, from reportage which suggests, among other things, that the Garda investigation had identified the probable culprits very quickly but that it then ran into difficulties. This reportage also suggests that the Garda did not receive all appropriate co-operation from the RUC, that the Irish Government did not press the British Government on this point, and that agents of

a friendly Government may have had a hand in planning and executing the crime. Some of the reportage presents evidence, which, on the face of it, seems very plausible, to support some of these allegations. These surviving victims and relatives have been relentless in their commitment to finding out the truth. They have gone to the High and Supreme Courts seeking Garda files in support of their case with the European Court of Human Rights — to no avail. While I understand the Garda Commissioner's stand in upholding the principle of the confidentiality of Garda files, this seems to have reinforced the belief of some of the victims that there has been and that there continues to be some sort of cover up.

It is, I believe, significant that Commissioner Wilson does not mention two internal Garda investigations, which followed the 1993 Yorkshire Television *First Tuesday* broadcast, and the 1995 RTÉ *Prime Time* broadcast. Despite the attempts by the Department of Justice and the Garda Síochána to underplay the material contained in both documentaries, it appears that Mr Wilson was more impressed by the 'very plausible' reportage of these and other investigative journalists.

Commissioner Wilson's report went on to say that similar concerns were expressed by victims of other outrages such as the Sackville Place and Liberty Hall bombings, which killed George Bradshaw and Thomas Duffy on 1 December 1972, and the murder of Seamus Ludlow, near Dundalk, on 1 May 1976.

His Conclusions and Recommendations, however, regarding the Dublin and Monaghan bombings (4.5.2) caused uproar amongst the families and wounded involved in the Justice for the Forgotten campaign. There was immediate controversy with the recommendation '... that the Government choose a former Supreme Court Judge to enquire privately into [the Dublin and Monaghan bombings]'

Despite the fact that he recommended that the eminent legal person conducting the inquiry would adopt, almost verbatim, the demands of the Justice for the Forgotten campaign statement as his or her terms of reference, the use of the word 'private' caused a storm of protest amongst many of the bereaved and wounded. In effect, it compounded their suspicions and hurt. While John Wilson did recommend that the Judge would 'publish a report on his/her findings', to them the whole idea of a 'private inquiry' was unacceptable and confirmed their suspicions of a 'cover-up' — suspicions acknowledged by the Commissioner in his report.

After a quarter of a century of abandonment by the Irish State, the Commissioner's recommendation was viewed with very deep disappointment.

Their disquiet was expressed by 75-year-old Frank Massey, at the launch of Mr Wilson's report. Frank Massey's daughter Anna died in South Leinster Street. He protested:

> We asked you for a public inquiry. What is the Government afraid of? We are not going to have some faceless person telling us that we can't attend the inquiry. We are part of this — an essential part!'

The day after the publication of the Victims' Commissioner's report, solicitor Greg O'Neill wrote to Walter Kirwan, a senior official at the Taoiseach's Department. He stated:

> Despite the negative reaction of the victims and relatives to the Commission's recommendation of a private enquiry, ... Justice for the Forgotten and the victims and relatives generally endorse and applaud the Victims' Commission's recommendations over a broad range of issues which unfortunately were not discussed at the press conference [for the publication].
>
> Our committee will be working with you in accordance with its original agenda, i.e., to work out the feasibility of establishing a Public Tribunal of Inquiry....

Frank Massey's angry sentiments were unanimously supported by all the families and wounded who comprised the now formidable Justice for the Forgotten Campaign. At a press conference held on 7 August, following a meeting of the bereaved and wounded, their lengthy four-page press statement said:

> We are, without reservation, deeply disappointed that Mr. Wilson has chosen to recommend a private inquiry.... For those who have been abandoned by the police and justice system in this State for twenty-five years, any inquiry which compromises the principles of openness, transparency and accountability will not have any credibility.

Speaking on behalf of the families, Greg O'Neill told the press:

> There are clearly matters of public interest to warrant a Tribunal of Inquiry under the Tribunal of Inquiries Act. The reluctance of the Government to do so is bizarre and in the view of many may be explicable only in terms of maintenance of secrecy over that which should be revealed. It adds insult to the injury suffered by the bereaved and wounded.

On the same day as the bereaved and wounded held their press conference to react to the Victims' Commission recommendation of a private inquiry, Dr Conor Cruise O'Brien directed a caustic rebuke at *The Irish Times* for failing to show a 'better sense of news values' in comparison to the *Irish Independent*. On the previous day, the latter had run with the headline, 'Terrorists unite to threaten new blitz' while *The Irish Times* had a heading which spanned, according to Dr Cruise O'Brien, 'five columns on the front page', and which read: 'Private inquiry likely into 1974 bombings'. Dr Cruise O'Brien continued:

> Which is more relevant to the lives of readers today, a report of a serious perceived threat in the here and now, or a report of a proposed inquiry into events of a quarter of a century ago? Probably more than half of the current readership of both newspapers were either not born, or not yet aware of news, in 1974. But what is happening right now, and threatening lives here and now ought to be a matter of acute concern to all readers.

For such grossly insensitive remarks to be made by someone who was a member of the Government's 'Security Committee' at the time of the Dublin and Monaghan massacre is, to say the least, extraordinary.

By mid-October 1999, after nationwide consultations with its members, the Justice for the Forgotten campaign formally notified the Government of their overwhelming rejection of Victims' Commissioner John Wilson's recommendation that the Government establish a private inquiry into the bombings.

At a meeting with officials from the Department of the Taoiseach on 14 October 1999, a senior official said he had recently met with Mr Wilson informally and had been told by him that the Dublin and Monaghan families or their representatives never used the adjective 'public' when they met the Commissioner in 1998. Lawyers for the victims rebutted this suggestion forcefully.

Barrister Cormac Ó Dulacháin referred to his submission to the Victims' Commission on behalf of the bereaved and wounded. In December 1998 Ó Dulacháin presented the Commissioner with a submission headed 'The Case for a Tribunal of Inquiry concerning the Dublin and Monaghan Bombings on the 17th of May 1974'. It clearly stated:

4.1 The victims and relatives of the Dublin & Monaghan bombings ... believe that a sworn *public* tribunal of inquiry is the only existing mechanism that can address their substantive needs in the absence of a formally constituted Truth Commission.

4.2 Accordingly the victims and relatives, on whose behalf this submission is made, seek the endorsement and recommendation of the Victims' Commissioner for a Tribunal of Inquiry.'

Ó Dulacháin's submission to the Victims' Commission also included a report from Professor Dermot Walsh, Director of the Centre for Criminal Justice, University of Limerick, which concludes:

If an inquiry is to overcome the accountability shortcomings ... and serve the needs of the victims ... it is essential that it should be a *public* judicial inquiry with full powers to call for persons, papers and records.

Furthermore, minutes from the campaign's meeting with the Taoiseach, Bertie Ahern, on 22 April 1999, at which the officials were present, clearly record Cormac Ó Dulacháin expressing the firm belief 'that the only legal mechanism possible is a public inquiry....' The minutes also record the following:

He [the Taoiseach] suggested that a sub-committee be set up which will include our legal team, Don and others to work with officials from his Department to work towards a public inquiry. He did not commit himself to a public inquiry: 'I can't give outright commitments without going to the Cabinet and Attorney General,' he said. He confirmed, in response to a question by Don Mullan, that he is not ruling out a public inquiry.

At the meeting in Government Buildings on 14 October 1999, the Justice for the Forgotten committee informed the Government of their unequivocal and unanimous rejection of the recommendation of a 'private' inquiry. A letter, addressed to the Taoiseach, stating the families' rejection, was handed to the officials at the meeting by solicitor Greg O'Neill. It stated:

Our clients wish it to be noted that at no stage did Mr. Wilson seek or canvas their views on a Private Inquiry. Indeed, it is not known where the idea of a Private Inquiry originated and what matters influenced Mr. Wilson in this recommendation. We know not who, if anyone, he consulted in regard to this recommendation.

    The recommendation of a Private Inquiry appears to be without substance or merit and serves to denigrate the concerns which our clients wish to be addressed in a Public Inquiry. In short, our clients' grievances have been added to by Mr. Wilson's recommendation concerning a Private Inquiry. After 25 years of privacy and secrecy, they cannot have any confidence in an Inquiry that is conducted other than in public and with statutory powers.

During an interview for TV3's flagship programme *20/20*, on the 9 November 1999, I asked Commissioner Wilson why he had recommended a 'private' inquiry when the bereaved and wounded clearly wanted a public inquiry. He responded:

... all the correspondence that I have and I've gone through them meticulously — an inquiry was mentioned, a tribunal of inquiry was mentioned, but a public tribunal of inquiry wasn't mentioned at all, and I just read it today for a second time and right through a tribunal is mentioned but the word public is not in it.

Greg O'Neill, reacting to Mr Wilson's assertion that a 'public' inquiry had not been requested, is quoted in *Ireland on Sunday*, on 11 November 1999, as follows:

Our submission explicitly and implicitly called for a Public Inquiry and anyone reading the content of what was submitted could have been under no other impression. I don't know how Mr. Wilson came up with the idea or who influenced him. There are clearly tensions there between the Department of Justice and the rest of the Government.

In a major boost to those campaigning for a full public tribunal of inquiry into the Dublin and Monaghan bombings and the murder of Seamus Ludlow, the eminent UK solicitor, Imran Khan, who represented the family of murdered black teenager, Stephen Lawrence, encouraged them to reject the idea of a private inquiry. He said on the *20/20* programme on 11 November:

There are many reasons why the public inquiry achieved what the Lawrences wanted.

The way witnesses gave evidence ... they knew what they were saying would be open to public scrutiny. They couldn't hide behind the fact that what they were saying wouldn't be in the public arena. They were under pressure to tell the truth and then the public could make up their own minds on what was being said.... Because the inquiry itself was under public scrutiny, the conclusions the inquiry came to reflected the evidence the public knew about.

If it's a private inquiry you'll have a situation in that those who'll have to come to conclusions could put a gloss on what actually had occurred rather than deal with the facts as the public had seen it.

Khan was scathing in his comments regarding the offer of 'private' inquiries:

If any government is offering a private inquiry, then I would suspect that there is something to hide. Something that will embarrass or otherwise concern the Government and I think it means there are more questions to be answered. For this reason it is even more important there is a full public inquiry where there is full access to information and scrutiny by all those that are outside the particular case.

Within days of the 1974 bombings, the involvement of British Intelligence was suspected, given the sophistication and military precision of the attack. In spite of the UVF's statement in 1993 claiming sole involvement in the operation, the suspicion has grown in intensity over the years. The unwillingness of the Irish Government and the Garda Síochána to pursue this 'very plausible' possibility (strengthened by the opinions of several experts and former Irish and British Intelligence operatives) is peculiar.

Conclusion

'Only it happened to me, I wouldn't believe it.'

These are the words of Tim Grace whose wife Breda was murdered in the Dublin and Monaghan bombings on 17 May 1974. They were spoken at Dublin City University at the beginning of a presentation about the trauma of his loss. Tim was not referring to the fact that his wife was killed, leaving him alone to raise their one-year-old son. He was referring specifically to the official silence, intrigue and lack of public accountability that have characterised the political and police response to the biggest mass-murder case in the history of the Irish State.

The focus of the families and wounded who are involved in the Justice for the Forgotten Campaign has perceptibly changed in the past few years. While they still wish to know the whos and whys concerning the bombings, their focus now is on official answers to very basic and simple questions regarding the nature, extent and adequacy of the Garda investigation, and the response of the Government of the day.

During February 1999, the bereaved and wounded wrote to every member of the Oireachtas who, the previous year, had packed the Dáil and Seanad chambers to rush through tough emergency legislation following the Omagh bombing. The letter invited patronage for their campaign and support for a public tribunal of inquiry. In both houses, little more than 20 per cent of members responded positively: 36 TDs from all parties, excluding the Progressive Democrats, and 12 senators. No reply was received from 101 TDs (60 per cent) and 45 senators (75 per cent).

The predictable response from key Government ministers repeated the official response of the Department for Justice, that a tribunal of inquiry would not be a suitable course of action as the Garda investigation files remained open.

An Taoiseach, Bertie Ahern, TD

During 1995, as leader of the opposition, Bertie Ahern, TD, launched a book at the Irish Film Centre entitled *Turning the Page without Closing the Book: the Right to Truth in the Irish Context*. In the course of his address, he said that the dogs in the street could bark the names of those behind the 1974 Dublin and Monaghan bombings.

On 5 March 1999 a delegation of the group, Relatives for Justice, met with the Taoiseach, Mr Ahern, at Government Buildings. As part of a broad discussion on the issue of people killed in the 'Troubles' by British State forces, the issue of the Dublin and Monaghan bombings was raised. According to those present, Mr Ahern said that before he became Taoiseach he had intended to open the files on the bombings. However, since coming to power he had discovered that there was nothing in the files that would have suggested or indicated who was responsible.

The Taoiseach later clarified to Dáil Éireann that he was referring to Government departmental files and not the files of the Garda Síochána, within which we know that the names of prime suspects are listed. On 22 April 1999, he became the first Taoiseach to receive a delegation from the Justice for the Forgotten Campaign in an official capacity. Twenty-four of the thirty-three victims who died lost their lives in his constituency.

The meeting, scheduled for forty-five minutes, lasted an hour and a half. The bereaved and wounded assured the Taoiseach that they would not give up their campaign until the Government acceded to their demand for a public tribunal of inquiry. It must be noted that the Taoiseach handled the meeting sensitively. The bereaved and wounded left with the feeling that he was genuine in his expressed desire to assist them in finding closure to their suffering and ordeal.

The Taoiseach did not rule out the possibility of establishing such a tribunal of inquiry, and asked the campaign to establish a working committee to meet with an interdepartmental group of Government officials to explore ways of advancing the issue to a satisfactory conclusion. The campaign agreed to engage constructively with him in this process.

The first and only meeting of the Taoiseach's interdepartmental group took place at Government Buildings on 12 August 1999. Participating in the meeting were representatives of the Department of An Taoiseach, the Department of Foreign Affairs and the Attorney General's Office. The Department of Justice and the Garda Síochána were not represented as it might 'give rise to a perception of a clash of interests'. During the meeting, a senior official at the Department of An Taoiseach, Mr Wally Kirwan, said, 'It has to be admitted the State did fall short' concerning the victims of the Dublin and Monaghan bombings. This was the first official admission that the State had failed in its duty to protect and uphold the human rights of the bereaved and injured to truth and justice.

By then, the Justice for the Forgotten Campaign had made public their decision to reject the Victims Commissioner's recommendation for a private inquiry. However, it became clear at the meeting that the Government was moving in favour of adopting Mr Wilson's recommendation. Furthermore, the Government officials attending questioned the role, necessity and continuance of the Taoiseach's interdepartmental committee.

Despite strong objections by Greg O'Neill, the solicitor for the Justice for the Forgotten Campaign, the Taoiseach announced on 29 September 1999 that the Cabinet had accepted Mr Wilson's recommendation. His announcement served only to compound the loss of faith in the State which the victims of the Dublin and Monaghan bombings had steadily developed over the years.

On 1 October 1999, Margaret Urwin, secretary to the Justice for the Forgotten Campaign, was informed that the interdepartmental committee's work would now be taken over by officials at the Department of Justice. This was an extraordinary turnaround and was viewed by the Campaign as a very worrying development. It threatened to kill whatever faith and hope the families and wounded had cautiously developed through their engagement with the Taoiseach.

At a meeting on 7 October 1999, with officials from the Taoiseach's Department and the Department of Justice, Margaret Urwin made a crucial intervention by raising the issue of the Government's call for a public inquiry into the murder of Pat Finucane. The Government's assessment, submitted to the Northern Ireland Office, had included a section which stated:

> A public inquiry is held when it is deemed that there are matters sufficient on the grounds of urgent public interest to warrant one... the term 'urgent' should not be taken to mean contemporary... nor should it be thought that new information is a requirement for an inquiry.... Generally inquiries are about matters in which the State or its agents are believed to have been involved either through acts of omission or commission. The value of an inquiry in terms of the society as a whole is that it seeks to locate where culpability lies and thus establish a basis on which society, through its democratic system, can set about rectifying identified faults.

The Irish Government's assessment on the Finucane case made reference to 'the compelling circumstantial evidence presented by the marked change in the pattern of loyalist killings between 1988 and 1994.'

Margaret Urwin argued that the sophistication of the bombs used in the Dublin and Monaghan attack equally pointed to 'a marked change in the pattern of loyalist bombs in the early 1970s'. As has been considered, several experts support this point of view.

Urwin further highlighted reference in the assessment to 'the belief that RUC officers failed to co-operate with and possibly sought to frustrate the Stevens investigation.' She pointed out that in the case of Dublin and Monaghan there is the belief that the RUC failed to co-operate with the Garda Síochána to the extent that one would expect from a 'normal' police force.

She also highlighted, in the Government's assessment, reference to 'the widespread belief in the nationalist community that members and units of the security forces were involved in systematic purposeful collusion'. Again she pointed out that in the case of the Dublin and Monaghan bombings there is a widespread belief that members of the British security services and security forces were involved.

Finally, Margaret Urwin drew attention to the conclusion of the Government's assessment which stated:

It has been a poignant characteristic of relatives who have lost loved ones in such circumstances that the desire for truth and justice reaches a particularly acute point during sustained peace.... The lack of corrective action denied them the normal solace of the pursuit and prosecution of those who inflicted such pain and loss. Those failures endorsed an existing sense among nationalists of being undervalued and unequal in the eyes of the law. However desirable in terms of political reconciliation it may be to draw a line under the past, victims' relatives will inevitably carry their burdens into everyone's present and to continue to do so unless they have answers that help reconcile them with their loss.... The pursuit of certain cases can serve to be representative of that process of candour and truth.

'What more appropriate representative case could be taken', Urwin asked the Government officials, 'than that of Dublin and Monaghan, the greatest single atrocity committed on this island since World War II?'

The Government was conscious that without the co-operation and support of the bereaved and the injured, any private inquiry would lack public credibility. Consequently, the implementation of the recommendations of the Victims' Commissioner was stalled. There is no doubt that this development owed much to the growing strength of the Justice for the Forgotten Campaign.

Joint Oireachtas Committee Hearing

Somewhat out of the blue, the campaign was invited to make a presentation before the Joint Oireachtas Committee on Justice, Equality, Defence and Women's Rights on 25 November 1999. At the end of the hearing several members of the Oireachtas Committee voiced a chorus of support for the families' demand for a public inquiry.

On 8 December, during the Taoiseach's Question Time, Labour Leader Ruairí Quinn, TD, suggested an Oireachtas Committee Inquiry into the Dublin and Monaghan bombings. This, he suggested, could be modelled on that of the Public Accounts Committee (PAC) into the DIRT scandal. The Taoiseach later expressed interest in Deputy Quinn's suggestion.

Following this, the Justice for the Forgotten campaign was invited to a meeting at Government Buildings to be held on 16 December 1999. The meeting was attended by officials from the Taoiseach's Department, and the Attorney-General, Michael McDowell, SC. It became clear, almost immediately, that there was one item on the agenda — Ruairí Quinn's proposal.

The Attorney-General acknowledged the rejection by the families and wounded of the Victim Commissioner's 'private inquiry' recommendation. He said that the Government was now considering a response similar to the Public Accounts Committee inquiry. Specific legislation would allow an investigation to take place, the findings of which would be reported to the Joint Oireachtas Committee on Justice, Equality and Women's Rights. It was proposed that Chief Justice Liam Hamilton, who was due to retire at the end of January 2000, would examine the evidence, together with researchers. It was envisaged that Mr Justice Hamilton's assessment would take between six and nine months to complete.

The Government agreed to a full right-of-audience for the relatives and wounded at the Public Hearing of the Oireachtas Committee. Before making their decision on whether to co-operate, the lawyers for the Campaign sought further clarification and reassurance on a number of points. One assurance involved a commitment from the Taoiseach that he would seek the full co-operation of the British Government in helping to establish the truth about what happened. This was agreed.

On 18 December 1999, 95 per cent of the bereaved and wounded agreed to co-operate with the initiative on the clear understanding that:

- This was a process of assessment of all files and evidence to be carried out by Mr Justice Hamilton and not a 'private inquiry'.

- Justice Hamilton's report, which would not draw conclusions or make recommendations and would be presented to the Oireachtas Committee on Justice would be considered in public session, at which they would be legally represented.

- They were of the firm opinion that a public tribunal of inquiry was still the proper course and they would, therefore, actively campaign for that objective in the months and years ahead.

The following day, the Taoiseach announced the initiative in a press release, which concluded by saying that the Government believed that this approach represented a genuine attempt to respond to the legitimate needs and concerns of those injured or bereaved as a result of these appalling outrages and to move towards closure for people who had suffered for too long.

In a press release issued at the same time as the Taoiseach's, Justice for the Forgotten welcomed 'the commitment of the Government, with the support of the Opposition Parties' to deliver Mr Justice Hamilton's report to the Joint Oireachtas Committee, and the commitment of the Government that 'the families will be fully represented at the public sessions....'

The Campaign regarded the process as 'the first stage in the establishment of a properly constituted public inquiry into all aspects of this case'. However, they expressed reservations about the fact that Mr Justice Hamilton would not also be investigating other important unsolved murders in the Republic, including the 1972 and 1973 Dublin bombings.

An important act of campaign solidarity occurred on 13 June 2000 when Justice for the Forgotten issued a joint press statement with the family of Seamus Ludlow and the families of the victims of the 1972 and 1973 Dublin bombings, and the 1975 Dundalk bombing. The previous week, the Taoiseach had called for an independent public inquiry into the murder of Portadown man, Robert Hamill. On 8 June, in an interview on RTÉ's *Morning Ireland*, former Taoiseach Albert Reynolds supported the Taoiseach's call, expressed the need for a process of public accountability that was open and transparent and expressed concern that no inquest would be held into Robert Hamill's sectarian murder.

The joint statement issued by the campaigns welcomed the Taoiseach's call for public inquiries into the murders of Robert Hamill and of human rights lawyers Pat Finucane and Rosemary Nelson, as well as his support for the new Bloody Sunday Inquiry. The statement also welcomed Albert Reynolds' remarks. 'However,' it continued, 'their calls for public inquiries into atrocities committed outside this jurisdiction ring rather hollow when compared with their continued reluctance to hold public inquiries in this jurisdiction into the murders of our loved ones who died in equally tragic and controversial circumstances.' The statement went on to say that Mr Reynolds' expression of concern over the failure to hold an inquest in the Robert Hamill case 'might carry more conviction if he was to express equal concern at the failure of this State to conclude inquests in the cases of the Dublin bombings of 1972, 1973 and 1974.'

The statement concluded by asking the media to 'challenge the Taoiseach and all politicians who express support for inquiries outside this jurisdiction to account for the glaring anomaly of their failure to address the demands of victims in this State.'

Independent Commission of Inquiry

Mr Justice Hamilton established his 'Independent Commission of Inquiry' on 31 January 2000, with an office in the Department of the Taoiseach. The Government, in consultation with the Attorney-General, also agreed to fund, for approximately three months, the legal costs of the victims' engagement with Mr Hamilton's assessment. The agreed terms of reference are:

- To undertake a thorough examination, involving fact-finding and assessment, of all aspects of the Dublin and Monaghan bombings and their sequel, including
    - the facts, circumstances, causes and perpetrators of the bombings;
    - the nature, extent and adequacy of Garda investigation, including the co-operation with and from the relevant authorities in Northern Ireland and the handling of evidence, including the scientific analyses of forensic evidence;
    - the reasons why no prosecution took place, including whether and, if so, by whom and to what extent the investigations were impeded; and
    - the issues raised by the *Hidden Hand* TV documentary broadcast in 1993.

International Support

There is growing support in the British parliament for cross-jurisdictional co-operation into the bombings investigation. In the lead-up to the twenty-fifth anniversary of the atrocity, twelve British MPs supported an Early Day Motion (EDM 644) sponsored by Dr Norman Godman, MP. The motion called for the House of Commons to commemorate the twenty-fifth anniversary of the Dublin and Monaghan bombings, to support the demands of the bereaved and wounded for a thorough investigation and 'to waive the prohibitions of the Official Secrets Act and agree to establish in co-operation with the Irish Government a full and independent investigation to establish the truth'.

On the occasion of the twenty-sixth anniversary of the bombings, the bereaved and wounded of Dublin and Monaghan were further encouraged by the growing international support for their campaign when six members of the United States Congress wrote to the Taoiseach calling for a public tribunal of inquiry.

Joint Chairperson to the Justice for the Forgotten Campaign, Michelle O'Brien, welcomed the Congressmen's intervention as 'by far the most important international support we have received in our long and lonely 26-year campaign for Justice.'

Conclusion

All citizens of the Republic of Ireland have the right to know whether there is any substance to the notation in Captain Fred Holroyd's forensically tested police notebooks from the period, that instructions were given to the Garda Síochána to stop their investigations into the mass murder. These are serious matters with serious implications for the democratic health of the Irish and British states. They had dire and devastating consequences for the lives of many innocent citizens of three European Union states in the months and years following.

What is most galling for the bereaved and injured is the knowledge that the prime suspects for the murderous bombings of 1974 were not pursued with the necessary determination and rigour. A number of those suspects continued to murder, north and south, with apparent impunity. How?

The full story may not be told unless and until all that was said and decided at the meetings of the Government, and its various departments and committees, in the days and weeks following the bombings, is revealed.

These are not matters to be considered in a 'private inquiry' or simply left to Mr Justice Hamilton's 'Independent Commission of Inquiry'. They are matters which require a sworn cross-jurisdictional public tribunal of inquiry.

Nothing less is acceptable.

Afterword: History of the Campaign

For many years the issue of the Dublin and Monaghan bombings was dead and buried, together with the thirty-three victims. No annual commemoration was held, no stone marked the sites of the bombings in Dublin — it was as if this terrible atrocity had never happened. At the bomb site in Monaghan a small plaque was erected in 1978 at the instigation of Mr Padge McKenna, Town Clerk. As recently as June 1993, the then Taoiseach, Mr Albert Reynolds, in response to independent TD Tony Gregory's plea for a fitting commemoration and memorial for the Dublin and Monaghan victims, replied that it would be 'invidious to single them out for special official commemoration'. Tony Gregory responded by reminding the Taoiseach that members of the Irish Government attended the Enniskillen commemoration every year. The families of the victims and the wounded were impotent and demoralised in their terrible loss — no counselling, or support of any kind, had been provided by official Ireland. Not one penny in funds was ever raised for them. They received only derisory statutory compensation.

However, there was one concerned citizen who had witnessed the dreadful carnage of that terrible May day and had not forgotten. When the tenth anniversary came and went without any recognition, Kevin Walsh of Ballyfermot, Dublin, a trade union official, began to lobby members of Dublin Corporation for a memorial to be erected. Finally, six years later, in April 1990, Kevin received a letter from Alderman Seán Haughey, Lord Mayor of Dublin, stating that he had raised the issue of a memorial and that the City Manager was examining the situation.

At about the same time, John Rogers of Cabra, now sadly deceased, accompanied Kevin Walsh to request the administrator of St Mary's Pro-Cathedral in Dublin, Rev. Dermod McCarthy, to celebrate a commemorative Mass for all the victims on the sixteenth anniversary of the bombing. Fr McCarthy readily agreed to this suggestion and also promised that, from then on, a Mass would be celebrated each year on the anniversary. This promise has been faithfully adhered to by the clergy of the Pro-Cathedral. To ensure maximum attendance of the families of the victims at that first commemorative Mass, Kevin Walsh, at his own expense, placed advertisements in the national newspapers and also wrote to the President, members of the Oireachtas and Dublin Corporation, inviting them to attend. Kevin and John were congratulated on their initiative by Alderman Tomás MacGiolla TD and Senator John Dardis. A commemorative Mass was also organised on this date by the Dublin '68 Committee and was held at the Capuchin Franciscan Church in Dublin's Church Street.

Kevin's hopes for the erection of a memorial were at last realised on the seventeenth anniversary when, at a ceremony attended by the Lord Mayor of Dublin and several councillors, a stone was unveiled near the Garden of Remembrance. In recognition of his immense contribution, Kevin Walsh was invited by both families and dignitaries to address those assembled. This memorial was replaced by Dublin Corporation in September 1997; a large monument, bearing the names of all the victims, now stands in Talbot Street, close to Connolly Station.

Meanwhile, other strands had begun to come together. Denise and Angela O'Neill, daughters of Edward, killed in Parnell Street, and sisters of Billy and Edward, Jr., who were seriously injured, had grown to adulthood. Denise came across a newspaper article in 1988 that suggested the involvement of British intelligence in the Dublin and Monaghan bombings. She contacted the Garda Press Office about the article and only then discovered, to her dismay, that nobody had ever been convicted, or even charged, in connection with the outrage. She was assured that the files were still open. Determined to raise the issue, she and Angela began writing to the then Taoiseach, Charles Haughey, and to TDs. They attempted to contact other families by placing advertisements in newspapers, looking up telephone directories and press cuttings and calling personally to addresses. In the summer of 1990 they made contact with the family of Anne Byrne (killed in Talbot Street), and succeeded, eventually, in bringing together seventeen or eighteen families. Denise spoke publicly for the first time at the commemorative Mass organised by Kevin Walsh and John Rogers in 1990.

Other concerned citizens were similarly incensed at the State's lack of response to the bombings. Journalist Frank Doherty published an article in *Now* magazine in May 1990, which alleged that the Gardaí had the names of several suspects and that they were reluctant to pursue enquiries because of Garda links with British Intelligence. One man who read this article with interest was John Conway, a Dundalk businessman, who had, for many years, been concerned about the lack of official interest in the bombings. Having watched Yorkshire Television's documentary on the Stalker affair he was moved to write to the television station stating that the Dublin and Monaghan bombings were a much bigger 'can of worms', and suggesting that they might consider producing a documentary on the subject. He enclosed Frank Doherty's article from *Now* magazine. Glyn Middleton of Yorkshire Television has confirmed to me that this was what first provoked his interest in the subject.

Meanwhile, Lieutenant Colonel John Morgan, who served as head of security G2 (Military Intelligence) at Army Headquarters in Dublin, had retired in 1986. The following year, he had begun to study the issues surrounding the Dublin and Monaghan bombings and, within a year, had come to definite conclusions. He stated in the *Sunday Business Post* of 11 July 1993 that his problem then was how to bring these conclusions to light. 'There was no interest anywhere. It was all dead and buried since 1974', he said. However, the Irish language newspaper, *Anois*, decided to publish his findings, articles by him appearing in March, April and May of 1990. In these articles he described how he believed the bombings to have been carried out, and by whom. He had high hopes of stimulating official interest but his hopes were dashed. He was met with disbelief and put-downs. However, John Conway got to hear of Morgan's work and put him in touch with Yorkshire Television, in the belief that it was the only television station in these islands likely to take on such a controversial matter. Lt Col. Morgan met with Glyn Middleton in a Dublin hotel in December 1990, at which time he handed over his written analysis of the bombings and spoke for four hours on tape.

The Yorkshire Television team, after some weeks of research, decided to go ahead with the production of a documentary. Their work on the project over two-and-a-half years resulted in *Hidden Hand: the Forgotten Massacre*, co-produced by Glyn Middleton and Mark Ackerman, and broadcast on Channel 4 television on 6 July 1993. The contents of this programme are comprehensively dealt with elsewhere in the book (Chapter 5). Suffice it to say here that the Irish people owe a huge debt of gratitude to Yorkshire Television which was prepared to highlight the immoral and illegal acts of some of its own fellow-citizens. Lt Col. Morgan eloquently salutes their courage: 'To love one's country enough to expose its wrongdoings is patriotism of a high order'.

By the time the documentary was broadcast, many of the families of victims and the injured had joined together as a formidable campaign calling for a public inquiry. A petition containing 40,000 signatures was handed into the Taoiseach's office and copies of the documentary were sent to American senators. A public meeting was held in a Dublin hotel on 7 July 1993 — the evening following the broadcast. Four TDs — Tony Gregory, Eamonn Gilmore, Joe Costello and Austin Currie — attended this meeting. However, the Government was steadfast in its refusal to consider any inquiry. The then Minister for Justice, Mrs Máire Geoghegan-Quinn, in response to questioning in the Dáil by Tony Gregory and Eamonn Gilmore, ignored the issues raised and concentrated, instead, on the question of obtaining evidence sufficient to convict the culprits. By delaying for almost two years a response to the issues raised, both Máire Geoghegan-Quinn and her successor, Nora Owen, ensured that public anger and concern would be diffused, and would, eventually, dissipate. It would be three months before the gardaí contacted the producers of the programme. This happened only after a telephone call to the Department of Justice from Glyn Middleton.

Bitter disappointment was, once again, to be the lot of the families of the victims. No inquiry was called, and weeks of inaction stretched into months. After the build-up to the programme and the publicity in the immediate aftermath, silence again descended on the issue. The producers of *Hidden Hand: The Forgotten Massacre* had returned to Leeds. The families, whose hopes had been raised so high, became disheartened. Disagreements developed over the way forward for the campaign, and an ensuing rift between the families, sadly, worked to the advantage of the Government.

In October 1993 members of two victims' families — Jackie Wade (sister of Talbot Street victim Collette Doherty who was nine months pregnant when she died) and Alice O'Brien (sister of Parnell Street victim Anna O'Brien whose husband and two baby daughters were also killed) — contacted the Irish National Congress.[1] The Dublin and Monaghan families hoped that the INC might be able to assist them in setting up a similar inquiry. Four members became involved initially: Robert Ballagh, Nora Comiskey, Thomas Cullen and myself. Lt Col. John Morgan was also, at this time, involved in helping the families.

Throughout 1994 strenuous efforts were made to organise an unofficial public inquiry. The structures were decided upon and potential jurists were contacted. However, the initiative failed through lack of funding. Efforts continued to have the matter raised in the Dáil as the families still awaited a response to the documentary. Hopes were still alive that an official public inquiry might be forthcoming when the Garda investigation was complete. These hopes were to be shattered. In a statement issued by the Department of Justice, on 17 May 1995, and provided to the families in meetings with the Minister for Justice, Nora Owen, it was stated that the latest Garda investigation had produced 'no evidence that would enable any person to be charged'. There was no mention of a public inquiry and, at face-to-face meetings with the families, the Minister refused to consider such an option.

---

1   The INC, whose aims are peace, unity and justice in Ireland, had a track record in raising concerns in relation to human rights abuses perpetrated against Northern nationalists. The organisation had instigated the establishment of an unofficial public inquiry into the shooting by the British Army of an unarmed civilian, Fergal Caraher, in Cullyhanna, Co. Armagh in December 1990. The inquiry, held in Cullyhanna in June 1991, was presided over by international jurors, including the British human-rights lawyer, Michael Mansfield QC. The inquiry put pressure on the British Government and the RUC, which resulted in the arrest of two soldiers who were brought to trial. They were, however, subsequently, acquitted.

On the day following the release of the statement from the Department of Justice, RTÉ broadcast a programme entitled *Friendly Forces?* which broadly endorsed the findings of Yorkshire Television. The programme, which was produced by Paul Larkin, also dealt with the vexed issue of British intelligence involvement with loyalist paramilitaries, and the even more controversial issue of direct links between British Intelligence and the gardaí. It came as no surprise to the families of the victims when, nine months later, the Minister for Justice stated that 'the Garda authorities were satisfied from their assessment of the *Prime Time* broadcast of May 1995 that no new evidence or witness had been identified which would provide a basis for further Garda investigations'.

However, despite the Government's negative response to both programmes, the families decided to fight on. Yorkshire Television had let the genie out of the bottle and it refused to go back in. In January 1996 the campaign succeeded in securing funding from a number of concerned citizens, thus enabling it to hire a legal team. Solicitor Greg O'Neill and Barrister Cormac Ó Dulacháin had shown a deep interest in the case. Having studied the issue thoroughly, they felt that there were grounds for a case to be taken to the European Court of Human Rights against the United Kingdom Government for a breach of Article 2 of the European Convention on Human Rights. Over the following two years, actions were taken in the High Court and Supreme Court for discovery of the Garda files on the bombings, in order to assist with the claims before the European Court. Unfortunately, the cases were lost and, in July 1999, the European Court declared the cases before them to be time-barred because of their six-month ruling.

In the interval between the High Court case and the Supreme Court appeal a meeting was facilitated by Deputy Brian Lenihan. It took place in October 1997, and was attended by a number of families and the Minister for Justice, Mr John O'Donoghue TD. The purpose of the meeting was twofold: to ask the Minister whether he was prepared to instruct the Garda Commissioner to release the Garda files to the European Commission; and to enquire whether he would consider the establishment of a public tribunal of inquiry, or — in view of the climate created by the ongoing Peace Process — a Truth

Commission. The Minister addressed only the issue of the Garda files, which, he said, was a matter for the Garda authorities. He stressed, however, that he was anxious to help the families and said that he would get back to the lawyers. Neither the lawyers nor the families ever heard from the Minister for Justice following that meeting.

Don Mullan, author of *Eyewitness Bloody Sunday,* offered his expertise to the campaign, in September 1998, at the instigation of Robert Ballagh. He was gladly welcomed on board as adviser, and his encouragement and support have played a large part in uniting the campaign and healing the rift that had developed. His skill as an investigative journalist has been of enormous help in sourcing evidence in the case and in asking awkward questions of both Government and Garda Síochána alike. A campaign mission statement evolved and was adopted. The new unity, determination and sharp focus of the campaign led to the securing of a meeting with the Taoiseach, Bertie Ahern TD, in April, 1999 — the first meeting between a serving Taoiseach and families of the victims of the greatest atrocity the State has ever endured. At that meeting the Taoiseach was left in no doubt about the campaign's single-mindedness in its demand for a public tribunal of inquiry. Since then, the momentum has continued to mount.

Following the publicity surrounding the twenty-fifth anniversary commemorations — a special Mass in the Pro-Cathedral and an ecumenical service in Our Lady of Lourdes Church in Seán McDermott Street, Dublin, and open letters in the newspapers — more families and injured contacted us and became involved in the campaign. At this stage, 85 per cent of the families who lost loved ones are on board. In August 1999, the Victims' Commission, which had been established by the Minister for Justice as a requirement of the Good Friday Agreement, recommended a private inquiry into the bombings. This was totally rejected by the campaign.

A historic meeting was held at the Hillgrove Hotel in Monaghan on 20 November 1999, where most of the families of the Monaghan victims met one another for the first time. The meeting was also attended by several of those injured in Monaghan, and the campaign mission statement was adopted by them. A decision was made to hold an ecumenical service in Monaghan in May 2000, to celebrate the twenty-sixth anniversary. Notwithstanding the fact that seven of its citizens lost their lives in the bombing, no commemorative service had ever been held there.

The Joint Oireachtas Committee on Justice, Equality, Defence and Women's Rights, under the Chairmanship of Deputy Eoin Ryan, invited the campaign to a public hearing on 25 November 1999. A written submission, entitled *A Trust Betrayed*, was presented to the Committee; it makes the case for a public tribunal of inquiry. (This submission had already been presented to the Taoiseach). Oral presentations were given by five family members, by our Junior Counsel, by Glyn Middleton of Yorkshire Television, co-producer of *Hidden Hand: The Forgotten Massacre*, and by Don Mullan. The members of the Oireachtas who attended this hearing agreed that a public inquiry was necessary.

In December 1999, as a result of the campaign's strong reaction against a private inquiry, the Government offered a new initiative. After a meeting with the Attorney General, Mr Michael McDowell SC, and subsequent negotiations with the Department of the Taoiseach, a way forward was agreed upon. Retired Chief Justice Mr Liam Hamilton has been appointed by the Government to 'undertake a thorough examination, involving fact-finding and assessment of all aspects of the Dublin/ Monaghan bombings and their sequel'. The campaign has agreed to co-operate with this examination on the basis that it is a first step towards obtaining a properly constituted public inquiry. To this end we will continue our determined and united campaign to highlight the issues of urgent public concern which require investigation and public accountability. The process of a public inquiry — where justice is not only done but also seen to be done — is a minimum requirement for the families and wounded who have endured a twenty-six-year search for truth, justice and closure. As Liz O'Donnell, Junior Minister for Foreign Affairs, stated persuasively in relation to the Pat Finucane case: 'The value of a public inquiry, in terms of the society as a whole, is that it seeks to locate where culpability lies and thus establishes a basis on which society, through its democratic system, can set about rectifying identified faults'.

Margaret Urwin

Appendix I: Extracts from Interview with Dr James Donovan, Director of the Forensic Science Laboratory, Dublin, 24 March 1999

DM: What position did you hold at the Irish State Laboratory in 1974?

JD: The formal position would be chemist. In essence what I did then was (a) toxicology, that is, I analysed human organs for suicides and (b) I analysed explosives — bulk explosives and explosives trace. I also checked fire debris for fire accelerants. There were always bits and pieces the gardaí wanted me to do ... so I would have done hit-and-run accidents and criminal damage and that sort of thing as well. But mostly it was toxicology and explosives.

DM: Was it mainly bulk explosives that you analysed?

JD: At that time it was bulk explosives.

DM: When the bombs went off in Dublin and Monaghan, who would have been in charge of the case? Was it the Garda Ballistic Squad?

JD: No.... Certainly I presume the Commissioner or the Chief Superintendent in the Criminal Detective Unit — he would have been in Dublin Castle — would have overall charge and under him there would be a number of people.

DM: Do you remember who that was?

JD: As far as I remember it was John Joy was the man's name and he would be in charge.... This was twenty-five years ago. He would have been in charge. Tony McMahon was the Chief Superintendent in the Technical Bureau. So he would have quite a say, for example, in sending material north of the border.

DM: Was it common that material would be sent north of the border for analysis?

JD: No, it wasn't common. It occurred. But particularly because a Garda inspector ... was rather taken by sending material north of the border.

DM: Do you know who he was and why he was so taken with sending material up north?

JD: I can't think of his name now.... [I] believe he believed that ... they were more competent than anybody else....

DM: Did you get the impression that there was a disagreement or a dispute within An Garda Síochána about how and where the bomb debris would be analysed?

JD: Oh yes, there was very definitely....

DM: Who had overall control of the bomb debris then?

JD: The overall person would be the inspector. He was the chap who had overall control and, as such, it was his authority if you like to bring them north of the border.

DM: Do you think ... maybe, there was an influence from outside the State?

JD: Quite frankly ... I hear what you say. To an extent, I don't think so in that he wanted a result and he felt that the British or Northern Ireland could give a result. The fact that they seldom did didn't seem to do too much for him.... Ted Jones brought me the [debris] of one bomb, Parnell Street. But the [debris] of the others then were quite different. They were taken north of the border and as far as I am aware, nothing came from them at all.... [Ted Jones] was very careful to do things properly and carefully..... In one way [the Inspector] irritated me in that everything imaginable was brought north.... And there were many other things unless I put down my foot and said, 'We will do it.' For example, Lord Mountbatten, when he was murdered, and some others, I was offered by the Northern Ireland Lab, on three or four or more occasions, facilities and help with analysis. On all occasions, I declined. I was glad of [the offer] and said 'Thank you very much'. But [I refused] on the basis that you can't build up a laboratory if you're running somewhere all of the time.

And this inspector ... was running north all the time but then [other gardaí] were also there. For example, on one occasion he went up on official business only to find [two others] ... inebriated with the RUC and he did not know that they were going up. Now, the point about the inebriation, it is very strongly my belief that [alcohol] was deliberately used to get information out of them and they couldn't see through it.

DM: If the inspector didn't know [they] were with the RUC, then they didn't have ... permission to be there?

JD: Well, you are talking about a definite line of authority and that should have been the case. When he queried them as to why they were there ... they said, 'Crime and security sent us up.' Now, crime and security is sort of anti-terrorism if you like and is one of these things you sort of fear. Now, he couldn't ask Crime and Security afterwards did they send them up, so he was in a way stuck out on a limb and it wasn't very satisfactory from anybody's point of view.

DM: And were the RUC officers drunk?

JD: No.... and it wasn't the first time and it wasn't the last time. There were many other occasions when I think the gardaí were fed drink deliberately to get information out of them.... It was something that went on. It wasn't just a once-off and it went on for quite some time and the gardaí were entertained....

It's something that I feel quite strongly about because I don't think it should happen. And I don't think that as an independent country, we can develop facilities of our own if we are dependent on another state....

DM: With regard to the Dublin and Monaghan bombings, who made the decisions regarding who analysed what? For instance, you got some debris from the Parnell Street explosion; Mr Hall in Belfast got all four sites. I presume that it was the Inspector who made the decision apart from Garda Jones who brought you debris from Parnell Street.

JD: No. I have no doubt that while Chief Superintendent Joy would have had some say, he would nevertheless be so stretched by worry and things like that that this inspector....

DM: He would delegate to him to make the decision?

JD: Yes ... he would just wave him away and say, 'Do whatever is required.' So it wouldn't be quite correct to say a decision at a high level — Commissioner level or something — was made to send it north.... It would, I think, more likely be made at the inspector level ... he was so used to going up there and he knew that....

DM: Are you talking about the RUC?

JD: Yes, he would deal with the RUC. The RUC have a reception area and he would go in there and hand the stuff over. But what frequently happened, there was a place on the way into Belfast — I can't think of the name — it was a firearms place, and he frequently went in there on the way and would have a cup of coffee.... [It] was a semi-military place and they would have a chat. I was taken in there once. I remember going up and we just had a cup of coffee but everybody was great friends.

So he would have gone there or maybe gone on directly to the laboratory to the reception area, which is policed by policemen, and he would then hand over the stuff....

DM: Were the samples you were given from the Parnell Street bomb adequate or would you have preferred more debris?

JD: To be fair to Ted Jones, he was a good case-and-crimes man and he had a good head on what was required, so he brought in quite an amount. At the same time, you see, we were not used to bombings and we hadn't any experience of looking for traces anyway, and he'd have even less. Okay, we could have done perhaps with a little bit more, but he did a good job.

DM: What about the bomb debris that was sent to Belfast?

JD: I absolutely know nothing whatsoever about what was sent to Belfast.

DM: Did you not get a copy of the report?

JD: I did not get a copy of the report — ever!

DM: I have a copy.

JD: You have a copy? Well I haven't a copy.... I was surprised not to be given a copy of the report considering I sent out copies of my report to four or five people, which is a usual thing....

DM: I'll send you a copy of what I have if you want.

JD: Well, obviously, I would very much like to know. Somebody said that they didn't find anything in the North of Ireland.

DM: I wouldn't be in a position to say that. That's why I would be interested in your opinion. I know Dr Hall was critical of the time lapse between the bombs exploding and getting the debris delivered to his laboratory. He mentioned that within hours the chemicals traces begin to disappear and so on.

JD: Oh yes.

DM: It was several days before they actually had them delivered. That's all in the report from Dr Hall.

JD: Yes. It's just — that seems to be strange because of the close contact between the gardaí and the people in Northern Ireland. Normally they would work hand in glove. Equally, the material I got from Ted Jones, within a few hours I found ovide prilles of ammonium nitrate which were blackened, which would be consistent with anfo. They were in the material of the back seat. It would be consistent with anfo material and it would be consistent of a few other things as well. But ... what I found I thought had a significance. In fact, the significance was, I was told subsequently, not by the gardaí or by the RUC — certainly not — but again by Ted Jones, that there was a group of UVF persons in County Fermanagh who had access to ovide prilles of ammonium nitrate.

DM: Fermanagh or Armagh?

JD: I thought he said Fermanagh. I could be wrong — it was a while ago. He also said that the story was that their capabilities came from a recently discharged member of the British Army and that he provided them with the know-how to do this.

DM: Did he name him?

JD: He did, and for the life of me I can't remember

DM: Recently discharged! I have a signed document from a former RUC officer who names a serving captain in the UDR, who is also linked to British military intelligence, who supplied explosives for Dublin and Monaghan ... and he also names an RUC reservist's home and identifies the location where the bombs were made....

JD: Well, I did hear another story which is not too far removed from that one ... [from] a garda who should be in the know and had something like that but certainly not that.

Quite frankly I just don't know, there are so many possibilities. I mean ... where [did] they get the expertise? I don't know where they got the expertise and I don't know if they [the Garda] know ... because you need competency from people to put the thing together and equally the fact that you could detonate simultaneously essentially a number of bombs is not easy. Equally that ... there was a fair degree of consistency.... It was that the [bombs] were consistent together. They were evenly spread. They were, I would say, well done. I mean, from my point of view and my experience of the use of bombs, they were well put together.

DM: Your opinion anyway was not sought.

JD: No, you are the first to actually ask my opinion in twenty-five years. Now, in that time, I've done huge quantities of explosive offences of all sorts, including traces. Never once was I accused of falsifying results or incorrectly getting the wrong result, [such as] finding nitroglycerine on hands that couldn't possibly have.... So I have always felt that ... I must have found something or done something which nobody else wanted to hear. I tried to raise it with Alan Hall whom I know or knew. He is now retired. He did not want to discuss it at all....

DM: Dublin/Monaghan?

JD: Yes. Which is a bit strange because normally you would as professionals.... Almost to the point of rudeness which is very unusual. He's not rude. So, from that point of view, it seems strange.

I mean, I feel that the ovide prilles of ammonium nitrate, blackened as they were, must have had some significance or else somebody would have come and talked to me. But when my own authorities did not do so, I find that strange.

DM: Why do you think they didn't come and talk to you?

JD: Well, they could say they had my report so they didn't need me. The only problem about that is, around about that time, I used to be taken to the Director of Public Prosecutions because of the novelty of the evidence I was given. It was unusual — they would bring me along to the DPP and let me tell the DPP what evidence I had.

Now, obviously, no one was apprehended for Dublin/Monaghan but nobody [came to talk to me]. I assume that somewhere there was an investigation. I'm not saying I should have been questioned, but it's just a little bit odd when so many people died. Whatever you think of it, I did find something. [What I found] may not be of any relevance, but I did find something and I was involved. I did have a fair degree of experience in bombings and yet nobody said 'What's going on?' or 'What do you know?'

DM: With regard to Dr Hall's Belfast report, I would have thought you would have been a natural person to run that by and your opinion sought.

JD: Yes. Well, that would be the normal thing. You must remember that the relationship between the gardaí and the RUC is quite unique. The RUC would have received Hall's report and it would then be given to the gardaí. So, you would have a circular system where the gardaí were being made aware of what was there, but that is the only thing. It's not very satisfactory.... But the scientist at the same time does have information and does have experience. [To be] left out of the equation entirely ... is very strange.

DM: I would have thought that if I'm relying on an expert in this jurisdiction and I receive a report from an expert in another jurisdiction, out of courtesy and also out of curiosity I would be interested in asking, 'What do you think of this? What's your opinion?'

JD: You're not the only one who would think that. Anybody reasonable would think that that should be done [when] you have experts in your own jurisdiction.... I've mentioned Mountbatten and I refused their offers of help and there were a number of other areas that I refused their offers of help. That did not go down well at all. They complained to the Department of Justice.

DM: Belfast did?

JD: Yes.... Now, to be fair to the people in Justice, when I said, 'I'm running a laboratory that can only be run independently. You can't have multiple things,' they sort of accepted it and supported me. But there was this [attitude], from their point of view in Northern Ireland, they had a right to come down here or to get the stuff sent up ... preferably the stuff sent up for Mountbatten. Okay, maybe I'm overcritical and maybe they felt that they should do something about Mountbatten. My view was that we were quite capable of doing it.

DM: Do you think if you had received all the bomb debris at that time you could have done the analysis as adequately as Belfast?

JD: Well, it's difficult to say 'yes'.... But we have quietly convicted a lot of people on trace evidence. If I got the [debris], the staff are trained, we could, I believe, have done that.

DM: Did you feel in some way shunned?

JD: Yes, I felt shunned in that, there we were, able to do something, and that something was whipped away from us to another jurisdiction.

DM: So you found it strange that this crucial evidence was sent north?

JD: Quite frankly, yes, I did. The main attitude I had was, why? The point is that during the seventies I was involved. I gave evidence in armed robberies and a whole host of things and people were convicted.... We have, in the past, with trace explosives, proved people in possession of explosives. I can only assume the Government sends the bigger things, the important things, up to Belfast.

DM: Were there alternative laboratories, perhaps in the United States or Europe, which might have been considered more politically independent?

JD: Look! It happened here in our jurisdiction. There is no reason whatsoever for it to go anywhere else other than to stay in this jurisdiction. We can do it and we have done it in the past.

DM: And you could have done it in 1974?

JD: Yes! I mean, we did bits. The bit we were allowed to do we found some prilles of ammonium nitrate. My information is that they didn't find anything in Northern Ireland. If that is the case....

DM: Where is the bomb debris today? Given the fact that it's still an open murder case it still should be in the possession of the State. Do you know if the debris was sent back from Belfast?

JD: No. Definitely not. All I can assume is that it is still in Belfast.

DM: Why would you assume that?

JD: I would assume that because that would be the norm. That they would retain custody of anything that came into their possession.

DM: But it is the property of the Irish State.

JD: Is it?

DM: It should be.

JD: The Irish State hasn't taken too much interest in it.

DM: Did the Garda Ballistic Squad act quickly enough in getting the debris to both you and to Belfast for proper analysis?

JD: Well my contact, Ted Jones, was quite good. He was good and I can't understand why it took so long to get to Belfast.

DM: I will get you the Belfast forensic report.

JD: I would appreciate that.

Appendix II: Extracts from Interview with John McCoy, 27 April 1999

DM: You spoke with Brendan O'Brien and Liam Clarke?

J McC: Yes. Brendan O'Brien took the whole thing out of context, just sitting where you are now, in fact. I was only at that time trying to help. He showed me a photograph [of Holroyd] and I said, 'I may have, probably yes, saw that before.' But if you see a photograph and you see it in a paper or something. I think it had appeared in the *New Statesman* long before that. I didn't know that until afterwards, but that's where it was from.

DM: I've spoken with Holroyd.

J McC: Oh ah. So have several others, I believe.

DM: He felt that you were being set up as the scapegoat.

J McC: Holroyd was talking to other ones and I know that another man — I know this since — that another man who has since retired too was using my name at the time. I know that.

DM: Another guard was using your identity?

J McC: I know that. I know that. Not only there was it used. But that's beside the point now. I was told that way back, years ago. Oh I took the brunt of it, for another reason. Liam McQuaid too, and Liam's dead now, two years ago today. But I can say now about Liam. Liam's not the man. Liam was one of the ones all right. But he knew Liam. But there's another man, whose name never came up.

DM: Was he more senior than you?

J McC: No. He wasn't. He was the same rank actually.

DM: Let me go through the information that Brendan O'Brien and Liam Clarke reported in the papers. There are questions arising out of those articles which I want to clarify.

Obviously you are not denying the fact that you had contact with British Military Intelligence?

J McC: Oh I am. I had contact with the RUC.

DM: So you are saying you didn't have contact?

J McC: No! No!

DM: Then why didn't you, as Detective Garda McCoy, when your name surfaced in the papers, take legal action to stop it?

J McC: I should have.

DM: Based on information I got from Holroyd. Based on information that I have gleaned from the newspapers, I think that everybody is under the impression that you are 'The Badger' because it has never been challenged.

J McC: I know that. I know that. And I am not going to challenge it now. Let it die to heck.

DM: I don't think it is going to die.

J McC: Well it can ride the way; I don't care what it does. That's it.

DM: Are you saying to me that you did not have contact with British Military Intelligence?

J McC: No, I did not.

DM: You told Brendan O'Brien that you met 'Bunny' Dearsley in 1972.

J McC: Bunny Dearsley.... Yeah. I forget that one now. Who was Bunny Dearsley?

DM: Bunny Dearsley was a British Army Intelligence officer who was working to MI6 and he would have been the predecessor of Fred Holroyd.

J McC: No. I don't remember now. I certainly don't remember that. But I certainly remember the Holroyd thing and the name and all that.

DM: But I must ask you again, arising out of the O'Brien interview, when in 1972 did you meet Bunny Dearsley?

J McC: I have no recollection of ever meeting Bunny Dearsley. I can't think of anybody of that name.

DM: But you can confirm with me that you did an interview with Brendan O'Brien in this same sitting room.

J McC: Yes, sitting here.

DM: He wrote an article which appeared in the *Irish Independent*...?

J McC: Yes correct.

DM: ...which he claimed was based on a conversation he had with you.

J McC: Yes. On one word. When he showed me a photograph of Holroyd and I said, 'I think I saw that man before'. I don't know to this day where but I certainly didn't meet him.

DM: So you are saying to me that you are denying the fact that you ever met Bunny Dearsley?

J McC: Yes.

DM: And are you denying the fact that a friend of yours, with connections in County Armagh, suggested to you that somebody there wanted to meet 'some kind of policeman' and consequently you travelled to Lurgan where you met Bunny Dearsley in a car park of Lurgan Hospital?

J McC: I don't remember that now.

DM: According to O'Brien, there were four people in a car. They were all plainclothed. One of them was Bunny Dearsley. They were all armed to the teeth. They identified themselves as British Army and said they wanted to exchange intelligence. And they said that they would give you whatever type of intelligence you wanted, presumably on loyalists who might pose a threat to the Republic.

J McC: Definitely I have no recollection of that at all. None whatsoever. I have recollections of meeting RUC men several times, definitely. Several times, but I don't recall that.

DM: What I find strange is that you, as a police officer, didn't take legal action against these articles if untrue. These reports were appearing in national newspapers, which identify you, in a very dangerous way. Why didn't you take legal action?

J McC: I didn't want to bring it into the whole realm of the court at all, to tell you the truth because my mother was alive and living up there [Crossmaglen] at the time. I said, to heck, I'll let it ride.

DM: But you were aware that guards were dealing with British Army Intelligence?

J McC: I wasn't, but from what I know now and what I heard afterwards. That thing was going on being investigated until a Chief Kelly came down to the station [Monaghan]. And that was after he had taken long statements from this Holroyd. And he laughed at the thing when he saw the description that Holroyd gave of me. I didn't think about it at the time, but there was another man afterwards who said to me, at a much higher rank (and it's not McMahon), and he wasn't my boss at all. He told me, 'You know who that is?' And I was that stupid, [it wasn't] until he told me, that the penny dropped.

The description that Holroyd gave of me. You didn't see that one, no?

DM: No.

J McC: And he also gave a funny one of [name withheld]. He said he knew [name withheld] too, and who else? [name withheld] I think he mentioned. I don't know who else he mentioned. But the other one that I know now wasn't mentioned. But, ah for heaven's sake, the thing is ludicrous in the extreme. Only it was so serious in one way, it was laughable.

J McC: Then Holroyd had me sealing off the whole border for him.... He talks about 'freezing areas'. Jesus! I was a mighty guard doing all that. Eh?

DM: Are you saying then that Holroyd is lying?

J McC: He's a pure spacer in my book. I mean, how in the name of heaven could anyone of Garda rank seal off a border? I mean — it was a laugh. I remember even guards saying that at the start they were dubious of me until they saw that.

DM: But if you, at Garda rank, were also acting with the full sanction of your superiors, that's not beyond the bounds of possibility?

J McC: My immediate superior would be my detective sergeant. At the time, Tom Gavin, I suppose. No way was Tom Gavin involved in anything like that. Not at all! That was ludicrous.

DM: In the Liam Clarke interview you seem to substantiate what you said to O'Brien.

J McC: I was standing out there in the hallway with Clarke. I was trying to get rid of him, I think, at the time. Who was with him? A brother of John Cushnahan. His brother must be a reporter. He was with Clarke. I was trying to get shut of them. But, Oh Lord! Only the thing was so serious with Holroyd.

DM: But surely your Garda superiors must have advised you to respond to such serious allegations.

J McC: They did investigate it themselves and they were satisfied that I was in the clear. There were two investigations. The second one was headed by Chief Kelly and he made a pure laugh of Holroyd. He said he had Holroyd's statement, I think it was a hundred and something pages, he had taken from him. [In it, Holroyd claims that] the first thing he notices when he went up to the Garda Depot was that he saw an RUC man in the forensic department. I mean — that was the first ludicrous thing that Kelly laughed at. And the next was the description that Holroyd had of me — 5' 8' and all guards were 5' 9' for a start. And he had me built like a tank. But I began thinking afterwards — all right about that part of it. And I never made any bones about the fact that I went to RUC stations, several times.

DM: According to O'Brien you said that you didn't know that Dearsley, Holroyd and others were working to MI6 and that if you had known, you wouldn't have got involved with them.

J McC: Look, all that I can remember about O'Brien is that he was in there playing tiddlywinks with my fellas who were young at the time and then he came in here and that was it. I was kind of sorry I said anything to him. But ah, it was pure ... Jesus! Holroyd!

DM: He also makes very serious reference to information being passed on that was being used for incursions into the Republic.

J McC: That's right. Ah! Green and all that too. I remember that.

DM: And you are denying any knowledge of that?

J McC: Denying it surely. Green's wasn't our patch at all actually for a start. That's Carrickmacross/Castleblayney district.

DM: He also writes about information that was passed on and was used by loyalists to attempt a cross-border kidnapping here in Monaghan.

J McC: So there was. A kidnapping and they were arrested.

DM: Surely the Garda authorities must have been concerned that information they were passing on to the security forces north of the border found its way into the hands of loyalists who attempted to kidnap Seamus Grew and Paddy Loughlin.... How did they know the streets and how did they know the address and how did they know exactly where to go?

J McC: Did they know where to go? I think they were lost. That was a laugh. No, not at all, they didn't know.

DM: It would appear from what is said that it was information that was passed on, giving the actual address of Seamus Grew and Paddy Loughlin.

J McC: I can remember well that. That was a laugh. There were two of them arrested and a third came looking for them and he was arrested. And they got something like seven years because I escorted them up [to Dublin]. I remember that.

DM: Are you also denying that British Military Intelligence gave you high-quality ordnance survey maps for use around the border?

J McC: We have our own maps here. We had the same maps.

DM: According to O'Brien, the Garda maps were inferior.

J McC: Not at all! We had the same maps here as they had below in the RUC station in Armagh. I saw them there. John Paul McMahon had the very same maps here. Not at all!

DM: He also says that you were, on one occasion, offered guarded recompense for your work and that you refused it and that you never accepted money for any of the information you passed on.

J McC: Money? I certainly didn't take money from anyone, RUC or anyone. I never took money in my life from anyone. Certainly not! I wouldn't be aware of any of them that were talking to British Intelligence either. Only the fact that — that thing about the Badger — when I saw the description, and someone said to me ... it tied up with another time that my name was used in a different context altogether. When my name and another man's name were used. They were actually put down in a register, as having stayed in the Ormond Hotel in Dublin by two other boys — it was nothing to do with this, it was another reason. It was women actually.

DM: Was it guards?

J McC: Yes. And we were all in Dublin for court cases. I used to come home every night and they would stay there. You would get some allowance for Dublin. The other man and I took our cars on alternative days. Now that has nothing to do with it.

DM: What you're saying is that somebody used your name?

J McC: Yes my name was put down in the Ormond Hotel register.

DM: What year was that?

J McC: That's the same year, the Billy Fox trial again — '74.

[The Ormond Hotel is now under new management. When I asked, I was told that the registers for the period in question are no longer in existence].

DM: And whose other name did they use?

J McC: I'll not mention it now, he's dead.

DM: You don't want to mention the name of the guards who did it but you know who they are? Was any internal investigation done or did you make an internal complaint?

J McC: No. I didn't because actually I knew them and it was more or less laughed off as a prank.

DM: How did you find out about it?

J McC: Well you find these things out.

DM: Somebody told you?

J McC: Yes.

DM: But you must have been annoyed.

J McC: Well, I fecked them off but that was about it. But it didn't jeopardise me in any other way. It was more a big laugh. The other end of it was the lad. His name was used elsewhere.

DM: But you're not aware of any guards being involved in cross-border contacts with British Military Intelligence?

J McC: Well, I have my suspicions.

DM: You think that some of them were?

J McC: Well, I have my suspicions all right about that.

DM: How do you feel about members of An Garda Síochána getting involved with British Military Intelligence?

J McC: I wouldn't like it, to put it that way. I mean it was accepted okay — contact with the RUC. I've a notion, from what I know, that it was drinking sprees and that's how they crept into it.

DM: I've been told through other sources that guards often went up and would be offered lots of alcohol by the RUC and it was part of a ploy to soften them up in order to get more information from them. Do you think that went on?

J McC: It may have. It didn't happen with me anyhow. I didn't start drinking yet.

DM: But yet you have your suspicions that that went on?

J McC: Well I have suspicions.

DM: When exactly did your contact with British Military Intelligence end?

J McC: It never started. If you ask me when my contact with the RUC ended, it was when I retired. I'd say for ages before that. Because so many came into the branch then, the whole thing had changed.

DM: Is Holroyd correct when he talks about areas being frozen in the Republic?

J McC: Well I don't know but who could freeze it only....

DM: Is he being mischievous?

J McC: I suppose ... he has to be ... sure unless he knew some super or chief ... sure nobody else could freeze an area.

DM: Is it possible that somebody in the Republic was freezing?

J McC: Yes! Yes, of course it is.

DM: To allow the British to actually come in?

J McC: Well, say that he knew whoever the superintendent was in the station. But, even I'd say if he knew the chief super, and that the chief could make some order some day, he could say that the guards had some operation there undercover. The chief could say that. I doubt if the super chief could do it. I have my doubts. He would be a very forceful man if he could....

DM: But is it possible that the guards may have frozen areas at a higher level to allow British Army and possibly RUC officers to engage in incursions into the territory of the Republic?

J McC: They couldn't unless they were crazy. No chief super would do that. It's ludicrous in my view.

DM: Are you aware of British Military intelligence ever visiting Monaghan Garda station?

J McC: I wouldn't think so.

DM: Did Holroyd ever meet you in Monaghan?

J McC: No. I think, if I remember right, somebody mentioned they met me somewhere in a wood near Banbridge.

DM: There was talk about cross-border roads.

J McC: Banbridge isn't near the border. I know where it is.

DM: What happened in Banbridge?

J McC: I forget, to tell you the truth.

DM: Who did you meet there?

J McC: I didn't meet anybody. That's what they are saying. I was through Banbridge and I don't believe I was ever stopped there in my life.

DM: Is it possible this could be dirty tricks and that they are using you in some way?

J McC: Well, it has to be. Just my point again. That's what this Kelly man ... that's the chief. When I was meeting him I didn't know what to expect and what allegations he was going to make. He made none whatsoever. He said, 'This thing is crazy but I have to meet you. You freezing off an area and you a guard. That's impossible!' And he showed me the [Holroyd] description of me, and said, the first time he saw me, 'By God, if anything was further from the truth, that's it there from the description.' And then he went on to say how Holroyd was saying there was an RUC man working above in the Garda Depot. So on those things alone he laughed it off. That's all I know.

DM: When I talked to Holroyd he told me that you were only the tip of the iceberg in terms of people in the guards that he had contact with. Is this true?

J McC: Well he didn't run *me* — that's all I'm saying.

DM: And how extensive were the Garda/British Army Intelligence contacts?

J McC: I don't know.

DM: Why did you decide to do the interview with Brendan O'Brien in January 1987 and then with Liam Clarke in May 1987?

J McC: Why did I do it with you? I never chased anybody then.

DM: You could have sent me away and you could have done the same with those.

J McC: I could. I could just tell you a story now. But I mean, as I said before, only it was so serious, it was pure pantomime the whole thing, and lots of the stuff I saw. Well, I'm talking about freezing the area. And the other one, what was it he said ... about the Commissioner, what do you call him? Garvey.

DM: But you don't deny that you did interviews with O'Brien and with Clarke.

J McC: Oh yes, interviews if you could call them that. O'Brien, he was deadly altogether. He was throwing out the things. I could have said the same to you.

DM: I'm just going to deal very honestly, based on information that is in the public domain. Did you ever meet Captain Robert Nairac?

J McC: Definitely not. Did he say he met me?

DM: No. Now going on to Liam Clarke's interview, is he accurate when he writes that you claimed senior officers knew of your links with the RUC, MI5 and MI6?

J McC: No. He's right about my links with the RUC.

DM: But you didn't tell him that you had links with MI5 and MI6?

J McC: I doubt at that time if I knew who MI5 or MI6 were. It's only when I started reading afterwards I took an interest, but at that time I wouldn't have known who they were.

DM: He also claims that you said you were only one of the string of guards who were doing the same thing?

J McC: I was only one of the strings who were meeting the RUC. That would be right.

DM: Again, I must ask, you must have at least suspected that Dearsley, Delius, Holroyd, Maynard were working for MI5 and MI6?

J McC: I don't know any of those. I know who they are now from not only you but everyone mentions their names. But Dearsley wasn't mentioned.

DM: O'Brien writes that you had a friend with connections in the North who suggested you travel after which you met Dearsley. Clarke writes, and I quote: 'McCoy travelled northwards to see him. There in the RUC station he was introduced to Bunny Dearsley who went with him to the car park of the nearby hospital to talk about subversives. Dearsley later passed him on to Captain Fred Holroyd who he vaguely remembers sitting in on meetings.'

J McC: No. That's wrong.

DM: You're denying Dearsley at that point?

J McC: Yes, that's ludicrous stuff there altogether.

DM: But it appeared in public and, again, I'm surprised that you didn't challenge it at the time or that your Garda superiors didn't challenge it. They are very serious allegations.

J McC: Yes. Yes. I know.

DM: Is Holroyd telling the truth when he says he met Assistant Commissioner Ned Garvey, and was Garvey involved in passing intelligence also?

J McC: I don't know. I never ... the only time I ever met Garvey was when he did the whole-country inspection. He was Commissioner and he came down here. Other than that I never met Garvey.

DM: With regard to the Dublin/Monaghan bombings, how did your intelligence sources fail you so appallingly? Presumably there was intelligence being exchanged with the RUC as well. How come if intelligence was being exchanged that nobody was tipped off in terms of Dublin and Monaghan? It was a major operation and not an amateur job.

J McC: No. It seems that.

DM: And the RUC didn't tip you off, did they?

J McC: The only thing that was amateur about Monaghan was where they picked was a Protestant pub.

DM: Well, I have information to suggest that they had planned to do another pub but a garda spotted them and moved them on.

J McC: Yes, but that's what I thought at the time ... but how many pubs? I suppose you have twenty or twenty-five in Monaghan and one Protestant one and that's the one they picked.

DM: Were you here that day?

J McC: I remember distinctly I was in Killeshandra that day. I can't remember what we were doing but it could have been an ordinary crime job. I heard the local sergeant's wife in Killeshandra who was after hearing it. I remember, naturally enough, those ones were kids at the time and would be down the town and I came back straight away. It didn't take me too long coming back but I was trying to think why I wasn't involved in the investigation. But we were in Dublin for nearly a month on the Fox Inquiry. It was a murder trial.

DM: Your own town and the capital were devastated. Surely you had questions. I'm presuming that you were involved in intelligence.

J McC: It just happened and that was it. Sure there had been one in Belturbet before.

DM: But did anybody have questions when you were in Monaghan garda station?

J McC: Well, I don't remember — as I say, I wasn't involved in the investigation.

DM: No questions about the quality of the intelligence that they were getting? The fact that nobody tipped them off? There's no way that loyalists could put this together without British Army Intelligence or RUC Special Branch not knowing that something was being prepared.

J McC: The bomb?

DM: The bombs, yes!

J McC: It was a terrible thing the Dublin one. I always heard after that the whole thing was done outside Whitehall Church.

DM: The fact that Peter Maynard and others were intelligence operatives in the Lurgan–Portadown area must have raised suspicions?

J McC: I don't remember that name. The only Maynard that I can remember is Maynard McBrierney who was at that time a Detective Sergeant in Armagh.

DM: Were the Garda told or tipped off and maybe failed to act?

J McC: That wouldn't happen if you were tipped off about something like that.

DM: I have been told by Commandant Paddy Trears that you and Peter Maynard travelled to his home in Castleknock, Dublin, during the August Bank Holiday weekend of 1974. He says he asked if you were there with the knowledge of your superiors. He says that you both said 'yes'. He also told me at a certain point you absented yourself from the meeting but the purpose of the meeting was for Maynard to try and enlist Commandant Trears as an agent.

J McC: I don't remember that. I remember Trears down here on bomb-disposal things but....

DM: Are you denying that you travelled to his house in Castleknock?

J McC: Yes.

DM: So you didn't accompany Maynard?

J McC: No. As I said, the only Maynard I can think of was Maynard McBrierney. Certainly I didn't go up with him to Trears' house. No. No.

DM: And who was Maynard McBrierney?

J McC: He was a detective sergeant in Armagh. That Maynard sticks out in my mind.

DM: But again, in an Irish Army Intelligence file given by Colonel Swan to the Garda Commissioner...

J McC: Yes, I heard about that at the time

DM: Apparently there is a report detailing you accompanying Maynard to Trears' house.

J McC: I remember that came up at the time with the garda investigation with Kelly. But he seemed to dismiss it too. I don't know why.

DM: Liam Flynn of *The Irish Times* wrote in relation to your interview with Liam Clarke, and I quote: 'In Gardaí circles, the interview is seen as a signal to more senior officers that Det. Garda McCoy may be prepared to disclose further details of garda liaison with the British Army at that time if any disciplinary action is taken against him'.

J McC: I never met Liam but I remember Flynn writing that. I'd forgotten.

DM: Were you aware that he was writing about you?

J McC: Yes, I knew that, and I saw that article in the paper. Somebody pointed it out to me.

DM: So you're denying that you travelled with Maynard to the home of Commandant Trears?

J McC: Yes, because I can remember Trears. There was some argument or a row with Trears around that time in Clones with guards. Trears and guards weren't on great terms that time. I know that. There was a stand-up row with the Chief Corbett who was here and Paschal McCarroll from Clones who was the local sergeant. There was a bomb in Clones and there was a big stand-up row. After that it was ... what was his first name? I think it was Boyle. He used to do the bomb work then after that. An Army man, Boyle, because there was a big row between Trears and guards. I remember that was all thrashed out in the investigation.

DM: When you accompanied Maynard to the house of Commandant Trears three months after the Dublin/Monaghan bombing, what did you understand to be the purpose of Maynard's visit?

J McC: I don't know who you're talking about when you talk about Maynard.

DM: Do you think somebody was using your name?

J McC: I don't know at the time, but I know it was used in other circumstances. I won't say it was used all the time. I don't know. I couldn't say that.

DM: So is it possible that a guard accompanied Maynard to Trears' house and introduced himself as John McCoy from Monaghan.

J McC: I don't know. It doesn't seem to add up.

DM: Did you absent yourself from Maynard and Trears when they were going to talk business? Did you absent yourself because you knew Maynard was going to attempt to enlist Trears as an agent?

J McC: Sure I wasn't there to absent myself.

DM: How do you explain your contacts and activities with British Intelligence to the families who had loved ones murdered in the Dublin/Monaghan bombings? Especially since there are suspicions that British Army Intelligence were involved?

J McC: I have no problem with that whatsoever. I knew Mrs White and her family. I'll tell you what I remember. I remember one man who was the last body to be identified. I was the longest here and would have a good local knowledge. I remember I made a mistake about the body and I actually brought a neighbour and he thought the same as I did and I went out to the house to notify the next-of-kin when the man answered the door.

DM: When was this?

J McC: After the bomb when I came back from Killeshandra. I went down to help out as best I could. It transpired it was a different man. He was like the man we thought it was. I can remember that part all right. I had no problem with meeting any of those people. We got on for forty-three years or so. My conscience is clear. I had nothing to do with it.

DM: I'm actually shocked from the point of view that I understood I was coming to meet 'The Badger'.

J McC: I know that and everyone else except my own officers knew well that it wasn't me and that's accepted. They were satisfied and they had their suspicions about who was wanted but couldn't prove it. I know. I went to the removal, exactly this day two years ago, to Liam McQuaid's funeral. But I know, and it's not because he's dead, but it was none of the other officers that would have been here at the time.

DM: I am going to have to go public with what you are telling me since it contradicts what's already in the public domain.

J McC: That's why the garda authorities investigated the thing and they cleared me.

DM: Do you feel that you've been exposed?

J McC: Oh yes! But I try to forget it.

DM: Unfortunately it's going to come back into the public domain and the Dublin/Monaghan is going to bring it back. The families who lost their loved have never been told the truth. To them there is some kind of a cover-up going on. People are not being honest with them in terms of the Garda authorities and the Government.

J McC: I wonder why you say there was an investigation but nothing came out of it. It was a very serious crime but there were other times of course that nothing came out of investigations I suppose. Did the guards not try their best at the time? I don't know.

DM: At one level I think the Special Branch initially did a superb job but it appears that once it went to the RUC Headquarters the trail went cold.

J McC: Is that right? I didn't realise at the time that that was the fact. That they met a black hole. I thought that it was just the police force wasn't available and intelligence wasn't sufficient. You just seem to think from what I read lately the RUC should have more intelligence ... beforehand.

DM: It says here: 'Holroyd says he ran two other Special Branch gardaí whose information was passed through the Badger. Holroyd said he met the Badger in the car park of a certain police station. On one occasion in his office or in a car near the border. He would make arrangements by phone to the Garda Station or to the Badger's house.' Now you are denying that he phoned you here.'

J McC: Yes.

DM: And you never phoned him?

J McC: Definitely not. I wouldn't have a clue. The only one I knew was the one in Armagh — that was the main one that you would be ringing and you would ask them for someone you'd know....

[I proceeded to give Mr McCoy copies of the articles I had used for the interview.]

J McC: I would have thought that it was long dead and gone from the time it was investigated fully by that Chief Kelly. But as I say, the way things went on, I know my name was used in places. Definitely.

DM: Do you think you may have been used as a kind of a patsy?

J McC: I don't know what I was used for but it was kind of a joke, I'd say. The other man's name in Dublin.... That was only a small thing putting your name down in a hotel register.

DM: And the other man whose name was used — he's dead now?

J McC: No. But the man that did it, he's dead.

DM: But the other man knows that his name was being used as well.

J McC: Yes.

DM: Could I just ask you ... one of the two guys who used your name is dead now ... was he the guard who used your name or was it the guard who is still alive?

J McC: I don't know. I wouldn't know that part but it was played as a joke. It's not the man ... the man that's dead is not the man I was told was the Badger — by one man.

DM: But you're saying there is a guy who is the Badger?

J McC: Well, it would surprise me if it went as far as Holroyd said. He certainly couldn't freeze areas anyhow.

DM: But there is a man who has been identified to you as the Badger within An Garda Síochána, but he's not you?

J McC: No. It's only from the description and all that as the time went on. It was just a man and didn't enlarge on it in any big way but everyone knows who the Badger is within the guards.

DM: What rank was the man who told you? He must have been more senior than you.

J McC: Certainly, much more senior. I'm not saying who he is.

DM: But at least he knew who the Badger was?

McCoy: I don't know whether he knew for certain but he had his own ideas. I'm not saying but he was much more senior to me.

DM: And he identified who he believed was the Badger?

J McC: And the funny thing is, another man, and that was a man who is retired, McMahon. He named the other man that's dead, that he always assumed was the Badger.

DM: The one who used your name when you were down in Dublin?

J McC: So, in other words, as far as they were concerned, I was clear and I'd say they were focusing on the other two, so I don't know what transpired then.

DM: So it seems that the guy that's dead was using your name?

J McC: Well, one man told me that it was the other man, but another senior officer was more or less fingering the man that's dead, Liam McQuaid.

DM: Liam McQuaid is the man that's dead and it was suggested that he was the Badger.

J McC: One man more or less thought he was the Badger.

DM: And where did McQuaid work?

J McC: Here in Monaghan. But I don't like dragging names — it's not right, I suppose.

DM: And were you conscious of McQuaid coming across?

J McC: Well, I know he would have been in Armagh station with me on occasions meeting RUC men.

DM: But what if Trears points at you?

J McC: I don't know what Trears is at. But there was a big thing with Trears and guards at that time which I saw myself in Clones one night. Trears and guards ... there was a bit of fighting there.

DM: Why did he finger you? Unless McQuaid introduced himself as McCoy?

J McC: I don't know. That's the only thing I remember about Trears and guards.

DM: I will probably ring Trears himself and say I've talked to Detective Garda John McCoy and he denies it. It's the close proximity to the Dublin/Monaghan bombings. That's the disturbing fact. It was three months afterwards.

J McC: Before or after?

DM: Three months after, he claims. That's the disturbing aspect. In fact, it's shocking. Maynard was a bomb intelligence officer, operating to MI5, and the fact that he was located in the very area were the attack emanated from.

J McC: Portadown?

DM: Yes. So how come Garda Intelligence failed? And why haven't the guards come out publicly and said this is a lie? That's what I find very strange. I can't understand why your superiors didn't say, 'This is a lie. You've got to take Trears to court.'

J McC: I don't know who was involved ... I couldn't think at the time why I wasn't [involved in the investigation] but it was only afterwards when I was thinking that the Fox trial was on at the time. The Fox trial was on in May and June. That would be the reason I wasn't involved. I would be up there [in Dublin] everyday.

DM: But you are denying all that was written in those articles?

J McC: I remember for some reason being in Lurgan RUC station and the name I remember there was Harvey. He was the detective sergeant at the time. Why I remember Harvey, he asked me about a White. The only White I knew in the RUC was killed in Newry after he left the RUC. He was working actually in the RUC station after he retired.

DM: There is going to be focus on you because of the twenty-fifth anniversary of the Dublin and Monaghan bombings and suspicions around British Army Intelligence. If what you are telling me is the truth, I think the garda authorities need to start coming in behind you.

J McC: You see all those ones are gone that were there that time.

DM: But still, it's important that your name is cleared and if your name was being used then that's a violation.

Appendix III: Telephone Conversations, 2 July 2000, with Suspected Parnell Street Bomber, and Owner of Farm Suspected of being Launch Base for the Dublin Bombings

On the afternoon of 2 July 2000, I spoke briefly by telephone with the suspected Parnell Street bomber who now resides in England. I could hear the sounds of a happy family gathering of adult children and grandchildren in the background. The suspected bomber, who was named in the 1993 Yorkshire Television documentary, Hidden Hands: The Forgotten Massacre *was a former UDR member who left Northern Ireland in 1975. Three separate eyewitnesses identified him from police photographs in the aftermath of the Dublin bombings. He is also named in the Holroyd notebooks. The following is an edited transcript of my conversation with him:*

DM: You're [name given] is that right?

Suspect: That's correct.

DM: I am currently writing a book about an event in 1974. You are probably aware of the event I am talking about because Yorkshire Television did a programme....

Suspect: Oh ah! Yes!

DM: Would there be a possibility of meeting you to discuss it?

Suspect: Discuss what? I have nothing to.... I have nothing to do with ... about anything like that.... Because they were all wrong about it because I got on to my solicitor and all and I was brought in and everything else was sorted out because I was released, no charge, nothing. So that's all. I can do nothing more. I don't want nothing to do with it.

DM: Are you saying that you were interviewed by the police?

Suspect: Yeah.

DM: By the RUC?

Suspect: Yeah.

DM: Given the serious allegations Yorkshire Television levelled against you ... why didn't you sue them?

Suspect: I was doing that through the solicitor and they couldn't get ... Legal Aid ... they couldn't get it ... so that's why. But I didn't have the money to fight it but I would have.

DM: What was your feeling about the overall programme?

Suspect: Bloody disgraceful to me ... where I was involved.

DM: Are you saying categorically that you had absolutely nothing to do with it?

Suspect: Nothing. Not one thing.

DM: And what about the other people that were named?

Suspect: Well, I don't know about them, to tell you the truth. I have no idea.

DM: Would there be a possibility that I could interview you in relation to this matter?

Suspect: No, I don't like anything.... I don't want anything brought up again about that. No!

DM: There is a new investigation going on....

Suspect: Yeah.

DM: ... in Ireland at the moment and it looks as though the families of the bereaved will be meeting Tony Blair's representative.

Suspect: Well, I'm not caring. I don't care. I've nothing to hide. So I'm not worried.... All right, so we'll leave it at that.

On the same afternoon I spoke with the suspected Parnell Street bomber, I also spoke by telephone with the County Armagh farmer and former RUC reservist whose farm is suspected of being the launch base for the Dublin bombing mission on 17 May 1974.

DM: Hello, [name withheld]?

Suspect: Yes.

DM: Your farm is located in [name of townland withheld], County Armagh, is that right?

Suspect: Yes.

DM: I'm working on a book at the moment about events that happened in 1974.

Suspect: Ah well, ah, I wouldn't know nothing about that. Ah ... ah ... ah ... you're putting a parcel of lies up.

DM: Who's putting a parcel of lies up?

Suspect: There's books out everywhere ... and I don't want to take part in it.

DM: Are you saying categorically that your farm was never used?

Suspect: Absolutely. Definitely not!

DM: Despite the fact that former RUC officers and Intelligence officers and others have....

Suspect: A lot of bloody liars.

DM: They're all liars?

Suspect: Aye! All a parcel of lies and writing it down in paper and they don't know what they're talking about, the half of them. It's all lies.

DM: Are you denying, therefore, that your farm was used as the launch pad for the Dublin and Monaghan bombings?

The farmer hung up the telephone without answering my question.

Appendix IV: Statement of Dublin/Monaghan Bombing Families and Wounded

On Friday, 17 May 1974, 33 people died and over 250 were injured in what has become known as the Dublin and Monaghan Bombings.

As victims of that outrage we have not been able to find closure to our suffering and bereavement even after 25 years.

Closure will only come once we have been told the whole truth and nothing but the truth.

Truth will only be established when the British Government and the Irish Government deal openly and honestly with our grievance.

Accordingly, in the context of the new political arrangements evolving within Northern Ireland, and between the Governments of the United Kingdom and Ireland, we the victims of the Dublin and Monaghan outrage, appeal for — and demand — our right to know the truth as to how and why our loved ones (including French and Italian citizens) lost their lives and so many of our fellow citizens were maimed.

Only when we know the truth can we find peace of mind and consequently allow all our loved ones to rest in peace.

Basic justice and humanity demands no less.

To this end we have resolved:

To demand the establishment of a cross-jurisdictional public tribunal of inquiry into the following matters:

1. the facts, circumstances and causes of the Dublin and Monaghan bombings;

2. the nature, extent and adequacy of the investigations conducted by the Garda Síochána;

3. the extent to which their investigations may have been impeded or frustrated;

4. any matters connected with or relevant to the establishment of the truth.

Adopted in Dublin on Saturday, 19 September 1998
Adopted in Monaghan on Saturday, 20 November 1999

Bibliography

Bew, Paul and Gordon Gillespie, *Northern Ireland — A Chronology of the Troubles 1968–1993*, Gill and Macmillan, 1993.

Bell, J. Bowyer, *In Dubious Battle*, Poolbeg, 1996.

Bureau, J.R., *Buchlyvie — A Village in Stirlingshire*, Stirling Library Services, 1996.

Casey, Michael (Ed.), *To Act Justly – Reflections of Ireland at the End of the Millennium*, Columba Press, 1999.

Chartes, John, Bert Henshaw and Michael Dewar, *Northern Ireland Scrapbook,* Arms and Armour Press, 1986.

Coogan, Tim Pat, *The Troubles — Ireland's Ordeal 1966–1995 and the Search for Peace*, Hutchinson, 1995.

Cusack, Jim, 'Evidence Links Timers to Bombs used by Loyalists', *The Irish Times,* 26 June 1999.

Cusack, Jim and Henry McDonald, *UVF*, Poolbeg Press, 1997.

Deutsch, Richard and Vivien Magowan, *Northern Ireland Chronology of Events 1968–1974* Vol. 3, Blackstaff Press, 1975.

Doherty, Frank, 'Dublin bombings: new revelations', *Sunday Business Post,* 4 April 1999.

Doherty, Frank, *The Stalker Affair*, Mercier, 1986.

Downing, Taylor (Ed.), *The Troubles — The Background to the Question of Northern Ireland*, Thames/Macdonald, 1980.

Elliott, Sydney and W.D. Flackes, *Northern Ireland — A Political Directory 1968–1999*, Blackstaff Press, 1999.

Faligot, Roger, *Britain's Military Strategy in Ireland — The Kitson Experiment*, Brandon, 1983.

Fisk, Robert, *The Point of No Return*, André Deutsch, 1975

Foot, Paul, *Who Framed Colin Wallace?*, Macmillan, 1990.

Hall, Michael, *20 Years — A Concise Chronology of Events in NI from 1968–1988*, Island Publications, 1988.

Hume, John, *Personal Views — Politics, Peace and Reconciliation in Ireland*, Town House, 1996.

Jordan, Neil, *Michael Collins*, Vintage, 1996.

McGuill, Paul, *Political Violence in the Republic of Ireland 1969–1997*, National University of Ireland, 1998 (MA Thesis, unpublished).

McKittrick, David, Seamus Kelters, Brian Feeney and Chris Thornton, *Lost Lives*, Mainstream, 1999.

McMahon, Theo, *Old Monaghan 1785–1995*, R. & S. Printers, Monaghan, 1995.

McPhilemy, Sean, *The Committee*, Roberts Rinehart, 1999.

Marrinan, Patrick, *Paisley: Man of Wrath*, Anvil Books, 1973.

Mullan, Don, 'Endgame?', *Magill,* May 1999.

Mullan, Don, *Eyewitness Bloody Sunday*, Wolfhound Press, 1997.

Murray, Raymond, *The SAS in Ireland*, Mercier Press, 1990.

Owen, Robert, Ben Emerson and Tim Otty, *The Murder of Pat Finucane and the Case for a Public Inquiry*, Amnesty International, 1999.

Parker, John, *Death of a Hero — Captain Robert Nairac, GC, and the Undercover War in Northern Ireland*, Metro Book, 1999.

Rolston, Bill and Mairéad Gilmartin, *Unfinished Business, State Killings and the Quest for Truth*, Beyond the Pale Publications, 2000.

Sutton, Malcolm, *Index of Deaths from the Conflict in Ireland 1969–1993* Beyond the Pale Publications, 1994.

Walsh, Dermot, 'The Capacity of Legal, Administrative and Political Mechanisms to call the Garda Síochána to account for its investigation into the Dublin and Monaghan Bombings', Justice for the Forgotten, 1998.

Wilson, John, *A Place and a Name*, Government Publications, 1999.

Wright, Peter and Paul Greengrass, *Spy Catcher*, Dell, 1988.

Forensic Reports of Dr James Donovan (23/28 May 1974)
Forensic Report of R.A. Hall (5 June 1974)
Summary notes of Yorkshire TV forensic investigation (1993)
YTV *Hidden Hand: The Forgotten Massacre*

Newspapers
Ireland on Sunday
The Evening Herald
The Evening Press
The Belfast Telegraph
The Irish News
The Irish Independent
The Irish Press
The Irish Times
The Derry Journal
The Northern Standard
The Observer
The Sunday Business Post
The Sunday Independent
The Sunday Press
The Sunday World

Other Publications
Magill Magazine
Combat Magazine
Hibernia
NOW

Government Publications
'Dublin and Monaghan Bombings 1974', Statement issued by Department of Justice, 17 May 1995.

Statement to RTÉ *Prime Time*, issued by Minister for Justice, 17 May 1995.

Index of Statements

Askin, Patrick, 123 — *killed, Monaghan, remembered by his wife, Patricia, and children, Patrick, Sonia and Sharon*

Barror, Denis, 58 — *wounded, Talbot Street*

Bergin, Bernadette, 74 — *wounded, South Leinster Street*

Bradley, Josie, 99 — *killed, Talbot Street, remembered by her sister, Sr Claude, RSM*

Butler, Marie, 86 — *killed, Parnell Street, remembered by her mother*

Byrne, Anne, 101 — *killed, Talbot Street, remembered by her daughter, Michelle O'Brien*

Byrne, Derek, 48 — *wounded, Parnell Street*

Byrne, John, 49 — *wounded, Parnell Street*

Campbell, Thomas, 125 — *killed, Monaghan, remembered by his sister, Mary*

Candon, Una, 49 — *wounded, Parnell Street*

Chetrit, Simone, 103 — *killed, Talbot Street, remembered by her hostess and friend, Helena Gunn; her brother, Elie Chetrit; sister-in-law, Carole; and niece, Sylvie*

Croarkin, Thomas, 126 — *killed, Monaghan, remembered by his brother, Jim*

Dempsey, Concepta, 106 — *killed, Talbot Street, remembered by her niece, Gertie Shields*

Doherty, Collette and Baby, 107 — *killed, Talbot Street, remembered by Collette's mother, Winifred, and sister, Jackie McCarthy Wade*

F, Mr, 52 — *eyewitness, Parnell Street*

Fay, Patrick, 88 — *killed, Parnell Street, remembered by his wife, Maura, and son, Pat*

Fitzpatrick, Bridget, 51 — *wounded, Parnell Street*

Fitzsimmons, Nora, 82 — *wounded, Monaghan*

Goss, Frank, 60	*wounded, Talbot Street*
Grace, Breda, 108	*killed, Talbot Street, remembered by her husband, Tim*
Harper, Archie, 126	*killed, Monaghan, remembered by his daughter, Iris*
Hegarty, Noel, 61	*wounded, Talbot Street*
Hourigan, Joan Ann, 76	*wounded, South Leinster Street*
Keane, Christopher, 62	*wounded, Talbot Street*
Keenan, Marian, 64	*wounded, Talbot Street*
Lawlor, Tom, 65	*eyewitness, Talbot Street*
Lawlor-Watson, Phil, 78	*wounded, South Leinster Street*
Magliocco, Antonio, 90	*killed, Parnell Street, remembered by his brother, Mario, and son, Tomassiono*
Marren, Anne, 112	*killed, Talbot Street, remembered by her sister, Margaret O'Connor*
Massey, Anna, 120	*killed, South Leinster Street, remembered by her father, Frank*
McCormick, Josie, 83	*wounded, Monaghan*
McKenna, May, 110	*killed, Talbot Street, remembered by her sister, Margaret McNicholl*
McLaughlin (née Clever), Catherine, 81	*wounded, South Leinster Street*
Molloy, John, 54	*wounded, Parnell Street*
Morris, Dorothy, 114	*killed, Talbot Street, remembered by her nephew, Maurice Redmond*
Mussen, Rosaleen, 66	*eyewitness, Talbot Street*
Ní Cearnaigh, Martessa, 67	*wounded, Talbot Street*
O'Brien Family, 89	*killed, Parnell Street, remembered by Anna's sister, Alice Doyle; John's sister, Linda Sutherland; and Anna's father, Paddy Doyle*
O'Hanlon, Bernie, 68	*wounded, Talbot Street*
O'Loughlin, Christine, 122	*killed, South Leinster Street, remembered by her husband, Kevin*
O'Neill, Edward, jnr, 56	*wounded, Parnell Street*
O'Neill, Edward, snr, 95	*killed, Parnell Street, remembered by his wife, Martha*

O'Neill, Joe, 70 — *wounded, Talbot Street*

Phelan, Marie, 116 — *killed, Talbot Street, remembered by her father*

Roe, Kevin, 72 — *eyewitness, Talbot Street*

Roice, Siobhán, 117 — *killed, Talbot Street, remembered by her sister, Liz Gleeson*

Sherry, Marie, 73 — *wounded, Talbot Street*

Shields, Maureen, 118 — *killed, Talbot Street, remembered by her daughter, Fiona Ryan*

Sullivan, Liam, 58 — *wounded, Parnell Street*

Travers, Jack, 128 — *killed, Monaghan, remembered by his sister, Eileen McCague*

Turner, Breda, 98 — *killed, Parnell Street, remembered by her parents*

Walshe, John, 118 — *killed, Talbot Street, remembered by his nephew, Gavin Corbett*

White, Peggy, 129 — *killed, Monaghan, remembered by her children, Marie, Brendan, Alan and Maurice*

Williamson, George, 129 — *killed, Monaghan, remembered by his nephew, Thomas Steenson, and niece, Margaret McAdam*

Picture and Text Acknowledgements

Front cover photograph: Courtesy Tom Lawlor (*The Irish Times*)
Back cover photograph: Courtesy D.J. McEnroe

Section 1
page 1, courtesy Irish Press plc
pages 2 and 3, courtesy of the families of the victims
page 4 (top), courtesy Irish Press plc; (bottom) courtesy Garda Press Office
page 5, courtesy *The Irish Times*
pages 6 and 7, courtesy of the families of the victims
page 8, courtesy Garda Press Office

Section 2
page 1, courtesy *The Irish Times*
page 2 (top), courtesy of the families of the victims; (bottom), courtesy Irish Press plc
page 3, courtesy Garda Press Office
page 4, courtesy D.J. McEnroe
page 5 (top), courtesy Pacemaker Press International; (bottom), courtesy D.J. McEnroe
pages 6 and 7, courtesy of the families of the victims;
page 8, courtesy Garda Press Office

The author and publishers have made every reasonable effort to contact the copyright holders of photographs reproduced in this book. If any involuntary infringement of copyright has occurred, sincere apologies are offered and the owners of such copyright are requested to contact the publishers. For permission to reproduce the copyright material, we gratefully acknowledge the above.

Of major value to the author in researching this work were the various newspapers and magazines which he has credited wherever quoted. If, however, he has inadvertently omitted to acknowledge any sources, he pleads pressure of time and deadlines and would ask the relevant editors to contact him via the publishers. In particular, he would like to acknowledge Yorkshire Television, TV3, Frank Doherty, the Finucane Family, Government Publications.